WITHDRAWN

DATE DUE

CONCEPTUAL SCHEMA and RELATIONAL DATABASE DESIGN

A Fact Oriented Approach

Conceptual Schema and Relational Database Design

A Fact Oriented Approach

G. M. Nijssen

T. A. Halpin

Department of Computer Science
University of Queensland

PRENTICE HALL

New York   London   Toronto   Sydney   Tokyo

Prentice Hall, Inc., *Englewood Cliffs, New Jersey*
Prentice Hall of Australia Pty Ltd, *Sydney*
Prentice Hall Canada, Inc., *Toronto*
Prentice Hall Hispanoamericana, SA, *Mexico*
Prentice Hall of India Private Ltd, *New Delhi*
Prentice Hall International, Inc., *London*
Prentice Hall of Japan, Inc., *Tokyo*
Prentice Hall of Southeast Asia Pty Ltd, *Singapore*
Editora Prentice Hall do Brasil Ltda, *Rio de Janeiro*

Typeset by
Midnight Express Professional Typesetting Pty Ltd, Cromer, N.S.W.

Printed and bound in Australia by
Globe Press Pty Ltd, East Brunswick, Victoria

Cover design by
Kim Webber

   3 4 5 93 92 91 90
ISBN 0 7248 0151 0 (paperback)
ISBN 0-13-167263-0 (hardback)

National Library of Australia
Cataloguing-in-Publication Data

Nijssen, G. M. (Gerardus Maria), 1938–
    Conceptual schema and relational database design.

    Includes index.
    ISBN 0 7248 0151 0.

    1. Information storage and retrieval systems. 2. Data bases - Design.
    I. Halpin, Terence A. (Terence Aidan). II. Title.

005.7'4

Library of Congress
Cataloguing-in-Publication Data

Nijssen, G. M.
    Conceptual schema and relational database design.

    Includes index.
    1. Data base design. 2. Relational data bases.
I. Halpin, T. A.   II. Title.
QA76.9.D26N55 1989 005.75'6   88-32545
ISBN 0-13-167263-0

 PRENTICE HALL

A division of Simon & Schuster

Contents

Foreword

It is a great pleasure to write the Foreword for this book, which has been long overdue. Prof. G. M. Nijssen, the originator of NIAM design method, had for a long time given a higher priority to working on new aspects of the method and advancing it, than to writing a textbook about it; but at last, here it is. The NIAM method was initiated in the early 1970s, at a time when most researchers in the data base and information system field still were discussing data modeling on the level of record structures. Only a few acknowledged the need for semantic data modeling. Among these few was Prof. Nijssen, who realized its enormous potential for the practice of data base and information system development.

One of Prof. Nijssen's greatest achievements was that at a very early stage in the development of the NIAM design method, he found that it is not sufficient to provide the designer with a system of metaconcepts and a suitable graphical notation for specifying models. He realized that it is equally important or even more important, to provide the designer with a design procedure, a "cookbook", which tells the designer how to develop a model, step by step, using the metaconcepts and the notation. This way of thinking has proved to be very successful in practise, and still distinguishes the NIAM design method from many other, so-called, "design methodologies".

The NIAM design method has been growing gradually over the years via extensive feedback from many information system development projects, from many workshops, as well as from many discussions with researchers. In 1983, Prof. Nijssen introduced the NIAM design method as a major computer science discipline at the University of Queensland, Australia. In 1986, Mr T. Halpin joined the Computer Science Department at the University and took charge of the first year program in information systems. His research efforts also contributed to the achievement of a mature design method, as it is presented now in this book.

We are convinced that semantic data modeling will become a more important part of data base and information system development. The NIAM design method, with its simple system of metaconcepts, powerful graphical type-oriented and instance-oriented notation and detailed design algorithms and heuristics, is a major contribution to the state of the art of semantic data modeling. We trust therefore that this book will be used by many practitioners of requirements analysis, information analysis and database design, as well as by many students in these disciplines.

Prof. E. D. Falkenberg
Department of Information Systems,
University of Nijmegen,
The Netherlands.
Member IFIP WG 2.6 (Databases).
Member IFIP WG 8.1 (Information Systems).
Chairman IFIP WG 8.1 TG FRISCO
(Framework of Information Systems Concepts).

Prof. R. A. Meersman
University of Brabant,
The Netherlands.
Chairman IFIP WG 2.6 (Databases).

Preface

This book is concerned with the design of information systems, focussing on high level data modeling and relational database systems. It is aimed primarily at students of computer science and/or informatics, as well as professional database designers. It should also be useful to anyone wishing to formulate the information structure of applications in a way readily understood by humans yet easily implemented on computers.

This is the first major work in English which deals with fact-oriented modeling, and, in particular NIAM (Nijssen's Information Analysis Methodology). The "cookbook" approach, use of intuitive and expressive diagrams, and numerous examples and exercises should enable even the general reader with an interest in databases to master the concepts and techniques. With this wider audience in mind, the authors have deliberately avoided a formalized, mathematical treatment of the subject. The language has been kept simple; and where necessary, relevant concepts from elementary logic and set theory are discussed prior to their application.

Many books have been written on database design, but these tend to focus on popular methodologies, such as entity-relationship modeling and normalization. While such methodologies are of value, we believe that fact-oriented modeling provides a simpler and more powerful approach. Some features of NIAM which we have found advantageous include: the use of only one data structure (the fact type), but many constraint types; explicit treatment of derived fact types; diagrams which are visually meaningful and easy to populate; the focus on starting with examples of relevant facts expressed in natural language; and smooth mapping from the level of human communication down to relational table structures.

Earlier versions of the material in the book have been tested with undergraduate students at the University of Queensland. The first 11 chapters formed the basis of a one semester subject, introducing first year students to the area of information systems. This is followed in the second semester by a subject which focuses on relational database systems, including practical work with SQL. Material from the later chapters has been taught in second year subjects.

The first chapter provides an historical background, and may be skipped by the reader familiar with computer systems. Chapter 2 provides a structural background, introducing a number of key concepts which are dealt with more thoroughly in later chapters. It should be read in full by the reader with little or no database experience.

Chapter 3 is fundamental and should be carefully examined. Sections 3.3 and 3.4 describe the first and most important step of the conceptual schema design procedure (expressing information examples in terms of elementary facts). While this material may seem trivial, it should not be rushed. The rest of this chapter introduces the graphical notation for conceptual schema diagrams and offers guidance on how to simplify schemas and identify information which should be derived rather than stored.

Chapter 4 begins the task of specifying constraints on the populations of fact types. The most important kind of constraint (the uniqueness constraint) is considered in detail. Chapter 5 discusses a number of strategies for checking that the fact types so far specified actually are elementary. These two chapters also introduce two notions that are fundamental to relational database theory (the join and projection operations).

Chapter 6 discusses further constraints, the most important of which is the mandatory role constraint. In this connection, subtyping is introduced to deal with certain cases where roles are not mandatory. Section 6.4 provides an introduction to simple set concepts and NIAM subtypes: the reader with a background in set theory may skip all but the last part of this section. In a very short course, where there is a need to omit significant portions of the material in this text, the whole of the work on subtypes could be deleted (sections 6.4 through 6.6). The other constraint types discussed in this chapter (entity type constraints and occurrence frequencies) should definitely be studied: they are common in practice and are easy to understand.

While reference schemes are discussed in many chapters, Chapter 7 deals with these schemes in greater depth. Although important, this material could be skipped or skimmed over in a short course. Chapter 8 examines several other kinds of constraints which may need to be specified. Of these, the most important are equality, subset, and exclusion constraints (section 8.2). The kinds of constraints discussed in sections 8.3 and 8.4 are less common, and in a short course these sections could be deleted.

Chapter 9 discusses final checks on the design. The treatment of implied redundancy (section 9.3) is somewhat advanced, and could be omitted on a first reading. Chapter 10 describes some of the basic transformations between conceptual schemas, which should be studied in detail. Chapter 11 shows how to map the conceptual schema onto a relational database schema. Sections 11.2 and 11.3 are vital. If wished, the summary discussion on normalization (section 11.4) could be omitted.

Chapter 12 provides an introduction to information flow diagrams. The reader should be aware that the data-oriented perspective provides only one, albeit the most important, dimension for specifying information systems. This chapter should be included in courses which address the process-oriented and behavior-oriented perspectives, but may be skimmed or omitted in courses focusing only on data modeling. Chapter 13 concerns the metaschema, which should be examined by anyone seeking to appreciate the full power of the methodology. However, because of its rather advanced nature, this chapter may be skipped in an introductory course. Chapters 14 and 15 provide some background and discussion indicating how NIAM relates to various other methodologies used for the design of information systems.

Answers to most of the exercise questions, particularly those in the earlier chapters, appear at the back of the book. Further answers, as well as related pedagogic material, are included in an accompanying Instructor's Guide. This guide is available to the classroom instructor.

T. A. Halpin
Prof. G. M. Nijssen
University of Queensland.

Acknowledgments

It is our great pleasure to acknowledge the numerous fruitful discussions which we have had with Prof. E. D. Falkenberg, while he was at the University of Stuttgart, Siemens Research and at the University of Queensland. Some of these discussions were enjoyed in "high places", such as the Rigi and Saas Fee, in Switzerland. Various ideas contained in the NIAM design method were originated by Prof. Falkenberg, for example, the basic set of concepts and some aspects of the design procedure, including an algorithm for designing subtypes.

While the "great debate" in 1974 between proponents of the CODASYL Network Model (C. W. Bachman) and of the Relational Model (Dr E. F. Codd) was the focus of attention in database research world, it was Prof. Falkenberg who said that: "The debate is irrelevant for semantic data modeling". Now, years later, the debate on semantic data modeling is indeed concerned with issues quite different from those emphasised in the conventional data models.

It is also a great pleasure to mention the contributions Prof. R. A. Meersman has made and is still making to the NIAM concepts and methodology. An evolving set of concepts and methodology can only be improved when new insights are gained. Prof. Meersman in particular contributed to the language RIDL, a language for the manipulation of knowledge represented in NIAM, and the connection with semantic networks.

Of particular importance is the acknowledgement of the late Dr Michael Senko's of IBM, contribution. His love for the binary model and his clear articles about retrieval and update aspects deserve more attention.

Also worthy of mention is the emphasis that Mr Frans van Assche put on natural language while he was a member of the Database Research Laboratory at Control Data, where many of the aspects were extensively discussed and further developed. Two other members of this Laboratory, Ms Suzanne Galand and Mr Roland Horne, were among the major contributors of the new update operators needed for a semantic data model, which distinguishes items from their names.

Another productive contributor to the fact-based approach is Mr William Kent of Hewlett Packard Research, Palo Alto. His lucid articles are a joy to read.

Prof. Nijssen wishes to express appreciation to the general manager of Control Data, Holland, Mr Rober Endert, who in 1967(!) gave him the opportunity to concentrate his work on fundamental aspects of data and advised him that for most applications, data are more important than the programs. Ms Maria Briers, Mr Endert's secretary at Control Data, contributed for over eight years her time and energy in producing the numerous diagrams which he used in many seminars and other presentations.

Many of the questions asked by students, both at the University of Queensland and in professional workshops for practitioners in Europe, the USA, China and Australia have had a healthy influence on the work. Indeed, teaching is a joy when one sees the two-way learning processes taking place.

In developing the text, the authors wish to acknowledge the useful feedback received from Steven Twine, David Duke and Dr Maria Orlowska, from the Department of Computer Science, at the University of Queensland, Australia. We also gratefully acknowledge permission granted by this Department to include a selection of our examination questions within the exercises. Ms Lois Fordham also of this Department, is to be commended for the expert work in producing the diagrams included in this text.

The order in which the author names appear on the title page does not reflect the division of the actual writing task, the bulk of which was completed by Mr Halpin.

Of eminent importance for any academic is a spouse who understands that research, teaching and writing can also be a hobby. We feel fortunate and privileged that our wives, Mia and Norma are such people.

1 **Introduction**

1.1 Why study information systems?

This book provides a modern introduction to information systems, with the emphasis on information design. Basically, information systems are used to maintain, and answer queries about, a store of information. Although such tasks can be performed manually, we confine our attention to computerized information systems. Most current information systems are called database systems. The database itself is the collection of facts (data) stored by the system. The system is used to define what kinds of data are permitted, to supervise the addition, deletion and modification of data, and to answer questions about the data.

In developed countries, a study of information systems is desirable for most careers. In terms of the dominant employment group, the Agricultural Age was supplanted late in the nineteenth century by the Industrial Age, which has now been replaced by the Information Age. The ongoing information explosion and mechanization of industrial processes indicate that the proportion of information workers will steadily rise in the foreseeable future. Computerization can lead to dramatic increases in productivity. Consider the following advantages of today's database systems over manual record-keeping systems:

time saver   — operations on data may be done much faster
space saver — data may be stored compactly on disk
corrector   — avoids many human errors, for example, in update and retrieval
reliever   — reduces repetitive, boring work for humans
organizer   — requires humans to develop organized model of data
formatter   — rapid display of information in several formats
centralizer — for multi-user systems, centralized control enables sharing of data, less
                       redundancy, tighter security

If an information-oriented business does not computerize, its production costs in terms of both money and time will typically far exceed those of competing companies that do use information technology. Imagine how long a newspaper firm would last if it tried to return to the methods used before word-processing and computerized typesetting.

Although most employees will need to be familiar with information technology, there are vast differences in the amount and complexity of information management tasks required of these workers. Until recently almost all technical computer work was the responsibility of an elite "high priesthood" of computer specialists such as programmers and systems analysts. This picture is changing, owing to the introduction of powerful but cheap PCs (personal computers) and the availability of software that can be readily mastered by the average, intelligent user. This decentralization of computing power has only just begun: its future impact will be significant.

During 1986 the first PCs using the Intel 80386 processor were released, providing minicomputer power in the form of a desktop PC. Within a few years, PCs as powerful as today's mainframe computers will be well within the budget of the average small business. These systems will be capable of running very sophisticated software that will enable end-users to perform most information management tasks, apart from complex design, without the need to consult professional computer experts.

It is clear then that most workers will need to learn how to utilize information systems. This trend toward more users "driving" their own computer systems rather than relying on expert "chauffeurs" does not eliminate the need for computer specialists. For the foreseeable future the current heavy demand for computer expertise is likely to continue. However, the nature of this expertise is evolving, with the emphasis shifting from programming skills in languages like COBOL and Pascal to higher-level skills such as logically designing complex information systems that can interact productively with average users.

Employment considerations beside, knowing how to utilize information systems can be of great benefit. Apart from those databases we may wish to construct for our own purposes (e.g. to keep track of songs on an extensive compact disk library), there is a growing number of large databases that we may want to access through our home computer or the local library computer. We may, for example, want to do some computer shopping, check the latest details on share prices, or research some topic. If knowledge is a form of power, then the ability to efficiently interact with information systems would seem to be generally advantageous.

Considerations such as these have led to the study of information systems being introduced in schools. For example, in Queensland, Australia, two such subjects are offered spanning the last two years of high school. One of these includes a treatment of conceptual schema design, which is the major topic dealt with in this text. Both include work with a relational database language such as SQL.

Apart from the immediate relevance of the study of information systems to careers and knowledge acquisition, our approach to this discipline seeks to develop skills in information design and problem solving that will hopefully have transfer value to a wider context. We trust that the further you delve into the discipline of information systems design, the more you will find it to be intellectually stimulating and satisfying.

1.2   The first four generations

This optional section provides an historical background. In terms of computer **hardware** we may identify at least four generations of digital computer systems. *First generation* computers were introduced shortly after World War II. These were based on *vacuum tube* technology, and in consequence were large, required lots of power, generated plenty of heat, and needed substantial maintenance.

Second generation computers were introduced in 1959, with the release of the IBM 7090. These used *transistors* instead of vacuum tubes, resulting in a dramatic decrease in cost, size and power consumption as well as an increase in reliability.

Third generation computers, introduced in 1964 with the announcement of the IBM 360, were the first to use *integrated circuits* (ICs). An IC consists of a large number of electronic circuits etched onto a single semiconductor chip. This use of microchips led to an even more dramatic drop in cost, size and power consumption and an increase in reliability.

By 1971, two advances in microchip technology had occurred. Firstly, the first general purpose processor-on-a-chip or *microprocessor* had been released: this represented a major breakthrough in chip architecture. Secondly, *large scale integration* (LSI) had been achieved: this represented a major increase in chip density (i.e. the number of circuit elements contained on the one chip). Although LSI led to size reductions, its primary purpose was to speed up processing by reducing the distances that electrons had to travel. These advances are often said to have introduced the *fourth generation* of computers. In 1975, *very large scale integration* (VLSI) was achieved. With VLSI, over 100,000 transistors may be packed onto a single chip. Packing densities of over 500,000 are now available.

Let us now turn to the related but distinct question of computer **software**. It is quite common to speak of generations of *computer languages*. We identify four such generations in this section. Computers were first programmed in *machine language*. Each machine language instruction consists of a sequence of binary digits (bits). For example, with an 8086 processor, the machine code instruction to add 7 to the AX register is: 00000101 00000111 00000000. The byte 00000101 indicates that the following 16 bit data word should be added to the AX register; you may recognize 00000111 as binary for the decimal number 7. The final 00000000 is the "high order byte" of the 16 bit representation of 7.

You can imagine how boring and error-prone it was to program in strings of 1s and 0s all the time. So humans invented a mnemonic code called *assembly language*. In macro-86, the assembly language for the 8086 chip, the previous machine instruction may be written as: ADDI AX, 7. The ADDI, or "add immediate", indicates that the number to be added is contained immediately within the instruction; so the 7 is interpreted as data instead of as an address holding the data. The AX part indicates the target variable for the addition.

Although humans can (with some difficulty!) read assembly code, the computer cannot understand anything but pure machine language. So a program called an assembler is used to translate from assembly language into machine language. Although modern assembly languages are considerably better than older ones, they are still rather painful to use. Besides being hard to understand, assembly language programs tend to be very long since each instruction corresponds to just one machine language instruction. In this sense, assembly language is very low level.

Most programmers nowadays work almost exclusively with high level languages, such as COBOL, Pascal and BASIC. These are easier to write in and understand because they are closer to English. Moreover, a high level program is typically much shorter than an assembly program because one high level instruction usually does the job of several machine language instructions. For example, the following Pascal instruction tells the computer to write out the square root of the value of x: write (sqrt(x)). The equivalent machine code would be quite lengthy. As with assembly language, higher level languages must be translated into machine language before they can be carried out by the computer.

Since higher level languages are so much easier to use, nowadays assembly languages tend to be used for only two reasons: to gain control over machine operations not accessible by high level languages; and for speed, for example, fast animation. Quite often, the bulk of a program is written in high level code and assembly code is used only for sections which require extra control or higher speed.

Some high level languages include *optimizers* to generate more efficient machine code, and some include facilities which come close to matching the power of assembly languages. Since high level code can be written and maintained much more easily than assembly code, the use of assembly languages has considerably diminished in recent years.

With respect to computer languages, machine language is *first generation*, assembly language is *second generation* and high level languages are at least *third generation*. Notice that it is wrong to define an nth generation language as one that runs on an nth generation computer. For example, even the later first generation computers could run the first three generations of computer languages (the first high level language, FORTRAN, was released in 1957).

There are literally hundreds of high level programming languages. Most of these languages are *procedural*, emphasizing the algorithmic side of programming (the procedures showing how a task is to be accomplished), and are generally classified as third generation. This is true even of the more recent procedural languages such as Modula-2 and Ada.

When applied to languages, the term *fourth generation* tends to be used only of database languages which fulfil certain conditions. Database languages are designed specifically to handle the large, complex databases typically found in business and various technical applications. Some database languages are third generation (e.g. dBase III) while others are fourth generation (e.g. SQL). Some database languages marketed as fourth generation are in fact only third generation. How do we tell the difference?

To begin with, fourth generation languages are primarily declarative in nature rather than procedural: the programmer essentially declares *what* has to be done rather than *how* to do it. Fourth generation languages (4GLs) are also highly interactive, supporting an ongoing dialogue between the human and the system. Ideally, a 4GL should be relationally complete, associative, interactive, and provide an integrated data dictionary, dynamic optimization, data sensitive privacy, a fully automatic recovery system and a relational screen interface.

The term "relationally complete" implies that all the data are stored in tables and that the operations of relational algebra are supported, while "associative" implies that columns in tables may be accessed and associated by name without needing to specify access paths. A database usually has information organized into tables. A single row of such a table is called a record. With 3GLs we need to specify how to access the information one record at a time. With a 4GL, a single statement can be used to perform operations on whole tables (i.e. sets of rows) at once. Hence 4GLs are *set-oriented* rather than record-oriented.

SQL is one of the few languages satisfying all the above criteria. Moreover, SQL has been accepted by ANSI (American National Standards Institute) as a standard 4GL, and is the language used in IBM's major database systems SQL/DS and DB2. Recent trends (e.g. OS/2) suggest that SQL will become the common language for communication between different database systems.

It should be appreciated that 4GLs represent a quantum leap beyond 3GLs for work with large, complex databases. Suppose we wish to extract some particular information from a database, and no program is on hand for our particular query. In a 3GL like Pascal or COBOL we would typically have to write pages of code, then compile and debug this until finally it could be run to yield the required results. In contrast, such an ad hoc query could typically be formulated easily in a single statement in SQL and the answer obtained immediately.

It has been estimated that approximately 80 percent of computer software applications fit into the information systems basket, with the emphasis on the data rather than the algorithm. Given the higher productivity of 4GLs in this area, it is clear that many programming tasks now performed in languages like COBOL would be better handled by languages like SQL.

It needs to be borne in mind however that there is still a place for 3GLs like Pascal or Modula-2. Sometimes an application is best coded partly in a 4GL and partly in a 3GL: recent developments are making it easier for these language generations to "talk to one another". And some programming problems cannot be handled efficiently by 4GLs (e.g. computer aided learning, theorem provers, advanced mathematical work, hardware control, and compiler construction). For most applications, however, the data-centred, set-oriented approach of languages like SQL point the way to the future. In this text you will learn how to design databases for use with 4GLs and future languages.

Exercise 1.2

1. For each of the following pairs select the item which most appropriately describes fourth generation database languages.

   A. low level   B. high level
   C. declarative   D. procedural
   E. algorithm-centred   F. data-centred
   G. set-oriented   H. record-oriented
   I. associative   J. must specify access paths

2. "An nth generation computing language is one that runs on nth generation computer hardware." Is this definition correct?

3. As a computer trivia question, the IBM 7090 was originally named the 709T, the "T" denoting the transistorized version of the old 709 model: can you guess why the name was changed?

1.3   The fifth generation

The first four generations of computers are based on the *von Neumann architecture*, which includes a CPU (central processing unit), main and secondary memory, and input and output devices. The CPU is the heart of the computer: it controls the actions performed by the system and computes the values required for arithmetic and logical operations. The main memory stores information which can be "immediately" accessed by the CPU, including the program (or program segment) being executed. The secondary memory stores (usually on disk or tape) information not being processed. An input device (e.g. keyboard) enables data to be sent from the outside world to the CPU, and an output device (e.g. monitor or printer) enables results to be communicated to the outside world.

The versatility of this model derives from the fact that the user can input the program to be processed by the CPU (this "stored program" concept is usually attributed, perhaps mistakenly, to John von Neumann) as well as the data to be operated on. This model is based on the notion of *serial processing* with at most one instruction being executed at any time.

In contrast, *fifth generation technology* incorporates large scale *parallel processing*, (many instructions being processed at once), different memory organizations, and new hardware operations specifically designed for symbol manipulation (not just number-crunching). Instead of one central processor, there may be literally thousands of processors working simultaneously on different aspects of the problem being processed. This new hardware organization is tightly coupled with a new approach to software, in which the notion of *knowledge representation* is central.

Fifth generation computer systems should become commercially available in the 1990s. As an example, Japan's fifth generation project aims to construct a system comprising a knowledge base, problem solving and inference module, and an intelligent human-machine interface. The knowledge base is essentially a relational database, with an aim of storing 1K of information for each of 100 million objects, as well as over 10,000 inference rules. Prolog has been chosen as the language for the inference system, with ultimate projected speeds of up to 1 billion LIPS (logical inferences per second), using parallel processing.

Although Japan was the first to announce its fifth generation project, several other countries have mounted massive research programs in fifth generation technology. As one example, researchers at the University of Syracuse in the United States are working with a language known as Super which includes both the relational capabilities of Prolog and the functional capabilities of Lisp. The language has been developed to exploit the potential of large scale parallel processing, and is being tested on a machine which includes 64,000 processors working in parallel. Some of the developments in supercomputer research are staggering. For instance, IBM's GF11 machine is designed to work at a speed of 11 gigaflops (11 billion floating point operations per second).

One might argue that a language such as Prolog or Super should be classified as a *fifth generation language* (5GL), since fifth generation system programmers will use such a language. It is more appropriate however to reserve the term 5GL for the language in which most users will communicate with such systems. What is this language? The human-machine interfaces are being designed to allow significant use of *natural*

Table 1.1   Five generations of computing languages

Generation	Language example	Sample code for same task
5	Formal English	List the name and size of the moons of planet Saturn in order of size
4	SQL	**select** name, size **from** Moon **where** planet = 'Saturn' **order by** size
3	Pascal	2 pages of code e.g. **for** i := 1 **to** n **do** writeln (names[i],size[i])
2	86 Assembler	Several pages of code e.g. ADDI AX, 1
1	86 machine code	Several pages of code e.g. 00000101 00000001 00000000

language and even images. In this sense, the fifth will be the *last* of the language generations (at least from the human verbal interface point of view).

In this and the previous section we have sketched the evolution of computer languages through five generations. Table 1.1 summarizes how each language generation might be used to program the computer to list the names and sizes of the moons of Saturn in order of size, assuming the information is stored in an astronomical database.

Since fourth generation, relational database systems are already available we henceforth ignore the less productive database systems based on 3GLs. Although fifth generation systems are not yet available, we need to take these into account in order to avoid wasting our time acquiring knowledge and skills that will rapidly become obsolete. Recall the impact of the electronic calculator on school mathematics curricula (e.g. the removal of the general square root algorithm).

With our preview of the fifth generation, we can see that there are basically two skills that will always be relevant to interacting with an information system. Both of these skills relate to *communicating* with the system about our particular application area: this area is technically known as our **universe of discourse** (UoD). The two requirements are to:

1. **describe** the universe of discourse;
2. **query** the system about the universe of discourse.

The first skill entails describing the structure or design of the UoD, and describing the content or *population* of the UoD: the design aspect is the only challenging part of this. The ability to clearly describe the UoD is critical if one wishes to add a UoD description to the system. Complex UoD descriptions should normally be prepared by specialists: these descriptions can then be made available as software modules to the end users who require them. Our main aim in this text is to introduce you to the fundamentals of information design: if you master the methodology discussed you will be well on your way to becoming an expert in the design of fourth and fifth generation information systems.

Issuing queries is often fairly easy using a 4GL, but even then the formulation of complex queries can become difficult. With a 5GL, query formulation will usually be much easier. Occasionally, the ability to understand some answers given by the system requires knowledge about how the system works, and in particular its limitations.

No matter how sophisticated the information system, if you give it the wrong picture of your UoD to start with, you can't expect to get much sense out of it. This is one aspect of the GIGO (Garbage In Garbage Out) principle. Most of the problems with various database applications today can be traced to bad database design. In this text we focus on how to design a UoD at the fifth generation level using natural language: this ensures the skills we develop here will still be relevant when fifth generation systems become available. To ensure that our design skill can be put into practice in the interim, we also study an algorithm to map our fifth generation design onto a fourth generation design suitable for working with today's relational database systems.

In this introduction, we have noted how the nature of computing has evolved over five generations. The first generation language was composed of binary numbers, and most early computing was confined essentially to "number crunching" tasks for mathematical and scientific applications. The word "compute" is commonly used to mean "perform a numerical calculation". But the word derives from the prefix "com" (from the Latin *cum*) meaning "with" or "together", and the Latin *putare* meaning "to think". Nowadays, computers are used for many non-numeric applications (e.g. word-processing and language translation). As computers become more intelligent and we communicate to them in languages we naturally think in, they will become in fact what their etymology suggests: extra "brains" to think with.

References

Evans, C. (1980), *The Mighty Micro* (London: Coronet Books).

Feigenbaum, E. A. and McCorduck, P. (1984), *The Fifth Generation* (London: Pan Books).

Halpin, T. A. (1985), "Teaching Computer Programming", *Proceedings of the 1985 Australian Computer Education Conference* (Brisbane: CEGQ).

Naisbitt, J. (1982) *Megatrends* (London: Futura Publications).

Nijssen, G.M. (1985), *Major Characteristics of a 4th and 5th Generation Language* (Dept. of Computer Science, University of Queensland: Brisbane).

Scientific American October 1987.

2 Information systems

2.1 External, conceptual and internal levels

Advanced information systems are sometimes described as "intelligent". Just what intelligence is, and whether fifth generation machines will be intelligent are debatable questions. In the classic "Turing test" of intelligence, an opaque screen is placed between a typical human and the object being tested for intelligence. The human can communicate with the object only by means of computer (with keyboard for input and screen for output). The human may communicate in natural language about any desired topic. According to Turing, if the human is unable to determine from the object's responses whether that object is an intelligent human or a machine, then that object should be classified as intelligent.

To date, no machine has passed the Turing test. Notice that two of the key conditions in the test are that natural language be used and that there be no restrictions on the topics chosen for discussion. Once we place restrictions on the language and confine the discussion to a predefined topic, we can find examples where a computer has performed at the level of a human expert (e.g. chess, diagnosis of blood diseases, and mineral

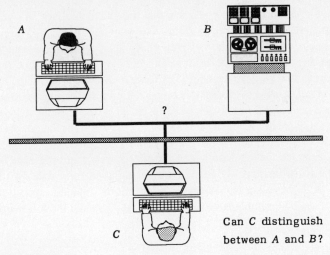

Figure 2.1   The Turing test

9

exploration). Such systems are called "expert systems" since they perform as well as a human expert in some specific domain of application. Expert systems have passed "restricted Turing tests" specific to particular universes of discourse.

Expert systems use sophisticated programs, often in conjunction with large but highly specific databases. A fifth generation information system (5GIS) is like a "user-definable" expert system in that it allows the user to enter a description of the universe of discourse and then conduct a conversation about this, all in natural language. Just how well the system handles its end of the conversation depends on how powerful its user interface, database management and inference capabilities are.

Although desirable, it is not necessary that a 5GIS always be able to operate at expert level when we communicate with it. It must, however, allow us to communicate with it in a natural, human way. This point is expressed (Nijssen, 1980) as follows:

> If two humans communicate about a certain UoD, replacing one human by a 5GIS should not fundamentally alter the language used by the remaining human to communicate.

Natural languages such as English and Japanese are so complex and subtle that it will be many years before an information system will be capable of conversing freely in unrestricted natural language. We will be content in the meantime if a 5GIS supports dialogue in a formalized subset of natural language and we refer to such a language as a Formal Natural Language (FNL). There will obviously be many FNLs, for example, one for English, one for Japanese, and so on. A 5GIS should be able to respond in the same FNL used by the human. For example, if you posed the following query:

What is the age of Selena?

and you received the reply:

junisai

this would not help much unless you knew that this is Japanese for "12 years old". Even if you can translate from Japanese to English you might still misinterpret the reply, because unlike the usual convention of giving people an age of zero years when born, the Japanese give them an age of one year. So an age of twelve years in the Japanese system corresponds to an age of eleven years in the Western system. Besides the requirement for a *common language*, effective communication between two speakers requires that each gives the *same meaning* to the words being used. This can be achieved by ensuring that both speakers (a) share the same context or universe of discourse, and (b) speak in sentences that are unambiguous with respect to this UoD.

With our example, the confusion over whether Selena's age is eleven or twelve years results from two different UoD frameworks being used, one relating to Western age conventions and the other to Japanese conventions. Natural speech abounds with examples that can be disambiguated only by context. Consider the following example:

Pluto is owned by Mickey.

This is fine if we treat the UoD to be the world of Walt Disney's cartoon characters. But suppose someone unfamiliar with Mickey Mouse and his dog Pluto interpreted this within an astronomical context, taking "Pluto" to refer to the planet Pluto: a more drastic communication failure!

It is clearly essential then, that we have a clear way of describing the UoD to the information system. An information system may be viewed from at least *three levels: external, conceptual and internal.* Since the conceptual level is the most fundamental, portraying the UoD in a way that is meaningful to humans, we focus on this level first. At this level, the framework of the UoD is called the **conceptual schema**, which describes the *structure* or *grammar* of the specific UoD (e.g. what types of object populate the UoD, what roles these play, and what constraints are in effect). In other words, the conceptual schema is a general design plan of the UoD.

Whereas the conceptual schema indicates the structure of the UoD, the **conceptual database** at any given time indicates the *content* or instances populating a specific *state* of the UoD. Although the term "information base" is more appropriate (ISO, 1982), we continue to use the briefer and more popular term "database". Conceptually, the database is a set of sentences expressing propositions asserted to be true of the UoD. Since sentences may be added to or deleted from the database, the database may undergo transitions from one state to another. However, at any particular time the sentences populating the database must individually and collectively conform to the application specific grammar or design plan which is the conceptual schema. To summarize:

> The conceptual schema completely specifies all the permitted states and transitions of the conceptual database.

To enforce this law we now introduce a third system component known as the **conceptual information processor**. This component is responsible for supervising updates to the database by the user and for answering user queries. The basic conceptual architecture of a 5GIS is set out in Figure 2.2. This diagram assumes the conceptual schema is already stored within the system. For each application area of choice, a different conceptual schema is entered.

Although the diagram may suggest that the user is interacting directly with the conceptual information processor, the user's interaction with the system is external rather than conceptual. The conceptual schema expresses the essential logical structure of

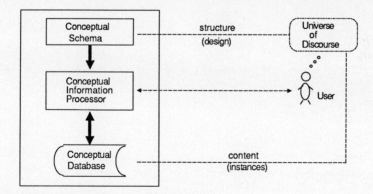

Figure 2.2   Information system: Conceptual level

the UoD. It is not concerned with providing convenient interfaces for various users, nor with the physical details of how the database can be efficiently maintained.

These concerns may be catered for by including corresponding external and internal components within the overall architecture, as shown in Figure 2.3. Here an **external schema** specifies the UoD design perceived by a particular user or group of users, and how it relates to the conceptual schema. At the external level we specify *what* kind of information may be viewed by users and *how* it is displayed. Often a user has access to only part of the information. This may be for *user convenience*. For example, it is simpler to issue queries if selecting only from the information relevant to one's needs. Sometimes, *security* reasons may require that only certain authorized users have access to sensitive information stored in the system.

The **internal schema** specifies the physical storage and access structures used to implement the whole conceptual schema efficiently (e.g. file packing, indexes, etc.). An important advantage of the conceptual level is that it is the most *stable* of all the levels. Changing a user-interface or altering the physical storage and access techniques have no effect on it. While there is only one conceptual and one internal schema, there can be several external schemata for the same UoD. The addition of external and internal levels to the architecture may be summarized as follows:

> *An external schema* prescribes a view of the database for a particular user. The database associated with this view is called an external database.

> *The internal schema* completely specifies the physical representation of each permitted database state. The physical representation of the database is called the internal database.

If a language is the object of study it is said to be the *object language*. The language used to study it is then called the *metalanguage*. For example, you might use English as a metalanguage to study Japanese as an object language. An object language may be its

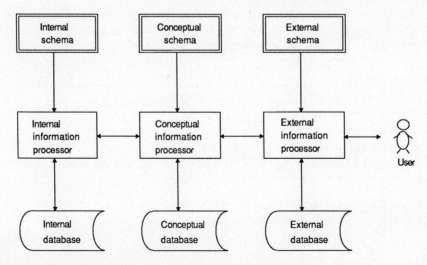

Figure 2.3   Three-level architecture of an information system

own metalanguage. English, for example, may be used to learn about English. Note that any conceptual schema may be expressed as a set of sentences and hence may be viewed as a database in its own right. This leads us to the *Meta Principle*:

> The conceptual schema may itself be treated as a database, the permitted states of which may be completely specified by a conceptual meta schema.

Embodied in a conceptual schema design aid, the conceptual meta schema may be used to help designers produce a variety of conceptual schemas. Let us agree to accept both "schemas" and "schemata" as plural of "schema". Although "data" is the plural of "datum" let us adopt the common practice of allowing "data" to be used in both singular and plural senses.

In the next section we develop a more detailed exposition of the conceptual level. The meta schema is discussed in a later chapter.

Exercise 2.1

1. Use the key:
   A. external
   B. conceptual
   C. internal
   to classify each of the following levels:

   (a) This level is concerned with the physical details of how data may be efficiently stored and accessed.
   (b) This level is concerned with providing a convenient and authorized view of the database for an individual user.
   (c) This level is concerned with representing information in a logically fundamental way.

2.2 The conceptual level

Given our emphasis on the conceptual level, we often abbreviate the term "conceptual database" to "database". All communication between humans and the information system at this level is handled by the **conceptual information processor** (CIP). This communication may be divided into three main stages:

1. If the conceptual schema is not already stored, the human describes the design of the UoD, subject to checking by the CIP. The CIP stores the accepted design as the conceptual schema.

2. The user updates the database by adding or deleting specific facts. The CIP accepts an update operation if and only if it is consistent with the conceptual schema.

3. The user queries the system about the UoD and is answered by the CIP. The CIP can supply information about the conceptual schema or the database, provided it has stored the information or can derive it.

In executing its task at these three stages the CIP is performing its roles as a *design filter, data filter* and *information supplier* respectively. In a more detailed analysis, the design filter could be treated as a separate unit involving a conceptual schema processor with read access to the conceptual metaschema.

When interpreted by humans, the conceptual schema and database both provide knowledge about the UoD. Hence the combination of conceptual schema and (conceptual) database may be described as the **knowledge base**. Thus the information system comprises a knowledge base and CIP. The knowledge base is a formal description of the UoD, and the CIP controls the flow of information between the knowledge base and humans.

In the overall construction of practical information systems, at least three categories of humans are involved. The *UoD expert* or domain expert is familiar with the application area, and can clarify any doubtful aspects of the UoD. For example, if a computerized accountancy system is required for a company, the company's accountant would probably be the UoD expert. The *designer* provides the formal specification of the CS (conceptual schema), is trained in schema design and regularly consults with the UoD expert in developing the CS. The *end user* makes use of the system once it has been developed (e.g. data entry operators, clerks and executives of the company). For a small system the domain expert, designer and user might be the same person. For a large system there might be several partial experts, a team of designers, and thousands of end users.

For simplicity let us agree that there is one designer but possibly several users. The designer inputs the CS to the system and has *read/write* access to the conceptual schema. A user who merely works with an already existing schema has *read-only* capability for the schema, but has read/write access to the database. Different external schemas might be created for different users so that some users have access to only part of the knowledge base. This situation is summarized in Figure 2.4.

To understand how the CIP deals with updates and queries, we need to know a little more about the conceptual schema. In this section we introduce many of the relevant ideas in an informal way. For our purposes we may consider the conceptual schema to consist of three sections as shown in Figure 2.5.

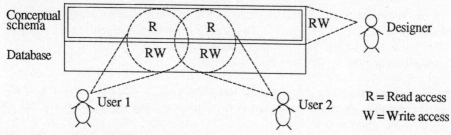

Figure 2.4 Access to the knowledge base

Stored fact types	Constraints	Derivation rules

Figure 2.5 The conceptual schema

Basically, the section on **stored fact types** lists the kinds of sentence or *fact* which may be stored in the database. Here we indicate what types of *entity* are permitted in the UoD (e.g. Person, Subject), how these are *referenced* by labels in the database (e.g. surname, subjectcode), and the various *roles* (e.g. studies, studied-by) played by them.

The **constraints** section lists various constraints or restrictions that apply to populations of the fact types. These may be either static or dynamic. *Static constraints* apply to every state of the database. For example, suppose a geographical database stores information about countries and their capital cities. Although a country may change its capital city (consider Japan), at any state of the database it has at most one city recorded as its current capital.

Dynamic constraints forbid certain *transitions* between states of the database. For instance, although a student may be enrolled in Year 9 at one time and in Year 11 at another time, a school would normally forbid the student to jump straight from Year 9 enrollment to Year 11 enrollment.

Constraints are also known as *validation rules* since they must be obeyed if the population of the database is to be a "valid population" (i.e. in agreement with the conceptual schema). Although most relevant constraints can be neatly represented on conceptual schema diagrams, some constraints, (e.g. transition constraints), need to be represented in other ways (e.g. by logical formulae, tables or graphs).

The **derivation rules** section provides a list of functions, operators and rules that may be used to derive information not explicitly stored in the database. These may involve *mathematical calculation* or *logical inference*. In practice, many operators and functions may be thought of as generic to particular data types: this permits a large variety of possible queries without the need to document each related derivation. Typical mathematical facilities provided include arithmetic operators, for example, +, -, * (multiply), and / (divide), set operators such as $\cup$ (union), as well as functions for counting, summing, and computing averages, maxima and minima.

In addition to such "open-ended" derivation facilities, specific *derived fact types* that are known to be required may be individually listed in the schema by means of rules. Some mathematically computed fact types and almost all logically inferred fact types fit into this category. Fact types derived by use of *logical inference* typically involve rules which make use of logical operators such as **if**.

Although derivable facts could be stored in the database it is usually better to avoid this. The reason for this is not so much to save storage space, but rather to avoid anomalies when updating the database. For instance, suppose we wanted to regularly obtain individual ages (in years) of students in a class, and, on occasion, the average age for the class. If we stored the average age in the database we would have to arrange for this to be recomputed every time a student was added to or deleted from the class, as well as every time the age of any individual in the class increased. As an improvement, we might store the number of students as well as their individual ages and have the average age derived only upon request. But this is still clumsy. Can you think of a better design?

As you probably realized, there is no need to store the number of students in a class since this can be derived using a count function. This avoids having to update the class number every time someone joins or leaves the class. Moreover, there is no need to store even the individual ages of students. It is better to store the birthdate of the students as well as the current date, and then have the system derive the age of any student upon request by using an appropriate date subtraction algorithm. Of course the date has to be changed daily but this is easily automated using the system clock. With this arrangement we don't have to worry about updating ages of students as they become a year older.

Sometimes, what is required is not the current age but the age on a certain date (e.g. entrance to schooling, age grouping for a future sports competition). In such cases where a single, stable age is required for each person, it may be appropriate to store it.

Before considering a derivation example using logical inference, it should be noted that we distinguish between *propositions* and *sentences*. Propositions are asserted by declarative sentences, and are always true or false (but not both). The same proposition may be asserted by different sentences (e.g. "Paris is the capital of France" and "The French capital is Paris"). While humans can deal with underlying meanings in a very sophisticated way, computers are completely literally minded and deal in sentences rather than their meanings. If we want the computer to make what to us are obvious connections, we have to be explicit and provide it with the background or rules for making such connections.

Suppose that facts about brotherhood and parenthood are stored in the database. For simplicity we assume that the only objects we want to talk about are people who are identified by their first names. We may now set out facts as follows:

Alan is brother of Betty.
Charles is brother of Betty.
Betty is parent of Fred.

As humans we can look at these facts and readily see that both Alan and Charles are uncles of Fred. In doing so we are using our understanding of the term "uncle". If we want a computer system to be able to make similar deductions we need to provide it with a rule which expresses this. For example, assuming the variables X,Y,Z range over people:

Given any X, Z:
    X is uncle of Z **if**   there is a Y such that
                        X is brother of Y **and** Y is parent of Z

This may be abbreviated to:

    X is uncle of Z **if** X is brother of Y **and** Y is parent of Z.

This rule is an example of a *Horn clause*. The head of the clause is derivable from the conditions stated on the right-hand side of the **if**. Partly because of its popularity (e.g. Prolog), we often make use of Horn clause notation when setting out derivation rules.

To appreciate how the CIP works, let's look at an example. The example is based on a fragment of an information system designed to test the influence of heredity on bodily properties. The CS notation used is simplified, awaiting a more detailed treatment of fact types in the next chapter. Moreover, the constraints on the brother and parent fact types are incomplete. The structure of the UoD is set out by means of the following conceptual schema:

Stored fact types:
    F1 Person is brother of Person
    F2 Person is parent of Person
    F3 Person has Height

Constraints:
   C1 Each person's height must be recorded
   C2 Each person has at most one height
   C3 Nobody is his/her own brother
   C4 Nobody is his/her own parent

Derivation rules:
   D1 avg(Height) returns the average of the recorded heights
   D2 X is uncle of Y **if** X is brother of Z **and** Z is parent of Y

Here the UoD is perceived to include two kinds of entity: Person and Height. Assume that people are identified by their firstname, and heights are measured in cm (strictly, such reference schemes are part of the schema).

At the fifth generation level each fact in the database is simple or elementary. We may **add** or insert a fact into the database, and we may **delete** a fact from it. However, we may not modify or change just a part of a fact. We refer to the operation of adding or deleting a single fact as an *elementary update* or *simple transaction*. In our informal input language, add and delete requests start with "add:" and "del:", and queries end with "?". The CIP either accepts updates or rejects them with an indication of the violation. The CIP answers legal queries and rejects illegal ones. Suppose now that we start populating our UoD as follows:

User: *CIP:*
add: Person Alan has Height 178   → accepted

The CIP recognizes the type of this sentence and sees that no constraints are violated; so it adds it to the database and issues the reply "accepted". If an update is inconsistent with the conceptual schema, the CIP rejects it, indicating the reason for rejection. You should now be able to follow the following dialogue:

   add: Person Alan is brother of Cat Felix   → rejected. Fact type
                                                   not recognized.
   add: Person Alan is brother of Person Sue → rejected. C1 violated
   add: Person Sue has Height 170   → accepted
   add: Person Alan is brother of Person Sue → accepted
   add: Person Alan is brother of Person Alan → rejected. C3 violated

Here for brevity we use constraint numbers to indicate the constraints violated. In practice of course, since the CIP response is intended to be meaningful to humans, the full text description of the constraint would be displayed. Now suppose that Alan has grown 2cm since we last updated his height. How would we record this change? Here are two incorrect attempts:

   add: Person Alan has Height 180   → rejected. C2 violated
   del: Person Alan has Height 178   → rejected. C1 violated

Is there any way of changing Alan's recorded height from 178 to 180cm? Yes. Sometimes it is convenient, or even necessary, to submit a whole bundle of elementary updates as a single group. This is referred to as a *compound transaction*. To indicate a compound transaction we use "begin" and "end" as brackets to open and close the transaction. It is important to note that with compound transactions the CIP considers only the total or *collective effect* of the transaction on the database. It is quite possible that the CIP will accept a compound transaction even if, taken individually, some of its component simple updates would be rejected. To change Alan's height we proceed thus:

```
begin
   del: Person Alan has Height 178
   add: Person Alan has Height 180
end                                        → accepted
```

The CIP accepts a transaction if and only if its overall effect is consistent with the conceptual schema. The user entered this compound transaction as a sequence of two elementary updates. It is more natural here to specify the delete before the add operation. However the CIP treats any compound transaction as a *set* of updates, disregarding the order of the components, and looks only at the total effect. So even if the add operation had been specified before the delete, this would have been accepted with the same result. Note that the CIP cannot accept just part of a compound transaction: it is case of "all or nothing". Here are a few more simple interactions:

```
add: Person Mary has Height 175            → accepted
add: Person Sue is parent of Person Mary   → accepted
add: avg(Height) = 174                     → rejected. Derivable
avg(Height)?                               → 175
Who is uncle of Mary?                      → Alan
Who is aunt of Mary?                       → rejected. Fact type
                                             not recognized
```

Now consider a larger UoD which is the same as that just discussed except that facts of the following kind are to be recorded:

F4 Person eats Food

subject to the constraint:

C5 Each person must be recorded to eat a food

Suppose we start with an empty database, and try to add the following fact. How do you think the CIP would respond?

add: Person Bob is brother of Person Ann

This update request is rejected. It actually violates two constraints (C2 and C5), since all people mentioned in the database must have both their height and at least part of their diet recorded. Later on we use the terminology "mandatory roles" to describe such constraints. In general, the order in which constraints are listed in the CS does not matter. However, if an update request violates more than one constraint, this order may determine which constraint is reported as violated. Usually, if a CIP finds a constraint violation then it reports this and doesn't bother looking for any more violations. In this case, the CIP would respond thus to the previous request:

rejected. C2 violated

Of course, it is possible to program the CIP so that it reports all constraint violations (e.g. "rejected. C2, C5 violated"), but this tends to be less efficient. As an exercise, convince yourself that the following sequence of updates is processed as shown:

add: Person Ann has Height 170 → rejected. C5 violated
begin
   add: Person Ann has Height 170
   add: Person Ann eats Food spinach
end → accepted
begin
   add: Person Bob has Height 175
   add: Person Bob eats Food apple
   add: Person Bob eats Food spinach
end → accepted
add: Person Bob is brother of Person Ann → accepted

We have now considered examples of how the CIP can use the conceptual schema to supervise updates of the database and to supply information in response to a query. We may think of the designer of the conceptual schema as the *"law giver"*, and the schema itself as the *"law book"* since it contains the laws or ground rules for the UoD. We may think of the CIP as the *"law enforcer"*, since it ensures these laws are adhered to whenever the user tries to make any changes to the database. Like any friendly policeman or policewoman, the CIP is also there to provide information on request.

We have mentioned the terms "consistency" and "inconsistency" a number of times. Before closing this section let's briefly examine these notions as they relate to the concept of a universe of discourse.

Whenever we communicate to a person or an information system we have in mind a particular UoD. Logicians divide states of such UoDs up into two general categories: *possible worlds* and *impossible worlds*. One possible world is a state of the *actual* or *real* universe, with all its billions of galaxies. Usually we want to confine our attention to much smaller worlds than this. We often choose as our UoD some small part of the real universe, for example, a particular business environment.

In rare cases we might choose a fictional UoD (e.g. one populated by comic book characters), or perhaps a fantasy world we have invented for a novel that we are writing. Such fictional worlds may or may not be (logically) possible. You can often rely on your own intuitions as to what is logically possible. For instance a world in which the moon is coloured green is possible, but a world in which the moon is simultaneously green all over and red all over is not. A possible world is said to be *consistent* and an impossible world is *inconsistent*.

As humans we carry prodigious amounts of information around in our minds. It is highly likely that somewhere in our personal web of beliefs some logical contradictions are lurking. In most cases it does not matter if our belief web is globally inconsistent, so long as the local portions of the web that we use to communicate about are internally consistent. When reasoning about a particular UoD however, consistency is essential. It can be easily shown that once you let a logical inconsistency into a UoD it is possible to deduce anything (including loads of rubbish) from it. Recall the GIGO (Garbage In Garbage Out) principle discussed earlier.

There are basically two types of garbage: logical and factual. Inconsistent UoDs contain logical garbage. Even though the CIP checks that the database is consistent with the world design of the conceptual schema, it is still possible to add false data into the knowledge base. For example, if we tell the CIP that Alan is the husband of Betty it will accept this even though in the actual world Alan may not be married to Betty. If we want our knowledge base to remain factually correct, it is still our responsibility to ensure that all the sentences we enter into the database express propositions that are true of the actual world.

The following exercise gives you an opportunity to test your understanding of the concepts discussed in this section. It also introduces some further constraint types that will be treated more formally later. At this early stage, the notations used to express the conceptual schema and user-CIP dialogue have been kept informal.

Exercise 2.2

1. (a) Assuming the conceptual schema is already stored, what are the two main functions of the CIP?
   (b) What are the three main components of the conceptual schema?
   (c) "The CIP will reject a compound transaction if any of its component update operations is inconsistent with the conceptual schema." True or False?

2. The following conceptual schema is stored by a 5GIS:

   Stored fact types:
   F1 Person has FitnessRating
   F2 Person plays Sport
   F3 Person is expert at Sport

   Constraints:
   C1 Each person has at least one fitness rating
   C2 Each person has at most one fitness rating
   C3 Fitness ratings are denoted by integers in the range 1..10
   C4 Each person is expert at at most one sport
   C5 X is expert at Y *is stored* **only if** X plays Y *is stored*

   Derivation rules:
   D1 count(_ plays Y) returns the number of players of Y
   D2 X is martial artist **if** X plays judo **or** X plays karatedo

   Note that constraints apply to the database. For example, C1 means that each person referred to in the database must have his/her fitness rating recorded there. C4 means that no person can be recorded as being expert at more than one sport, and C5 means that X can be recorded as being an expert at Y only if (the same) X is also recorded as playing (the same) Y.

   The database is initially empty. The user now attempts the following sequence of updates and queries. For each update, circle the letter if the update is accepted. In cases of rejection supply a reason (e.g. state which part of the conceptual schema is violated). For queries, supply an appropriate response from the CIP.

   (a) add: Person Ann has fitness rating 9
   (b) add: Person Fred plays sport tennis
   (c) add: Person Bob has fitness rating 7
   (d) add: Person Ann has fitness rating 8
   (e) add: Person Chris has fitness rating 7
   (f) add: Person Fred has fitness rating 15
   (g) add: Person Ann plays sport judo

(h) add: Person Bob is expert at sport soccer
(i) add: Person Ann is expert at sport judo
(j) add: Person Ann programs in language SQL
(k) add: Person Ann plays sport soccer
(l) add: Person Chris plays sport karatedo
(m) del: Person Chris has fitness rating 7
(n) begin
    add: Person Bob has fitness rating 8
    del: Person Bob has fitness rating 7
  end
(o) add: Person Ann is expert at sport soccer
(p) add: Person Bob plays sport soccer

{ assume that queries (q)–(u) are legal }
(q) Person Ann plays sport judo?
(r) Who plays sport karatedo?
(s) count(_ plays soccer)?
(t) Who is martial artist?
(u) What fitness ratings are permitted?
(v) What is the meaning of life?

3. The UoD design is given by the following conceptual schema:

Stored fact types:
  F1 Student is enrolled in Degree
  F2 Student has MaritalState

Students are identified by first names, degrees by degree codes, and marital states by marital codes.

Constraints:
  C1 Each student is enrolled in exactly one degree
  C2 Each student has at most one marital state
  C3 Only the following marital states are permitted: single, married, widowed, divorced
  C4 Only the following marital transitions are allowed: ("1" indicates allowed)

From \ To	*single*	*married*	*widowed*	*divorced*
single	0	1	0	0
married	0	0	1	1
widowed	0	1	0	0
divorced	0	1	0	0

Recall that constraints apply to the database, not necessarily to the real world being modelled. Although each student in the real world may in fact have a marital state, for this application it is optional as to whether a student's marital state is recorded. There may be good reasons for this (e.g. to respect the wishes of particular students to keep their marital states private). Constraint C1 may be considered as a conjunction of two weaker constraints, since "exactly one" means "at least one, and at most one".

The database is initially empty. The user now attempts the following sequence of updates and queries. For each update, circle the letter if the update is accepted. In cases of rejection supply a reason. For queries, assume these are legal and supply an appropriate CIP response.

(a) add: Student Fred is enrolled in degree BSc
(b) add: Student Sue has marital state single
(c) begin
    add: Student Sue has marital state single
    add: Student Sue is enrolled in degree MA
end
(d) add: Student Fred is enrolled in degree BA
(e) add: Student Fred is studying subject CS112
(f) What marital states are possible?
(g) add: Student Bob is enrolled in degree BSc
(h) add: Student Sue has marital state married
(i) begin
    del: Student Sue has marital state single
    add: Student Sue has marital state married
end
(j) add: Student Bob has marital state single
(k) begin
    del: Student Bob has marital state single
    add: Student Bob has marital state divorced
end
(l) Is student Sue enrolled in degree BSc?
(m) Which students are enrolled in degree BSc?
(n) Which students are enrolled in degree MA?
(o) add: 3 students are enrolled in degree BE

What is the final state of the database?

4. In a particular UoD, people are the only entities allowed. People are designated by their first names. Partly to avoid introducing gender as another entity type, gender information is coded by means of two unary predicates. The conceptual schema is shown below:

Stored fact types:
    F1 X is male
    F2 Y is female
    F3 X is parent of Y

Constraints:
    C1 Each entity is either male or female
    C2 No entity is both male and female
    C3 Each entity has at most 2 parents
    C4 Nobody is his/her own parent

Derivation rule:
    D1 X is grandparent of Y **if** X is parent of Z **and** Z is parent of Y

The database is initially empty. The user now attempts the following sequence of updates and queries. For convenience we use an abbreviated notation for compound updates (for example, see (a)). For each legal update write "accepted". For each illegal update write "rejected" and supply a reason. For queries (assumed legal), supply an appropriate response.

(a) add: Terry is male; Norma is female; Paul is male;
David is male; Linda is female; Selena is female.
Alice is female; Chris is female.
(b) add: Bernie is parent of Terry.
(c) add: Terry is parent of Selena; Norma is parent of Selena.
(d) add: David is parent of David.
(e) add: Norma is parent of Paul; Alice is parent of Terry.
(f) add: Chris is male.
(g) add: Chris is parent of Selena.
(h) Who is grandparent of Selena?

Formulate your own derivation rules for the following:

(i) X is father of Y
(j) X is daughter of Y
(k) X is grand-daughter of Y

5. Consider the following UoD, where employees are identified by surname and departments and languages by name.

Stored fact types:
F1 Employee works for Department
F2 Employee speaks Language

Constraints:
C1 Each employee works for at least one department
C2 Each employee works for at most one department
C3 Each employee speaks at least one language

(a) Provide an update sequence to add the facts that Adams and Brown, who both speak English, work for the Health Department.
(b) Invent some database populations which are inconsistent with the conceptual schema.

2.3 Links between fourth and fifth generation approaches

In this section we provide a brief overview of fourth generation information systems and indicate some ways in which they can be used to implement conceptual schemas. While small database systems include simple file managers and free-format database systems, the large database systems of today may be broadly categorized into three main types: relational, hierarchic and network. Of these, only *relational database systems* are truly fourth generation, freeing the user of the need to specify access paths, so we confine our attention to these.

A relational database is made up of named *tables*, which may be divided horizontally into unnamed *rows* and vertically into named *columns*. A particular row-column location is a field. Each field contains only one data value. Table 2.1 shows a table with three rows, five columns and fifteen fields. The table name, column names and field values have been omitted.

Table 2.1 A table

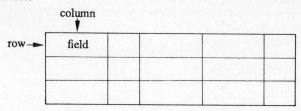

Table 2.2 Two tables containing information about employees

Employee:	Name	Sex	Dept	Speaks:	Employee	Foreign language
	Adams	F	sales		Adams	Spanish
	Bond	M	sales		Cooper	French
	Cooper	F	service		Cooper	Spanish

In spreadsheet work where both rows and columns are named, the term "cell" is often used for "field". In contrast to our usage, the term "field" is often used in the sense of "column".

Relational database systems are based on the relational model of data developed by E. F. Codd. In this model, duplicate rows are not allowed and the order of the rows doesn't matter. We may treat a table as a set of rows, and each row as a sequence or *tuple* of data values (actually columns are "ordered" by their names rather than by position). So a table is a set of tuples. Since a relation may be defined mathematically as a set of tuples, each table is a *relation*: hence the name "relational database".

In Table 2.2 we have two tables, named Employee and Speaks. The first might be used by a company to record the sex and department of its employees, and the second to record any foreign languages spoken by these employees. The arrow running between the tables indicates that any employee referenced in the second table is named in the first table. We discuss this example further shortly.

At the fourth generation level, the main *database operations* are:

Data definition
Data manipulation: Retrieval;
                      Maintenance: Insertion;
                                    Deletion;
                                      Modification
Data presentation: Data display
                      Report writing

Data definition means declaring the relational schema: here we create the table structures and specify various constraints on them. Tables so created are empty until data are inserted into them. Data definition reveals the design of the database.

Data manipulation covers both retrieval and maintenance of data. The operation of data retrieval typically involves three steps: the user requests information; the system searches the database and/or the schema to locate the relevant information, and uses this

Table 2.3 An output report

Employee	Gender	Dept	Foreign languages
Adams	F	sales	Spanish
Bond	M	sales	
Cooper	F	service	French, Spanish

to obtain the required result; the system then outputs this result. The second stage may involve sorting data and/or deriving results (e.g. an average value).

Unlike data retrieval, which leaves the database unaltered, the three *data maintenance* operations involve changing the database. Once a table has been declared, rows of data may be inserted into it. The removal of a whole row from a table is deletion. It is also possible to change just part of a row, by altering one or more of its field values: this is modification. Although in SQL "update" means "modify", we use the term "update" generically to include insert, delete and modify operations.

The maintenance operations are automatically supervised, to an extent dependent on the system, in an effort to ensure the database population is in accord with the schema. Checks on the *integrity* or correctness of the database are often quite limited at the fourth generation level. If a database is badly designed it can easily pick up errors when updated.

Data presentation refers to special techniques for displaying information on the screen (data display) or for producing formatted printed output (report writing). We use the term *"output report"* generically to include screen and hard copy reports. Other database operations include catalog manipulation, procedure execution and security enforcement. An important front end skill is the design of *input forms* to capture the data.

In this text the primary relational database operation discussed is data definition. As we show later, if we first design the conceptual schema for a UoD, it is easy to map this down onto a relational schema. To illustrate why we need to be careful in designing tables, and to introduce some of the connections between the fifth and fourth generation approaches, let's return to UoD of Table 2.2. To begin our design task, we won't have the database structures provided, but with the help of the UoD expert we can find or create an example of the kind of information required. Let's suppose we come up with the output report shown in Table 2.3.

In later chapters, we show how to use an output report like this to arrive at the conceptual schema and display it in graphical form. For now, we merely set out the conceptual schema informally, omitting details of reference schemes:

Stored fact types:
  F1 Employee has Gender
  F2 Employee works for Department
  F3 Employee speaks Foreign language

Constraints:
  C1 Each employee has at least one gender
  C2 Each employee has at most one gender
  C3 Each employee works for at least one department
  C4 Each employee works for at most one department
  C5 Gender is referenced by labels 'F', 'M'

Notice that the fact types are elementary. The constraints allow that some employees may speak no foreign language (e.g. Bond), some may speak many (e.g. Cooper), and many may speak the same foreign language (e.g. Spanish). The conceptual database for this schema contains three tables, one for each fact type. Some important consequences of this approach are that the schema is easy to understand, it is automatically free of redundancy, and constraints are easy to specify.

In contrast, a relational database allows facts of different types to be grouped into the same table. For example, Table 2.2 groups the three fact types into two tables. The Employee table caters for fact types F1 and F2, while the Speaks table caters for fact type F3. The first row of the Employee table expresses two facts: Adams has gender "M"; and Adams works for the sales department. In general, *each row of a table in a relational database expresses one or more elementary facts.*

With relational databases, care is needed in grouping facts into tables. In a later chapter we provide a simple procedure for mapping a conceptual schema onto a relational schema. This procedure shows that the choice of tables in Table 2.2 is correct. Suppose however, we chose the table design of Table 2.4. Can you see any problems with this?

Here we have put all the information into one table. Unlike the output report, only one value is allowed per field, so we need two rows to cater for Cooper speaking two foreign languages. But the facts that Cooper is female and works for the service department have been recorded twice. This redundancy leaves the database open to update anomalies. For example, suppose Cooper is transferred to the sales department and, to record this change, we replace "service" with "sales" on the third row but forget to do this for the fourth row. The database is now inconsistent with the conceptual schema, since Cooper is now recorded as working for two departments.

Such issues will be discussed in detail later, but from this preview a number of points should already be clear. Firstly, even if an output report comes in tabular form, this may differ from the table design actually used in a relational database. Secondly, each table of a relational database corresponds to one or more fact types of the conceptual schema. Thirdly, good table design is crucial to avoiding database errors.

Note that the row modify operation of a relational DBMS can be expressed conceptually in terms of adding, deleting or replacing elementary facts. For example, changing "service" to "sales" on the third row of the Employee table of Table 2.2 corresponds to deleting the fact that Cooper works for the service department and adding the fact that Cooper works for the sales department. If this seems tedious, remember that we are talking about the conceptual level, not the external level where the user actually communicates. At the external level, a 5GIS may permit the user to simply modify values in a table row displayed on the screen: conceptually however, such an operation would be

Table 2.4 A badly designed table

Employee:	Name	Sex	Dept	Foreign language
	Adams	F	sales	Spanish
	Bond	M	sales	
	Cooper	F	service	French
	Cooper	F	service	Spanish

translated into the appropriate delete and add operations on elementary facts before being passed on to the CIP.

We now have some idea of how the stored fact types of a conceptual schema are handled in terms of table definitions in a relational DBMS. In a later chapter, we see that these definitions can also be used to specify some of the constraints, but in practice many constraints have to be coded separately. As regards derivation rules, some of these may be handled by defining virtual tables (called "views" in SQL) or by parametized stored queries or routines. If a query type is commonly used and requires derivation, then it is explicitly included in the derivation rules section of the conceptual schema. In contrast, ad hoc queries are catered for by including derivation functions and operators in the query language itself, so that the user may express the required derivation rule within the query formulation itself.

In a relational database language like SQL it is fairly easy to express many mathematical and logical derivation rules (e.g. averages, or grandparenthood derived from parenthood). Some derivation rules cannot be expressed in SQL, but can be easily expressed in other languages. For example, the following Prolog rules recursively define ancestry in terms of parenthood:

X is ancestor of Y **if** X is parent of Y.
X is ancestor of Y **if** X is parent of Z **and** Z is ancestor of Y.

Languages like Prolog and Lisp are used extensively in artificial intelligence (AI) research, while SQL has become the standard relational language for large commercial databases. In the past, AI systems tended to work with small populations of a large number of complex fact types, and database systems worked with large populations of fewer and simpler fact types. More recently, there has been a growing realization of the benefits of powerful inference and efficient database management capabilities to both AI systems and commercial database systems. This synthesis of relational DBMSs and inference systems is a promising move toward fifth generation information systems. Commercial products such as IBM's Prolog/SQL/DS are already proving their worth.

Even if we have a very sophisticated 5GIS in which formulating queries in the system's language is almost as easy as expressing the query in natural language, the mental task of first coming up with appropriate queries in natural language may remain difficult. Moreover, certain problems are of such a nature that their solution cannot be fully automated, even in principle. Apart from the human skills and responsibility involved in specifying the design of a UoD there will always remain room for human creativity at the query level when interacting with an information system.

References

Codd, E. F. (1970), "A Relational Model for Large Shared Data Banks", *CACM* 13, 6.

Date, C. J. (1986), *An Introduction to Database Systems*, Vol. 1, 4th ed. (Reading, MA: Addison-Wesley), Chaps 1–3.

Falkenberg, E. D. (1982), "Foundation of the Conceptual Schema Approach of Information Systems Management", *Lecture Notes for Database Management and Applications* (Amsterdam: North Holland-Publishing Co.).

Nijssen, G. M. (1985), "On Experience with Large Scale Teaching and Use of Fact-Based Conceptual Schemas in Industry and University", in R. Meersman and T. Steel Jr (eds) *Database Semantics: Proc. IFIP Conf. on Database Semantics* (Amsterdam: North-Holland Publishing Co.).

Van Griethuysen, J. J. (ed.) (1982), *Concepts and Terminology for the Conceptual Schema and the Information Base*, ISO Report TC97/SC5/WG3.

3 Fact types

3.1 The software life cycle

In this chapter we look at the first few steps in designing a conceptual schema: here we examine how to identify and graphically portray the fact types relevant to the UoD. As a background to this we first consider the overall task of software development, then provide an overview of the full conceptual design procedure.

Developing an information system is essentially a *problem solving* process. This general process may be broken down into four main stages: define the problem; devise a plan; execute the plan; evaluate what happened. Two of the most generally useful problem solving strategies are: try a *simpler* version of the problem first; divide the problem into a number of *subproblems* and deal with these individually. When the problem solving process involves the development of computer software, it may be refined into the 5-stage **software life cycle** shown in Figure 3.1.

The arrows indicate the cyclic nature of the process. If a need for change is detected at a later stage of the cycle it is often necessary to return to one of the earlier stages. Unless a decision is made to cease work on the software, the cycle may be perpetual. While this cycle applies to software development in general, we now focus on information systems.

Specification involves saying clearly what you want the system to do. This often involves careful analysis of the environment and assessment of user needs. At this stage the various functions or tasks expected of the information system are delineated. A cost/benefit analysis is often advisable to determine, at least roughly, whether the needs are likely to be best satisfied by continuing with the project. This stage is sometimes described as "systems planning and analysis".

The second stage is the **design** of the software to meet the specifications. With large information management tasks, subproblems of a more manageable size might be

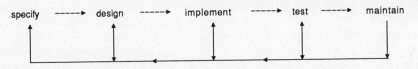

Figure 3.1   The software life cycle

29

selected and a conceptual subschema designed for each. The various *subschemas* may then be *integrated* within an overall conceptual schema. In our methodology, the specification phase blends into the design phase, since we begin our design procedure by looking at information examples obtained in the planning and analysis stage.

In this text, the problems we discuss are small enough to enable us to design the whole conceptual schema without the need to first design subschemas. We will, however, break the design process up into various stages. For example, we identify the fact types before adding constraints to them.

In a recent survey of information systems design methodologies (Olle et al., 1988), three different perspectives are identified. The *data-oriented perspective* focusses on what kinds of data are stored in the database, what constraints apply to these data, and what kinds of data are derivable. This perspective is expressed at the highest level by the conceptual schema, and because of its fundamental nature is the perspective given emphasis in this text.

The *process-oriented perspective* is concerned with the processes or activities performed in the application area. This perspective may help humans to understand the way a particular business operates. Processes are described, and the direction in which information flows between processes and other components is made clear. Often, a complex process is refined into several subprocesses. We use a graphical formalism known as *information flow diagrams* to display this perspective.

The *behavior-oriented perspective* is concerned with how events in the real world trigger actions in the information system, and in general with what temporal or "causal" constraints apply between *events*. The distinction between "process" and "event" is somewhat fuzzy, and in some cases an activity analysis may be rephrased in terms of an event analysis, or vice versa. The most important thing is to specify the information needed and conditions sufficient for a process to execute or "fire". For example, the process of producing an account balance might be triggered by the event of a client requesting his or her account balance, and require input of information from the client (e.g. client number and account name) and the relevant database table.

Further discussion of the process and behavioral perspectives is postponed until much later in the text. For the next several chapters we concentrate on the data perspective.

The *formalization* or *semantic modelling* phase is completed once we have developed the overall conceptual schema: if we have done this correctly (unfortunately there is no algorithm for this), any state of the UoD (the relevant portion of the real world) can now be formally described by a state of the knowledge base. We then consider the *mapping* phase, which introduces the design aspects needed to transform the conceptual design into the practical realities of the internal and external levels.

With most methodologies, the formalization phase is heavily dependent on human creativity. The schema design procedure discussed in this text essentially removes this creativity requirement from all but the *first step* of the design process. The rest of the formalization phase and the mapping phase can be automated almost entirely. Later we discuss an algorithm for mapping the conceptual schema onto an "optimal normal form" relational schema for implementation on fourth generation systems such as IBM's DB2.

The **implementation** or construction stage involves writing the actual code to add the schema to the actual hardware system. This stage usually overlaps with the **testing** stage. The software is run using carefully chosen databases. Sometimes a simplified version of the software known as a *prototype* is developed and tested first to make sure the overall project is feasible. With certain types of software (e.g. military security systems), *correctness proofs* may be developed to ensure the program meets its specifications.

The term software **maintenance** refers to the modification of software after it has been initially released. This maintenance may be of three main types: *corrective* (eliminate bugs); *adaptive* (alter software to cater for changes in the environment or UoD); and *perfective* (add improvements). Most software maintenance tends to fall into the perfective category.

In developing information systems, various factors are considered generally important. These include practicality (is use of a computer the best way to solve the problem?), correctness, clarity (code should be readable and well documented), efficiency (memory requirements, speed, production costs), portability, user-proofing and support.

For large commercial software projects using third generation languages, maintenance typically involves over half of the total cost. The transition from third to fifth generation systems is associated with a *shift of emphasis towards* the first two stages of the software life cycle. If the *specification and design* are done properly, there is comparatively little programming, testing and maintenance required. Use of fourth generation software with fifth generation design techniques can dramatically reduce the total costs, with specification and design becoming the most costly stages.

With this overall picture of the software production cycle, we now direct our focus to the specification and design of conceptual schemas. In doing so, we use the term *conceptual schema design* (CSD) to cover both specification and design aspects.

3.2 Overview of conceptual schema design procedure

When presented with the task of developing an information system, our first steps are to specify what is required and produce a design to meet these requirements. For reasons outlined earlier, we first develop this design at the conceptual level. That is, we attempt to formally describe the UoD in terms of a conceptual schema.

To solve this problem we use a **conceptual schema design procedure** (CSDP) that was originally developed by Professors G. M. Nijssen (University of Queensland) and E. D. Falkenberg (Katholieke Universiteit, Nijmegen). The idea to base conceptual schema concepts on elementary *natural language* sentences was proposed by Falkenberg, and was influenced by the work of the linguist C. J. Fillmore (1968). The fundamental approach of building a design by *starting with specific examples*, and thereafter following a well-defined procedure using visually meaningful diagrams easily populated for validation purposes, was originally developed by Nijssen while working at Control Data: this methodology was called NIAM (Nijssen's Information Analysis Methodology) by Control Data.

Over the years, NIAM has evolved owing to the research contributions of Nijssen, Falkenberg and others. In particular, several revisions and extensions to the methodology as presented in this text were developed by T.A. Halpin (University of Queensland). Because of its emphasis on fact types, NIAM is also called *fact-oriented modeling*.

Table 3.1   The conceptual schema design procedure

---

1. Transform familiar information examples into elementary facts, and apply quality checks.
2. Draw a first draft of the conceptual schema diagram, and apply a population check.
3. Eliminate surplus entity types and common roles, and identify any derived fact types.
4. Add uniqueness constraints for each fact type.
5. Check that fact types are of the right arity.
6. Add entity type, mandatory role, subtype and occurrence frequency constraints.
7. Check that each entity can be identified.
8. Add equality, exclusion, subset and other constraints.
9. Check that the conceptual schema is consistent with the original examples, has no redundancy, and is complete.

Although similar in some respects to the Entity-Relationship model proposed by Chen (1976), we believe that NIAM provides a simpler and more natural approach to semantic modeling. Moreover, NIAM provides a high level procedure for relational database design that has many advantages over the traditional "normalization" technique. A comparison between NIAM and these other methodologies is presented in a later chapter.

In order to divide what in principle could be a very complex task into manageable stages, the CSDP is presented as a sequence of **nine steps**, as set out in Table 3.1. The procedure begins with the analysis of examples of information to be output by, or input to, the information system. Basically, the first three steps are concerned with identifying the fact types (stored or derived). In later steps we add constraints to the stored fact types. Throughout the procedure, checks are performed to ensure that no mistakes have been made. In the rest of this chapter we consider the first three steps in detail.

3.3   CSDP step 1: From examples to elementary facts

To specify what is required of an information system, we need to answer the question: *What sort of information do we want from the system*? This is closely connected with deciding what sorts of queries we wish to issue. Clearly, any information to be output from the system must be either stored in the system, or be derivable by the system. To get a detailed and clear picture of how this should be done, we use a conceptual schema design procedure. Our first step is to *begin with familiar examples* of relevant information, and *express these in terms of elementary facts*.

CSDP *step 1: Transform familiar information examples into elementary facts*

If we are designing a conceptual schema for an application that was previously handled either manually or by computer, information examples will be readily available in the form of reports, documents etc. Two of the most important types of examples are output reports and input forms. These might be in tabular, graphical, template or textual form. A simple tabular report was discussed in the previous chapter. Another example is shown in Table 3.2. This is an extract from the tutorial listings printed by a system used to help allocate students to tutorial groups.

Table 3.2 An output report indicating tutorial allocations

Tutorial group	Time	Room	Student#	Student name
A	Mon 3 p.m.	CS-718	302156	Bloggs FB
			180064	Fletcher JB
			278155	Jackson M
			334067	Jones EP
			200140	Kawamoto T
..	..	..	..	..
B1	Tue 2 p.m.	E-B18	266010	Anderson AB
			348112	Bloggs FB
..	..	..	..	..

Here we would begin by trying to read off the information contained on the top row in terms of elementary facts. To help us in this task we introduce the *telephone heuristic*. That is, imagine you are on the phone and have to convey the information, in simple sentences, to the person at the other end of the line. Try this for yourself now, before checking your answer with the list shown. Here the facts are still expressed somewhat loosely—we will provide a more rigorous treatment shortly.

> Tute group A meets at Time Mon 3 p.m.
> Tute group A is held in Room CS-718.
> Student 302156 belongs to Tute group A.
> Student 302156 has Name 'Bloggs FB'.

Since this verbalization involves some interpretation on our part it is important that the kind of example is *familiar* to us or to another person (e.g. the UoD expert) who is assisting us with step 1. There are many features in this example that rely on interpretation. For instance, we have assumed that if a student number and student name occur on the same row then they refer to the same student. The report itself does not tell us this: we use our background familiarity with the situation to make this assumption. If we are not familiar with the kind of example we should resolve any doubts by consulting a person who is familiar with the UoD.

We stress that communication with the UoD expert and end-users should be by means of examples familiar to these people. Although we as schema designers might be expert in expressing ourselves at a formal, type level the same cannot be said of the average user for which the application is being designed. By working with examples familiar to the user we can tap that user's implicit understanding of the UoD without forcing the user to abstract and express, perhaps incorrectly, the structure we are seeking.

Input forms are used for data capture (i.e. getting specific information into the database). Sometimes information not appearing in the final output reports is required as data to enable the actual results to be computed. For instance, input forms for tutorial allocation would usually seek information on student preferences, for example, students may indicate their first, second and third preferences regarding which tutorial time is suitable for them. If this information is to be taken into account in determining tutorial allocations it must be stored in the system. An example of such an input form is shown in Table 3.3.

Table 3.3   An input form for collecting tutorial preferences

CS112 Tutorial preferences form

Please complete the form below to assist in tutorial allocations.
Tutorials are of 1 hour duration, and are available at these times:

Monday	Tuesday	Thursday
		10 a.m.
		11 a.m.
		12 noon
	2 p.m.	2 p.m.
3 p.m.		3 p.m.

Student number	
Student surname	
Student initials	
Tutorial preference 1	
Tutorial preference 2	
Tutorial preference 3	

To perform step 1 here, you should fill out the form with some examples first. If
"302156" and "Mon 3 p.m." are entered in the first and fifth fields, this expresses the fact
that Student 302156 chooses as second preference the time Mon 3 p.m. Notice that this
input form lacks some of the information needed for the output report, namely, the codes
and rooms of tutorial groups which can be offered at the times indicated. This reduces the
chance of students entering wrong data (they enter the times they prefer directly rather
than indirectly through associated group codes), and allows flexibility in offering many
tutorials at the same time.

Taken individually, the output report and the input form reveal only partially the kinds
of information needed for the system. In combination however, they might be enough for
us to arrive at the structure of the UoD. In this case the pair of examples is said to be
significant. In general, a set of examples is said to be significant or adequate with respect
to a specific UoD if it illustrates all the relevant sorts of information and constraints
required for that application. With complex UoDs, considerable attention is needed to
ensure that the set of examples is significant.

With our current application, if a student can be allocated to only one group then
Table 3.2 is significant in this respect. However, if more than one group can be held at the
same time, Table 3.2 is not significant in this other respect. A further row would be
needed to illustrate this possibility within the UoD (e.g. a row including the fact that tute
group B2 meets at time Tue 2 p.m.). We explore the notion of significance relative to
various constraints in later chapters.

It will become obvious later that no set of examples can be significant with respect to
derivation rules or subtype definitions. In such cases the use of a UoD expert is essential.

With the current application, we have made no mention of the rules used to arrive at the tutorial allocations. If in addition to storing information about preferences and allocations, the information system was also required to compute the allocations in a nearly optimal way which respected preferences and other practical constraints (e.g. on size of groups), the design of the derivation rules becomes the challenging aspect of the schema. While such automation can be achieved (e.g. by examining intermediate output reports used by human experts to perform the allocation, and questioning them about their strategies) another alternative is to divide the task between the human expert and the system. The use of powerful 4GLs like SQL facilitates such co-operative solutions.

Provided we include output reports relevant to intermediate stages of computation, all the information structures can be determined. Hence a comprehensive set of output reports can eliminate the need to examine input forms. Output reports tend to be easier to interpret, especially if the input forms have been poorly designed. Once the conceptual schema has been specified, it is clear to the analyst just what kinds of information need to be input. However care is still needed in the design of the input forms to make them clear and simple for the people entering the data.

Sometimes information examples appear in formats other than tables or text. For example, Figure 3.2 might be used to display information about what flight connections are provided by a particular airline, with the arrowheads indicating the direction of the flights. As an exercise, perform step 1 for this graph. If no output reports, input forms, data diagrams etc. already exist (e.g. you may be working on a new application) then you should begin by getting the user to write down some examples, and then work from these.

Assuming we have a significant set of familiar examples, we translate these examples into elementary facts. Recall that at the conceptual level the database consists of a set of elementary facts. It is time we defined more precisely what an elementary fact is.

To begin with, an elementary fact is a simple assertion about the UoD. The word "fact" indicates that the system is to treat the assertion as being true of the UoD (whether this is actually the case is of no concern to the system). Although in everyday speech, unless something is true of the real world it cannot be a fact, in computing terminology we resign ourselves to the fact(!) that it is possible to have "false facts" in the database (just as we agree to use the word "statement" for so many things that aren't really statements in procedural languages like Pascal).

Recall that the UoD is the portion of the (typically) real world relevant to our application. We may think of the UoD as a *set of objects playing roles*. Elementary facts

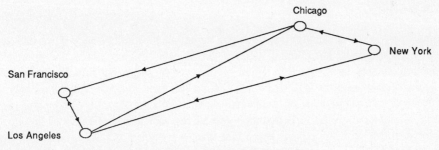

Figure 3.2 A graph showing flight connections between cities

are assertions that particular objects play particular roles. The simplest kind of elementary fact asserts that a single object plays a given role. For example:

1. Ann smokes

Here we have one object (Ann) playing a role (smokes). We will shortly demand a more rigorous scheme for identifying objects (e.g. "Ann" is expanded to "the person with firstname 'Ann'"). With sentences like (1) the role played by the object is sometimes called a *property* of the object. Here an elementary fact asserts that a certain object has a certain property. In practical information systems, such facts are rare. Typically an elementary fact asserts that certain objects participate in a *relationship*. For example:

2. Ann employs Bob

Here we have two objects (Ann and Bob) participating together in a relationship (an employment instance). In this relationship Ann plays the role of employer and Bob plays the role of employee.

The adjective "elementary" indicates that the fact cannot be "split" into smaller units of information which collectively provide the same information as the original. Basically, *an elementary fact asserts that a particular object has a property, or that one or more particular objects participate together in a relationship.* Hence elementary facts do not involve the use of logical connectives (e.g. *not, and, or, if*) or logical quantifiers (e.g. *all, some*). For example, none of sentences (3)–(8) are elementary facts.

3. Ann smokes **and** Bob smokes
4. Ann smokes **or** Bob smokes
5. Ann does **not** smoke
6. **If** Bob smokes **then** Bob is cancer prone
7. **All** people who smoke are cancer prone
8. **If any** person smokes **then that** person is cancer prone.

All of these sentences express information. Proposition (3) is a logical conjunction: it should be split into two elementary facts:

Ann smokes.
Bob smokes.

Proposition (4) is a disjunction, and (5) is a negation. It would be nice if we had some way of storing this information, and of having the system make the appropriate deduction: in this case, that Bob smokes. However most current information systems, including those based on SQL or Prolog, are not designed to work with such examples. With respect to negation, work with most database systems operates under the *closed world assumption* (CWA): it is assumed that all relevant information about the UoD is captured in the knowledge base. If the fact that Ann smokes is not stored or derivable, then under CWA it is understood that Ann is not a smoker.

Conditional facts like (6) are almost never encountered in practical systems, but universally quantified conditionals like (7) and (8) are. Actually (7) and (8) are equivalent, and may be catered for either in terms of a subset constraint (see later) or by a derivation rule. Such rules can be specified readily in SQL by means of a view, and are also easily coded in Prolog. For example:

cancer_prone(X) **if** person(X) **and** smokes(X)

Actually, it is possible to express negations, disjunctions, conditionals, and quantified sentences in such a way that they can be handled by relational systems like SQL. However the method is somewhat advanced, and is not considered in this introductory text. Note that for commercial applications it is almost always sufficient to work with databases that are conjunctions of elementary facts. For most cases it would be either needless or impractical to attempt to store disjunctive or negative facts. Negative information about objects might be irrelevant and too large to store; so for efficiency reasons the closed world assumption is usually warranted. Like SQL systems, our methodology allows either a closed or open world approach (or both).

Before refining our notion of elementary facts, it will help to discuss some related terminology. Recall that *entities* are the basic objects or things that we want to talk about. Entities belong to the UoD, and are represented by terms in the knowledge base. An entity may be a tangible object (e.g. the person Felix) or an abstract object (e.g. the subject CS112). A *type* is the set of all possible *instances*. Each entity is an instance of a particular **entity type** (e.g. Person, Subject). For a given UoD, the entity type Person is the set of all people we might possibly want to talk about during the lifetime of the information system. Note that some authors use the word "entity" for "entity type": we sometimes expand "entity" to "entity instance" to avoid any confusion.

In any UoD, we demand that each entity plays at least one role. One way of formalizing this is to say that each entity instantiates at least one logical *predicate*. The simplest sort of predicate is a *unary* predicate (i.e. a property which may be possessed by entities taken individually). For instance, if Felix smokes we may attribute the property of smoking to Felix. To represent a predicate we may use a descriptive phrase, for example, "smokes" or "is cancer prone". A singular term is a phrase which refers to exactly one object. A singular term which refers to an entity is an entity designator. Syntactically then, a unary predicate may be represented as a *sentence with one hole in it*, where the hole or placeholder is to be filled in by an entity designator. For instance, we might represent the smoking predicate as:

. . smokes

For a binary predicate, two entities are usually required. For example, the fact that Felix studies CS112 involves the binary predicate "studies". A binary predicate may be shown as a *sentence with two holes*. For example:

. . studies . .

where the holes are to be plugged in by entity designators. Notice that the *order* in which entities are represented here is important. For example while it may be true that Felix studies CS112, it is nonsense to say that CS112 studies Felix. Sometimes a binary predicate may involve just one entity type. For example, with ". . likes . ." defined over Person we might have "Felix likes Mary" or even "Felix likes Felix".

For a *ternary* predicate three entities are usually required. A ternary predicate may be shown as a *sentence with three holes*. For instance, the fact that Terry has worked in the Computer Science Department for three years involves the predicate:

.. has worked in .. for ..

In general, an *n-ary predicate* may be viewed as a sentence with n holes, each of which is to be filled in by an entity designator. Since the order of these holes is significant, and the same entity designator may sometimes be repeated in the one sentence, we may regard an n-ary predicate to be associated with a *sequence* of n entity designators. The value of *n* is said to be the *arity* of the predicate. Predicates of arity ≥ 2 are said to be polyadic. Unary predicates are often called properties, and polyadic predicates are sometimes called relations (the word "relation" is used in several different senses).

In natural language, there are two main ways of referring to entities. One method uses *proper names*: here a **label** is used to denote a particular object (e.g. "Margaret Thatcher"). The other method is to use a *definite description* (e.g. "the Prime Minister of the UK" or "the Prime Minister called Maggie"). One advantage of proper names is that they tend to be shorter than definite descriptions. So to reduce keystrokes as well as computer storage, we might consider representing each entity simply by a label. But consider the following sentence:

Sydney is located in Wales.

Just exactly what is meant by this? Sydney might be a city, a person or even a horse. Wales might be a country, a hotel or a stable. To avoid this type of referential ambiguity, we need to provide the *context* in which the sentence is to be interpreted. To begin with, we demand that the entity type be mentioned, for example:

The city Sydney is located in the country Wales.

This brings to mind the old joke:

Q. Did you hear about the man with the wooden leg named "Smith"?
A. No. What was the name of his other leg?

Here the responder mistakenly took the label "Smith" to refer to an entity of type WoodenLeg rather than of type Man. Recall the similar example:

Pluto is owned by Mickey.

Mentioning the entity types removes the ambiguity discussed. Compare:

The dog Pluto is owned by the mouse Mickey.
The planet Pluto is owned by the person Mickey.

Sometimes, even the combination of label and entity type is not enough to provide an unambiguous reference. Suppose our UoD concerns a hospital and the following sentence is stated:

The patient Lee has a temperature of 37.

Now imagine that the UoD contains two patients named "Lee Jones" and "Mary Lee". There is more than one person to which the label "Lee" might apply. Worse still, there may be some confusion about the units being used to state the temperature: 37 degrees Celsius is normal bodily temperature but 37 degrees Fahrenheit is freezing! We could resolve this ambiguity by demanding that the **reference mode** (i.e. the manner in which the label refers to the entity) always be mentioned. Compare the following two sentences:

> The patient with firstname 'Lee' has a temperature of 37°C.
> The patient with surname 'Lee' has a temperature of 37°F.

A more common way around the potential confusion caused by overlap of firstnames and surnames would be to demand that the full name be used instead to label people (e.g. "Lee Jones", "Mary Lee"). In some cases however, even full names may not be unique, and another naming convention must be employed (e.g. PatientNr). To avoid confusion with the word "No", we use "Nr" or "#" to abbreviate "Number" instead of "No.". From now on, we usually demand that each entity designator involve three components:

entity type	e.g. Person	Temperature
reference mode	surname	Celsius
label	'Lee'	37

This is the simplest kind of entity designation scheme; and we restrict ourselves to it for quite some time. An elementary fact may now be thought of as asserting a proposition of the form:

$$R (e_1, \ldots ,e_n)$$

where R is a predicate of arity n, and $e_1 .. e_n$ are n entities, not necessarily distinct; moreover, with respect to the UoD the proposition must not be splittable into a conjunction of simpler propositions. Defined in this way, the predicate is instantiated by a sequence of entities, and so the order of the entities is important. Syntactically, we have a sentence in which the predicate and the entities are designated by identifying phrases. This formal definition ties in closely with the notation of *predicate logic*. For naturalness, we write predicates in distfix form (i.e. distributed among their terms). For example, here are two elementary facts:

> The STUDENT with *student#* '302156'
> **studies**
> the SUBJECT with *code* 'CS112'.

> The SCIENTIST with *surname* 'Einstein'
> **moved to**
> the COUNTRY with *acronym* 'USA'
> **during**
> the YEAR 1933 *AD*.

Table 3.4   Some languages and their designers

Designer	*Language*
Wirth	Pascal
Kay	Smalltalk
Wirth	Modula-2

For exposition purposes, the names of the entity types are in upper case, the reference modes in italics, and the predicates in bold type. Step 1 of the CSDP involves translating relevant information examples into sentences like this. For instance, consider the output report of Table 3.4.

Try now to express the information in the first row in the form of elementary facts. Imagine you have to convey the information over the telephone to someone. In performing this visual to auditory transformation, listen first for the entity types and the predicates. Then make sure you fully specify each entity in terms of entity type, reference mode and label. In reports like this the column headings and table names or captions often give a clue as to the entity types and predicates. The column entries typically provide the labels. Here is one way of translating row 1 as an elementary fact:

9. The PERSON with *surname* 'Wirth'
   designed
   the LANGUAGE with *name* 'Pascal'.

Here the entity types are Person and Language, and the reference modes are Surname and Name. Notice that these are all represented by nouns. The predicate is Designed. Notice that the predicate appears as a verb. This is fairly typical for the binary case.

In translating row 1 into the elementary fact shown above, we read the row from left to right. If we like, we could read it in a different order. Reading it from right to left, we would probably come up with something like this:

10. The LANGUAGE with *name* 'Pascal'
    was designed by
    the PERSON with *surname* 'Wirth'.

Notice that, although reordered, the entity designators have remained the same; but we have a different predicate, namely, was-designed-by. In reversing the order of the entity designators we also reversed the predicate. We speak of was-designed-by as the *inverse* of the predicate Designed.

Although semantically we might regard sentences (9) and (10) as expressing the same fact, syntactically they are different. Most logicians would describe this as a case of two different sentences expressing the same proposition. Linguists like to describe this situation by saying the two sentences have different *surface structures* but the same *deep structure*. For example, one linguistic analysis might portray the deep structure sentence as comprising a verb phrase (Design), various noun phrases (the entity designators) each of which relates to the verb in a different case (e.g. agentive for Wirth, and objective for Pascal), together with a modality (past tense).

Different viewpoints exist as to the "correct" way to portray deep structures (e.g. what primitives to select), and the task of translation to deep structures is often complex. In practice, most information systems can be designed without delving further into such issues. It is important however, that we do not treat sentences like (9) and (10) as different, unrelated facts. Our approach is to choose a single, consistent way of expressing facts in natural sentences, but to demand that the entities be carefully identified, and the roles they play be made clear.

This approach can be implemented in different ways, and we do not wish to argue that one of these ways is the best. Each fact type must eventually be given a distinct name. Surface sentences are ordered, and so are logical predicates. If we choose to make use of logical predicates, then faced with sentence (9) or (10) we choose one of these to determine the predicate, for example, if we choose (9) the predicate is "Designed". If we make predicate names distinct we can choose these as the fact type names. For a given fact type, if all the entity types are different the names of the entity types might be used to clarify the roles; if not, the positions in the predicate can be used.

Instead of using this logical predicate representation, one may treat a fact as a *named set of (entity,role) pairs*. Each entity is paired with the role that it plays in the fact. We might set this out thus:

$$F \{ (e_1, r_1), \ldots, (e_n, r_n) \}$$

At the syntax level, F is replaced by the fact type name, each e by an entity designator, and each r by a role name. For example, both (9) and (10) might be translated as the following elementary fact:

Design { (The Person with surname 'Wirth', *designed*),
         (The Language with name 'Pascal', *designed by*) }

Here the role names are italicized. Obviously, there is considerable choice regarding names for fact types and roles. Our preference is to use verb phrases for role names, but one might have used adjectives (e.g. "agentive", "objective") or noun phrases (e.g. "Designer", "Language"). The latter choice relates closely to typical choices of column names in output reports. Notice that by naming the roles we have made the position of the entity-role pairs irrelevant: this is closer to the relational database approach (the order of the columns is irrelevant).

When two or more roles in a fact type are played by the same entity type, it is incorrect to use the name of the entity type for these roles. In general, the name of each role must be unique within its fact type. As a simple example, consider the report shown in Table 3.5.

We might translate row 1 as follows:

Table 3.5   An output report concerning marriages

Husband	Wife
Alan	Betty
Colin	Sue

Marriage { (The Person with firstname 'Alan', *husband of*),
 (The Person with firstname 'Betty', *wife of*) }

Basically, a role is a part played by an entity in some relationship (let us widen the term "relationship" to include unary relationships). To avoid messy problems with symmetric relationships, we demand that each role in a relationship is played by exactly one entity. For example, here we used the role names "husband of" and "wife of", not "spouse of" and "spouse of".

When choosing role names, we generally try to keep them unique to the conceptual schema; but with large schemas this becomes impractical. Since role names must be unique within their own fact type, the combination of the role name and the fact type name serves to identify the role within the context of the conceptual schema.

In this text we make extensive use of the concept of roles, since this concept greatly simplifies the expression of constraints. Two ways of implementing the representation of roles in an information system have been discussed: naming all roles and disregarding order; naming one ordered predicate. In discussing examples, we will pick whichever way of representing roles feels the most convenient. Naming just a single predicate saves writing and matches the approach of logic programming languages such as Prolog. Naming all the roles simplifies query formulation, and is the approach adopted by RIDL (Reference and Idea Language), and effectively by SQL. We discuss this further in Chapter 11.

Note that we have distinguished between entities and labels on the basis that labels are essentially just character strings (names, codes, numerals etc.) which are used to refer to entities. Roughly speaking, the distinction between entities and labels is the distinction between things and their names. This distinction is not absolute however, but relative to the UoD. Sometimes we may wish to regard labels as entities in their own right. Consider the following two sentences:

Australia is a large country.
"Australia" has nine letters.

Here we have an illustration of what logicians call the use/mention distinction. In the first sentence the word "Australia" is being used simply as a label. In the second sentence the word "Australia" is being mentioned, and is talked about as an entity itself: in such cases we may regard labels as referring to themselves.

Exercise 3.3

1. Assuming suitable entity types and reference modes are understood, which of the following sentences express exactly one elementary fact?

    (a) Adam likes Eve.
    (b) Bob does not like John.
    (c) Tom visited Los Angeles and New York.
    (d) Tom visited Los Angeles or New York.
    (e) If Tom visited Los Angeles then he visited New York.

(f) Sue is funny.

(g) All people are funny.

(h) Some people in New York have toured Australia.

(i) Brisbane and Sydney are in Australia.

(j) Brisbane and Sydney are in the same country.

(k) Who does Adam like?

2. Perform CSDP step 1 on rows 1 and 2 of the tutorial group table discussed in this section (these rows are reproduced below). In other words, express the information contained on these two rows in terms of elementary facts. Set your answer out as sentences in English.

Tute group	Time	Room	Student#	Student name
A	Mon 3 p.m.	CS-718	302156	Bloggs FB
			180064	Fletcher JB

3.4   Quality checks on elementary facts

Once we have translated the information examples into elementary facts we should check our work by asking ourselves the following questions:

Are the entities well identified?

Can the facts be split into smaller ones without losing information?

Recall that an entity designator typically involves an entity type and reference mode as well as the label. If we are reading the facts from a table we should ask ourselves what kind of thing (entity type) each column refers to and what kind of naming convention (reference mode) is being used for it.

One way of checking that we have included all components in our elementary facts is to draw a *fact type - instance table*. The top section of this table indicates the fact type being considered, by showing the entity types, reference modes and roles. Thus the top portion of the table deals only with the conceptual schema. The bottom section of the table contains the actual labels stored in the database. When read in conjunction with the top section, the rows in the bottom provide instances of elementary facts. Let's consider a few examples, beginning with the report shown in Table 3.6.

Let's try step 1 on the first row. We might at first consider expressing this information in terms of the following sentence (we adopt the common practice of omitting quotes around numeric labels):

The Person with surname 'Wirth' **designed** the Language with name 'Pascal' **in the** Year 1971 AD.

If this is correct we have a ternary fact type with the predicate:

.. designed .. in ..

Table 3.6

	Designer	Language	Year
	Wirth	Pascal	1971
	Kay	Smalltalk	1972
	Wirth	Modula-2	1979

But recall that an elementary fact must be *simple* or *irreducible*. It cannot be split into two or more simpler facts in the context of the UoD. The appearance of the word "and" in a sentence usually indicates that the sentence may be split into simpler facts. Here we have a sentence without an "and"; but clearly this fact may be split into the following two elementary facts:

> The Person with surname 'Wirth' **designed** the language with name 'Pascal.
> The Language with name 'Pascal' **was designed in** the Year 1971 AD.

If we know these two facts then we also know the original ternary fact we started with. So the ternary can be split. This results in two fact type - instance diagrams (see Figure 3.3).

Now consider the output report of Table 3.7, and try to express the information contained in its top row in terms of one or more elementary facts. Here the table itself has a name ("Results"), which can help us with the interpretation.

Entity types:	Person	Language
Reference modes:	surname	name
Roles:	designed	was designed by
Labels:	Wirth Kay Wirth	Pascal Smalltalk Modula-2

Entity types:	Language	Year
Reference modes:	name	AD
Roles:	was designed in	is design year of
Labels:	Pascal Smalltalk Modula-2	1971 1972 1979

Figure 3.3   Fact type - instance diagrams

Table 3.7   A sample of student performance

Results:	Student	Subject	Rating
	Bright S	CS112	7
	Bright S	CS100	6
	Collins T	CS112	4
	Jones E	CS100	7
	Jones E	CS112	4
	Jones E	MP104	4

After the previous example, you might have been tempted to try to split the information into two facts. For example:

The Student with name 'Bright S' **studies** the Subject with code 'CS112'.
The Student with name 'Bright S' **scores** a Rating with rating# 7.

This approach is incorrect because it results in loss of information. Since Bright studies more than one subject, we don't know for sure from these two facts that Bright's 7 rating is for CS112. In some cases a ternary which is not splittable into two facts may be split into three facts. Here we might try to split the ternary into the previous two facts as well as:

A Rating with rating# 7 **is obtained in** the Subject with code 'CS112'.

However even these three facts don't guarantee that Bright got a 7 for CS112. For example, Jones studied CS112, Jones scored a 7, and a 7 was obtained for CS112, but Jones did not score a 7 in CS112. If a ternary can't be split into three binaries without information loss, then it is definitely unsplittable. We may formulate the ternary fact as:

The Student with name 'Bright S' **scores** a Rating with rating# 7 **in** the Subject with code 'CS112'.

Here the predicate is ".. scores .. in ..". We leave it as an exercise for you to draw up the relevant fact type - instance table. This will have three columns. As a final example, try your hand at step 1 on the report shown in Table 3.8.

One of the tricky features of this table is the final column. Entries in this column are sets of degrees, not single degrees. You should phrase your sentences to include only one degree at a time. When applied to the first row, step 1 results in four facts which may be set out as follows:

Table 3.8   A staff profile

Lecturer:	Name	Birthyear	Age	Degrees
	Adams	1946	42	BSc, PhD
	Ferguson	1940	48	BE, MSc
	Summers	1946	42	BA, BSc, PhD

The Person with surname 'Adams' was born in the Year 1946 AD.
The Person with surname 'Adams' has an Age of 42 years.
The Person with surname 'Adams' holds the Degree with code 'BSc'.
The Person with surname 'Adams' holds the Degree with code 'PhD'.

Here we have three fact types. The reference mode for the entity type Year is AD (rather than e.g. BC). The reference mode for the entity type Age is years, indicating that age is measured in years (rather than e.g. months). Notice that the entity type Year is essentially a location in time, whereas Age is a duration in time.

After you have had plenty of practice at step 1, you may wish to write the elementary facts down in abbreviated form. To start with, we might drop articles such as "the". Then we might shorten the names of reference modes (so long as the names are still meaningful to us) and place them in brackets after the names of the entity types. To help distinguish the entity types we start their names with a capital letter. This would give us something like:

Person (surname) 'Adams' was born in Year (AD) 1946.
Person (surname) 'Adams' has Age (y) 42.
Person (surname) 'Adams' holds Degree (code) 'BSc'.
Person (surname) 'Adams' holds Degree (code) 'PhD'.

Once a standard reference scheme has been detected for an entity type it could be stated once only and thereafter assumed by default. Besides saving writing, this notation helps prepare us for the next step which is to draw a first draft of the conceptual schema diagram. Although this abbreviated notation is useful, please remember to express the facts fully in English, as you would if stating the information over the telephone, before writing them down. Communication with the user should always be in full natural English.

Although it might sound hard to believe, if you have performed step 1 properly, you have completed most of the "hard part" of the conceptual schema design procedure. The remaining steps may seem difficult at first, but, apart from the problem of detecting unusual constraints and derivation rules, once you learn the techniques you can carry out those steps almost automatically. With step 1, however, you will always need to draw upon your human interpretation skills.

Exercise 3.4

Perform step 1 of the CSDP (Conceptual Schema Design Procedure) for the following output reports. In writing down the elementary facts, you may restrict yourself to the top row of the table unless you feel that another row reveals a different kind of fact.

1. (a)

Athlete	Height (cm)
Jones EM	166
Pie QT	166
Smith JA	175

(b)

Athlete	Height (cm)
Jones EM	400
Pie QT	450
Smith JA	550

2.

Person	Height (cm)	Birth year
Jones EM	166	1955
Pie QT	160	1970
Smith JA	175	1955

3.

Advisory panel	Internal member	External member
Databases	Kowalski Turner Frederickson	Ienshtein Spock
Logic programming	Kowalski Colmerauer	Robinson

4. Amsterdam:
   - Born: Colin, David, Gus, Fiona
   - Living: Colin, Eve, Fiona
   - Working: David, Ann, Fiona

   Rotterdam:
   - Born: Ann, Bill
   - Living: David, Bill
   - Working: Bill, Colin, Gus

   The Hague:
   - Born: Eve
   - Living: Ann, Gus
   - Working: Eve

5.

Parents	Children
Ann, Bill	Colin, David, Eve
David, Fiona	Gus

6.

Country	Friends	Enemies
Disland	Oz	
Hades		Oz Wundrland
Wundrland	Oz	Hades
Oz	Disland Wundrland	Hades

Table 3.9

Drives:	*Person*	*Car*
	Adams B	235PZN
	Jones E	235PZN
	Jones E	108AAQ

3.5   CSDP step 2: First draft of conceptual schema diagram

Once we have translated the information examples into elementary facts, and performed quality checks, we are ready for the next step in the conceptual schema design procedure.

CSDP *step 2: Draw a first draft of the conceptual schema diagram and apply a population check*

The major work in this step consists of drawing a diagram which shows all the *fact types*. To do this we need a convention for illustrating entity types, label types and roles. By way of introduction, we first consider the sample output report of Table 3.9.

Let us agree that the information in this report can be expressed by the following three elementary facts, using "reg#" as an abbreviation for "registration number":

The Person with name 'Adams B' drives the Car with reg# '235PZN'.
The Person with name 'Jones E' drives the Car with reg# '235PZN'.
The Person with name 'Jones E' drives the Car with reg# '108AAQ'.

Before looking at the conceptual schema diagram for this situation we first present an *occurrence diagram*, as shown in Figure 3.4. Such diagrams are used to illustrate particular occurrences or instances of facts. Taking advantage of the concrete nature of the entities in this example, we have used cartoon drawings to denote the actual people and cars. The labels are shown as character strings. A particular fact or Drives relationship between a person and a car is shown as a solid arc. A particular reference between a label and an entity is shown as a broken arc.

On both occurrence diagrams and conceptual schema diagrams, an *entity type* is depicted as an *ellipse*: this may be a circle (the simplest form of an ellipse). The name of the entity type is written either inside the ellipse or just beside it. Using flattened ellipses often makes it easier to include the name inside. On an occurrence diagram, individual entities of a given population are explicitly portrayed (e.g. by cartoon symbols or dots). However on a conceptual schema diagram, individual entities are never shown: recalling that a type is the set of permitted instances, we may imagine that entities of a particular type are represented as points inside the ellipse.

We represent a *label type* as a *broken ellipse*, together with the name of the label type. The name of the label type may be the same as the name of the reference mode (e.g. "reg#") or it may differ (e.g. "personName"). Given the name of the entity type and the name of the reference mode it is a trivial matter to choose a name for the label type. In those rare cases where labels of a particular type are to be both used and mentioned (as discussed in Section 3.3), we have a label type which is also an entity type. For example we may wish to compare the nationality of various people with the linguistic origins of their names. Here the names would be used to refer to people as well as be talked about in their own right. Such a case may be depicted by means of a broken ellipse surrounding an unbroken one.

Entities and labels are both examples of *objects*. On a *conceptual schema diagram*, the *roles* played by objects are explicitly shown as *boxes* (see Figure 3.5). The name of the role is placed inside or beside the box. A line segment or *arc* joining a role box to an object type ellipse indicates that the role is played by (at least some) objects of that type. Recall that an *n*-ary fact type involves *n* roles. Diagrammatically, we represent an *n*-ary fact type as a contiguous sequence of *n* role boxes, each of which is connected to exactly one entity type.

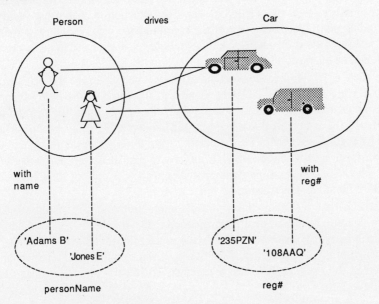

Figure 3.4 An occurrence diagram

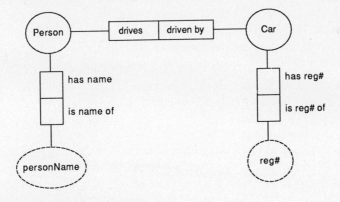

Figure 3.5 A conceptual schema diagram

Table 3.10

Person	Licence#	Cars driven
Adams B	A3050	235PZN
Jones E	A2245	235PZN, 108AAQ

A relationship between entities is an example of a *fact* whereas a relationship between a label and an entity in which the former is used only to help identify the latter is an example of a *reference*. References provide the bridge between the world of things and the world of labels. In Figure 3.5 we have one fact type and two reference types.

For this UoD each person has exactly one name, and each person name refers to exactly one person. Moreover, each car has exactly one registration number, and each registration number refers to exactly one car. This situation is seen most clearly in the occurrence diagram, Figure 3.4. Each of the two reference types is said to provide a *1:1 reference scheme*. This is the simplest kind of reference scheme and in most cases such a scheme should be adopted, where practical.

When such a 1:1 naming convention exists we may indicate the reference mode simply by placing its name in *parentheses* next to the name of the entity type. This is similar to the shorthand scheme for writing down fact types introduced in the previous section. Hence the conceptual schema depicted in Figure 3.5 may be displayed more concisely by Figure 3.6. Unless we specifically want to illustrate the reference schemes, this concise form is to be preferred. Until otherwise indicated, you may assume that all reference schemes in our examples and exercises are 1:1. Step 7 of the CSDP considers other kinds of identification scheme.

As a check that we have drawn the diagram correctly, we should *populate the diagram* with some of the original facts for each fact type. We do this by adding a *fact table* for each fact type, and entering the labels in the relevant columns of this table. The resulting diagram is called a *schema-base diagram*, since not only the schema but various facts stored in the database are shown together. To illustrate this, consider the output report of Table 3.10.

Let us interpret "licence#" as identifying the person's driver's licence. Performing step 1 reveals that there are two binary fact types involved (check this for yourself). We can now draw the conceptual schema diagram. As a check, we populate it with the original data to produce the schema-base diagram shown in Figure 3.7.

Being able to easily populate the conceptual schema diagram is useful not only for detecting schema diagrams that are nonsensical, but also for discussing constraints (as we will see later).

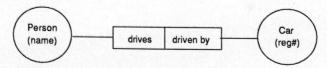

Figure 3.6   1:1 reference schemes are shown in parentheses

Table 3.11

	Smokers	*Nonsmokers*
	Pat	Norma
	Lee	Shir
		Terry

Nowadays most nonsmokers, if given a choice, would select a smoke-free environment in which to work, travel, eat and so on. So for many applications, a table like that of Table 3.11 is relevant. As an exercise, perform step 1 on this table before reading on.

One way of expressing the facts on row 1 is:

Person (firstname) 'Pat' is smoker.
Person (firstname) 'Norma' is nonsmoker.

Each of these facts is an instance of a different *unary fact type*. With a unary fact type, there is only one role. The two fact types are shown on the diagram of Figure 3.8.

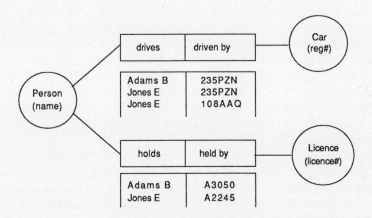

Figure 3.7   A schema-base diagram for the UoD of Table 3.10

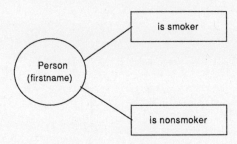

Figure 3.8   Schema diagram for Table 3.11 (unary version)

Here we have two roles, but they belong to different fact types. This is shown visually by having blank space between the role boxes. For reasons to be made clear later (e.g. to simplify the enforcing of constraints), we rarely make use of unary fact types. Any schema with unary fact types may be transformed into an equivalent one using binaries instead. For example, the two unary fact types above can be replaced by a single *binary fact type* by introducing SmokingStatus as another entity type. This status may be represented by means of a code with the possible values "S" for smoker and "N" for non-smoker. So the two facts above could be represented as:

Person (firstname) 'Pat' has SmokingStatus (code) 'S'.
Person (firstname) 'Norma' has SmokingStatus (code) 'N'.

This leads to the conceptual schema diagram shown in Figure 3.9. For checking purposes this has been populated.

Notice the brief role names. For simplicity and convenience, you can choose role names as short as you like, so long as they are meaningful to you. If you adopt the approach of identifying a role by its position in a named predicate, then to keep predicate names distinct you may need to use longer names such as ". . has smoking status . .". If you adopt the approach of naming all the roles, then in textual communication you actually need to identify each fact type by a fact type name: we don't bother about this here since we can identify a fact type by its position on the diagram.

A conceptual schema diagram serves two purposes. Firstly, it provides a clear, simple picture of the UoD for humans. With this purpose in mind, we can be quite relaxed about omitting some names from the diagram (e.g. fact type names and inverse role names) if they are obvious from what is displayed. The second purpose is to provide a formal specification of the knowledge base in terms which can be conceptually handled by the computer system. This requires that such names are provided. For most of the diagrams in this book we have the first purpose in mind.

With each of the above binary examples, there were two different entity types involved. Fact types involving different entity types are said to be *heterogeneous fact types*. Most fact types are of this kind. Consider however the schema-base diagram of Figure 3.10. Here we have only one entity type (Person). In cases like this where each role in the fact type is played by the same entity type we have a *homogeneous fact type*.

Now consider the output report of Table 3.12. This is a briefer form of an example discussed in the previous section.

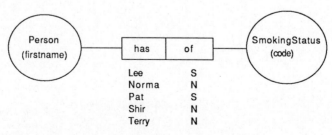

Figure 3.9   Schema-base diagram for Table 3.11 (binary version)

Table 3.12

Student	Subject	Rating
Adams	CS100	4
Brown	CS100	4
Brown	CS112	5

As discussed earlier, here we have a *ternary fact type*. The elementary fact on the top row could be expressed as:

Student (surname) 'Adams' **for** Subject (code) 'CS100' **scores** Rating (rating#) 4.

On a conceptual schema diagram, a ternary fact type appears as a sequence of three role boxes, each of which is attached to an entity type, as shown in Figure 3.11.

With a ternary fact type we could write in names for the three roles. However, apart from involving a lot of writing, it is often difficult to come up with role names which are natural and unambiguous. Instead, we will usually write a single predicate name as shown. To ensure that the order of the roles is clear we write the predicate name in or besides an end role box: this box indicates the first position in the predicate, and the other positions are ordered according to the box-sequence on the diagram. We also adopt this approach with longer fact types such as quaternaries. Of course, this is merely a simple convention to help humans understand the diagram: in adopting this approach we do not

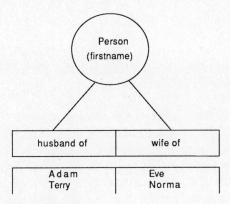

Figure 3.10   A homogeneous fact type

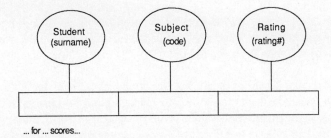

Figure 3.11   A ternary fact type

commit ourselves to the view that the textual specification of the schema must assume any ordering of roles by position in a predicate.

There are two commonly used notations used for describing the "length" or *arity* of a fact type. We have set these out for the first four cases. Our preference is the notation shown on the left. When the right-hand notation is used, the term "adicity" or "adinity" is used instead of "arity".

1.	unary	monadic
2.	binary	dyadic
3.	ternary	triadic
4.	quaternary	tetradic

In a later chapter we devote considerable attention to methods of transforming a conceptual schema diagram into different but semantically equivalent conceptual schema diagrams. At this point we introduce one mechanism for performing such a transformation. The mechanism is known as **nesting**, and basically amounts to treating a relationship between objects as an object itself. For instance, consider once more the information contained in:

Student	*Subject*	*Rating*
Adams	CS100	4

Instead of expressing this as a single sentence, we might convey the information in the following two sentences:

Person (surname) 'Adams' enrolled in Subject (code) 'CS100'.
This Enrollment scores a Rating (rating#) 4.

Here "this enrollment" refers back to the enrollment relationship between the specific person and the specific subject mentioned in the first sentence. It is quite natural to relate a rating to particular enrollment or a student-subject combination of this kind. Any such enrollment may be treated as an object in its own right. The label for such an *objectified relationship* combines the labels for the entities involved. For example, the enrollment of Adams in CS100 may be identified with the use of the compound label "Adams CS100". We say we have a *nested fact type* since the enrollment relationship is nested inside the scoring relationship.

With nested fact types, the objectified relationship is indicated by an ellipse surrounding the relevant roles. This is now treated as an object type in the usual way. The conceptual schema diagram is shown in Figure 3.12. It has been populated with the facts of Table 3.12.

We recognize three kinds of objects. Entities are the simple objects in the UoD about which we wish to talk. Labels are the lexical objects found in database tables that are used to refer to entities. Both these kinds of objects are simple. Finally, we allow relationships between objects to be treated as objects themselves: these are compound objects.

Although we have stressed the practice of populating conceptual schema diagrams for checking purposes, such fact populations do not form part of the conceptual schema diagram itself. In the following exercise, population checks are not requested. However we strongly suggest that you populate each fact type with at least one row as a check on your work.

Exercise 3.5

1. The names and gender of various people are indicated in the following output report:

   Male: Fred, Tom
   Female: Ann, Mary, Sue

   (a) Express the information about Fred and Ann in terms of unary facts.
   (b) Draw a conceptual schema diagram based on this choice.
   (c) Express the same information in terms of binary elementary facts.
   (d) Draw a conceptual schema diagram based on this choice.

Note: For the rest of this exercise, avoid using unary facts.

2. Draw a draft diagram of the conceptual schema for the UoDs of:

   (a) Exercise 3.4, Question 1
   (b) Exercise 3.4, Question 2
   (c) Exercise 3.4, Question 3
   (d) Exercise 3.4, Question 4
   (e) Exercise 3.4, Question 5
   (f) Exercise 3.4, Question 6

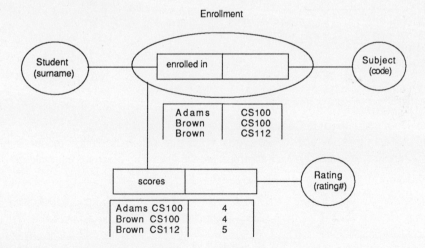

Figure 3.12 A schema-base diagram for a nested fact type

3. Perform steps 1, 2 of the CSDP for the following output report:

Retailer	Item	Quantity sold
CompuWare	SQL+	330
	Zappo Pascal	330
	WordLight	200
Softwareland	SQL+	330
	Zappo Pascal	251

4. Perform steps 1, 2 of the CSDP for the following output report:

Item	Retailer	Quantity sold
SQL+	CompuWare	330
	SoftwareLand	330
Zappo Pascal	CompuWare	330
	Softwareland	251
WordLight	CompuWare	200

5. Perform steps 1, 2 of the CSDP for the following output report:

Tute group	Day	Hour	Room
A	Mon	3 p.m.	69-718
B	Tue	2 p.m.	42-B18
C1	Thu	10 a.m.	69-718
C2	Thu	10 a.m.	67-103

6. Perform steps 1, 2 of the CSDP for the following output report: (*Hint*: Use a nested fact type)

Subject	CreditPts	Semester	Enrolment	Lecturer
CS100	8	1	500	PP
CS102	8	2	500	GR
CS112	8	1	300	TH
CS113	8	2	270	TH
CS380	16	1	50	PB
CS380	16	2	45	AL

7. (a) Does diagram (d) in Question 8 represent a ternary fact type?

(b) Assuming A, B and C are entity types for which reference modes may be supplied, and that r1, r2, r3 are roles, are the following diagrams equivalent?

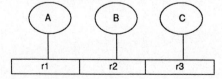 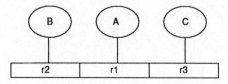

8. Assuming appropriate names may be supplied for entity types, reference modes and roles, which of the following conceptual schema diagrams are legal? Where illegal, briefly explain the error.

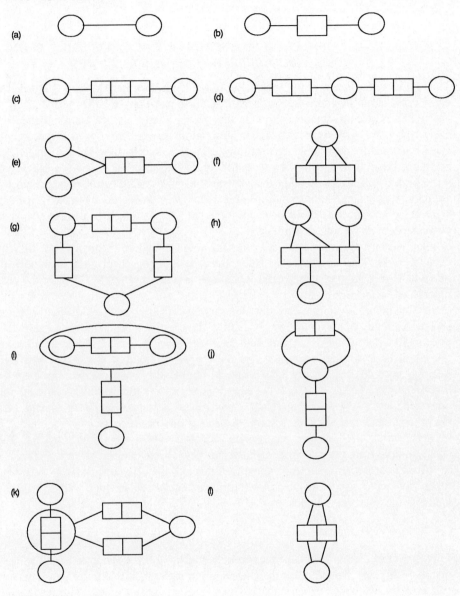

3.6   CSDP step 3: Trim schema and find derived fact types

Having drawn our first draft of the conceptual schema diagram and performed a population check, we now perform the next step in our design procedure.

CSDP *step 3: Eliminate any surplus entity types and common roles, and identify any derived fact types*

The first part of this step is to look around to see if we have introduced any unnecessary entity types in our diagram. Our basic approach is to partition the UoD in such a way that each entity is grouped into exactly one entity type; roughly, entities are grouped into the same type if we want to record similar information about them. So, in selecting **entity types** we should ensure they are **mutually exclusive**, that is, they have no instances in common. Note that this applies to entity types, but not necessarily to label types. Actually, we will need to qualify this statement even in regard to entity types, when we consider subtypes in a later chapter. However, for the moment we may take it that entity types should not overlap. So if you spot some entity types which do overlap you should combine them into a single entity type.

One reason for suspecting that two entity types should be combined is if they both have the *same unit-based reference mode*. Here the entity is conceived as a quantity of so many units (e.g. kilograms or years). Let's look at a few examples. Consider the output report of Table 3.13.

At first glance, we might consider representing the design of this UoD by the diagram shown in Figure 3.13. Note however that the three entity types Wholesale price, Retail price and Markup all have the same unit-based reference mode ($). Moreover, looking at the instances in the table we note that $50 appears as both a wholesale price and a markup: since this same entity is an instance of both entity types *the entity types overlap and hence should be combined*. If the table population is significant the set of retail prices does not overlap the set of markups; nevertheless, it is *meaningful to compare* retail prices and markups since they have the *same unit or dimension* (i.e. dollars). For instance, article A1 has a retail price which is three times its markup. These considerations lead us to collapse the three entity types into one, as shown in Figure 3.14.

There is one other point to be noted with this example. If you look back at the output report you will notice that the following mathematical relationship holds between the values in the last three columns:

Markup = Retail price - Wholesale price

In other words, the markup value may be derived from the wholesale and retail values by means of this rule. To minimize the chance of human error it is usually best to have the system derive this value rather than have humans compute and store it. This also saves on storage. So let us agree to add this rule into our derivation section. We could represent the derived fact type in a formal notation. For example:

A has-markup M **if** A has-wholesale-price W
        and A has-retail-price R
        and M = (R - W)

Table 3.13

Article	Wholesale price ($)	Retail price ($)	Markup ($)
A1	50	75	25
A2	80	130	50
A3	50	70	20
A4	100	130	30

but let us agree to allow **derived fact types** to be expressed informally in any obvious notation (such as the earlier simple arithmetic formula). *Derivation rules may be written below the schema diagram.*

With the rule for deriving markups noted, there is strictly no need to include the derived fact type on the diagram. However, it can be useful for the schema designer to include derived fact types on the diagram so that they can be seen at a glance: this is particularly the case if the number of derivation rules is small. If a derived fact type is shown on the diagram it must be identified as such, to distinguish it from the stored fact types. Our convention is to *place an* **asterisk** *beside any derived fact type that is included on the diagram*, as shown in Figure 3.14.

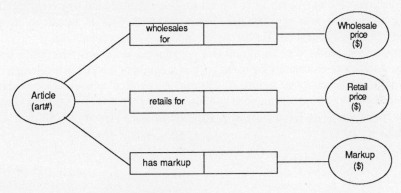

Figure 3.13   A faulty conceptual schema

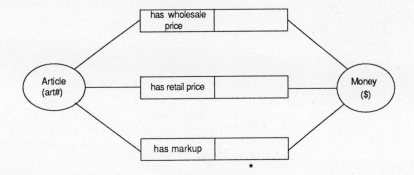

Figure 3.14   The result of applying step 3 to Figure 3.13

Table 3.14

Poster	Height (cm)	Width (cm)	Area (cm²)
P1	40	30	1200
P2	200	60	12000
P3	80	40	3200
P4	20	10	200

Notice that the markup formula allows any one of the three values to be derived from knowledge of the other two. So there is in principle a degree of choice as to which value is selected as the derived one. For instance, we might have chosen Retail price to be derived from Wholesale price and Markup. Our choice of Markup as the derived value is a pragmatic one based on the assumption that it will probably be required less frequently than the other two values in retrieval requests.

Let's consider now a somewhat similar example. Look at the output report of Table 3.14, and try constructing a conceptual schema for it before reading on.

As you probably guessed, we can get by with less than four separate entity types here. Seeing that the values shown in the last three columns are all numbers, you may have been tempted to combine Height, Width and Area into one entity type. You might argue that Height and Width overlap since the value 40 is common, and that Height and Area overlap since each has a value 200. But notice that Area is measured in square centimetres, which is quite a different unit or dimension from centimetres.

Heights and widths may be meaningfully compared with each other since both are lengths: a length of 40 cm may be an instance of a height or a width. But a length of 200 cm is not the same entity as an area of 200 cm². If our final column was Perimeter, we could collapse three headings into one entity type as for the previous example. But since Area is fundamentally a different type of quantity, we must keep it separate, as shown in Figure 3.15.

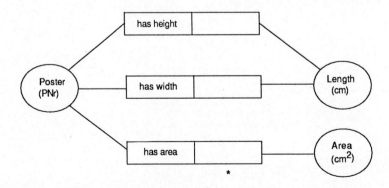

Figure 3.15   Schema diagram for Table 3.14

Notice that we have classified the Area fact type as derived, since area can be computed as the product of height and width. A rule such as the following should be included within the derivation section:

Area = Height × Width

Now consider the conceptual schema diagram shown in Figure 3.16. Here the entity types Cat, Dog and Mouse have a similar reference mode (name) but this is not unit-based; so this is no reason to combine the types. Notice however the "common role" being played by each of the three entity types Cat, Dog and Mouse. Each plays the "role" of having a gender. Actually, this is speaking a bit loosely. A more accurate way of describing this situation is that the *same kind of information* (having a gender) is to be recorded for each.

In cases like this we can arrange for the "common role" to appear just once by combining the entity types playing this role. Here the specific animal types are united into one general animal type, as shown in Figure 3.17.

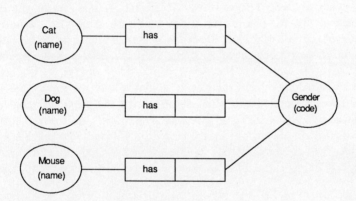

Figure 3.16   Another faulty conceptual schema

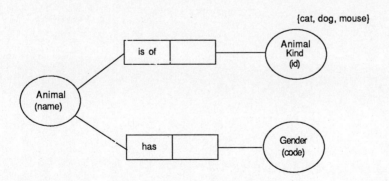

Figure 3.17   The result of applying step 3 to Figure 3.16

Notice that this move effectively combines three label types (CatName, DogName, MouseName) into one (AnimalName). Our use of "(name)" for Animal asserts that there is a 1:1 reference scheme between Animal and AnimalName. The schema of Figure 3.16 permits a dog and cat to have the same name (e.g. "Felix"), but the new schema does not. If the original label types did overlap we would now need to either rename some animals to ensure their names are distinct e.g. "Felix1" and "Felix2", or identify animals by the combination of their name and kind.

To preserve the distinction between the different kinds of animal we introduced a new entity type AnimalKind with reference mode "id" (i.e. identifier). The associated label type AnimalKind-id would have the permitted values "dog", "cat" and "mouse" (or shorter forms if desired). We discuss such "lexical constraints" in detail in Chapter 6. As an exercise, you may wish to invent a small population for this UoD and populate both schemas.

The new schema is simpler than the old one since it has replaced three binary fact types with two binaries. If we had several animal kinds (e.g. bird, cat, dog, elephant, koala, etc.) the saving would be even more worthwhile. If we have only two kinds of animal (e.g. cat and dog) both schemas would have the same number of fact types: but even in this case we choose the new version. There are two main reasons for this. Firstly it is fundamental that we group entities for which the same kind of information is required into the same entity type. Secondly, as will be apparent much later, if both schemas are mapped onto a relational database, the newer schema usually results in fewer tables.

To ensure you are not reading the phrase "common role" too strongly, we had better consider one more example. Have a look at the schema of Figure 3.18. Notice that both the roles played by Person have been given the name "has". Moreover, the roles played by Gender and Height are each given the name "of". Should we treat this as a case of "common roles"? For example, should we collapse Gender and Height into, say, Feature, with an attached fact type to indicate the kind of feature? Think about this before reading on.

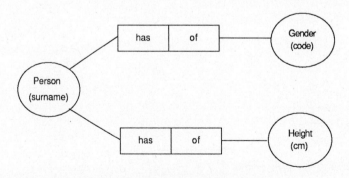

Figure 3.18   Is this schema wrong because of "common roles"?

We hope you decided to leave the schema as it is. Recall that roles are defined not just by their local names but also by the fact type in which they occur. Consider first the roles played by Person. We clearly have two different kinds of information that are to be recorded for Person, so from this viewpoint it would be quite wrong to collapse the two fact types into one.

Consider now the roles played by Gender and Height. By analogy with the animal example, it might be argued that the same kind of information has to be recorded for both Gender and Height (namely, which people possess them) and hence these entity types should be combined! We now have two arguments with contradictory conclusions. Which is correct?

Subjectively, most people would agree that Gender and Height are included in the schema to provide information about Person, and not the other way around. Formally, this intuition can be supported in the following way. Firstly, notice that a person has only one gender and one height, but not vice versa. Secondly, the entity type Person typically plays many more roles than Gender or Height play (the latter often play only one role, as in this case). For such reasons, gender and height are often described as "attributes" of Person.

Thirdly, if we did allow such "attributes" to be collapsed to one entity type we would lose our simple means of enforcing strong typing. In particular the naming conventions would become unwieldy. Here we would have to bundle gender codes (e.g. "M") into the same label type as height numerals (e.g. "180"). With the Poster example, if we combined Area and Length into, say, Measure, the label type for measure would somehow have to distinguish between cm and cm^2 values. So the schema of Figure 3.18 should be left as it is.

In choosing names for reference modes we may use whatever is meaningful enough for our purposes. With dimensionless quantities we often use the reference mode name "Nr" instead of longer names such as "decimal whole number". Strictly speaking, a number is an abstract entity whereas a numeral is a label for a number (e.g. "3" is the decimal (base 10) numeral for the decimal number 3, while "11" is the binary numeral for the same number). Such distinctions will be made explicit only if needed to clarify the intent. We will also loosely speak of labels such as "E1" as "employee numbers" etc. even though such labels are neither numbers nor even numerals.

In performing step 3 of the CSDP, the relevant questions to ask ourselves may be summarized thus:

1. Can the same entity be a member of two entity types?
   If so, combine the entity types into one.

2. Can entities of two different types be meaningfully compared (e.g. to compute ratios)?
   If so, combine the entity types into one.

3. Can all instances of two different entity types play the same role?
   If so, combine the entity types into one, and if necessary add another fact type to preserve the original distinction.

4. Is a fact type derivable from others?
   If so, mark the fact type with "*" and provide a derivation rule.

Exercise 3.6

Perform steps 1–3 of the CSDP for the following output reports.

1.

Project	Project manager	Project budget	Salary	Birth year
P1	Smith J	28000	14000	1946
P2	Jones	42000	10000	1935
P3	Brown	42000	28000	1946
P4	Smith T	36000	12000	1950
P5	Collins	36000	12000	1956

2.

Dept	Budget	NrEmployed Employee	Salary	Sum of salaries
D1	60000	2		35000
		E01	20000	
		E02	15000	
D2	75000	3		42000
		E03	20000	
		E04	12000	
		E05	10000	
D3	75000	2		65000
		E06	45000	
		E07	20000	

3.

Employee	Project	Hours spent so far	Expenses so far
E4	P8	24	200
E4	P9	26	150
E5	P8	14	100
E5	P9	16	110
E6	P8	16	120
E6	P9	14	110

4.

Complexion	Name	Height (cm)	Eye colour
Blonde	Marilyn	160	blue
Blonde	Eve	165	green
Brunette	Ann	160	blue
Redhead	Suzy	170	brown

References

Chen, P. (1976), "The Entity Relationship Model: Towards a Unified View of Data", *ACM TODS* 1, No. 1.

Falkenberg, E. D. (1976), "Concepts for Modelling Information", in G. M. Nijssen (ed) *Modelling in Database Management Systems* (Amsterdam: North-Holland Publishing Co.).

Fillmore, C. (1968), "The Case for Case", in E. Bach and R. T. Harm (eds) *Universals in Linguistic Theory* (New York: Holt, Rinehart & Winston).

Haack, S. (1978), *Philosophy of Logics* (Cambridge: Cambridge Uni. Press) See Chap. 5 for logicians' approaches to proper names and descriptions.

Nijssen, G. M. (1986), "On Experience with Large-scale Teaching and Use of Fact-based Conceptual Schemas in Industry and University", *Proc. IFIP Conference on Database Semantics*, R. Meersman and T. Steel (eds) (Amsterdam: North-Holland Publishing Co.).

Olle, T. W. et al. (1988), *Information Systems Methodologies: A Framework for Understanding*, IFIP CRIS 3 Task Group.

4 Uniqueness constraints

4.1 CSDP step 4: Uniqueness constraints

So far, our conceptual schema design procedure has focussed on specifying the elementary fact types, both stored and derived. The rest of the CSDP is concerned mostly with specifying **constraints**. As we saw in Chapter 2, constraints apply to the database, and may be either static or dynamic. Many kinds of static constraints may be readily indicated on a conceptual schema diagram. On the other hand, dynamic constraints are expressed in natural language or other formalisms such as transition tables. In this text our treatment of constraints focusses on static constraints. In this chapter we look at **uniqueness constraints**. These play a pivotal role when the conceptual schema is later mapped onto a relational schema.

For brevity we often describe static constraints as being "constraints on the fact types". More accurately, *static constraints apply to every possible state of the database*. Here "every state" means "each and every state, taken one at a time". In other words, static constraints apply to all possible *populations* of the fact types. Recall the following example from Chapter 2:

F1: Employee works for Department
C1: Each Employee works for at most one Department

During the lifetime of the information system, the database goes through a sequence of states. In one of these states, the employee Jones may be recorded as working for the sales department. In another state, Jones may be recorded as working for the production department. In no state however may Jones be recorded as working for both of these departments. This is how a constraint like C1 should be interpreted.

In this chapter we learn how to specify uniqueness constraints on the conceptual schema diagram. As we will see shortly, each stored fact type must be assigned at least one uniqueness constraint. Strictly speaking, we could ignore derived fact types in our discussion of constraints since, given the constraints on the stored fact types, such "derived constraints" are implied by the derivation rules. For example, with regard to the derived markup fact type considered in an earlier chapter, if each article has only one wholesale price and only one retail price, the derivation rule (markup = retail price - wholesale price) now implies that each article has only one markup price. However, for exposition purposes we often include uniqueness constraints for derived fact types as well.

CSDP *step 4: Add uniqueness constraints for each fact type*

In this section we learn how to represent uniqueness constraints that apply to a single fact type of arity 1 or 2. The next section considers fact types of arity 3 or above. After that we treat uniqueness constraints that involve more than one fact type.

Unary fact types are the easiest, so let's look at them first. Suppose as part of a fitness application we are interested in which people are joggers. This can be handled with a unary fact type, as shown in Figure 4.1. A sample population is included.

From the conceptual viewpoint the population of this fact type is the set containing the following facts:

The Person with surname 'Adams' jogs.
The Person with surname 'Brown' jogs.
The Person with surname 'Collins' jogs.

Given that these facts are recorded in the database, what would happen if we tried the following update operation?

add: The Person with surname 'Adams' jogs.

The database is a variable whose value or population at any state is a set of elementary facts. Since the fact that Adams jogs is already present in the database, if this fact was now added the population would remain unaltered (sets are insensitive to repetition). In other words the two fact tables shown in Figure 4.2 are equivalent if we look at each as a set of instances:

From this point of view, there is no problem with accepting the update. However, from the internal view, when an elementary fact is added to a database it is typically stored in a previously unallocated space. So accepting the update operation above would mean that the fact that Adams jogs is actually stored twice, in two physically separate locations. This is an example of **redundancy**. If redundancy occurs we need to view the database as a *bag* of facts rather than a set of facts. Informally, a bag or multiset is just like a set except repetition of its members is made significant. For example, although the sets {1} and {1,1} are equal the bags (1) and (1,1) are different.

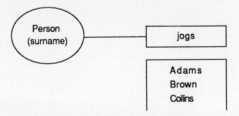

Figure 4.1 A schema-base diagram for a unary fact type

Figure 4.2 Identical sets but different bags

Let us review our reasons for wanting to avoid redundancy in a database. The most important reason is to maintain the integrity of the database by simplifying the correct handling of update operations. For instance, suppose the fact that Adams jogs was stored twice in the database. If we later wanted to delete this fact then we would have to make sure we deleted both the recorded instances of this fact. Managing updates could become very difficult if we allowed redundancy in the database. A second reason for avoiding redundancy is to save space (computer systems have finite storage capabilities).

On the other hand, redundancy can be useful in making retrieval of information more efficient, and sometimes to make information systems work fast enough it may be necessary to allow certain kinds of controlled redundancy, particularly with derived fact types. However, for the purposes of conceptual schema design we will demand that *no redundancy may occur* in the knowledge base.

We will have more to say about redundancy in a later chapter. For now, we simply note that for any state of the database no elementary fact can be repeated. Since each row of a conceptual fact table corresponds to one elementary fact, this means that *no row of a fact table may be repeated*. With our current example, this means that the fact table on the right is illegal, since the Adams row is repeated (see Figure 4.3).

Here, for any particular state of the database, each person can be recorded as being a jogger *at most once*. We represent this *uniqueness constraint* by placing a **double headed arrow** above the fact table as shown in Figure 4.4. This indicates that each entry in the column must be unique.

Notice that the uniqueness constraint also appears next to the role. We can show the constraint on the conceptual schema diagram alone by placing the arrowed bar next to the role (see Figure 4.5).

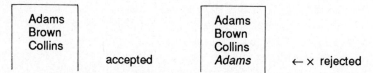

Figure 4.3   Duplicate rows are not allowed

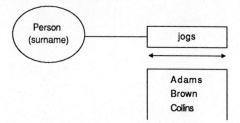

Figure 4.4   Arrowed bar notation for uniqueness constraint

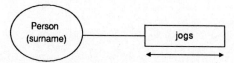

Figure 4.5   Uniqueness constraints are shown next to the role(s)

It doesn't matter on what side (top or bottom) of the role we place the constraint symbol. Moreover, for unary predicates a simple bar may be used instead of an arrowed bar. In this text we always include the arrow tips. Since elementary facts are unique to the database, and each unary fact involves just one entity it is clear that all unary fact types appearing in a conceptual schema diagram should be marked with a bar.

So much for unaries. Now let's consider *binary* fact types, beginning with a schema-base diagram for a familiar example (see Figure 4.6). First note that no whole row of the fact table is repeated. This must be the case, since each row corresponds to an elementary fact, and we have agreed not to repeat facts in our database.

Although each row is unique, we cannot say the same for each student. For example, the student Adams appears twice in the first column. Nor is the subject unique; for example, CS112 occurs twice in the second column. This is an example of a *many to many* (or *m : n*) relation. A student may study many (i.e. at least two) subjects, and a subject may be studied by many students. This feature is shown more clearly in the occurrence diagram of Figure 4.7.

For this fact type then, the strongest uniqueness constraint which applies to every one of its possible populations is that the *combination* of student and subject is unique. We depict this uniqueness constraint by means of an arrowed bar which spans both columns of the fact table (see Figure 4.8).

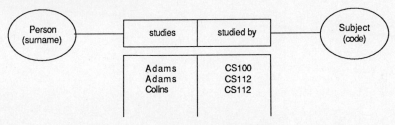

Figure 4.6   A schema-base diagram for a binary fact type

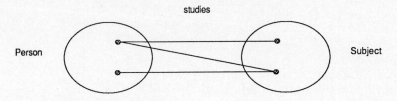

Figure 4.7   A many to many relation

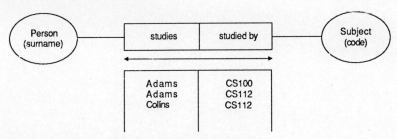

Figure 4.8   Uniqueness constraint across whole row only

We may show the uniqueness constraint on the conceptual schema diagram alone by placing the arrowed bar next to the roles (just remove the fact table from Figure 4.8). As with the unary case, we may use a plain bar to mark the uniqueness constraint on a binary fact type.

Now consider the example shown in Figure 4.9. For this UoD, although many students may enroll in the same degree, no student may be enrolled in many degrees.

This situation may be depicted as shown in Figure 4.10. Many people may enroll in the one degree, but many degrees may not be enrolled in (simultaneously) by the one person. We say that the predicate "..is enrolled in.." is *many to one* (or *n : 1*). The inverse predicate "..is enrolled in by.." is said to be *one to many* (or *1 : n*).

If you look at the fact table you will see that the constraint that each person may enroll in at most one degree amounts to saying that each entry in the Person column must be unique: no surname can be duplicated in that column. We indicate this uniqueness constraint by placing a constraint bar over that column, as shown in Figure 4.11.

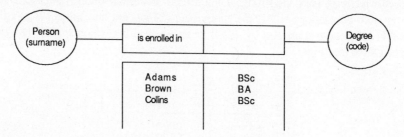

Figure 4.9   Many students may be enrolled in the same degree

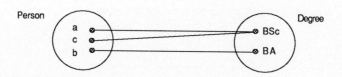

Figure 4.10   A many to one relation

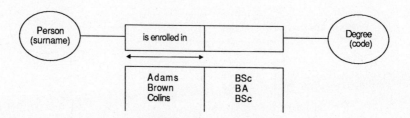

Figure 4.11   Entries in marked column must be unique

Notice that some instances in the Degree column are repeated (here "BSc"). So we do not place a uniqueness marker over this column. As usual, we show the constraint on a conceptual schema diagram by omitting the fact table from this result (see Figure 4.12).

Although the terms "many to one" and "one to many" are often used in describing uniqueness constraints on binaries, this terminology is confusing to many people. A common error is to interpret the "many" side as the "one" side and vice versa. Our convention of showing both roles, and marking the constraint beside the relevant role, clearly indicates the column where entries must be unique.

Now consider the schema-base diagram shown in Figure 4.13. Here we use "PM" to abbreviate "Prime Minister". At any point in time, a person can be Prime Minister of at most one country, and each country can have at most one Prime Minister. For a little variety, we have shown the entity types connected to the top of the role boxes instead of the sides.

For any state of the database, any one person can be recorded as PM of only one country, and vice versa. Hence each population of this fact type is said to be a one to one (or 1:1) relation. The occurrence diagram of Figure 4.14 illustrates the idea.

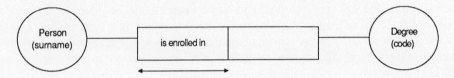

Figure 4.12 Each person is enrolled in at most one degree

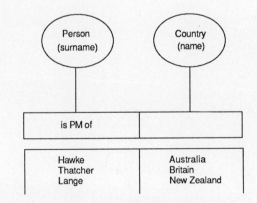

Figure 4.13 What are the uniqueness constraints?

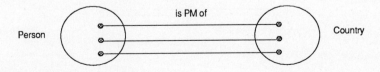

Figure 4.14 A one to one relation

With 1:1 relations no repetition is allowed in either column of the fact table. Here each person is referenced only once in the first column, and each country is referenced only once in the second column. So we mark uniqueness constraints above each of these columns (see Figure 4.15). The conceptual schema diagram for this fact type is obtained by removing the fact table.

If one of the object types involved in a 1:1 relationship type is a label type we have a 1:1 naming convention. For such cases we usually just name the reference mode in parentheses. However, if desired we may set out 1:1 reference schemes more fully as shown in Figure 4.16.

Note that here we have a reference type rather than a fact type. When there is only one means of referring to an entity type, and this reference is 1:1, the uniqueness constraints are the responsibility of the user rather than the system to enforce. For example, we had better ensure that there really is only one degree with the code "BA". If two 1:1 naming conventions could be used (e.g. code or title) we choose one as our standard reference type for identification, and treat the other like any other fact type. We discuss such cases further in a later chapter.

We have now considered the four possible types of uniqueness constraints that may be applied to a binary fact type (many to many, many to one, one to many, and one to one). Each of the examples has involved a heterogeneous fact type (different entity types). Let's look now at some schema-base diagrams for a few homogeneous fact types (only one entity type). In these examples Person is the entity type, and we assume that a person's first name provides a 1:1 naming convention.

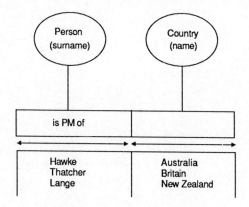

Figure 4.15   Entries in each column must be unique

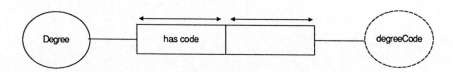

Figure 4.16   A 1:1 naming convention shown explicitly

For our first example we consider parenthood (see Figure 4.17). As the sample fact table reveals, a person may have many children. Moreover a person may have many parents. The column entries need not be unique but the whole row must be. So the uniqueness constraint spans the whole row.

Contrast this with motherhood (see Figure 4.18). Although a mother may have many children each person has only one mother. Entries in the second column (as ordered in the figure) of the fact table must be unique to that column. So we mark the constraint as shown.

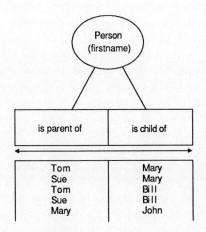

Figure 4.17   Parenthood is many to many

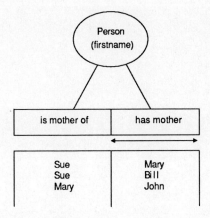

Figure 4.18   Each person has only one mother

The example shown in Figure 4.19 is consistent with the marriage convention known as monogamy: at any time each man has at most one wife and each woman has at most one husband. This means that entries in each column must be unique.

As an exercise, draw a schema-base diagram for each of the following marriage conventions: polyandry (a woman may have many husbands but not vice versa); polygyny (a man may have many wives but not vice versa); and polygamy (the unrestricted case where a man may have many wives, and a woman may have many husbands).

To understand our convention for marking uniqueness constraints we should see them as being placed in the context of a whole schema-base diagram, in the way we have introduced them in this section. With this understanding we may consider that for a given fact type **each role is associated with a corresponding column of the fact table**. If we think of fact types in terms of logical predicates, the role boxes are the "holes" in which the entities are entered for a given fact; for a set of facts of this type the holes expand to columns. With heterogeneous fact types, we tend to make a strong connection between columns and their entity types. For example, with "Einstein was born in 1879" we think of Einstein as a person and 1879 as a year. With homogeneous fact types we tend to focus on the roles. For example, with "Tom is parent of Mary" we think of Tom and Mary as playing the roles of parent and child respectively.

Marking a single role with a uniqueness bar means that entries in the associated column must be unique to that column, that is, no duplicates are allowed in that column. A uniqueness bar that spans a whole row means that each whole row entry is unique to the table. Since we never allow whole rows to be repeated, this whole row constraint will be true of any fact type that we consider.

If we have a stronger uniqueness constraint then the whole row constraint is implied by this and hence is redundant. For this reason, we never mark the whole row constraint across a fact type unless that is the only uniqueness constraint that applies. With this understanding, we must choose exactly one of the four constraint patterns shown in Figure 4.20 to specify the uniqueness constraint for any binary fact type. For brevity we ignore reference schemes, and think of the facts as being of the form aRb (a bears the relation R to b, or a Rs b).

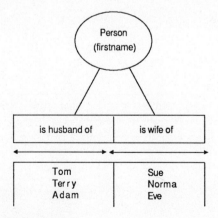

Figure 4.19   Monogamy is one to one

Table 4.1   An output report of doubtful significance

Referee	Paper
Jones	1
Smith	2

Provided a significant fact table is supplied, the uniqueness constraints can be determined simply by looking for duplicates. If we are not familiar with the application, we may be unsure as to whether the population of the fact table is significant. Consider for example the output report of Table 4.1.

Suppose this report is presented as an example of one kind of information to be provided by an information system to assist in running a conference. Part of the task involves getting qualified people to referee (assess the suitability of) papers submitted by people who hope to present a paper at the conference. Let us agree that the information in the table may be dealt with by the fact type shown in Figure 4.21.

Which of the four binary uniqueness constraint patterns should be specified for this fact type? If the population of Table 4.1 is significant then clearly we have a 1:1 situation, and constraints should be marked on each role. This means that each person referees at most one paper (good news for the referees), and each paper is refereed by at most one person (bad news for the people submitting the papers).

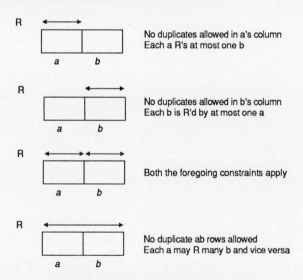

Figure 4.20   The four uniqueness constraint patterns for a binary

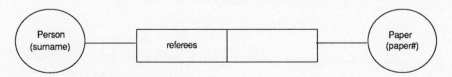

Figure 4.21   The fact type for Table 4.1

Now while this arrangement is possible, we would probably have some doubt as to whether this constraint pattern is really intended. One way of resolving our doubts is to add another fact which makes the population inconsistent with the doubtful constraint pattern, and ask the UoD expert whether the new population is permitted. For example, suppose we suspect that the fact type is really many:many. To test our hypothesis we add a carefully chosen row to the schema-base diagram, as shown in Figure 4.22.

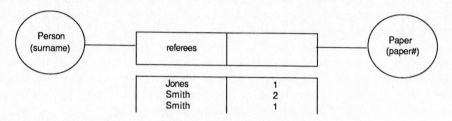

Figure 4.22 A population to test the many to many hypothesis

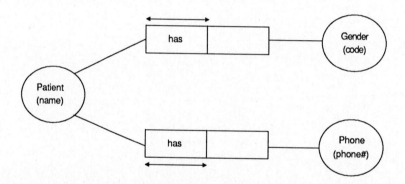

Figure 4.23 The conceptual schema actually used

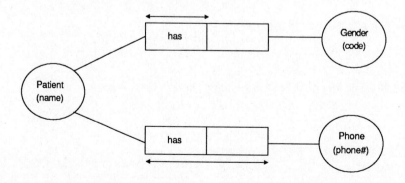

Figure 4.24 A different "real world schema"

If this change is accepted, we know that the many to many constraint pattern should be specified. If not, there are still three possibilities left (one to one, one to many, many to one): we leave it to you as an exercise to provide further rows to test these three hypotheses.

Remember that all constraints on fact types are to be interpreted as applying to what is recorded in the database, not necessarily to the real world. We can program an information system to enforce constraints on what can be stored in its database, but we cannot program it to enforce constraints within the actual world. The constraint schema for the "real world" need not be the same as for the "recorded world". For example, consider the conceptual schema of Figure 4.23.

What do these uniqueness constraints actually say? For any particular state of the database, each patient is recorded as having at most one gender and at most one phone. Now it may be the case in the real world being modelled here that some patients have more than one phone (e.g. a home phone and a business phone). We might display this "real world schema" as in Figure 4.24.

For some reason, the designer of the information system has decided that no patient will be recorded to have more than one phone. Hence the constraints in the first schema (Figure 4.23) are accurate for the information system. *When we speak of a conceptual schema without qualification we always mean the recorded world schema.*

Nevertheless, we often use our background knowledge of the "real world schema" when designing the conceptual schema. With respect to uniqueness constraints we typically observe the following principle: *for a given fact type, the uniqueness constraint should be at least as strong as that which applies to the fact type in the real world.* For the case being discussed we know that in the real world each person has at most one gender: so we should enforce this in our schema. With the phone fact type, we need to consciously decide whether a stronger constraint than the real world constraint is required.

Exercise 4.1

1. For a given fact type, a sample population is significant with respect to uniqueness constraints if all the relevant uniqueness constraints can be deduced from the sample. An incomplete schema diagram is shown for a binary fact type. The names of reference modes and roles have been omitted for simplicity.

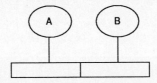

For each of the following cases, add the uniqueness constraints to the diagram assuming the population provided is significant.

(a)

a1	b1
a2	b2
a1	b3

(b)

a1	b1
a1	b2
a2	b1

(c)

a1	b1
a2	b2
a3	b3

(d)

a1	b1
a2	b2
a3	b1

2. In a given department, employees are identified by employee numbers "e1", "e2" etc., and projects are identified by project numbers "p1", "p2" etc. Draw a schema diagram for the fact type Employee works on Project, and provide populations which are significant with respect to the following constraint patterns:

   (a) 1:many   (b) many:1   (c) many:many   (d) 1:1

3. Add the relevant uniqueness constraints to the conceptual schema diagrams for the Exercise questions listed below. For some of these questions the output report provided in the question might not be significant with respect to uniqueness constraints. However, by using common sense you should be able to avoid adding uniqueness constraints which are likely to be violated by a larger population.

   (a) Exercise 3.5 Question 1b   (b) Exercise 3.5 Question 1d
   (c) Exercise 3.5 Question 2   (d) Exercise 3.5 Question 5
   (e) Exercise 3.6 Question 1   (f) Exercise 3.6 Question 2
   (g) Exercise 3.6 Question 4

4.2   Constraints on longer fact types

In this section we consider how to specify uniqueness constraints on fact types of arity 3 and beyond. Let's begin with an example. In the schema-base diagram of Figure 4.25 we have a *ternary fact type* of the form Person scores Rating for Subject.

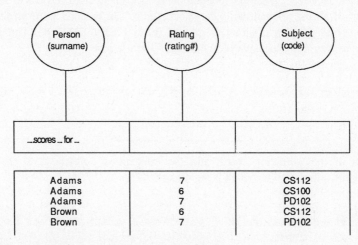

Figure 4.25   What are the uniqueness constraints?

To determine uniqueness constraints from a fact table, we should look first at each column individually. Here, with each column there is at least one value that is repeated. So no column by itself has a uniqueness constraint. We see later that this must be true of any ternary fact type.

Now let's look at pairs of columns. For ease of reference here, we number the columns 1,2,3 in the order shown in the diagram. Beginning with columns 1 and 2 we note that the pair (Adams,7) is repeated. With columns 1 and 3, each pair is unique, that is, each (Person,Subject) combination occurs on only one row of the table. With columns 2 and 3 the pair (7,PD102) is repeated. There are only three ways of pairing the columns in a ternary. So if the population of the fact table is significant, the only pairwise constraint is that each (Person,Subject) pair must be unique to the table.

If we are familiar with the application, we can usually decide whether the population is significant in this regard simply by using common sense. With the present example, this constraint means that for each (Person,Subject) combination, at most one rating may be obtained. This agrees with our background knowledge about the UoD and so the uniqueness constraint suggested by the table is accepted.

Sample fact tables may be obtained from output reports (which often represent a combination of separate fact tables) or from simple factual knowledge about the UoD. Unless the population is large, or well chosen, it is unlikely to be completely significant with respect to all uniqueness constraints. For instance, suppose row 3 was deleted from the table in Figure 4.25. For the smaller sample, both the column 1,2 pair and the column 2,3 pair would then show no duplicates. The table would then suggest a uniqueness constraint for all three column pairs.

So we need to be wary of relying on just a sample fact table to determine uniqueness constraints. We should *ask ourselves whether any suggested constraint really makes sense*. A uniqueness constraint on the column 1,2 pair would mean that a person-rating combination could occur for at most one subject: this would forbid somebody obtaining the same rating for two subjects—an unrealistic restriction! Similarly, the suggested constraint on the column 2,3 pair must be rejected as unrealistic (it would forbid two people to score the same rating for a particular subject).

Uniqueness constraints may often be determined simply by background knowledge about how the UoD works. As we saw in the previous section, real world uniqueness constraints usually determine the weakest uniqueness constraints that may be considered for the actual database. If we know the fact table is significant then we can always generate the constraints from it. Usually however, we won't know in advance that the table is significant and we will have to use some of our background or semantic knowledge. If we lack such knowledge we should consult the UoD expert about any doubtful constraints. As discussed, one effective way of questioning the UoD expert is by adding further facts to the population and asking whether these should be accepted or rejected.

With a ternary fact type, the constraint spanning all three columns is always implied, since no whole row may be repeated. We mark this constraint if and only if no other uniqueness constraint holds. For our current example then, we mark just the constraint for the column 1,3 pair, indicating that each person-subject pair is assigned at most one rating. Since the two role boxes involved are not adjacent, we use a divided constraint bar as shown in Figure 4.26.

Notice that this time we must include the arrow heads. If we omitted them we would interpret the bars as two separate constraints, one for each of the two columns. To avoid confusion, let us agree to always include arrow heads on constraint bars for any fact type longer than a binary.

We use the term *n-role constraint* for a constraint that spans *n* roles. The constraint in Figure 4.26 is a 2-role constraint since it spans two of the three roles involved in the fact type. With a binary fact type we had three basic constraints (two 1-role and one 2-role) which gave rise to four possible cases. In the next chapter we show that *no (elementary) ternary fact type can have a 1-role uniqueness constraint.* So with a ternary fact type there are four basic uniqueness constraints to be considered: three 2-role constraints and one 3-role constraint (see Figure 4.27).

With a ternary fact type, you should systematically test each of the three 2-role constraints to see which ones hold. Only if none of these hold should the 3-role constraint be specified. There is only one way of having a 3-role uniqueness constraint. There are three ways of having precisely one 2-role constraint, and three ways of having precisely a pair of 2-role constraints. Finally there is one way of having three 2-role constraints. Thus there are eight different uniqueness constraint patterns that may arise with a ternary fact type. Four of these involve just one constraint (Figure 4.27) and four involve combinations (see Figure 4.28).

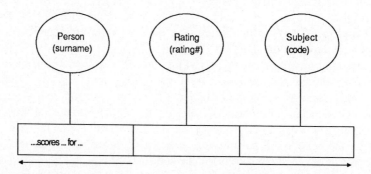

Figure 4.26   Each (Person,Subject) combination is unique

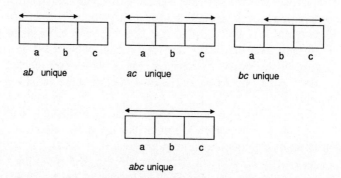

Figure 4.27   Allowed basic uniqueness constraints for a ternary

All other constraint patterns for a ternary are illegal (i.e. disallowed). Some examples of these are shown in Figure 4.29.

The general approach we have introduced for specifying uniqueness constraints applies to fact types of any arity. In Figure 4.30 a *quaternary fact type* is portrayed. In this case we have a 3-role uniqueness constraint indicating that each *acd* combination must be unique to the fact table, where *a*, *c* and *d* occur on the first, third and fourth columns on the same row of this table.

A small but significant population of the fact table is shown. Verify for yourself that this is consistent with the indicated uniqueness constraint. We show in the next chapter

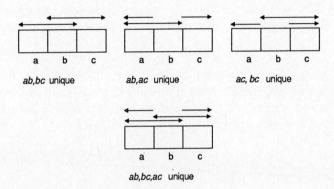

Figure 4.28   Allowed constraint combinations for a ternary

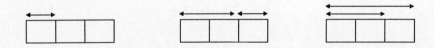

Figure 4.29   Some illegal constraint patterns

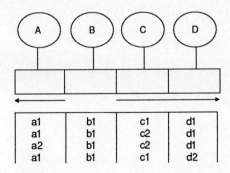

a1	b1	c1	d1
a1	b1	c2	d1
a2	b1	c2	d1
a1	b1	c1	d2

Figure 4.30   Each *acd* combination occurs on at most one row

that any uniqueness constraints in a quaternary must span at least three roles. We leave it as an exercise for you to explore all the possible cases. Since elementary fact types are almost never longer than quaternaries, we do not illustrate any such examples here.

To visualize the connection between roles and columns of the fact table, think of the role boxes as the holes in which the entities get placed to complete the fact. No matter what the arity of the fact type, a uniqueness constraint across a combination of role boxes means that any instance of that column combination that does appear in the table must occur on one row only, and hence can be used to identify that row.

Since a role combination governed by a uniqueness constraint thus provides a "key to unlock" any row of the fact table, this combination is sometimes referred to as a *key* for that table. In later work when we consider the (often non-elementary) tables used in relational databases we will have substantially more to say about this notion.

Exercise 4.2

1. An outline for the conceptual schema of a ternary fact type is shown, minus the names for the reference modes and roles. For each case, add the uniqueness constraints, assuming that the population shown is significant in this regard.

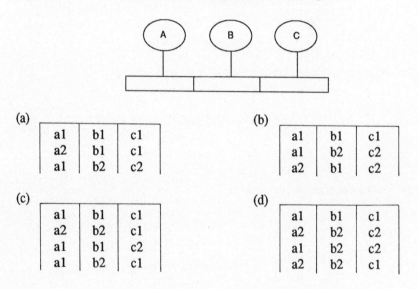

(a)

a1	b1	c1
a2	b1	c1
a1	b2	c2

(b)

a1	b1	c1
a1	b2	c2
a2	b1	c2

(c)

a1	b1	c1
a2	b2	c1
a1	b1	c2
a1	b2	c1

(d)

a1	b1	c1
a2	b2	c2
a1	b2	c2
a2	b2	c1

2. Perform steps 1–4 of the CSDP for the following output report:

Department	Staff category	Number
CS	Professor	3
CS	Senior lecturer	6
CS	Lecturer	10
EE	Professor	3
EE	Senior lecturer	7
EE	Lecturer	7

3. Perform steps 1–4 of the CSDP for the following output report:

Year	Branch	Profit ($)	Total profit ($)
1987	New York	100 000	
	Paris	50 000	
			150 000
1988	New York	150 000	
	Paris	100 000	
			250 000

4.3 Constraints involving joins or nesting

Before discussing some more complex cases of uniqueness constraints it will be useful to discuss the notion of two tables being *joined* to produce another table. In Figure 4.31 we have two fact types sharing a common entity type, *B*. We assume the reference modes for *B* are the same for each table.

The *natural inner join* of tables T1 and T2 is obtained by pairing rows of T1 with rows of T2 where the *B* column values match, and arranging for the final *B* column to appear just once in the result. For example, row (a1,b1) is paired with rows (b1,c1) and (b1,c3) to give rows (a1,b1,c1) and rows (a1,b1,c3). The final result of this join operation is shown in Figure 4.32.

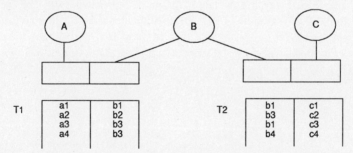

Figure 4.31 Tables T1 and T2 share a common entity type

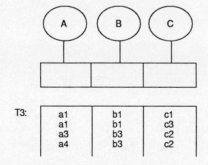

Figure 4.32 Table T3 is the natural inner join of T1 and T2

Table 4.2   An output report about high school students

Student:	student#	name	class
	001	Adams J	11A
	002	Brown C	12B
	003	Brown C	11A

Notice that the final *B* column is the intersection of the original *B* columns. The term "natural join" or even "join" is often used without qualification to mean the natural inner join. Of less importance is the *natural outer join*. This is obtained by adding to the inner join those rows (if any) where the join column value occurs in just one of the tables, and replacing the missing entries of such rows with *null values*. We use "?" to denote a null value with the meaning of "not recorded". See Figure 4.33. The final *B* column is the union of the original *B* columns.

We now consider uniqueness constraints that involve more than one relationship type. An output report for a UoD concerning high school students is shown in Table 4.2. As an exercise, perform step 1 for the top row of this report before reading on.

You should have set out the information for row 1 in terms of two elementary facts:

The Student with student# '001' has name 'Adams J'.
The Student with student# '001' is in the Class with code '11A'.

The first of these facts is a relationship between an entity and a label. The entity is represented in the usual way, but the label "Adams J" represents itself. The second fact is in the usual form. Note that in this UoD, students are identified by their student numbers. As rows 2 and 3 show, it is possible for two different students to have the same name ("Brown C"). We might now draw the schema-base diagram as in Figure 4.34.

T4:	a1	b1	c1
	a1	b1	c3
	a2	b2	?
	a3	b3	c2
	a4	b3	c2
	?	b4	c4

Figure 4.33   T4 is the natural outer join of T1 and T2

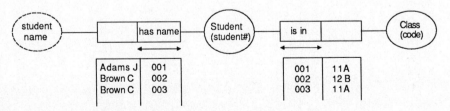

Figure 4.34   The conceptual schema diagram for Table 4.2

Table 4.3   The output report with uniqueness constraints added

Student:	*student#*	*name*	*class*
	001	Adams J	11A
	002	Brown C	12B
	003	Brown C	11A

Let us agree that the population supplied is significant. It follows that each student has at most one name, and each student is in at most one class. These uniqueness constraints have been captured on the schema diagram. However, there is another uniqueness constraint that we have missed. What is it?

The output report has been reproduced in Table 4.3, with uniqueness constraints marked over its columns. Notice that the combination of name and class is unique. So although a student's name need not be unique to the UoD it is unique to the student's class. While there are two students named "Brown C" there can be only one student with this name in class 12B, and only one student with this name in class 11A.

Each row of the output report splits into two elementary facts. To specify the name-class uniqueness constraint on the schema diagram we need to involve two fact types. The relevant role boxes to which the constraint applies are joined by dotted lines to a *circled "u"*, as shown in Figure 4.35. The "u" stands for "uniqueness".

Because this is a constraint between fact types it is called an "inter-fact-type constraint". The usual uniqueness constraint is an intra-fact-type constraint. The uniqueness arc joining the two role boxes shown indicates that for each student the *combination* of student name and class is unique: given any student name and class code from the tables, there is at most one student# which is paired with both. For instance, given "Adams J" and "11A" there is only one student# sharing rows with both (001). Given "Adams J" and "12B" there is no student# paired with both.

One useful way of understanding this kind of constraint is to say that if we perform the natural *join* operation on the two fact tables, then the resulting table has a uniqueness constraint across the (name,class) column pair. Note that when we join the two fact tables we obtain the table in the original output report (Table 4.3). So the join operation provides a simple way of relating this schema constraint to the corresponding constraint on the original report. To ensure you understand this kind of constraint, see if you can explain why the population shown in Figure 4.36 is *not* a valid population for this schema.

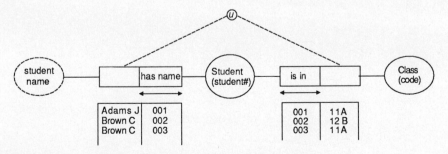

Figure 4.35   u-notation for inter-fact-type uniqueness constraint

The extra row added to each table provides a counterexample to the constraint, since given "Adams J" and "11A" there are two student# entries which are paired with these entries (001 and 004). This breaks the rule that student names within a given class are unique to that class, since in class 11A two students (001, 004) have the same name ("Adams J"). More simply, if we join these two tables the combination ("Adams J","11A") occurs on two rows, thus violating the uniqueness constraint.

The general case is summarized in Figure 4.37, where A, B and C are any object types, and T1 and T2 are the associated fact tables.

We now turn our attention to *nested fact types*. With these, uniqueness constraints need to be marked on the objectified relationship type as well as the outer relationship type. Recall our example about people enrolled in subjects scoring ratings for those subjects. This was shown in flattened form in the previous section (Figure 4.26), and is shown here in nested form (Figure 4.38).

Adams J	001		001	11A
Brown C	002		002	12B
Brown C	003		003	11A
Adams J	004		004	11A

Figure 4.36   A population inconsistent with the schema

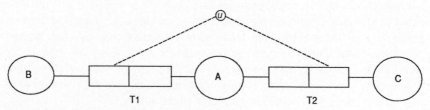

Given any *b, c* in the tables, there is at most one *a* paired with both.
Given any population, T1 join T2 has *bc* unique.

Figure 4.37   An inter-fact-type uniqueness constraint

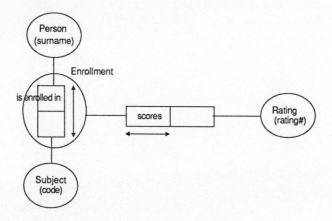

Figure 4.38   Uniqueness constraints on a nested fact type

Table 4.4

	Person	Subject	Position
	Adams	CS112	3
	Adams	CS100	10
	Adams	PD102	3
	Brown	CS112	10
	Brown	PD102	5

Here each (Person,Subject) enrollment is treated as an object which scores a rating (e.g. the enrollment (Adams,CS112) scores a 7). The uniqueness constraint on the objectified fact type indicates that each person may enroll in many subjects and the same subject may be taken by many people. The other constraint indicates that each (Person,Subject) enrollment scores at most one rating.

Because of its simplicity the flattened version (Figure 4.26) is preferable unless there is a good reason for nesting (e.g. if we want to enter enrollment information at the start of a semester and add the ratings at the end of semester, then we need to nest). If nesting is chosen, the *uniqueness constraint on the objectified relationship type must span it*. For example the uniqueness constraint on the Enrollment relationship type of Figure 4.38 must be many to many. We justify this rule in the next chapter.

As a more complex case, consider a UoD in which persons enroll in subjects but are given subject positions (i.e. 1st, 2nd, 3rd etc.) rather than subject ratings. Moreover no ties may occur (i.e. for each position in a subject there is only one student). A sample output report for this UoD is shown in Table 4.4.

Performing step 1 on the first row, we might express the information as the following ternary: Person (surname) "Adams" is placed in Subject (code) "CS112" at Position (Nr) 3. This leads to the schema shown in Figure 4.39.

Notice the overlapping uniqueness constraints. Check these with the population and make sure you understand them. Now suppose we instead adopted a nested approach. For example we might have expressed the information on row 1 as follows: Person (surname) "Adams" enrolled in Subject (code) "CS112"; this Enrollment achieves Position (Nr) 3. This leads to the nested schema shown in Figure 4.40.

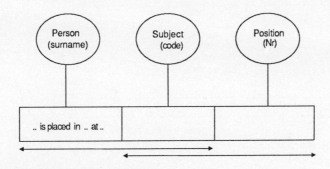

Figure 4.39 A schema diagram for Table 4.4

Table 4.5

	Person	*Subject*	*Rating*	*Position*
	Adams	CS112	7	3
	Adams	CS100	6	10
	Adams	PD102	7	3
	Brown	CS112	6	10
	Brown	PD102	7	5

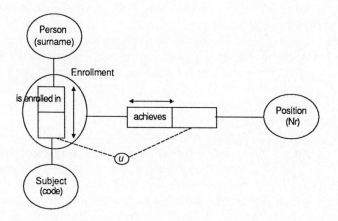

Figure 4.40   Another schema diagram for Table 4.4 (nested version)

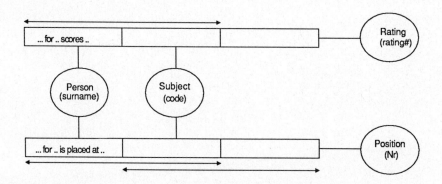

Figure 4.41   A schema diagram for table 4.5

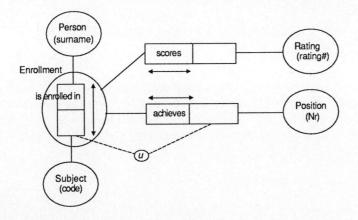

Figure 4.42 A better schema diagram for Table 4.5

The uniqueness bar constraints are similar to our earlier rating example, and together are equivalent to the constraints spanning the first two roles in the ternary version. The additional uniqueness constraint corresponds to the constraint spanning the last two roles in the ternary version (i.e. each (Subject,Position) combination is unique). In other words, if we flatten the nested fact type into a ternary then any given (Subject,Position) pair occurs on at most one row of the ternary table. To help understand this we suggest you add the fact tables to the diagram. The fact table for the outer relationship type effectively matches that of the output report.

As you may have gathered from these examples, nesting tends to produce a more complex constraint picture. For this example, the flattened version is to be preferred. However, if the position information is optional (e.g. to be added later) then we would choose the nested approach.

Another reason for nesting is to avoid a kind of redundancy when the same relationship type is embedded within more than one fact type. Consider for example a UoD in which we have to record both a rating and a unique subject position for each student taking any given subject. A sample output report is shown in Table 4.5.

One might be tempted to describe this UoD in terms of two ternaries, as shown in Figure 4.41.

Note however that all (Person,Subject) combinations appearing in one fact table must also appear in the other. As discussed in a later chapter, it is better to objectify the relationship type between Person and Subject and attach rating and position roles to this (see Figure 4.42). This approach corresponds to reading the information on row 1 of the table as: Person (surname) "Adams" is enrolled in Subject (code) "CS112"; this Enrollment scores Rating (rating#) 7; this Enrollment achieves Position (Nr) 3.

Exercise 4.3

1. Add the uniqueness constraints to the conceptual schema diagrams for:

(a) Exercise 3.5 Question 6   (b) Exercise 3.6 Question 3

2. Many manufactured products contain parts which may themselves be products of even smaller parts. The structure of one such product is shown below, by two equivalent representations (a tree or hierarchy, and an indented explosion). For instance, at its first level of decomposition the product A contains 2 B parts and 1 C part.

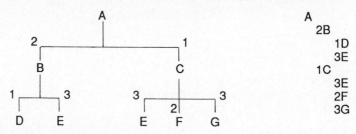

Draw a conceptual schema diagram for this UoD, including uniqueness constraints. Provide two solutions as follows:

(a) Make no use of nesting   (b) Use nesting

3. A car dealer maintains a database on all the cars in stock. Each car is designated by the car number engraved on the compliance plate. For each car the dealer records the model (e.g. Pulsar XT), the year of manufacture (e.g. 1987), the retail price (e.g. $15,000) and the colour (e.g. blue). Because of space limitations the dealer will never have in stock more than one car of the same model, year and colour at the same time.

The dealer also keeps figures on the number of cars of a particular model and colour that are sold in any given year. For example, in 1986, five blue Pulsar XTs were sold.

Draw a conceptual schema diagram for this database, including all uniqueness constraints.

5 Arity checking

5.1 CSDP step 5: Arity checks

In step 1 of the CSDP we tried to express information examples in terms of elementary facts. At that stage we relied on familiarity with the UoD to determine whether a fact type was simple or compound (splittable). We now conduct a more thorough and formal check in this regard.

CSDP *step 5: Check that fact types are of the right arity*

If we have been careful in our earlier steps, this step is not really required. However, until we have had considerable experience at conceptual schema design, it is possible that some of the fact types we have included in our schema are either too long or too short.

By "too long" we mean that the arity of the fact type is higher than it should be. In this case we must split the compound fact type up into two or more simple fact types. For example, the fact type Scientist was born in Country during Year should be split into two fact types: Scientist was born in Country; Scientist was born during Year.

By "too short" we mean that the arity of some fact types is too small, resulting in loss of information. We have wrongly split an elementary fact type. In this case we need to combine the relevant fact types into one of higher arity. For example, given that scientists may lecture in many countries in the same year, it is wrong to split the fact type Scientist lectured in Country during Year into the fact types: Scientist lectured in Country; Scientist lectured during Year. This kind of error is comparatively rare, but serious nevertheless.

In checking the arity of the fact types in our conceptual schema there are at least three methods that may be of use. These are listed below:

1. Use your common sense or background knowledge of the UoD to decide if information is lost by splitting a fact type (can the fact type be expressed as a conjunction of smaller ones?).
2. Use the splittability rules about the shortest key (see later).
3. Provide a significant fact table for the fact type, split this by projection (see later) then recombine by natural join: if new instances appear then the fact type is unsplittable in this way. Test until a split is found or all ways are exhausted.

Table 5.1

Person	Degree	Subject	Rating
Adams	BSc	CS112	7
Adams	BSc	CS110	6
Adams	BSc	PD102	7
Brown	BA	CS112	6
Brown	BA	PD102	7
Collins	BSc	CS112	7

Table 5.2

Person	Degree	Subject	Rating
Adams	BSc	CS112	7
Adams	BSc	CS110	6
Adams	BSc	PD102	7
Brown	BA	CS112	6
Brown	BA	PD102	7
Collins	BSc	CS112	7

The first method may be less formal but it is really the best. It ties in strongly with step 1, and with the notion of deciding "which columns relate to which" in an output report. Let us review this approach briefly before we look at the other methods. Consider the output report of Table 5.1.

Using our background knowledge of the UoD, we interpret the first row as stating that the person Adams is enrolled in the degree BSc and studies the subject CS112, scoring a rating of 7 for that subject. Is this piece of information simple or compound? The "and" strongly suggests that we have a conjunction of two facts here, which we can set out as:

Person (surname) 'Adams' seeks Degree (code) 'BSc'.
Person (surname) 'Adams' enrolled in Subject (code) 'CS112', scoring Rating (Nr) 7.

We use the word "seeks" to mean "is enrolled to obtain the qualification". In the first fact we see that a Degree relates or "hooks on" to a Person. In the second fact we see that a Rating relates to a Person-Subject enrollment. As a temporary, shorthand way of displaying these relationships we may connect the relevant table columns by arcs, as shown in Table 5.2.

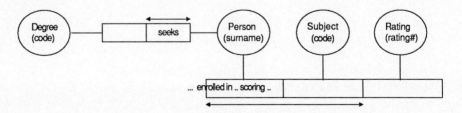

Figure 5.1   A schema diagram for Table 5.2 (flattened version)

The first fact type is obviously a binary. If Rating must be recorded for each (Person,Subject) enrollment, as suggested by the sample population, then the second fact type is best represented as a flat ternary (see Figure 5.1).

As discussed in earlier work, the ternary fact type is elementary. For example, if we tried to split the fact that Adams scored a rating of 7 for CS112 into the facts that Adams enrolled in CS112 and that Adams scored a 7 we would have lost the information that the 7 was for CS112 rather than some other subject. If a fact is elementary (with respect to the UoD) it can't be split into shorter facts without information loss.

As previously discussed, if it is desired to allow at least some (Person,Subject) enrollments to be recorded without a Rating, then the second fact type should instead be represented in nested form, as shown in Figure 5.2. Please note however that *nesting is not to be regarded as splitting*. Each Enrollment object is an objectified relationship or compound object involving two simple objects of type Person and Subject. So each Enrollment scored Rating relationship involves three simple objects, not two. In contrast, if we wrongly split the ternary into two or three of the fact types Person enrolled in Subject, Person scored Rating, and Subject resulted in Rating, each of these would involve two simple entity types.

Provided we take care with the early steps of the CSDP, and don't treat too lightly the task of interpreting an output report, use of our background knowledge in deciding what relates to what should ensure that our fact types are of the right arity. Using our insight into the semantics of the UoD, we should be able to decide whether a given fact type can be expressed as a conjunction of smaller fact types. If it can, we split the fact type into these conjuncts. If not, splitting would result in information loss, so we leave the fact type as it is.

If you still find you have some doubt about your interpretation of just what the (elementary) fact types are, and these doubts cannot be removed by questioning the UoD expert using critical examples, the methods described in the next two sections should be of assistance.

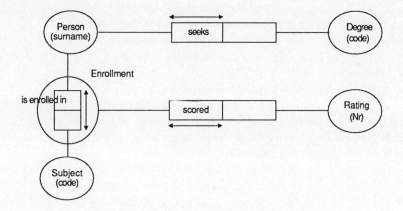

Figure 5.2   Another schema diagram for Table 5.2 (nested version)

5.2   Key length check

In the previous chapter we saw that, for a given fact type, any combination of roles spanned by a uniqueness constraint is called a "key" for that fact type. Each role is associated with a column of the fact table for the fact type. Unless the fact type is unary, it is possible for it to have more than one key. Consider the cases shown in Figure 5.3.

Here the binary has two 1-role keys, the middle ternary has two 2-role keys, and the other ternary has one 3-role key. Of course, the first two fact types also have uniqueness constraints across their whole length, but we don't show these because they are implied by the stronger constraints shown. We do *not* use the term "key" for such longer, implied constraints.

The *length* of a key or fact type is the number of roles included in the key or fact type respectively. A key of length 1 is a *simple key*. All other keys are *composite*. The following rule provides us with a useful splittability check: *an n-ary fact type can be split if it has a key of length less than n-1*. Since keys must have a length of at least 1, the condition specified in this rule can be true only for fact types of length 3 or greater. We can set this result out in tabular form thus:

fact type of *length*	can be split if it has a key of *length*
3	1
4	1 or 2
5	1, 2 or 3
:	:
n	$1 .. n\text{-}2$

So if a fact type is elementary, all its keys must be of the same length. Either there is exactly one key and this spans the whole fact type, or there are one or more keys and each is one role shorter than the fact type. To start with the simplest case, a *ternary fact type can be split if it has a simple key*. Consider for example the output report of Table 5.3.

We interpret the first row thus: the Person with surname "Adams" seeks the Degree with code "BSc" and has Gender with code "M". The presence of "and" in this translation of row 1 strongly suggests that the fact is splittable. Suppose however that we foolishly ignore this linguistic clue, and schematize the report in terms of a ternary, as shown in Figure 5.4.

Our familiarity with the UoD tells us that, for any state of the database, each person seeks at most one degree and has at most one gender. So there is a uniqueness constraint on the Person column of the fact table. The population of Table 5.3 shows that there is no such constraint on Degree or Person, either singly or in combination. So we mark the constraint on the diagram as shown.

Now let's apply the splittability rule mentioned earlier. Here the key has length 1, which is 2 less than the length of the fact type. So the condition of the rule is satisfied, and we can split the fact type. But *how do we split it*? Examining our English translation of row 1, we find a conjunction of two facts about the same person. Assuming our interpretation of the output report is correct, we must split the fact type into two as shown in Figure 5.5.

Table 5.3

Person	Degree	Gender
Adams	BSc	M
Brown	BA	F
Collins	BSc	M

Here the key entity type is Person, and we say we have "split *on* Person". If we have correctly captured the semantics of the output report in step 1 then it would be wrong to split this fact type in any other way. Before considering this point further, let us try to see why the splittability rule works in this case.

Look back at Table 5.3. A uniqueness constraint on the Person column means that, given any state of the database, no person can be referenced more than once in this column. Each person seeks at most one degree and each person has at most one gender. So for any given person, if we are given as separate pieces of information that person's degree and that person's gender we can reconstruct that person's row in the output report. Since the ternary fact type of the output report can be split and recombined without information loss it is not elementary.

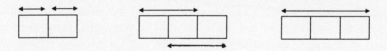

Figure 5.3   A fact type may have one or more keys

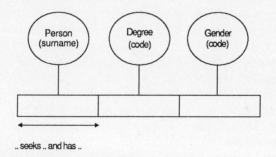

.. seeks .. and has ..

Figure 5.4   A splittable fact type

Figure 5.5   Two elementary fact types

Table 5.4   Is this population significant?

Person	Degree	Gender
Adams	BSc	M
Brown	BA	F
Collins	BSc	M

Before considering other ways of splitting, it is convenient to introduce some terminology commonly used in traditional approaches to database design. For a given fact table, let Y denote a single column, and X denote either a single column or combination of columns. Then we say that Y is *functionally dependent on* X if and only if, for each value of X there is at most one value of Y. In other words, Y is a *function of* X. A function is just a many:1 relation. If Y is a function of X, then X is said to (functionally) determine Y. We often abbreviate "functional dependency" to "FD".

Now let us return to the output report of our example. For your convenience, this has been reproduced in Table 5.4. If this population is significant, then any functional dependencies should be exposed here. Note that Degree is functionally dependent on Person, since for any given person there is only one degree. Moreover, Gender is a function of Person since for any given person there is only one gender. But can you spot any other functional dependencies?

If the population is significant, then Gender is a function of Degree, and Degree is a function of Gender! Does this make sense? To answer this question we need to know more about the semantics of the UoD. Spotting a functional dependency within a population is a formal game. Knowing whether this dependency reflects an actual constraint in the UoD is not. To assume the population is significant begs the question. Only someone familiar with the UoD can resolve the issue.

If one column is functionally dependent on another column, this reflects a 1:many relationship type which can be given a meaningful name by the UoD expert. For example, suppose the UoD expert informs us that row 1 of the output report should actually be read as: the Person with surname "Adams" seeks the Degree with code "BSc", and the Degree with code "BSc" is sought by people of Gender with code "M". Here we have two facts about the same degree, and so we split on Degree rather than Person (see Figure 5.6). If Gender really is a function of Degree, then any given degree is restricted to one gender (e.g. only males can seek a BSc). If Degree really is a function of Gender then all people of a given gender seek the same degree (e.g. all females seek just a BA). These two FDs are captured in Figure 5.6 by the two uniqueness constraints on the relationship type between Degree and Gender.

Now while such a UoD is possible, our knowledge about degree awarding institutions makes this interpretation highly unlikely. The best way to resolve our doubts is to add test rows to the population. For example, if the UoD expert accepts the population of Table 5.5 as being consistent with the UoD, then no FDs occur between Degree and Gender.

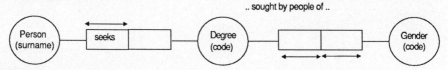

Figure 5.6   A weird UoD where Degree and Gender are functions of each other

Table 5.5   A counterexample to any FD between Degree and Gender

	Person	*Degree*	*Gender*
	Adams	BSc	M
	Brown	BA	F
	Collins	BSc	M
	Davis	BSc	F

Table 5.6

	Lecturer	*Dept*	*Building*
	Halpin	CS	69
	Okimura	JA	1
	Nijssen	CS	69
	Wang	CH	1

This by itself does not guarantee that our earlier schema (Figure 5.5) is now correct. For example, the schema of Figure 5.6 with the 1:1 constraint changed to a many to many constraint is still a remote possibility; but it would be silly to have a report so open to redundancy (e.g. the fact that the BSc is sought by males would be shown twice already). Of course, if we simply checked our interpretation at step 1 with the UoD expert, we could have avoided all this hassle.

While the notion of FD is sometimes useful, it is impractical to treat fact tables in a purely formal way, hunting for FDs etc. The number of dependencies to check increases very rapidly as the length of the fact type grows. While our conceptual focus on elementary fact types constrains this length, the search for such dependencies can still be laborious. We short-circuit this work by taking advantage of human knowledge of the UoD. As another simple example consider the output report of Table 5.6.

Suppose that, with the help of the UoD expert, we express row 1 thus: the Lecturer with surname "Halpin" works for the Department with code "CS" which is located in the Building with building# "69". Is this fact splittable? Here the pronoun "which" introduces a non-restrictive clause about the department that may be stated separately. So we have two facts about the department (Halpin works for the CS department; and the CS department is located in building 69). So we split on Department to get two fact types as shown in Figure 5.7. If the population is significant then each lecturer works for only one department, and each department is located in only one building. If these constraints are confirmed by the UoD expert we add them to the schema as shown.

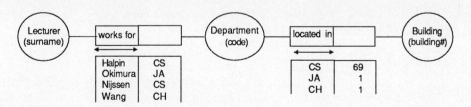

Figure 5.7   Schema-base diagram for Table 5.6

If the population of Table 5.6 is significant then Building is a function of Department, which itself is a function of Lecturer. This means that Building is transitively dependent on Lecturer. An alternative design methodology known as "normalization" uses this formal feature to decide that the ternary table of Table 5.6 should be split in two. This formal reliance on FDs rests on the assumption that the population is significant, which can only be confirmed informally by access to natural semantics, such as the interpretation provided by the UoD expert. We feel that it is simpler and safer to work with these semantics right from the start.

In this book we provide a practical design procedure that can be readily understood and mastered. Since the book is aimed at the average practitioner we generally omit rigorous mathematical justifications. However it may be of use here to sketch an outline proof of the splittability rule. An *n*-ary fact type with a key of length < *n-1* has at least two columns in its fact table that are functionally dependent on this key. Split the table by pairing the key with exactly one of these columns in turn. Recombining by join on this key must generate the original table since only one combined row is possible (otherwise the common key portion would not be a key). Although the *n*-ary fact table is thus formally splittable in this way, in practice the splitting might need to be made on part of the key or even a nonkey column if an FD applies there (consider the previous examples).

As an example of a *quaternary* case, look back at Table 5.2 discussed in the previous section. Suppose we did a bad job at step 1 and schematized this situation as in Figure 5.8.

Notice the uniqueness constraint. Here we have a fact type of length 4, and a key of length 2. *Since two roles are excluded from this key, we must split the fact type.* Using either natural semantics or the FD of Degree on Person, we now split it on Person into a binary and ternary as shown in Figure 5.1. Any quaternary splits if it has a key of length 1 or 2.

Now consider the schema-base diagram shown in Figure 5.9. Suppose that our interpretation of the UoD is correct. For example, suppose the first row of the output report giving rise to this schema really does express the information: the Person with surname "Adams" seeking the Degree with code "BSc" studies the Subject with code "CS112". Should the ternary fact type be split?

Since this ternary has no simple key, our splittability rule does not apply. We said that a ternary can be split **if** it has a simple key. However, we did *not* say "a ternary can be split **only if** it has a simple key". The ternary in this example does actually split. The best way to see this is to *try to rephrase the information in terms of a conjunction*. Initially we expressed the information on the first row using the present participle "seeking". But this information may be rephrased as:

The Person with surname 'Adams' seeks the Degree with code 'BSc'
and studies the Subject with code 'CS112'.

which is equivalent to:

The Person with surname 'Adams' seeks the Degree with code 'BSc'
and
the Person with surname 'Adams' studies the Subject with code 'CS112'.

This is obviously a conjunction with Person common to each conjunct. So the ternary should be split on Person into two binaries (see Figure 5.10). From this approach the following formal rule may be derived: *given a significant fact table, the fact type is splittable if a column is functionally dependent on only some of the other columns.* By "only some" we mean "some but not all". With our present example, Degree is functionally dependent on Person only; so it should not be combined with Subject information.

Another way of testing for splittability is to *perform a redundancy check* by determining whether some information is (unnecessarily) duplicated in the fact table. For example, in Figure 5.9 the tuple (Adams,BSc) occurs three times. Using our semantical insight we see that this tuple corresponds to a fact of interest (Adams seeks a BSc degree). Since this fact has been duplicated, the ternary is not elementary. Redundancy is not a necessary requirement for splittability. For example, the ternary table of Table 5.5 has no redundancy but is splittable. We examine redundancy checks in more detail in a later chapter. Whichever method we might have used to spot the splittability of the ternary, we still need to phrase the information as a conjunction of two binaries, as shown in Figure 5.10.

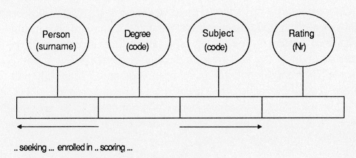

Figure 5.8   A quaternary fact type that is splittable

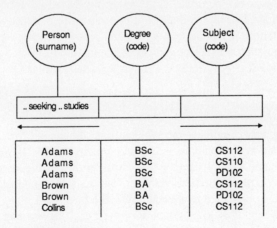

Figure 5.9   Is this ternary splittable?

Table 5.7

	Subject	CP	Lecturer
	CS100	8	DBJ
	CS109	5	?
	CS112	8	TAH
	CS113	8	TAH

Notice how the redundancy within the ternary has been eliminated by splitting it into two binaries. Although we may allow redundancy in output reports, we should avoid redundancy in the actual tables stored in the database.

Our examples so far have avoided nested fact types. Recall that nesting is not the same as splitting. If nesting is used, the following rule can be used to avoid splittable fact types:

The uniqueness constraint on an objectified relationship type must span the whole of this relationship type.

This is basically our earlier rule adapted to the nested case (if the constraint on the objectified relationship type was shorter, there would be at least two roles excluded from the constraint when the nested type was transformed by flattening). For example, consider the output report of Table 5.7. Here "CP" indicates the credit points for a given subject. The "?" on the second row is a null value, indicating that a real value is not recorded (e.g. a lecturer for CS109 might not yet have been assigned). Although null values are forbidden in conceptual fact tables, they often appear in output reports.

Now let's play the part of an inexperienced, and not very clever, schema designer, so that we can learn by the mistakes made. Looking just at the first row, we might be tempted to treat the information as a ternary:

Subject (code) 'CS100' worth CreditPts (Nr) 8 is lectured by Lecturer (initials) 'DBJ'.

If we drew our schema diagram now and populated it we would discover an error, since the information on the second row doesn't fit this pattern (remember we don't allow null values in our fact tables). On looking at the second row we see that we need to be able to record the credit points for a subject without indicating the lecturer. So we then rephrase the first row as follows:

Subject (code) 'CS100' is worth CreditPts (Nr) 8.
This Offering (code-Nr) is lectured by Lecturer (initials) 'DBJ'.

This approach certainly overcomes the problem with the second row, since we can now express the information there simply as: Subject (code) "CS109" is worth CreditPts (Nr) 5. Using this approach, we now develop the schema shown in Figure 5.11. Assuming the population of the output report is significant, we mark the uniqueness constraints as shown. Note that the objectified relationship type is a binary but it has a simple key. This breaks our new rule: an objectified relationship type can't have a key shorter than itself. So we know something must be wrong. Since the schema diagram follows from our handling of step 1 this means that we must have made a mistake at step 1.

Have another look at the way we set out the information for row 1. The second sentence here is the problem. In this UoD each subject has exactly one credit point value, so this is independent of who lectures the subject. So there is no need to mention the credit point value of a subject when we indicate the lecturer. In FD terminology, the CP column is functionally dependent on the Subject column alone. The information on the first row can be set out in terms of two simple binaries:

Subject (code) 'CS100' is worth CreditPts (Nr) 8.
Subject (code) 'CS100' is lectured by Lecturer (initials) 'DBJ'.

leading to the correct schema shown in Figure 5.12. Note that Lecturer depends only on Subject, not CreditPts. With the nested schema we incorrectly suggested that Lecturer was dependent on both, by relating Lecturer to the objectified relationship type.

With this example, Lecturer was a function of Subject, but this had no bearing on the splittability. We should use two binaries even if the same subject can have many lecturers. It is the functional dependency of CreditPts on Subject which is important.

One lesson to be learned from this section is that it pays to look out for uniqueness constraints even when performing step 1. Consider the output report of Table 5.8. If you are told that the population is significant, how would you set out the conceptual schema?

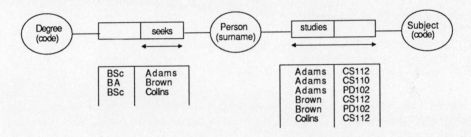

Figure 5.10 The correct schema-base diagram for Figure 5.9

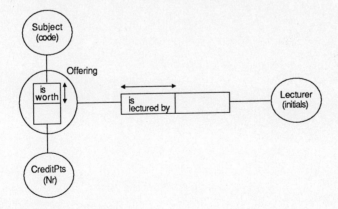

Figure 5.11 A faulty schema diagram

Table 5.8

	Person	*Subject*	*Rating*
	Adams	CS112	7
	Brown	CS112	7
	Collins	PD102	5

If you used either a ternary or a nested fact type you have made a mistake! Although similar to a UoD discussed earlier, the UoD being described by this table is more restricted. Given that the population is significant, the lack of duplicates in the Person column indicates that, at any given time, each person can be enrolled in only one subject (e.g. these people might be your employees, and you are funding their studies and want to ensure they don't take on so much study that it interferes with their work performance).

Since we store information only about the current enrollments, and each person is enrolled in only one subject it follows that each person can get only one rating. So if we know the subject in which a person is enrolled and we know the rating obtained by the person, we do know the subject in which this rating is obtained by the person. To begin with, we might express the information on the first row of the table in terms of the ternary: Person (surname) "Adams" scores Rating (Nr) 7 for Subject (code) "CS112". However, because of the uniqueness constraint on Person we should rephrase this information as the conjunction:

Person (surname) 'Adams' studies Subject (code) 'CS112'
and
Person (surname) 'Adams' scores Rating (Nr) 7.

leading to a conceptual schema diagram with two binary fact types. Because of this uniqueness constraint, the ternary has the same truth value as the conjunction of binaries for all possible states of this UoD.

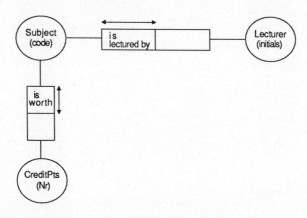

Figure 5.12   The corrected schema diagram for Figure 5.11

Exercise 5.2

1. The keys for certain fact types are as shown. On this basis, which of these fact types are definitely splittable?

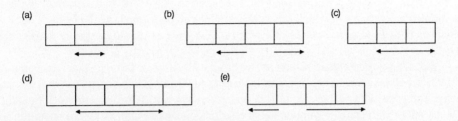

2. The following output report provides information on aeroplane flights between cities. The population of this table is significant with respect to uniqueness constraints.

FlightNr	Origin	Destination
T74	Paris	London
A52	Paris	London
B80	Sydney	New York
T23	London	Paris
B45	New York	Sydney

A student information designer expresses the information on the first row in terms of the following ternary:

Flight (F#) 'T74' **goes from** City (name) 'Paris' **to** City (name) 'London'.

Discuss the correctness or otherwise of this approach, and draw a correct conceptual schema diagram, including uniqueness constraints.

3. Executives may be contacted at work on one or more phone numbers and at home on one phone number. The following output report provides a sample population for this UoD.

Executive	Work phone	Home phone
Adams A	235402	837900
Adams A	235444	
Adams S	235444	837900
Brown T	235300	578051

A student information designer notes that this ternary table lacks a simple key, and on this basis decides to schematize in terms of a single ternary fact type. Evaluate this approach, and draw a correct conceptual schema diagram.

5.3   Projection-join check

In the previous section we discussed two *sufficient* conditions for splitting a fact type: a fact type can be split if it has more than one role excluded from a key; an objectified relationship splits if it has a shorter key. Since these are not *necessary* conditions for splitting, in some cases further analysis is required to make a definite decision. We have examined a few ways in which this analysis might be performed. At the heart of such an analysis is the question: *can the fact type be rephrased as a conjunction of smaller fact types?*

With a bit of experience behind us, we can usually answer this question fairly quickly. In this section we discuss a formal procedure for addressing this question in a systematic way. The procedure makes use of two operations known as "projection" and "joining", which are of considerable importance in relational database work. The *join* operation has already been discussed, and involves combining two tables by matching values referencing the same entity to form a new table (review Section 4.3).

The *projection* operation also produces a table, but it is performed on a single table. We project on one or more columns of a table by choosing just these columns and then deleting any resulting duplicate rows, that is:

> Remove all other columns;
> then remove any duplicate rows from the result.

Notationally, we list the columns on which a projection is made in square brackets after the table name, separated by commas (e.g. T[i,j] is a projection on columns i and j of table T). See Table 5.9 for some examples.

Notice that Scores[person,subject] is a projection on the key, and hence must have the same number of rows as the original table (Why?). Now that we know about joins and projections, the following method for checking whether a doubtful fact type is splittable may be discussed:

> Provide a significant fact table for the fact type
>
> **repeat**
>   split the table by projection then recombine by natural join;
>   **if** the result is the same as the original
>   **then** the table is splittable in this way
>   **else** the table is not splittable in this way
> **until** found to be splittable **or** all splitting ways tried
>
> **if not** found to be splittable **then** fact type is unsplittable.

Let's see how this algorithm works by considering some examples for which the key length rule doesn't apply. Consider first an example from the previous section which is reproduced in Table 5.10.

Recall that we first tried to represent this information in terms of the ternary: Person seeking Degree studies Subject. Using our semantic understanding of the UoD, we saw that this could be rephrased as the conjunction: Person seeks Degree **and** Person studies Subject. Suppose however that we only suspect that the ternary can be split into two binaries in this way, and we want some way of testing our intuition. The best way is

Table 5.9 Some projection examples

Scores =	*person*	*subject*	*rating*
	Adams	CS112	7
	Adams	CS110	6
	Adams	PD102	7
	Brown	CS112	6
	Brown	PD102	7
	Collins	CS112	7

Scores[person] =	*person*	Scores[rating] =	*rating*
	Adams		7
	Brown		6
	Collins		

Scores[person,subject]

person	*subject*
Adams	CS112
Adams	CS110
Adams	PD102
Brown	CS112
Brown	PD102
Collins	CS112

Scores[person,rating]

person	*rating*
Adams	7
Adams	6
Brown	6
Brown	7
Collins	7

simply to ask the UoD expert (who was needed anyway to confirm that the fact table is significant). If the UoD expert is not currently available we can use the projection-join test. To start, we split on Person by projecting on two columns, with Person being common to both projections (see Table 5.11).

We then recombine into a 3-column table by performing the natural join on these two projections. As an exercise, perform this join. The result is the same as the original table. So no information loss is caused by the splitting. So the fact type is splittable in this way. The correct schema involves two binary fact types, one for each projection. Refer to the previous section for the schema diagram.

While the application of this technique is purely mechanical, a brief explanation of why it works is in order. With the current example, the technique was used to test the following equivalence:

In this UoD, given any Person, Degree and Subject:

Person seeking Degree studies Subject **iff**   Person seeks Degree
and
Person studies Subject

Here "iff" abbreviates "if and only if". Assuming predicate names are supplied, the projection corresponds to the conditional: *if* the ternary is true *then* the conjunction is true. The join corresponds to the conditional: *if* the conjunction is true *then* the ternary is true.

Table 5.10

	Person	Degree	Subject
	Adams	BSc	CS112
	Adams	BSc	CS110
	Adams	BSc	PD102
	Brown	BA	CS112
	Brown	BA	PD102
	Collins	BSc	CS112

Table 5.11   Two projections of Table 5.10

Person	Degree		Person	Subject
Adams	BSc		Adams	CS112
Brown	BA		Adams	CS110
Collins	BSc		Adams	PD102
			Brown	CS112
			Brown	PD102
			Collins	CS112

Now consider our familiar ternary example about people scoring ratings for subjects. Look back at the fact table at the top of Table 5.9. Suppose we suspect that this ternary is splittable on Person. For example, we might feel that in this UoD the following equivalence holds:

Person scores Rating for Subject **iff**   Person studies Subject
                                       and
                                       Person scores Rating

To test this way of splitting, we form the two binary projections shown in Table 5.9, and then recombine by joining on Person. The result is shown in Table 5.12 (as an exercise, confirm this result). In forming the join, several new rows (marked "X") appeared which were not present in the original table. Any one of these new rows is enough to prove that the fact type can not be split in this way (i.e. on Person).

Consider for instance the information on the first row of our original table: Adams scores a 7 in CS112. We have attempted to split this fact into the two separate facts: Adams studies CS112; Adams scores 7 (see first rows of the two projections). If this splitting is legitimate the two separate facts must, in combination, be equivalent to the original fact. However they are not. Knowing that Adams scores a 7 does not tell us the subject in which this rating is scored. It could be any of Adams's subjects (CS112, CS110 or PD102) Joining the projections causes all such possibilities to be listed. Since some of these were not present in the original we can tell at a glance that information has been lost in the splitting. So the original fact type cannot be split in this way.

The forward conditional of the equivalence does hold (*if* ternary *then* conjunction). However, the backward conditional fails (it is not generally true that: *if* conjunction *then* ternary). If you use a bit of insight it should be clear that trying to split on Subject or Rating or all three would be pointless. In this case we could conclude that the fact type is unsplittable, and leave it as a ternary. If this is not clear then you can use the algorithm to test all possibilities. You would find that none of them work and then conclude that the fact type is unsplittable.

Table 5.12 The join of the binary projections in Table 5.9

	Person	Subject	Rating
	Adams	CS112	7
X	Adams	CS112	6
X	Adams	CS110	7
	Adams	CS110	6
	Adams	PD102	7
X	Adams	PD102	6
	Brown	CS112	6
X	Brown	CS112	7
X	Brown	PD102	6
	Brown	PD102	7
	Collins	CS112	7

In general, for a ternary A-B-C there are four ways in which it might split: A-B, A-C; B-A, B-C; C-A, C-B; A-B, A-C, B-C. In the fourth case the schema diagram is triangular in shape: this is referred to as 3-way splitting. As an exercise, draw these four possibilities. With 3-way splitting the join should be done in two stages. For example, first join A-B and A-C (with A common); then join the A-B-C result of this join with B-C (with B and C common).

A classic example of testing for 3-way splitting involves the fact type: Agent sells Product for Company. Even if the key spans the whole fact type, the fact type can be split into three binaries if a derivation rule allows the ternary to be deduced from the binaries. This example is discussed in Section 11.4. Such examples are very rare in practice.

Although the projection-join test for splittability works (provided the original sample population is significant) it is quite tedious. For an n-ary fact type, with no intuitions to guide you as to which splitting ways can be ruled out, some work may be saved by first trying the n-way split. If the n-way split fails (by generating new rows in the final join) then all other ways of splitting can be ruled out too: the fact type is unsplittable.

In practice, the projection-join test should only be used as a last resort. If you have access to the UoD expert, then you should instead work directly with this expert, using meaningful names for the fact types. This is much better than playing formal games with populations (whose significance depends anyway on the UoD expert).

Exercise 5.3

1. A ternary fact type is outlined below (minus meaningful names). The population shown in the fact table is significant.

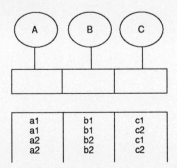

a1	b1	c1
a1	b1	c2
a2	b2	c1
a2	b2	c2

(a) Add the uniqueness constraints for this fact type.
(b) Use the projection-join test to show that this fact type cannot be split into two binaries with C as the common node.
(c) Use the projection-join test to show that this fact type can be split into two binaries with B as the common node.
(d) Draw a schema outline for this result.

6 More constraints

6.1 CSDP step 6: More constraints

So far we have learned how to proceed from familiar information examples to a conceptual schema diagram in which the elementary fact types are clearly set out, with the relevant uniqueness constraints marked on each. In practice there are usually several other kinds of constraints that need to be considered. The most common of these are: entity type constraints, mandatory roles, subtype constraints and occurrence frequencies. Adding these constraints is the next step in our design procedure.

CSDP step 6: Add entity type, mandatory role, subtype and occurrence frequency constraints

In this chapter these constraints are explained, and notations are introduced to specify them on conceptual schema diagrams. There are good reasons for considering the constraints in the order listed. To help clarify our discussion of these and later constraints, we now introduce a shorthand notation for talking about *populations*.

In computing, various data structures such as sets, arrays and trees are used to store information; and each data structure has various operations defined on it. At the conceptual level, there is essentially only one data structure with associated update and retrieval operations: this is the fact type. For a *given state* of the database and a given fact type *F*, we define *pop(F)*, the population of F, to be *the set of facts of type F that are stored in the database.*

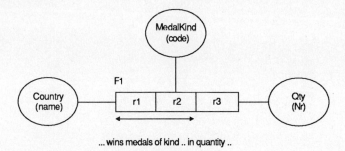

... wins medals of kind .. in quantity ..

Figure 6.1 A fact type for Olympic Games results

109

For a given schema, types are fixed or unchanging. For a given state of the database, the *population* of a given type is the set of instances of that type which are recorded in the database. So as the database is updated, the population of any given type may change. For example, suppose the ternary shown in Figure 6.1 is used to store information about medals won by countries in the next Olympic Games. The fact type and roles are numbered for easy reference.

Initially the fact table for F1 is empty, since so far no sporting results are known. Let us use "{ }" to denote the *empty set* (or *null set*), i.e. the set with no members. To begin with then, pop(F1) = { }. Now suppose that the database is to be updated after each sporting event, and that in the first event the gold and bronze medals are won by USA and the silver medal by Japan. The new state of the fact table is shown in Figure 6.2, using "G", "S", "B" for gold, silver and bronze. Now the population of the fact type contains three facts. The population grows each time the results of an event are entered.

It is convenient to speak of the *population of a role* or column. Given any role *r* and any state of the database:

$pop(r)$ = population of role *r*
 = set of instances referenced in the fact column for *r*

In Figure 6.2, pop(r1) = {USA,Japan}, pop(r2) = {G,S,B} and pop(r3) = {1}. Role populations may be used to define *entity populations*. In any schema, each role is played by exactly one entity type. If an entity type plays exactly one role then the population of the entity type equals that of its role. With our current example, if r1 is the only role played by Country then pop(Country) changes from { } to {USA,Japan} after the first event. The entity type Country is the set of all countries which might possibly compete in the Games: this set contains many countries.

We may also speak about the population of label types. If we need to emphasize the distinction between entities and labels we surround the labels in quotes. For example, at this state of the database we have pop(countryname) = {"USA","Japan"}.

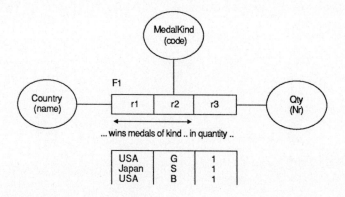

Figure 6.2   The results of the first event

In general, an entity type may play more than one role. The following definition handles the general case: *the population of an entity type equals the union of the populations of its roles*. For example, consider the UoD schematized in Figure 6.3. Here we are interested in the countries with the largest natural gas and coal reserves (1982 figures are shown). The unit symbols "Gt" and "Gm^3" stand for gigatonnes and giga cubic metres (giga = 10^9, i.e. 1,000,000,000).

Notice that a dictionary is provided for role names. This is an alternative to writing the names beside the role boxes, and is quite useful with large schemas. When using this notation we often use a predicate name for the role name. For this state of the database, only the top three countries in each category have been recorded. Here the entity type Country plays the roles r1 and r2. So its population is the set of all the instances referenced in either the r1 column or the r2 column. We could set this out formally as:

pop(Country) = pop(r1) ∪ pop(r2)
              = {USSR, Iran, USA} ∪ {USSR, USA, China}
              = {USSR, Iran, USA, China}

We use ∪ as an operator for *set union*. The union of two sets is the set of all the elements in either one or both. For instance {1,2} ∪ {2,3,4} = {1,2,3,4}. In the above case, USSR and USA occur in both role populations while Iran and China occur in only one.

6.2 Entity type constraints

Consider once more the ternary fact type reproduced in Figure 6.4. The entity type Country is the set of all countries that might possibly be included in our UoD. In practice, it may be impossible to specify this entity type exactly. For example, next week a new country might be formed from the amalgamation of two others. For this entity type, and many others (e.g. Employee, Department, Project, EnergySource) we are often unable to list all the possible members (from the real world viewpoint).

However, there are some entity types whose membership we can specify realistically (e.g. there are only three kinds of Olympic medal: gold, silver and bronze). This restriction on MedalKind is one example of an *entity type constraint*. In this section we discuss how to specify such constraints on our conceptual schema diagram.

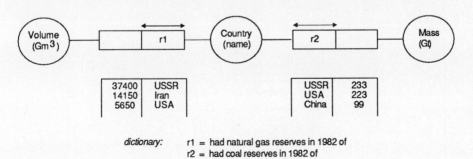

Figure 6.3 A schema-base diagram with a dictionary

Conceptually, the constraint that the kinds of medal are limited to gold, silver and bronze is independent of the reference scheme. We could specify MedalKind using names (e.g. {gold,silver,bronze}) or codes (e.g. {G,S,B} or {Go,Si,Br}) and so on, so long as this identifies the entities for the humans reading the schema. However, we have already chosen a reference scheme in setting out our schema-base diagrams, so it is convenient to use this. Here, the three kinds of medal are referred to by the codes "G", "S" and "B". The set of possible medalkinds may now be *listed* or enumerated as {G,S,B}, and placed besides the entity type (see Figure 6.4).

The members of a set are collectively known as the *extension* of the set. When a set has few members, it is practical to define the set by listing all its members individually. With larger extensions this may be impractical. For example, suppose that there are 200 events in the Olympic Games and that a gold, silver and bronze medal are to be awarded for each event (we assume there are no ties). Since it is logically possible (although highly unlikely) that the same country may win all medals of a given kind, the largest value for Qty is 200. What is the smallest value?

If we want to store facts indicating that a country wins 0 medals of a given kind, we would choose a lower limit of 0. However, if we want to minimize the size of the database we would store only facts about actual wins: this is the approach suggested by our sample population. In this case Qty has a lower limit of 1. Taking the closed world assumption, the fact that a country has won 0 gold medals could then be derived from the absence of a stored fact about that country winning some gold medals.

In principle, we could specify this restriction on Qty by listing the numbers 1, 2, 3 and so on up to 200. However this would be a lengthy description. Happily there are two aspects of this case which enable us to adopt a convenient shorthand notation.

Firstly, because the values we are talking about are integers, they have a clearly defined *order* (e.g. 1 is less than 2 which is less than 3 and so on). Secondly, we are talking about a *continuous* range of integers, that is, we wish to include all the integers in the range from 1 to 200, without leaving any gaps that can be filled by other integers. So we may safely indicate the integers from 1 to 200 simply as "[1..200]" where the ".." abbreviates the integers in between. This is analogous to a *subrange definition* in a

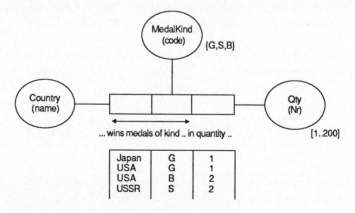

Figure 6.4   Constraints are specified for MedalKind and Qty

language like Pascal. The use of square brackets rather than braces specifies our intention to treat the values as numbers rather than character strings (e.g. we may want to total all the medals won by a country). The constraint is marked beside the entity type (see Figure 6.4).

We have now constrained the entity types MedalKind and Qty. What about Country? If the UoD is only about one Olympics, and we do know which countries are competing, we could provide a full listing for Country. However this list would be too long to include on the schema diagram. If we are to enforce this constraint it should be specified separately.

Recall that although we originally conceive of constraints within the UoD or real world, the information system can only enforce constraints on the knowledge base, that is, the formal model of the UoD. So an "entity type constraint" is actually implemented as a constraint on the label type used to reference entities of that type.

With our example, the entity types MedalKind and Qty are well defined in the real world; so it is easy to capture them with a precise lexical constraint. For many entity types however, we have no precise way of listing them. Often the best we can do is to adopt an artificial lexical constraint, which effectively places an upper bound on what populations are permitted for the entity type. For example, we might specify that each country must have a unique name consisting of a *character string up to a certain length*. For example, we might allow up to nine characters to name a country, and specify this as <c9>.

In practice many different kinds of constraints can arise for label types, and a large variety of notations would be needed to enable all to be specified formally. For instance, in Queensland, Australia, car licence plates have codes comprising a sequence of three decimal digits followed by three letters: we might specify this constraint as <dddaaa> where "d" denotes a decimal digit ("0".."9") and "a" a letter (alphabetic character). We discuss such schemes further in Chapter 7.

We will often omit entity type constraints from our diagram examples unless they are important for clarification. As we will see later however, they may be needed to provide definitions for subtypes, and are sometimes required in making schema transformations. In such cases they must be clearly indicated..

Exercise 6.2

1. Draw a conceptual schema diagram for the UoD described by the following sample output report about elementary particles. Include uniqueness and entity type constraints, assuming no particle has a mass greater than 2000 amu.

Family	Particle	Charge	Mass (amu)
lepton	neutrino	0	0
lepton	electron	-	1
lepton	positron	+	1
meson	eta	0	1074
baryon	proton	+	1836
baryon	neutron	0	1839

Table 6.1

Patient	Sex	Phone
Adams C	F	2057642
Brown S	F	?
Collins T	M	8853020

6.3 Mandatory and optional roles

Consider the output report of Table 6.1. The question mark "?" denotes a null value, indicating that an actual value is not stored. For instance the patient with name "Brown S" may actually have a phone but this information is not recorded, or she may simply have no phone.

A schema base-diagram for this situation is shown in Figure 6.5. Here we have two binary fact types. If this population is significant, we must record the sex of each patient but it is optional whether we record a phone number for a patient.

To formally specify whether or not certain information *must be recorded*, we indicate, for each role on the diagram, whether it is mandatory or optional. A role is **mandatory** if and only if, for all states of the database, it must be recorded for every member of the population of the attached entity type; otherwise the role is **optional**. Which of the four roles in Figure 6.5 are mandatory and which are optional?

To answer this question we need to know whether the diagram includes all the fact types to be recorded for the UoD, or only some of them. Is it the *whole schema* diagram or only a *subschema* diagram (a schema fragment)? For large applications, subschemas are often developed first and later merged to produce the whole schema. In this text, unless otherwise indicated, you may assume the diagrams are whole schema diagrams.

Now consider the two roles played by the entity type Patient. For the database state shown, pop(is of) = {Adams C, Brown S, Collins T} and pop(has) = {Adams C, Collins T}. Since these are the only roles played by Patient, pop(Patient) = {Adams C, Brown S, Collins T}. The first role is played by all recorded patients, and the second role is played

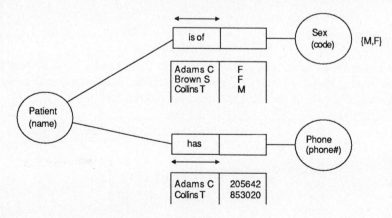

Figure 6.5   A schema-base diagram for Table 6.1

by only some recorded patients. By "played" we mean "recorded in the database". Assuming the output report is significant in this regard, we conclude that the first role is mandatory and the second is optional.

Trivially, the roles played by Sex and Phone are mandatory since each is the only role played by that entity type. So three of the four roles in the schema are mandatory. To indicate explicitly that a role is mandatory we add a *mandatory role dot* to its attached entity type, at the point where the arc from the role meets the entity type. If we do this for each mandatory role, the absence of a dot then indicates that the role is optional. Thus the mandatory role constraints for the UoD under discussion may be specified explicitly as shown in Figure 6.6.

In NIAM, no entity type may be specified unless it is included in a fact type. There is little point in talking about an entity unless it has some role to play (other than its identifying reference role, e.g. has-name). Given this understanding, *if a primitive entity type plays only one role, this role is mandatory*. Here "primitive" excludes objectified relationship types and subtypes (see later), which may have a single role that is optional. So if we have a role attached to a primitive entity type, and this is the only role attached, there is actually no need to include a mandatory role dot since this constraint is implied by the above metarule. So the schema diagram may alternatively be shown as in Figure 6.7.

This implicit specification is usually preferable. It highlights the mandatory role constraints that are really important, that is, the ones we need to enforce. Moreover, the

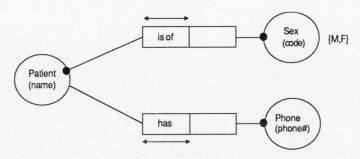

Figure 6.6 All mandatory role constraints specified explicitly

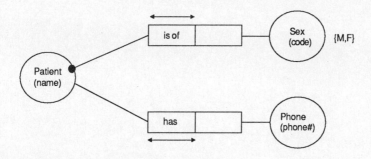

Figure 6.7 Implicitly, right hand roles are mandatory

diagram is easier to draw (e.g. fewer dots to be added), and if the schema is later merged with another there are usually fewer changes to make. However, the explicit specification may be preferred if we wish to draw the attention of a human reader to the implied constraints. In this text we include examples of both approaches.

If a role is mandatory, its population always equals the total population of its attached entity type. For this reason, a mandatory role is sometimes said to be a *total role*. Given an entity type *A* and an attached role *r*, here are three different ways of expressing the constraint that *r* is *mandatory* or *total*:

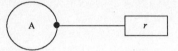

For each state of the database:

pop(r) = pop(A)

Each member of *pop(A)* is recorded as playing *r*

For each member of *A*, if any role is recorded for it then *r* is

Note that this does *not* mean that all members of the entity type *A* are recorded as playing *r*. Mandatory role constraints are enforced on populations rather than types.

If you look back at Figure 6.7 you will notice that the is-of role is both mandatory and unique. Can you think of a concise way of expressing the combination of these constraints? The uniqueness constraint tells us that each patient has *at most one* sex recorded. The mandatory role constraint tells us that each recorded patient has *at least one* sex recorded. In combination these two constraints thus indicate that each recorded patient has **exactly one** sex recorded. This is an illustration of the general result that *at least one + at most one = exactly one*.

In our discussion about uniqueness constraints we contrasted the UoD (real world portion of interest) with the knowledge base (the formal model of the UoD). As with other constraints in our conceptual schema, mandatory role constraints are interpreted in terms of the database. With our current example, it is optional whether a patient has a phone. This simply means that we do not need to record a phone number for every patient. In the real or actual world maybe each patient does in fact have a phone. To ensure this point is understood, consider the schema of Figure 6.8.

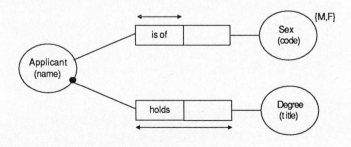

Figure 6.8   Recording the sex of an applicant is optional

Table 6.2

	Patient	Sex	Phone
	Adams C	F	2057642
	Brown S	F	?
	Collins T	M	8853020

This schema could be used to describe a UoD in which applicants for a position are given the choice whether to have their sex recorded or not, but must provide details about their degrees. In this case it is optional whether sex is recorded for an applicant. This contrasts sharply with the real world where of course all applicants are of a particular sex.

With respect to mandatory roles, the relationship between the real world and the knowledge base is simply this: *if a role is optional in the real world, then it is optional in the knowledge base, but the converse need not apply*. Equivalently, if a role is mandatory in the knowledge base then it is mandatory in the real world, but not conversely.

Do *not* read a mandatory role constraint as saying "if an entity plays that role in real life then we must record it". While this might be a constraint we wish to place on ourselves as conceptual schema designers, it is obviously not a constraint that the system is capable of checking. Only humans can enforce such a constraint.

To help ensure that we have correctly specified the mandatory role constraints, we can apply the following checking procedure. For each mandatory role: is it mandatory in the real world? (if not, make it optional). For each optional role: is it optional in the real world? (if not, what reasons are there for making it optional? . . . we will have more to say about this in the section on subtypes).

You may recall from Section 2.2 that when an entity type plays more than one role, special care needs to be taken in updating the database to take account of mandatory roles. Suppose we wanted to add the information contained in the sample output report (reproduced in Table 6.2) into the database described by the conceptual schema of Figure 6.7.

Consider the following interactions between the user and the conceptual information processor, where for simplicity reference modes have been omitted.

User	*CIP*
add: Patient 'Adams C' is of Sex 'F'	accepted
add: Patient 'Adams C' has Phone '2057642'	accepted
add: Patient 'Collins T' has Phone '8853020'	rejected: sex of each patient must be recorded

To add the third fact into the database we must either first record the fact that Collins is a male, or at least include this fact with the phone fact in a compound transaction.

Now consider the sample output report of Table 6.3. Such a report might relate to a database maintained by a retailer of software items. This is similar to an example considered in an earlier chapter. Abbreviating cost price and sales price as "CP" and "SP" we may describe this UoD by the conceptual schema shown in Figure 6.9. Note that both the roles is-CP-of and is-SP-of are connected to the same dot on their attached entity type. This means that the *disjunction of these roles is mandatory*.

Table 6.3

	Software	CostPrice ($)	SalesPrice ($)	Profit ($)
	Modula 3	200	300	100
	OS/3	300	400	100
	WordLight	400	599	199

In other words, each amount of money that is recorded in the database must appear *either* as the cost price of a software item *or* the sales price of a software item *or both*. For example, with the sample provided, $200 occurs as a cost price, $599 occurs as a sales price, and $300 occurs as both a cost price and a sales price.

In contrast, both the roles played by software are mandatory. For each item of software in the database we must record both the cost price and the sales price. An update here requires a compound transaction.

Note that the roles of the derived fact type are both optional, since these are derived rather than recorded. Although not recorded, the profit of each software item must be known: but this "mandatory knowledge" constraint is implied. *Derived roles should always be shown as optional.* The uniqueness constraint shown on the derived fact type may also be omitted since it is implied by the derivation rule: however, we usually include it for clarity.

Figure 6.10 indicates in general how we may explicitly specify that a disjunction of roles $r_1, r_2, \ldots, r_n$ is mandatory. As usual, we use "or" in the inclusive sense; so we accept the possibility of some member of *pop(A)* being recorded as playing all the roles $r1 \ldots r_n$.

In Figure 6.10, we specified the constraint that each member of *pop(A)* is recorded as playing *at least one* of the roles $r_1..r_n$. Contrast this with the much stronger constraint pictured in Figure 6.11. Since each role is depicted as mandatory this means that each member of *pop(A)* is recorded as playing *all* the roles $r_1..r_n$. For example, with our software schema recorded software items had to have both their cost price and selling price recorded.

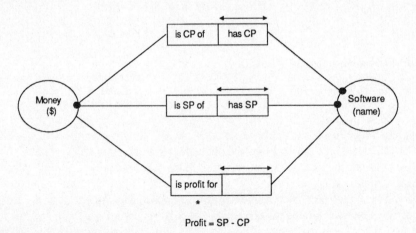

Profit = SP - CP

Figure 6.9   Each recorded money amount is a cost or sales price

As an example involving a homogeneous fact type, consider the schema-base diagram of Figure 6.12. Here each person referenced in the database is recorded as playing either (or both) of the two roles. As an aid to understanding, try representing each of the people as a point inside the Person ellipse, and draw appropriate links through the roles to picture the relationships recorded in the table. For instance, in this UoD Terry is recorded as being a child of Alice and Bernie, and as being a parent of Selena.

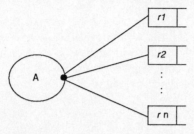

For each state of the database:

$$pop(r1) \cup pop(r2) \cup \ldots \cup pop(r_n) = pop(A)$$

Each member of *pop(A)* is recorded as playing *r1* or *r2* or ... or *r_n*

Figure 6.10   The role disjunction is mandatory (explicit version)

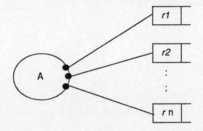

Figure 6.11   All roles played by A are mandatory

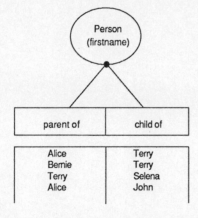

Figure 6.12   Role disjunction is mandatory (explicit version)

Since any entity type must play at least one role, it is always the case that *the disjunction of roles played by any primitive entity type is mandatory*. Objectified relationship types and subtypes (see next section) are not primitive: they may play a single, optional role. If mandatory disjunction is the strongest mandatory role constraint on a primitive entity type, there is no need to show this explicitly. For example, in the schema diagram of Figure 6.13 the constraint that the role disjunction is mandatory is implied by this metarule.

The explicit version of specifying mandatory role disjunctions often leads to awkward looking diagrams, since arcs from several entity types may need to twist around before joining at the dot. Hence the simpler, implicit version is usually preferred. Of course, if we need to specify a mandatory disjunction among just some of the roles played by an entity type then this must be shown explicitly.

Exercise 6.3

1. Draw a conceptual schema diagram for the UoD described by the following sample output report. Include uniqueness and mandatory role constraints.

Country	Coal reserves (Gt)	Oil reserves (Gt)
USSR	233	8.6
USA	223	4.1
China	99	2.7
Australia	59	?
West Germany	59	?
GDR	23	?
Saudi-Arabia	0.1	23

2. Set out the schema for the UoD indicated by the following output report. Include uniqueness and mandatory role constraints, and the entity type constraint for Rating. Identify any derived fact type(s).

Subject	Year	NrEnrolled	Rating	NrStudents	%	Lecturer
CS121	1982	200	7	5	2.50	P.L.Cook
			6	10	5.00	
			5	75	37.50	
			4	80	40.00	
			3	10	5.00	
			2	5	2.50	
CS123	1982	150	7	4	2.67	L.P.Green
			6	8	5.33	
			5	60	40.00	
			4	70	46.67	
			1	6	4.00	
CS121	1983	250	7	10	4.00	A.B.White
			6	30	12.00	
			5	100	40.00	
			4	80	32.00	
			3	15	6.00	

3. In the game of cricket a *six* is scored if the ball is hit over the field boundary on the full. If the ball reaches the boundary after landing on the ground a *four* is scored. In either case, a "boundary" is said to have been scored. A cricket fan maintains a record of boundaries scored by Australia, India and New Zealand in their competition matches. Although it is possible to score a 4 or 6 by running between the wickets, such cases do not count as boundaries and are not included in the database. A sample output report from this information system is shown below.

Year	Australia			India			New Zealand		
	4s	*6s*	*total*	*4s*	*6s*	*total*	*4s*	*6s*	*total*
1984	120	30	150	135	23	158	115	35	150
1985	112	33	145	110	30	140	120	25	145
1986	140	29	169	135	30	165	123	35	158

Here "*4s*" means "number of 4-boundaries" and "*6s*" means "number of 6-boundaries". Draw a conceptual schema diagram for this UoD, including uniqueness constraints and mandatory roles. Indicate any derived fact types. Use nesting.

6.4 Sets and subtypes: Some formal background

So far we have found it convenient to make use of the notions of *set* and *type* to explain various aspects of our design procedure. Since the next section involves a detailed discussion of subtypes, and the reader may not be familiar with set theory, we take time out here to examine some background theory about sets and to introduce the subtype notation for schema diagrams. In the interests of providing a comprehensive summary of the required background, some ideas met earlier are included.

Intuitively, a set is a well-defined collection of items. The items may be either concrete (e.g. people, computers) or abstract (e.g. numbers, points), and are called *elements* or *members* of the set. Sets themselves are abstract: they are numerically definite in the sense that each has a definite number of elements. Earlier we defined a *type* as a set of possible items. Each item of a particular type is an instance or element of that particular set.

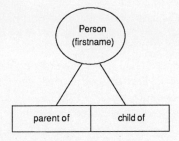

Figure 6.13 Role disjunction is mandatory (implicit version)

The members of a set collectively constitute the *extension* of the set. While a set may contain members it does not consist of those members. For example, the set of Martian moons is an abstraction over and above its members (Phobos and Deimos) and consequently has no physical properties such as mass or volume. Although sets (unlike heaps) are not to be equated with their members, they are determined by their members, since two sets are *identical* just in case they have the same extension. Using "iff" to abbreviate "if and only if", the Law of Extensionality may be stated thus:

Given any sets A and B,   A = B iff A and B have the same members.

Since sets are determined by their members, one simple way of *defining* a set is to enumerate the elements of the set. In so doing we often use braces as delimiters and commas as item separators (e.g. A = {3,6}). Here A is defined to be the set containing just the elements 3 and 6. One consequence of the Law of Extensionality is that a set is not changed by *repeating* any of its members. For instance, if B = {3,6,6} it follows that A = B since both sets contain precisely the same members (3 and 6).

When enumerating sets it is usual not to repeat the members; however it is sometimes useful to permit this. For example, when stating general results about the set variable {x,y} it may be handy to include the case x = y. Sometimes repetition of members occurs undetected. For instance, some people do not realize that the entity set {Morning Star, Evening Star} contains just one member (the planet Venus). Of course, the label set {"Morning Star", "Evening Star"} contains two members.

If repetition is made significant, we have a *bag* or multiset. To help distinguish between bags and sets it is advisable to use different delimiters (e.g. parentheses for bags and braces for sets). For instance the bag (3,6,6) has three members while the set {3,6,6} has two. One use of bags is in collecting values for statistical work. For example, the set {3,6,6} has an average of 4.5 but the bag (3,6,6) has an average of 5. Bags are frequently used with languages like SQL.

Another consequence of the Law of Extensionality is that the *order* in which elements are listed is irrelevant. For example, if A = {3,6} and B = {6,3} then we may conclude that A = B, since each set contains the same members. Bags are also insensitive to order, as in (3,6) = (6,3). If order is made significant we have an "ordinal set". Usually, when order is made significant, so is repetition. In this case we have a *sequence* or list or permutation, that is, a sequence is an ordered bag. One way to distinguish between sequences and bags is to use angle brackets as sequence delimiters (e.g. the sequence <6,3,6> has three members and is different from the sequence <3,6,6>). However, parentheses are often used as sequence delimiters (e.g. Cartesian coordinate sequences, argument sequences for relations, functions and procedures). In practice several different notations are used, for example, square brackets are used as set delimiters in Pascal and list delimiters in Prolog.

Although when a set is enumerated in full the ordering does not matter, frequently a natural ordering provides an obvious pattern: in such cases a partial enumeration will serve to define the set. For example, the set of decimal digits may be shown as {0..9}, where the ".." indicates the missing digits. Infinite sets may be represented with ".." at one end, for example, the set of natural numbers may be shown as {1,2,3..}.

The preceding set definitions enumerate, wholly or partially, the extension of the set and are thus examples of an *extensional definition*. Another way to define a set is by means of an *intensional definition*. Here an identifying description is provided which is held by just those members of the set, that is, a description is given which constitutes both a necessary and sufficient condition (an "iff condition") for an item to belong to a set. For example, the set A which is defined extensionally as {1,2,3} may be defined intensionally as:

A = the set of natural numbers which are less than 4

This definition may be recast in set builder notation as {x: x is a natural number less than 4 } or more briefly as {x: x ∈ N & x < 4} where "∈" abbreviates "is a member of", and N is the set of natural numbers. In set builder notation a stroke "|" may be used instead of a colon, e.g. {x|x<4}. The number of elements in a set is called the *cardinality* of the set, e.g. the set {2,4,6} has a cardinality of 3.

Some set operations result in propositions while others result in sets. We note the following proposition-forming operators: =, ≠, ⊆, ⊂, ⊇, and ⊃. These are read respectively as "equals", "is not equal to", "is a subset of", "is a proper subset of", "is a superset of" and "is a proper superset of".

Given any sets A and B, we say that A is a **subset** of B iff every member of A is also a member of B. For example, {1,3} ⊆ {1,2,3}. An equivalent definition is: A is a subset of B iff A has no members that are not in B. This second definition makes it easy to see that the *null set* is a subset of every set. The null or empty set has no members and may be represented as { } or ∅.

Note also that every set is a subset of itself, for example, {1,3} ⊆ {1,3}. We say that A is a *proper subset* of B iff A is a subset of B but is not equal to B, for example, {1,3} ⊂ {1,2,3}. We say that A is a **superset** of B iff B is a subset of A, and that A is a proper superset of B iff B is a proper subset of A (e.g. {1,2,3} is both a superset and a proper superset of {1,3}).

For the case of two sets, such relationships are most easily depicted by means of Hypothetical Euler Diagrams (HEDs). Before discussing HEDs, let's briefly look at *standard Euler diagrams*. As developed by the Swiss mathematician Leonhard Euler, these were spatial and existential (these terms are now explained). Each set is pictured as a set of points inside an ellipse. This enables the relationship between the sets to be "seen" by the spatial arrangement of the ellipses. For example, placing ellipse A inside ellipse B shows that A is a proper subset of B (see Figure 6.14).

Here we can see that every element of A is also an element of B (so A is a subset of B). Moreover, the existential viewpoint implies that each of the regions in the above Euler diagram are assumed to contain some elements. So B has some elements not in A. So A is a proper subset of B.

If we want to express the relationship that A is a subset of B on standard Euler diagrams we need to use a disjunction of two diagrams, as shown in Figure 6.15. The right hand diagram caters for the possibility that A = B.

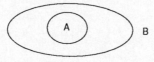

Figure 6.14 Euler diagram for: A is a proper subset of B

It turns out that the notion of subsethood is a more useful one than proper subsethood. Partly to enable such relationships to be shown on a single diagram, we introduce a notation which we call *Hypothetical Euler Diagrams* (HEDs). Here an asterisk is placed in a region to show something exists there, while shading the region indicates that it is empty. If a region is unmarked the question of whether any elements exist there is left open or hypothetical. Figure 6.16 sets out the HEDs for the most important kinds of relationship between two sets.

Case 1 is that of *equality* or identity (e.g. A = B = {1,2}). In case 2, A and B are disjoint or *mutually exclusive*, that is, they have no members in common (e.g. A = {1}, B = {2}). In case 3, A is a *subset* of B (equivalently, B is a superset of A). In case 4, A is a *proper subset* of B (equivalently, B is a proper superset of A). For example both A = {1}, B = {1,2} and A = {1}, B = {1} are instances of case 3, but only the former is an instance of case 4. Case 5 is that of *overlap*, that is, the sets have some members in common. Case 6 is that of *proper overlap*, that is, the sets have common as well as extra members. For example, both A = {1,2}, B = {2,3} and A = {1}, B = {1,2} are instances of overlap but only the former is a case of proper overlap.

Let us now turn to set-forming operations in which the result is a set rather than a proposition. Given any sets A and B, and reading "or" inclusively, we define A ∪ B (i.e. A *union* B) to be the set of all elements in A or B. We define A ∩ B (i.e. A *intersect* B) to be the set of all elements common to both A and B. Each of these operations is commutative, so the order of the operands doesn't matter (i.e. A ∪ B = B ∪ A and A ∩ B = B ∩ A).

Figure 6.15   Euler diagram disjunction for: A is a subset of B

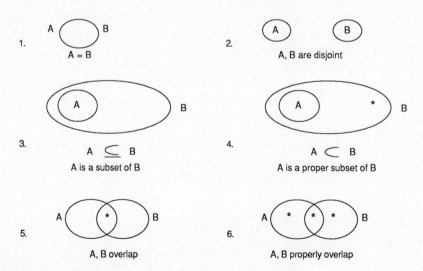

Figure 6.16   Hypothetical Euler Diagrams for set comparisons

The set *difference* (or relative complement) operation is defined thus: A – B (i.e. A minus B) is the set of all elements that are in A but not in B. This operation does not commute (i.e. cases may arise where A – B ≠ B – A). If we let U = the universal set (i.e. the set of all elements under consideration) we define the *complement* of A as A' = U – A.

Various other set operations may be defined. For example, the symmetric difference between A and B is the set of elements in just one of A or B (i.e. the union minus the intersection). For our purposes the three most important set-forming operations are union, intersection and difference. These are depicted in Figure 6.17 by means of *Venn diagrams*, using shading to indicate the result of the operation. Unlike Euler diagrams, the ellipses in Venn diagrams always overlap. Like HEDs, Venn diagrams adopt the hypothetical viewpoint.

As examples of these operations, if A = {1,2,3} and B = {2,4} then A ∪ B = {1,2,3,4}, A ∩ B = {2}, A – B = {1,3} and B – A = {4}. There are literally dozens of different diagram methods for working with sets. However, most of these methods become extremely unwieldy as soon as the number of sets exceeds three. For instance, a Venn diagram for four sets is shown in Figure 6.18.

We have used Hypothetical Euler Diagrams to explain various relationships between sets, and Venn diagrams to explain various set-forming operations on sets. So long as the number of sets involved is quite small, these diagrams are well suited for these purposes.

In the next section we will see that in designing a conceptual schema we may need to introduce subtypes, and in so doing spell out clearly what is a subtype of what. Since one entity type may have several subtypes we need a method that is not going to become

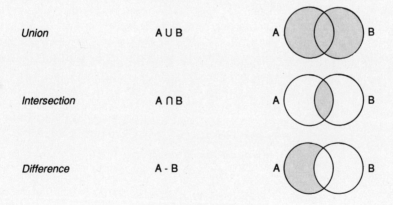

Figure 6.17   Venn diagrams for set-forming operations

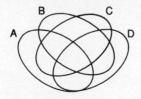

Figure 6.18   A Venn diagram for four sets

hopelessly complicated when the number of types that are to be compared becomes large. For this purpose, a radically different diagram technique is used in which the subtypes are shown *outside* their supertype. This ensures that space is available to clearly indicate subtype connections and subtype names. The basic idea is shown in Figure 6.19.

Here A and B are object types (e.g. A = Employee and B = Manager). The type Employee is the set of all employees about which facts might possibly be recorded in the database. The **subtype** Manager is the set of all managers about which facts might be recorded in the database. At any given state of the database, pop(Employee) and pop(Manager) are respectively the set of employees and set of managers actually referenced in the database.

Look carefully at the definition provided in Figure 6.19. Given this, and the fact that A ≠ B (NIAM never allows an object type to be duplicated in the schema) it follows that B is a *proper subtype* of A. The directed arc or "arrow" going from B to A indicates that B is a proper subtype of A, or equivalently, A is a proper supertype of B. For brevity we usually omit "proper" when speaking about subtypes and supertypes in NIAM.

In contrast, we should *not* use the adjective "proper" when describing the corresponding *population* comparison. It is possible that at various states of the database pop(A) = pop(B). For example, before any facts about A have been entered both pop(A) and pop(B) equal { }; and with the example given, there is nothing to stop us entering information about managers before the other employees. Although the graph in Figure 6.19 is often read as "B is a subtype of A", it is more precisely defined by the population constraint given at the right of the graph.

Now consider the subtype graph shown in Figure 6.20. Here we might have A = Person, B = Woman, C = AsianPerson, D = JapaneseWoman. We say that A is a *common supertype* of B and C, and D is a *common subtype* of B and C. In general, a common supertype is at least the union of its subtypes; if it is the union of its subtypes then its subtypes are said to *exhaust* it. In our example, B and C do not exhaust A. In general a

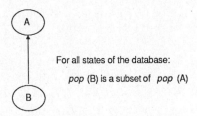

Figure 6.19   Subtype notation for schema diagrams

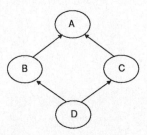

Figure 6.20   D is a subtype of B and C, which are subtypes of A

common subtype is at most the intersection of its supertypes. In our example, B ∩ C = AsianWoman, and D is a proper subset of this.

Since B is attached directly to its supertype A, we say that B is a *direct subtype* of A. Since D is a subtype of B, and B is a subtype of A it follows that every member of D is also a member of A: we say that D is an *indirect subtype* of A. In general, the relation of subtypehood is *transitive*, that is, given any sets X, Y and Z, if X ⊆ Y and Y ⊆ Z then X ⊆ Z. We should omit explicit marking of indirect subtype relations since these are implied by transitivity.

A type may have many direct subtypes and a subtype may have many direct supertypes: so in general we have a graph rather than a tree. The subtypes are referred to as the *nodes* of the graph. Since the arrowheads provide direction we have a directed graph. Since no type can be a proper subtype of itself it follows that no cycles or loops are permitted. Thus in NIAM, any pattern of type-subtype relationships forms a *directed acyclic graph*.

An entity type which is not a proper subtype of any other entity type in the schema is said to be a **primitive entity type** for the schema. The JapaneseWoman subtype might occur in a schema whose primitive entity types include Person, Sex, and Country. Within a conceptual schema it is possible to have several distinct subtype graphs. Each subtype graph must stem from exactly one primitive entity type, which is the common supertype, or *head*, for that graph (e.g. Person).

Subtype graphs have only one head since, as we know from earlier work, *primitive entity types are mutually exclusive*. In contrast, subtypes in a graph necessarily overlap with their supertype(s), and may even overlap with one another (e.g. Woman and AsianPerson). Since primitive types are mutually exclusive, there can be no overlap between subtypes that belong to different subtype graphs.

Recall that two sets are mutually exclusive iff they have no elements in common, and that sets B and C exhaust A iff B ∪ C = A. Now consider the subtype graph of Figure 6.21. Although we have a nice clean picture telling us that B and C are (proper) subtypes of A, there is no indication here as to whether B and C exhaust A, or whether B and C are mutually exclusive. This is not really a disadvantage, since information on exhaustion and exclusion can be expressed in a conceptual schema by the subtype definitions and other constraints. How this is done is discussed in the next section.

It is worth noting that many different subtyping schemes have been proposed for various purposes. In NIAM, subtypes are introduced to express constraints on what is recorded in the database, rather than to provide a complete picture of natural classification in the real world. This important feature of NIAM will be expanded on in the next section.

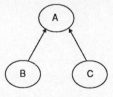

Figure 6.21   Are B and C mutually exclusive? Do they exhaust A?

Exercise 6.4

1. (a) For each of the following NIAM subtype graphs assume that type A = {1,2,3}. Provide examples for the subtypes to complete a satisfying model for each diagram.

(i)   (ii)

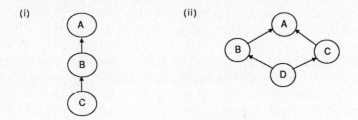

(b) Explain what is wrong with each of the following NIAM subtype graphs.

(i)   (ii)   (iii)

(iv)   (v)

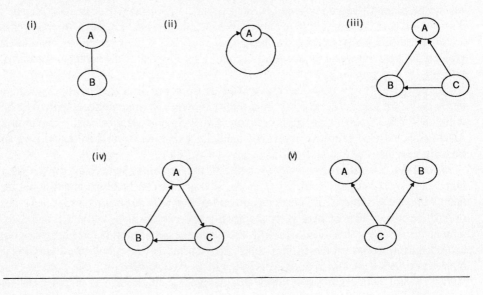

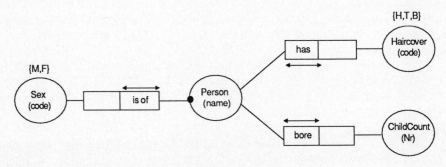

Figure 6.22   A conceptual schema diagram for Table 6.4

Table 6.4

Person	Sex	Haircover	NrChildren
Jones E	F	-	2
Smith J	M	T	-
Blow J	M	B	-
Lane L	F	-	0
Blossom B	F	-	5

"-" = "not to be recorded"

6.5 Subtypes

Consider a UoD in which all the people are adults, and hence may be classified as men or women. Because men are much more likely to go bald we are interested in recording the amount of haircover just for the men. Let us agree that this has three possible states: H (hairy); T (thin); and B (bald). Only women bear children, and we wish to record the number of children just for the women. A sample output report for this UoD is shown in Table 6.4.

Note the use of a *hyphen* "-" to indicate that a particular fact is *deliberately never recorded*. This is quite different from "0". For the woman identified as "Lane L" we do not record haircover but we do record the fact that she has no children. We have previously used "?" as a general null value indicating an actual value is not recorded: this did not rule out the possibility that at some later state of the database a value might be assigned to that position. The hyphen "-" is a special kind of null value to indicate that an actual value will *never* appear in that position. Suppose we now schematize the UoD as in Figure 6.22.

Rather than take the output report to be significant, we used our knowledge about the UoD to assign uniqueness constraints (we permit duplicates in the columns for Haircover and NrChildren). Notice that Person has one mandatory and two optional roles. The sex of each person must be recorded, but the haircover and number of children borne are optionally recorded. If we take this to be the finished schema it is clear that we have missed out the constraints that haircover is recorded just for the men and NrChildren borne is recorded just for the women. One way of including these constraints in the schema would be to add sentences like the following below the diagram:

Haircover is recorded just for Persons of sex 'M'
ChildCount is recorded just for Persons of sex 'F'

Here the expression "*just for*" means "*for and only for*" (i.e. "for all and only"). By "Persons" we mean "persons referenced in the database". So for men, Haircover must be recorded and ChildCount must not be; for women, Haircover must not be recorded and ChildCount must be. While such sentences would suffice, it would be preferable if we had some way of seeing these constraints simply by looking at the diagram. Such a way is provided by introducing subtypes, as shown in Figure 6.23.

Here we added two subtypes: Man and Woman. The entity type Person is a supertype of both of these. Since subtypes inherit the reference mode of their supertype there is no need to repeat this for them. Because we have chosen meaningful identifiers for the subtypes we can see at a glance what the recording constraints are.

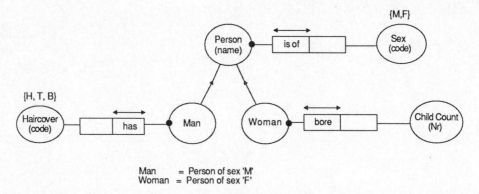

Man   = Person of sex 'M'
Woman   = Person of sex 'F'

Figure 6.23 A more complete conceptual schema for Figure 6.22

Recall that primitive entities for which the same roles are recorded are grouped into the same entity type. This basic idea is extended to subtypes. Now however, the subtype definitions provide a formal means of enforcing these recording constraints.

The subtype arrow going from Man to Person indicates that haircover is recorded *only for* men. The mandatory role dot on Man indicates that this is recorded for all men in *pop*(Person). Taken together, this subtype arrow and mandatory role dot indicate that haircover is recorded *just for* men, that is, the men in *pop*(Person). Similarly the subtype arrow and mandatory role dot on Woman indicate that NrChildren is recorded just for women.

In this example, by introducing subtypes we are left with no optional roles. This is what usually happens. In some cases however some roles may remain optional. For instance, suppose with our current example that additionally we want to record a phone number only for men. If not all men have phones then we will be left with an optional has-phone role attached to the subtype Man. We do not create a further subtype of Man since we have no good way of defining which men have phones.

It is even possible that a subtype may have just a single role, and that this is optional. For this reason, if the role played by a subtype is mandatory for that subtype then the mandatory role dot should always be included. So, *if they apply, mandatory role constraints must be specified explicitly for subtypes and objectified relationship types.* The implicit scheme applies only to simple, primitive entity types.

In NIAM we do not introduce a subtype unless there is at least one specific role recorded only for that subtype. For example, we have not introduced subtypes for BaldPerson or ChildlessWoman. As with primitive entity types, we demand that each subtype must have an attached role.

While specific fact types are attached to the relevant subtype, common fact types are attached to the supertype. In this example, the sex fact type must be recorded for all persons, so we attach it directly to Person. In general, each subtype inherits all the fact types associated with its supertype(s). Even though we draw a subtype outside its supertype it needs to be realized that the subtype is actually totally contained inside the supertype. So the previous diagram indicates that entities of type Man or Woman have their sex recorded. By attaching this fact type to the supertype rather than the subtypes we have avoided duplicating the fact type.

To determine membership of subtypes, we demand that *each subtype must be defined in terms of at least one role played by its supertype(s)*. With the present example, the sex fact type is used to determine membership in Man and Woman. The subtype definitions are shown below the diagram. Please be careful not to use circular definitions. In other words, don't try to define a subtype in terms of itself. For example, we would be guilty of circularity if instead of Woman and our associated definition we introduced a subtype ChildBearingPerson and then defined this subtype as: Person bearing some ChildCount. The constraint that ChildCount is recorded only for ChildBearingPerson could not then be enforced (Why not?)

In very rare cases, the role used to define a subtype may be a reference role. For example, we might record some fact only for people whose surname begins with the letter "Z". In almost all practical situations however, the subtype defining roles will belong to fact types.

For the schema of Figure 6.23, the subtype definitions make it clear that the division of Person into Man and Woman is a **partition**: Man and Woman are *mutually exclusive and collectively exhaustive*. We may display this situation on a HED as shown in Figure 6.24 (we include this only for illustration: it is not required for the schema).

The subtype names "Man" and "Woman" are meaningful to us, and our background understanding of these terms helps us to see this partition. However such names are only character strings to the computer system, so how is the partition formally captured in the knowledge base? Look back at Figure 6.23. The constraint that Man and Woman are mutually exclusive is formally implied by the definitions supplied for Man and Woman together with the uniqueness constraint on the is-of-sex role (nobody can be recorded to be both male and female). The constraint that Man and Woman exhaust Person is implied by the subtype definitions, the {M,F} constraint, and the mandatory role dot on Person (each person referenced in the database must be recorded as male or female).

Since the exclusion and exhaustion constraints are thus taken care of by the subtype definitions and the other constraints we don't need to clutter up the schema diagram with any further notations to express subtype exclusion and exhaustion. In contrast to the system, we can take advantage of our own background understanding of meaningful subtype names to immediately see whether subtypes are exclusive or exhaustive. This short cut for us depends on a judicious choice of subtype names. For example, if it is not clear that the terms "Man" and "Woman" cover all people in the UoD (e.g. we might want to include children) then the exhaustion constraint might be more appropriately seen by using the subtype names "Male person" and "Female person" instead of "Man" and "Woman".

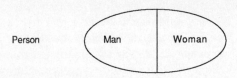

Figure 6.24 A partition of Person

Table 6.5

Animal	AnimalKind	Gender	Nr Cars chased	Nr mice caught
Fido	dog	M	12	-
Felix	cat	M	-	1
Fluffy	dog	F	0	-
Tweetie	bird	F	-	-

"-" = "not to be recorded"

Having discussed this example in some detail, we now summarize the basic method for deciding on whether subtypes need to be introduced. Assuming that all roles on our schema diagram have been classified as mandatory or optional, we proceed as follows:

Subtype Introduction Procedure (SIP):

For each optional role:

   if this role is to be recorded only for a *well-defined* proper subtype of the attached entity type

   then specify a subtype with this role attached; apply the SIP to this subtype

   else leave it as is.

For now, we take "well-defined" to mean that within the information system the subtype can be precisely defined in terms of other roles attached to its supertype(s). The procedure is recursive: since a subtype may itself have optional roles we apply the procedure to it to see if we need to form subtypes of it.

In most cases the subtypes will not be hard to spot. Let's look at a couple more simple examples before going on to harder cases. To begin with, consider Table 6.5 which lists a sample weekly report about animals belonging to a certain household. Before looking at the diagram provided, see if you can work out the conceptual schema for this UoD. You may assume that the population is significant with respect to AnimalKind.

From the table it should be obvious that there are four fact types to be recorded for the animals. Gender and AnimalKind are recorded for all the animals. The number of cars chased is recorded just for dogs, and the number of mice caught is recorded just for cats. This leads to the schema of Figure 6.25.

The subtype definitions are obvious in this case. Rather than defining a formal grammar for subtype definitions we use any clear notation. We do not introduce Bird as a subtype because there is no specific role to be recorded only about birds. Each bird however still has the common information (Gender and AnimalKind) recorded for it. Since a Bird subtype was not created, the subtypes created are not exhaustive, though they are mutually exclusive, as indicated by the uniqueness constraint on the is-of-kind role. The HED shown in Figure 6.26 portrays the supertype-subtype relationships clearly. The asterisk indicates that some animals other than dogs and cats exist in the *type* Animal. Of course it is still possible for some states of the database that pop(Animal) might contain only dogs and cats.

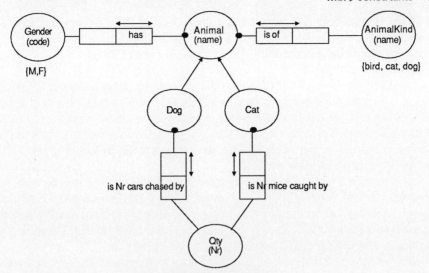

Cat = Animal of AnimalKind 'cat'
Dog = Animal of AnimalKind 'dog'

Figure 6.25 The conceptual schema for Table 6.5

Figure 6.26 Dog and Cat are exclusive and non-exhaustive

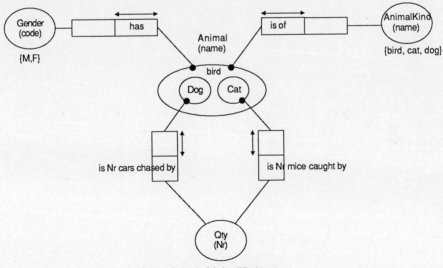

Cat = Animal of AnimalKind 'cat'
Dog = Animal of AnimalKind 'dog'

Figure 6.27 A hybrid diagram

In our schema diagrams, subtypes are drawn outside their supertypes. Don't forget however that every member of a subtype is also a member of its supertype(s). To emphasize this point, the previous schema diagram may be interpreted in terms of the hybrid diagram of Figure 6.27.

Compare this diagram with Figure 6.25. Although a hybrid diagram is helpful to humans for explanation purposes, it is unwieldy for complex subtyping configurations, and should not be looked upon as offering an alternative subtype notation for conceptual schema diagrams. We make no further use of such hybrid diagrams; however as an optional exercise you may wish to draw the corresponding hybrid diagrams for other subtype schemas presented in the book.

Consider now a UoD peopled just by lecturers and students who may be identified by name. Gender and PersonKind (L = Lecturer; S = Student) is recorded for all persons, salary is recorded just for lecturers, and course of study is recorded just for students. In this UoD it is possible for a person to be both a lecturer and student. Draw the schema diagram for this UoD yourself, then compare it with Figure 6.28.

Here we have two subtypes: Student and Lecturer. That these subtypes are exhaustive is clear from the {L,S} constraint. That these subtypes overlap is clear from the absence of a uniqueness constraint on the is-of role (a person may be both student and lecturer). The type-subtype relationships are further illustrated on the HED shown in Figure 6.29.

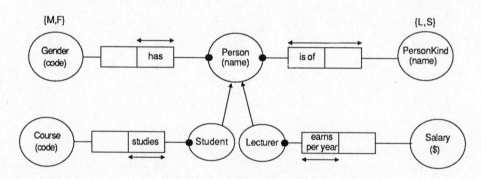

Student = Person of PersonKind 'S'
Lecturer = Person of PersonKind 'L'

Figure 6.28   In this UoD a student may be a lecturer

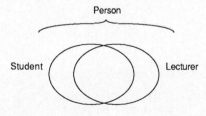

Figure 6.29   A person is either a student or lecturer or both

Table 6.6

Person	Age	Favourite group
Sue	13	Dire Straits
Fred	12	–
Bill	17	Abba
Mary	20	–
Tom	19	Beatles

If we modify this UoD to include people who are neither lecturers nor students (e.g. add administrative staff), but do not record specific roles for them (we still record their gender and person-kind) the schema diagram would need to be modified by changing the {L,S} constraint to {L,S,A} using A = Administrative staff member. This indicates that the two subtypes are no longer exhaustive. The HED of Figure 6.30 illustrates this changed situation: the subtypes overlap but are nonexhaustive.

Sometimes we have to look very carefully at an output report to determine the criterion being used to decide whether a fact type is recorded or not. Consider for instance the report of Table 6.6.

A database population for a UoD is said to be *significant* with respect to some kind of constraint if and only if all the relevant UoD constraints of that kind may be deduced from the population. We have already seen that obtaining a sample population which is significant with respect to uniqueness constraints can be rather tedious; but at least it can be done in a modest amount of time. Unfortunately, no decision procedure is available to automatically churn out the correct subtype definitions. To appreciate this, look at Table 6.6. Favourite group is recorded only for some subtype of Person. See if you can come up with a definition for this subtype before reading on.

One pattern that fits the sample data is that favourite group is recorded for a person if and only if that person is aged between 13 and 19 inclusive, that is, if and only if the person is a teenager. This is not the only pattern which fits however. For instance, maybe favourite group is recorded only for people with odd ages (13, 17 and 19 are odd numbers). While these might be argued to be the two most "obvious" patterns, there are very many patterns that are consistent with the data. Just based on age we could specify any set of natural numbers minus the set {12,20} and within the age range set for the UoD.

If we remove the restriction that a computer system has finite memory then we open ourselves out to the problem that for any finite set of data there will always remain an infinite number of possible patterns which fit the data. This is the basis of the philosophical "problem of induction". Rather than get bogged down in philosophical speculation at this point we adopt the following pragmatic approach to finalizing subtype

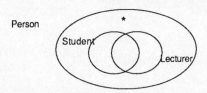

Figure 6.30   A person can be a student, a lecturer, both, or neither

definitions: look carefully at the data, use your "common sense" to spot what you feel is the simplest pattern, then check with the UoD expert whether this pattern is the one intended. Since the subtyping constraints reflect the decision of the UoD expert on what should be recorded for what, the UoD expert will always be able to resolve the matter. In the next section we discuss an algorithm to arrive at the subtype graph in complex cases; but finalizing the subtype definitions is still a matter to be sorted out by humans.

As an exercise, you may wish to draw the conceptual schema diagram for the UoD just discussed, assuming the subtype is Teenager.

Exercise 6.5

1. Draw the conceptual schema diagram for the UoD described by the following sample output report. Include uniqueness, mandatory role and subtype constraints. Provide a definition for any subtypes.

Computer	Company		CPU	
		Maker	*Kind*	*Frequency (MHz)*
AT	IBM	Intel	80286	–
Deskpro25	Compaq	Intel	80386	25
Mac	Apple	Motorola	–	–
PS/2 80	IBM	Intel	80386	16
PS/2 70	IBM	Intel	80386	25

"–" means "not to be recorded"

2. Examples of two output reports for a particular UoD are given in the two labels below. Draw the conceptual schema for this UoD, including uniqueness, mandatory role and subtype constraints. Provide a definition for any subtypes.

Employee Nr	Social Security Nr	Gender	Involved in project	Parking permit
E1	312	F	P1	–
E2	608	M	P1	–
			P2	
E3	471	M	P2	–
E4	488	M	P1	–
E5	216	M	P2	–
E6	196	M	P2	612
E7	740	F	P1	315

Project name	Project Nr	Budget	Manager	Project worker
Expo	P1	750 000	E7	E1
				E2
				E4
Fitness	P2	190 000	E6	E3
				E2
				E5

"–" means "not to be recorded"

6.6 Subtype matrices

If we have access to the UoD expert we can resolve any doubts about subtyping requirements. In the absence of the UoD expert we can, in simple cases, make a good guess as to the required subtypes merely by looking closely at a "significant" example that has been provided. We considered cases of this in the previous section.

In some cases, however, we may be presented with a situation where (a) we are expected to determine the subtype configuration from an output report, and (b) this configuration is not immediately obvious. In such a situation a technique known as *subtype matrix analysis* can be used to automatically determine the subtype graph, provided the output report is significant with respect to this graph.

A *matrix* is a rectangular array of elements. For example, a drawn game of "noughts and crosses" is a 3 × 3 matrix of "0" and "X" marks. There are two kinds of matrix that may be used to determine the subtype graph. We focus our attention on one of these: the *partition\details matrix*. The other matrix is briefly discussed at the end of the section.

Suppose that we have isolated some entity type A for which a subtype graph is required. We begin by dividing A into groups where each member of any given group has exactly the same roles recorded. These groups are mutually exclusive, and collectively exhaustive of A, that is, they form a *partition* of A. The term "partition" conveys the idea of dividing something into parts, as in slicing a cake. The Euler diagram of Figure 6.31 pictures A being partitioned into five groups.

The details recorded for each member of A forms the *recording pattern* for that member. Although members of the same group have the same recording pattern, different groups must have different recording patterns. Having partitioned A into groups on the basis of recording patterns, we display this on a partition\details matrix. To do this we begin by drawing up a table of the form shown in Figure 6.32.

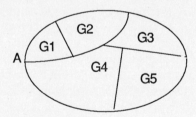

Figure 6.31 A is partitioned into five groups.

detail / group	d1	d2	d3
G1			
G2			
·			

Figure 6.32 The form of a partition\details matrix

Table 6.7 An output report resulting from a media survey

Person	Age (y)	Television viewing (h/wk)	Newspaper reading (h/wk)	Favourite channel	Favourite newspaper	Preferred news source
5001	41	0	10	–	The Times	–
5002	60	0	25	–	The Times	–
5003	16	20	2	9	The Times	–
5004	18	20	5	2	Daily Mail	TV
5005	13	35	0	7	–	–
5006	17	14	4	9	Daily Sun	–
5007	50	8	10	2	Daily Sun	NP
5008	33	0	0	–	–	–
5009	13	50	0	0	–	–

As row headings we list the groups G1, G2 etc. which comprise the partition. We may list these groups simply as "(1)", "(2)" etc. or, if their nature is obvious, we may use a descriptive name for each. As column headings we list all the details which are to be recorded for at least some groups. Each of these details relates to a role played by A, but we name the detail by asking what kind of information has to be recorded for the group members (e.g. weight, age, sports played, sports enjoyed).

If there are n groups and m details we have an $n \times m$ grid of cells which we now fill in with either a "1" or a "0" using the following rule:

1 = this detail must be recorded for this group
0 = this detail must not be recorded for this group

Here "this detail" and "this group" mean the detail and group for that cell's column and row respectively. Thus the recording pattern for each group is indicated by the pattern of 1s and 0s on its row. When the whole table has been filled in we have an $n \times m$ matrix of 1s and 0s.

Let's discuss an example. Suppose that as a result of a media survey, an output report like Table 6.7 is generated. As usual, "–" means "not to be recorded". In the final column "TV" and "NP" abbreviate "television" and "newspaper". People are identified by form numbers (each person is given a different survey form, each with a distinct serial number). Only a small extract from the report is shown, involving nine people. Let us assume that it is significant with respect to recording patterns. As always we begin with step 1, where we express the information in terms of one or more elementary facts. Do this for row 4 before reading on.

You should have arrived at six binary facts, all involving Person (e.g. Person (form#) "5004" has Age (y) 18). Disregarding subtyping for the moment, and excluding the referential has-form# role, Person plays six roles, of which three are mandatory (those relating to Age, TV viewing and Newspaper reading). The roles relating to favourite channel, favourite newspaper and preferred news source are optional: our task is to determine the subtype graph (if any) for these optional roles.

In constructing the partition-details matrix we divide the people up into groups according to their recording pattern. For example, the persons with form numbers 5001 and 5002 go into the same group because they have exactly the same details recorded.

Table 6.8 The partition\details matrix for Table 6.7

	Age	TVviewing	NPreading	FavChannel	FavNP	PrefNSource
(1)	1	1	1	0	1	0
(2)	1	1	1	1	1	0
(3)	1	1	1	1	1	1
(4)	1	1	1	1	0	0
(5)	1	1	1	0	0	0

Table 6.9 The subtype nodes are labelled A..D

	Age	TVviewing	NPreading	FavChannel	FavNP	PrefNSource
(1)	1	1	1	0	1	0
(2)	1	1	1	1	1	0
(3)	1	1	1	1	1	1
(4)	1	1	1	1	0	0
(5)	1	1	1	0	0	0
		A	A			
	A			B	C	D

Equivalently, they have exactly the same details *not* recorded. Clearly, *rows with the same pattern of "–" values go into the same group.* This yields the matrix in Table 6.8, using some obvious abbreviations.

Here persons 5001 and 5002 form group (1); 5003 and 5006 form group (2); 5004 and 5007 form group (3); 5005 and 5009 form group (4); and 5008 forms group (5). Confirm this partition and the recording patterns for yourself. It is a good idea as you assign a member to a group to write down the group name beside the row. With our example, this gives:

(1) 5001 ...
(1) 5002 ...
(2) 5003 ...
(3) 5004 ...
(4) 5005 ...
(2) 5006 ...
(3) 5007 ...
(5) 5008 ...
(4) 5009 ...

This provides a check that we haven't missed any rows.

Having obtained the matrix we now find the subtype graph as follows. **Each node in the subtype graph corresponds to a distinct column pattern in the matrix.** By "column pattern" we mean the sequence of 1s and 0s in the column. We *label the different column patterns* as "A", "B" etc. Matching columns correspond to the same node, and are given the same label. Work from left to right: if a column pattern is new, write its label two spaces below the column; if the column matches an earlier one, write the earlier label one space below the column. With our example only the first three columns match, so this yields Table 6.9.

To understand why this procedure yields the nodes of the subtype graph, recall that the head of the graph has the common role(s) attached, and each subtype node has some specific role(s) attached. With our example, the column pattern for Age, TVviewing and NPreading shows that these are recorded for all the groups. So these three details correspond to the common roles attached to the head of the graph. So A is the head node.

Looking at column B we see that FavChannel is recorded *only for* groups (2), (3) and (4). So provided there is a *well defined* way of determining membership in the union of groups (2), (3) and (4), we must make a proper subtype out of these groups. Since we are assuming throughout that the output report is significant in this respect, this indicates that there is a subtype node with the has-FavChannel role attached. So B is one of the subtype nodes.

Similarly, we can prove that there is a subtype node with the has-FavNP role attached, and a subtype node with the has-PrefNsource role attached. So C and D are the other subtype nodes. Note that in general, **the details recorded for the nodes are indicated by the column headings for the nodes.**

Before we start drawing the schema however, we still have to *determine the subtype relationships between the nodes*. This can be easily done by comparing the column patterns for the nodes. Clearly, the groups included in a node are those heading the rows where the node's column value = 1. With our example, node A includes groups (1)–(5), node B includes groups (2)–(4), node C includes groups (1)–(3), and node D includes group (3). One node is a subset of another node iff all its groups are included in the other node. So, given two nodes X and Y, *X is a subset of Y iff for every row where X = 1, Y = 1*.

We use this rule to determine the proper subtype relationships between the nodes. To be systematic, we work our way through all such relationships, beginning with the largest node. Try this yourself with our example, then check your answer with that provided below:

A has proper subtypes B, C, D
B has proper subtype D
C has proper subtype D

These relationships are portrayed by the subtype graph of Figure 6.33. To help you understand the example, we have also listed the groups included in each node.

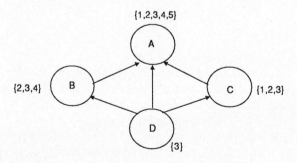

Figure 6.33   The subtype graph obtained from Table 6.9

The next step is to **delete all transitively implied subtype relationships**. Figure 6.33 includes an arrow to explicitly show that D is a subtype of A. But this is transitively implied, since D is a subtype of B, and B is a subtype of A. So we delete this redundant link from the graph. This gives the reduced subtype graph shown in Figure 6.34. At last we have the subtype graph for our example. With larger examples there may be more than one transitively redundant link to delete.

At this stage we can begin drawing the conceptual schema, since we know the subtype graph and also which roles to attach to each node. We can sketch this in outline as shown in Figure 6.35.

As discussed earlier, the head node A is the entity type Person. But we still need to **provide definitions and meaningful names for the subtypes**. To do this we go back to the original output report and ask ourselves what criteria are used to determine whether a specific subtype role is recorded. For any given subtype these criteria must be expressed in terms of one or more roles attached to its supertype(s).

So for node B we look at the roles recorded for A. There are potentially four roles that might be involved: the reference role (has-form#) and the three fact type roles involving Age, NPreading and TVviewing. It is highly unlikely for a standard reference role to be involved in a subtype definition, and after a moment's thought we can usually eliminate this as a candidate. For example, although in principle one might want to record a specific role only for persons with a form number above a certain value (e.g. 5002), we have no good reason for adopting such an unlikely criterion here.

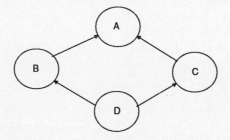

Figure 6.34 The subtype graph with transitive links deleted

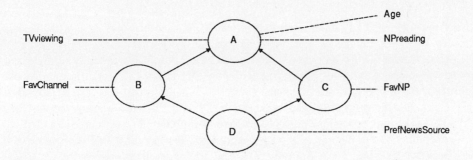

Figure 6.35 Details to be recorded for the nodes are added

Table 6.10   The original output report

Person	Age (y)	Television viewing (h/wk)	Newspaper reading (h/wk)	Favourite channel	Favourite newspaper	Preferred news source
5001	41	0	10	–	The Times	–
5002	60	0	25	–	The Times	–
5003	16	20	2	9	The Times	–
5004	18	20	5	2	Daily Mail	TV
5005	13	35	0	7	–	–
5006	17	14	4	9	Daily Sun	–
5007	50	8	10	2	Daily Sun	NP
5008	33	0	0	–	–	–
5009	13	50	0	0	–	–

This leaves the Age, NPreading and TVviewing roles. The specific detail recorded only for node B is favourite channel. Using our background knowledge about the terms involved (e.g. we would normally interpret "channel" as "TV channel") we zero in on the TVviewing column straight away. The sample output report has been reproduced in Table 6.10 for your convenience. See if you can define when the FavChannel detail is to be recorded, before reading the answer provided.

If you compare the FavChannel column with the TVviewing column, you will notice that the "–" values for FavChannel occur on just those rows where TVviewing has the value 0. So it is reasonable to conclude that information about a person's favourite channel is recorded only if that person is recorded as viewing at least some TV. To capture this meaning for humans, we now choose a meaningful name for node B, e.g. "TVviewer". The definition of this subtype can be set out in any clear notation. For example:

TVviewer = Person viewing TV for PeriodRatio > 0

Before reading on, see if you can come up with a definition and meaningful name for node C. The specific detail recorded for Node C is favourite newspaper. By similar reasoning to that for node B, you should have seen that the favourite newspaper detail is recorded only for people who are recorded as reading newspapers. So we may define subtype C as:

NPreader = Person reading newspapers for PeriodRatio > 0

Now we only need to define node D, for which the specific detail is preferred news source. See if you can define D before reading on.

First note that D is a subtype of both B and C. Recalling that a common subtype is at most the intersection of its supertypes, we know that D is either equal to or a proper subset of B ∩ C. So for a start we make a guess or hypothesis that D = B ∩ C. Now B ∩ C is just the set of people who both watch TV and read newspapers. To test our hypothesis we look to see if all such people have their preferred news source recorded.

According to our sample, the people who both view TV and read newspapers are 5003, 5004, 5006 and 5007. But only 5004 and 5007 have their preferred news source recorded. Either of these provides a counterexample to our original hypothesis. We need to modify our hypothesis to fit the data. What is the relevant difference between the people 5004 and 5007, for whom preferred news source is recorded, and the people 5003 and 5006?

The difference has to be expressible in terms of one of the roles attached to node A, that is, Person. Discounting the reference role (has-form#), we are left with the Age, TVviewing and NPreading roles. In this case, there might be a number of different "reasonable" patterns which could be hypothesized, all of which fit the data. For example, one difference is that 5004 and 5007 are at least 18 in age (i.e. they are adults), whereas 5003 and 5006 are below 18 in age. Another difference is that 5004 and 5007 read newspapers for at least five hours per week. You may like to suggest other possible criteria.

Confronted with more than one hypothesis which fits the data, how do we select the right one? In many cases, we can rely on our own intuitions as to which is the "simplest" hypothesis, and pick that one. In cases of doubt we should consult the UoD expert for confirmation. After all, the expert knows, at least implicitly, what the recording criteria are.

If the UoD expert finds it difficult to communicate about this directly, we can adopt a number of approaches to resolve the matter. Firstly, we can request more examples. A larger sample population will usually enable us to find counterexamples for all but the right hypothesis. Secondly, we can generate some test examples of our own based on the competing hypotheses, and ask the expert whether these are consistent with the UoD: by seeing which of these examples get rejected we can usually eliminate the wrong hypotheses.

A third approach which is particularly relevant to defining subtypes is to request a sample of the input forms which are used to capture the data. The information we need is usually provided clearly on such forms. This idea will be discussed a little later in this section.

Let us suppose that, by one means or another, we are able to determine that the hypothesis requiring adulthood was the right one. We can now define the subtype node D as follows:

TV&NPadult = TVviewer ∩ NPreader having Age ≥ 18

We are now in a position to set out the conceptual schema, as shown in Figure 6.36. The subtype definitions are written below the schema diagram. Note that the nodes in the subtype graph are quite different from the groups that were formed in the original partition. It is obvious from the entity type constraints and subtype definitions that TVviewer and NPreader are neither exclusive nor exhaustive. If desired, a check on exclusion and exhaustion constraints can be made by examining exclusion and exhaustion between the column patterns of the subtype nodes in the matrix: this optional check depends on the sample being significant with respect to these constraints.

For the subrange constraints shown we have made educated guesses as to what is reasonable (e.g. upper limit on Age of 140). The upper limit of 168 on PeriodRatio allows for the possibility of somebody watching TV every hour of the week (Aaagh!). It is somewhat debatable whether {TV,NP} is exhaustive (e.g. should radio be included?). Doubtful cases should be referred to the UoD expert.

Having illustrated the matrix technique by means of an extended example, we now provide a brief summary of the procedure.

Subtype matrix procedure:

1. *Construct the partition\details matrix for A:*
   List the details recorded for any members of A as column headings.
   Partition A into groups according to their recording patterns, and list these groups as row headings.
   Enter the recording pattern for each group (1 = detail recorded, 0 = detail not recorded)

2. *Sketch the subtype graph and attached details:*
   Label the different column patterns as nodes A, B etc.
   Determine the subtype relationships between the nodes as follows:
      node X is subset of node Y iff for each row where X = 1, Y = 1.
   Draw the subtype graph and delete any transitively implied arcs.
   Attach to each node the role(s) indicated by its column heading(s).

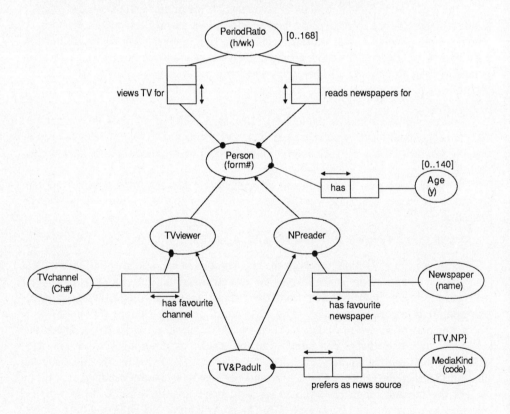

TVviewer   = Person viewing TV for PeriodRatio > 0
NPreader   = Person reading newspapers for PeriodRatio > 0
TV&NPadult = TVviewer ∩ NPreader having Age ≥ 18

Figure 6.36   The completed conceptual schema

3. *Provide definitions and meaningful names for the subtypes:*
   Define each subtype in terms of one or more roles attached to its supertype(s).

4. *Complete the conceptual schema:*
   Fill in the fine details of the schema diagram, with the subtype definitions listed underneath.

As indicated earlier, the subtyping configuration can often be determined in practice from a sample input form. Survey forms, application forms, taxation forms etc. often have optional sections which are clearly identified. For instance, an input form for our media survey example might look something like Figure 6.37. As an exercise, go through this form and check that it is consistent with the subtyping arrangement arrived at earlier.

We conclude this section by briefly mentioning an alternative matrix which can be used to determine the subtype graph. This is called the *detail\detail matrix* because the details recorded for any member of the head supertype are listed both as row and column headings. To fill in the values of the matrix we ask the following question for each cell: *for each entity for which we record the row detail, must we record the column detail? If the answer is Yes we enter a "1", else we enter a "0".*

As an example, the detail\detail matrix for the media survey UoD is shown in Table 6.11, using further abbreviations. It should be obvious that the diagonal running from the top left corner to the bottom left corner must always be filled in with 1 values (Why?). As with the earlier matrix, matching columns correspond to the same node, and different column patterns correspond to different nodes in the subtype graph.

Form#: 5001

1. Age (years): . . . .

---

2. Nr hours spent per week watching TV: . . . .

    if you answered 0 then go to Question 4

3. What is your favourite TV channel? . . . .

---

4. Nr hours spent per week reading newspapers: . . . .

    if you answered 0 then go to Question 6

5. What is your favourite newpaper? . . . .

---

6. Answer this only if you do watch TV and read newspapers and are at least 18 years old.

    Which do you prefer as a news source?
    (Tick the box of your choice)

    ☐ television   ☐ newspaper

Figure 6.37   An input form for the schema of Figure 6.36

Table 6.11   A detail\detail matrix

	Age	*TVview*	*NPread*	*FavChnl*	*FavNP*	*PrefNS*
Age	1	1	1	0	0	0
TVview	1	1	1	0	0	0
NPread	1	1	1	0	0	0
FavChnl	1	1	1	1	0	0
FavNP	1	1	1	0	1	0
PrefNS	1	1	1	1	1	1
		A	A			
	A			B	C	D

In a similar manner to the other matrix, subtype relationships between the nodes are determined by comparing the column patterns of the nodes, and the details recorded for the nodes are given by the column headings for the nodes. Check for yourself that this matrix gives the same result as the earlier one.

Unlike the partition\details matrix, the detail\detail matrix cannot be used to check on exclusion and exhaustion constraints. It is also somewhat less intuitive. However it is quite simple to compute, and it is idempotent with respect to boolean multiplication (i.e. when multiplied by itself using logical rather that arithmetic operations, the product is identical to the original matrix). This property may be used as a check on the matrix. Testing this property is tedious and is best handled by automation.

To use the detail\detail matrix instead of the partition\details matrix, replace steps 1 and 2 in the subtype matrix procedure with the method just described. Whichever kind of matrix is used, remember that the result depends on the sample being significant with respect to the subtype graph.

Exercise 6.6

1. Provide the conceptual schema for the following output report, including uniqueness, mandatory role and subtype constraints. Include definitions for subtypes. Make use of a partition\details matrix to determine the subtype graph. Here "supervisor" means supervisor of an employee rather than supervisor of a department. You may find it helpful to draw a tree showing who supervises whom.

Employee	Dept	Supervisor	Marital status	Home phone	Marriage year	Nr of children
Jones	D1	Johnson	M	3715821	1964	2
Edwards	D1	Jones	S	3715337	–	–
Giles	D1	Jones	M	3715437	1975	3
Fegan	D1	Edwards	M	3783437	1973	0
Crane	D1	Fegan	M	–	1967	–
Bell	D1	Fegan	S	–	–	–
Adams	D1	Giles	M	–	1959	–
Spencer	D2	Johnson	S	3786245	–	–
Smith	D2	Spencer	M	–	1971	–
Purcell	D2	Spencer	S	–	–	–
Johnson	D1	*	M	3781234	1964	4

N.B. "*" = "non-existent"
    "–" = "not to be recorded"

2. For a particular department, information of the kind indicated by the following output report has to be maintained. Departmental offices are identified by a room number. If you are unfamiliar with the metric system, note that 1 inch is about 2.5 cm (e.g. 5′ 10″ = 175 cm). Although small, the population shown is significant.

Note: "–" means "not to be recorded"

Member	Sex	Smoker?	StarSign	Height (cm)	Office	Sport
Adams	F	Y	Aquarius	–	–	–
Brown	M	Y	–	170	–	–
Collins	M	N	–	190	308	basketball
Davis	F	Y	Gemini	–	–	–
Evans	M	Y	–	190	–	–
Fomor	M	N	–	180	505	basketball, tennis
Gordon	F	N	Aquarius	–	406	–
Hastings	M	Y	–	165	–	–
Iveson	M	N	–	165	305	–
Jones	M	N	–	179	502	–

Draw the conceptual schema diagram for this universe of discourse, including the subtype graph, uniqueness constraints, and mandatory roles. Provide definitions for each subtype as well as relevant constraints on entity types involved in these subtype definitions.

3. A loan agency records information about clients borrowing loans. The following output report is extracted from this information system. Each client is identified by Client#. Marital codes have the following meaning: D = divorced; M = married; S = single; W = widowed. Residential codes have the following meaning: B = home buyer; O = home owner; R = home renter. The value "–" means "not to be recorded".

Client#	Marital status	Residential status	Number of dependants	Home value ($)	Spouse's income ($)	Spouse's share of home (%)
103	M	O	3	80000	40000	50
220	M	R	3	–	0	–
345	S	O	–	90000	–	–
444	W	B	2	70000	–	–
502	D	R	0	–	–	–
600	S	R	–	–	–	–
777	M	B	0	80000	0	40
803	D	B	1	40000	–	–
905	W	O	0	70000	–	–
etc.						

Each client has borrowed one or more loans. Any given loan can be borrowed by at most one client. The following output report from the same information system provides details on loans.

client#	Loans borrowed		
	loan#	amount	term
103	00508	$15000	7 yrs
220	00651	$15000	7 yrs
	00652	$ 2000	1 yr

Draw a conceptual schema diagram for this UoD. Include uniqueness, mandatory role and subtype constraints, as well as entity type constraints that are relevant to subtype definitions. Provide meaningful names and definitions for each subtype. The subtype graph may be determined from the first output report alone.

4. The following tables are sample output reports from an information system which maintains data about the following bodies in our solar system: the Sun, the naked eye planets and their moons. The names of these bodies may be assumed to conform to a simple 1:1 naming convention. Note that planets travel in roughly circular orbits around the Sun. A planet is in inferior conjunction if it is directly lined up between the Earth and the Sun. A planet is in opposition if the Earth is directly lined up between it and the Sun.

Note: "–" means "not to be recorded"
   "*" means "does not exist"

Sun:

Name	Mass (M_e)	Radius (km)
Sun	340000	690000

Planets:

Name	Nr of moons	Mean distance from Sun (AU)	Mass (M_e)	Radius (km)	Orbital period (y d)	Next inf. conj. (mth)	Next oppos. (mth)	Atmosphere (main gases)
Mercury	0	.39	.06	2440	0y 88d	Dec	–	*
Venus	0	.72	.81	6050	0y 224d	Jan	–	CO_2
Earth	1	1.0	1	6378	1y 0d	–	–	N_2,O_2
Mars	2	1.5	.11	3095	1y 322d	–	Feb	CO_2
Jupiter	16	5.2	318	71400	11y 315d	–	Sep	H_2,He
Saturn	23	9.5	95	60000	29y 167d	–	Sep	H_2,He

Moons:

Name	Planet orbited	Radius (km)	Orbital period (y d)	Mean apparent magnitude
Luna	Earth	1737	0y 27.3d	-13.0
Phobos	Mars	6	0y 0.3d	11.5
Deimos	Mars	4	0y 30d	12.0
Io	Jupiter	1867	0y 1.7d	5.5
etc.	...	...	...	...

Draw a conceptual schema diagram for this UoD, including uniqueness, mandatory role and subtype constraints. Use a subtype matrix.

6.7 Occurrence frequencies

In this section we consider various kinds of constraints on the number of times that an entity of a given type may be recorded as playing a given role. These are known as **occurrence frequency constraints** since they place restrictions on the frequency or number of times that labels may occur in a given fact column.

The most common kind of occurrence frequency constraint indicates that entries in a column must occur an *exact* number of times in that column. Consider a fact type where the role *r* is played by entities of type *A*. The following notation may be used to specify that, for every state of the database, every entry in the fact column for *r* occurs exactly n times in that column.

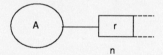

Each entry in *r*'s column occurs exactly n times in that column.

Clearly, if n = 1 then the occurrence frequency constraint is just a uniqueness constraint, i.e.

Since we already have a special, more convenient notation for uniqueness constraints we will use the new occurrence frequency constraint notation only for cases other than n = 1. Such cases usually arise when we need to record facts *for all instances* of some small, enumerated entity type. For example, suppose that a given company sells three kinds of computer storage devices (hard disk drives, floppy disk drives, and tape drives) and wishes to record yearly sales for each of these three kinds of drive. The conceptual schema for this UoD is shown in Figure 6.38, together with a sample population.

Notice that an occurrence frequency of 3 has been placed beside the role played by Year. This indicates that each year entry in the column for that role must occur there exactly three times. The entity type constraint implies that there are only three kinds of drive, and the uniqueness constraint ensures that each Year-DriveKind combination in the table occurs exactly once. So, taken together, these three constraints imply that, for each year that is recorded in this table, we must record the sales for all three kinds of drive. Thus we are able to specify that any yearly data of this kind is *complete* in this regard: no kind of drive can be omitted.

Hence, a *compound transaction* must be used for updating this fact type. For example, to add the figures for 1988, the compound transaction would provide for three facts to be added. If we tried to just add a single fact about how many hard disk drives were sold in that year this simple transaction would be rejected.

In this example, the role with the occurrence frequency constraint is mandatory. The combination of these two constraints means that every year recorded in the database must occur three times in this table. Suppose however, that this role is optional. For example, let us also record the year in which each kind of drive was invented. The schema for this larger UoD is shown in Figure 6.39.

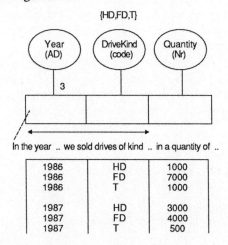

Figure 6.38   Complete sales figures are recorded for each year

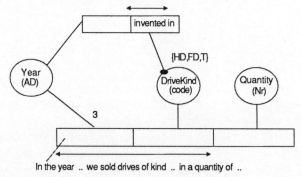

Figure 6.39   Invention year is recorded for each kind of drive

Although the disjunction of roles played by Year is mandatory, each of these two roles is optional. For instance we might not have any sales in a year in which a drive device was invented. In this case it is not true that every year recorded in the database occurs three times in the sales table. However, each year that is recorded in the sales table must occur three times in (the relevant column of) that table. This is what the occurrence frequency constraint means.

As a slightly harder example, suppose the company selling computer drives has two warehouses, one in Los Angeles and one in Tokyo, and the company wishes to record how many drives of each kind (HD, FD or T) are in stock in each warehouse. The warehouses are not given a name but the two cities are identified by their popular names "LA" and "Tokyo". See if you can set out a diagram for the relevant fact type, including constraints, before looking at the solution provided.

A schema-base diagram for this UoD is provided in Figure 6.40. The occurrence frequency of 3 indicates that each city recorded in the column for that role occurs there three times (once for each kind of drive). The occurrence frequency of 2 indicates that each kind of drive in the table occurs twice (once for each city). In the context of the entity type constraints and the uniqueness constraint, these occurrence frequencies imply that if any fact of this type is recorded, all such facts must be recorded. So if the table is populated at all, it must have six facts in it. Again, this implies a compound transaction is needed to initially populate the table. Any subsequent update to the table will be a compound transaction consisting either of an equal number of deletions and additions, or of six deletions (Why?).

Sometimes we need to specify an occurrence frequency constraint that spans two or more roles of a fact type. In this case we draw an arc linking the relevant roles, and write the number beside this. For example, suppose that within a fact type the roles $r1$ and $r2$ are played by entity types A and B. Let us use ab to indicate a pair of instances of A and B respectively that are recorded *on the same row* of this fact table. The diagram in Figure 6.41 indicates that, for each state of the database, each such ab combination has to occur exactly n times in the table, that is, there are n rows on which a is in column $r1$ and b is in column $r2$.

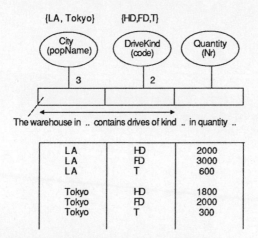

LA	HD	2000
LA	FD	3000
LA	T	600
Tokyo	HD	1800
Tokyo	FD	2000
Tokyo	T	300

Figure 6.40 Sales are recorded for all drives and all cities

When n = 1, this is equivalent to a uniqueness constraint spanning the relevant roles (see Figure 6.42). We retain the old, cleaner notation for uniqueness constraints, using the new notation only for cases where n > 1.

In most cases, any constraints of this kind are implied by other constraints. For example, suppose the company mentioned earlier wishes to maintain yearly records of sales in both Los Angeles and Tokyo for the three kinds of drive. For this UoD we have a quaternary fact type as shown in Figure 6.43. A sample population is provided.

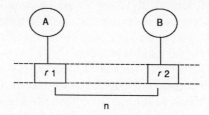

Figure 6.41   Occurrence frequency constraint on a role pair

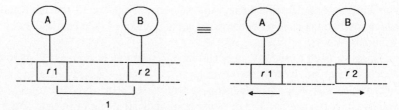

Figure 6.42   Use uniqueness bars if occurrence frequency = 1

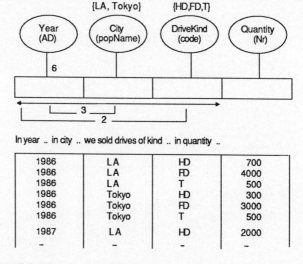

In year .. in city .. we sold drives of kind .. in quantity ..

1986	L A	HD	700
1986	L A	FD	4000
1986	L A	T	500
1986	Tokyo	HD	300
1986	Tokyo	FD	3000
1986	Tokyo	T	500
1987	L A	HD	2000
..	..	-	..

Figure 6.43   Are all these occurrence frequencies needed?

Here the occurrence frequency of 3 indicates that each Year-City combination in the table occurs three times (once for each kind of drive). The occurrence frequency of 2 indicates that each Year-DriveKind combination in the table occurs twice (once for each City). The occurrence frequency of 6 indicates that each Year in the table occurs six times. Given the entity type constraints on City and DriveKind, and the uniqueness constraint, this 6 implies that for each year in the table all possible City-DriveKind combinations must be recorded. So the *occurrence frequencies of 3 and 2 are implied by the other constraints, and hence should be omitted.*

For the example just considered, complete sales information was required for each year. Suppose we now weaken this requirement as follows. For each year in the table, sales information must be recorded for *at least one city*; and if a city is recorded for a given year then its sales for all three kinds of drives must be recorded for that year. For this UoD we now have to include an occurrence frequency constraint spanning more than one role. Why? Check your answer with the solution provided in Figure 6.44.

Occasionally the need arises to specify occurrence frequency constraints which involve more than one frequency. To indicate a continuous range of integer frequencies we use the subrange notation introduced earlier:

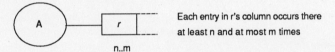

Each entry in r's column occurs there
at least n and at most m times

For example, consider a UoD in which each student is allocated to exactly one tutorial group, where each tutorial group must contain at least 10 students but no more than 30 students. We may model this as in Figure 6.45.

Here each tute group entry in the table must appear there between 10 and 30 times (inclusive): once for each student in the group. Care must be taken to position the occurrence frequency constraint beside the relevant role. If we put "10..30" next to the is-in role, this would say that each student in the table is in 10..30 tute groups instead of just one.

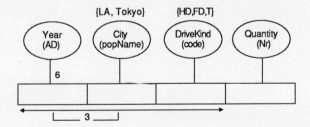

Figure 6.44   Yearly sales figures may omit a city but not a drive

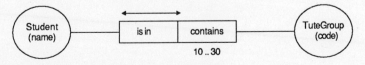

Figure 6.45   Each group contains 10 to 30 students

As another example, consider the schema fragment shown in Figure 6.46. Here the dotted line at the left indicates there is some other fact type with a role that is mandatory for Person. See if you can clearly express what is meant by the constraints on the fact type that is shown, then check your interpretation with the description provided in the next paragraph.

For this UoD, it is optional whether a person is on a committee. However, those persons who are (recorded as being) on a committee may be on at most three committees. Each committee includes exactly seven members.

If we want to specify only a lower limit, of n say, on an occurrence frequency we could show this as "n..". To specify an upper limit of m we use "1..m". Since occurrence frequencies apply only to entries in columns, a lower frequency of 1 is the smallest possible. So it does not make sense to specify an occurrence frequency with a lower limit of 0.

Note also that a numerical occurrence frequency constraint may be specified for a set of roles only if a uniqueness constraint spans these roles and at least one other (Why?).

Very rarely, other varieties of occurrence frequency constraints may arise. For example, groups of a particular kind might need to have 10 or 13 members but not 11 or 12. In this case we could use the notation "10,13" instead of 10..13. This comma notation could be extended to handle more values (e.g. "4,7,10" for "4 or 7 or 10").

As another example, a group might simply require an odd number of members, (e.g. to ensure a non-tied vote). In this case we could use some descriptor such as "odd". Further examples could be listed but since these situations are so rare we leave it to your own common sense to provide a suitable way of representing such an occurrence frequency constraint if and when the case arises.

Exercise 6.7

1. The following annual report provides information about sales of two kinds of database systems ("R" denotes Relational and "NR" Non-Relational) for each of the four seasons.

Database	Season	Nr sold
R	spring	50
NR	spring	70
R	summer	60
NR	summer	60
R	autumn	80
NR	autumn	40
R	winter	120
NR	winter	15

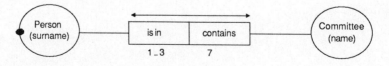

Figure 6.46   What do these constraints mean?

Draw a conceptual schema diagram for this UoD, including uniqueness, mandatory role, entity type and occurrence frequency constraints. In case the population is not significant, use your common sense.

2. A software retailer maintains a database about various software products. Two sample output reports are shown below.

Product: WordLight 4.0   **List price:**   *ex tax*   *with tax*
Functions: word processor $500 $600

	Poor	*OK*	*Good*	*Excellent*
Performance			■	
Documentation				■
Ease of learning			■	
Ease of use			■	
Error handling				■
Support			■	
Value				■

Release date: 1988 Feb
Next upgrade (if known):   ?

Product: PCjobs 1.0   **List price:**   *ex tax*   *with tax*
Functions: word processor $1000 $1200
               spreadsheet
               database

	Poor	*OK*	*Good*	*Excellent*
Performance			■	
Documentation	■			
Ease of learning		■		
Ease of use	■			
Error handling		■		
Support			■	
Value		■		

Release date: 1987 Oct
Next upgrade (if known):   1988 Jun

There is a sales tax of 20 percent on all software. The *ex tax* price excludes this tax; the *with tax* price includes it. The functions of a software product are the tasks it can perform. A "■" indicates the rating of the product for the criterion listed on that row (e.g. both products have a good performance). A "?" denotes a null value.

Draw a conceptual schema diagram for this UoD, including uniqueness constraints, mandatory roles, entity type constraints, occurrence frequencies and derived fact types. Do not attempt to nest or subtype. Try to capture the information about product evaluation (ratings for performance etc.) in terms of a single fact type.

3. (Acknowledgement: This question was originally devised by Prof. E. D. Falkenberg, and is used by permission).

Within a database, information of the kind as specified in the following lists has to be stored. For each list, a small, sample population is shown. Here "–" means "not to be recorded".

List of communities (cities, towns, villages):

Community name	Number of inhabitants	Longitude *	Latitude *	Size (sq km) **	Lord mayor Firstname ***	Surname ***
A	900 000	–	–	145	Fred	Bloggs
B	90 000	+120°50'	+48°45'	12	–	–
C	9 000	+120°50'	+48°40'	–	–	–

Notes:
*   Only recorded for villages and towns (at most 100 000 inhabitants).
**   Only recorded for towns and cities (more than 10 000 inhabitants).
***   Only recorded for cities (more than 100 000 inhabitants).

Lord mayors are uniquely identified by the combination of their first name and surname. A person can be lord mayor of only one city. A city has exactly one lord mayor.

List of roads:

Road number	Kind of road *	Connection Community **	Community **	Length (km)	Average travel time ***	Maximum steepness (%) ****
11000	f	A	B	25	0 h 20 m	–
11500	h	A	B	22	0 h 25 m	2
11561	p	B	C	17	0 h 20 m	2
11562	d	B	C	15	–	15

Notes:
*   f: Freeway; h: Highway; p: Paved connection road; d: Dirt road.
**   All connections are two-way, i.e. the order of the connected communities is irrelevant.
***   Only recorded for freeways, highways and paved connection roads.
****   Only recorded for dirt roads, paved connection roads and highways.

Assume that each road connects *exactly* two communities. Design the conceptual schema for this universe of discourse. Include uniqueness, mandatory role, subtype, and occurrence frequency constraints.

7 Reference schemes

7.1 Reference

In earlier chapters we took pains to distinguish between things (entities) and their names (labels). To facilitate early progress we restricted our attention to simple identification schemes. It is a challenging task to provide a consistent and complete account of reference schemes for use in information systems. Considerable research is still being conducted to provide such an account. In this chapter we examine some of the relevant issues, and discuss some cases of a more complex nature. In this section we illustrate some aspects of reference, using as an example the output report of Table 7.1.

Let us interpret the information on row 1 as follows:

Person with surname 'Adams' lives in City with name 'Brisbane'.
Person with surname 'Adams' has height of Length 175 cm.
Person with surname 'Adams' has chest circumference of Length 100 cm.
Person with surname 'Adams' weighs Mass 77 kg.
Person with surname 'Adams' has IQ of 100.

Here we have five facts. The first fact type is set out in Figure 7.1. In this UoD each person is identified by his/her surname, and each city is identified by its name. Correctly matching up an entity with its name is of course a human rather than a system responsibility. The presence of quotes around "Adams" and "Brisbane" indicates that the reference scheme for Person and City is literal rather than numeric (we expand on this point shortly). At this stage we have not specified any lexical constraints.

We use the term "label" to mean an entry in a fact column. For example, on row 1 of Table 7.1 the first three labels are: "Adams", "Brisbane", and "175". In this sense, every label is a self-referencing character string. For any UoD we could take the set of all possible character strings to be a universal label type, which we call "Label". Each specific label type is then a subtype of Label, and is defined by its lexical constraint. For

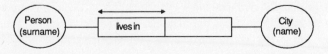

Figure 7.1 One of the fact types from Table 7.1

157

Table 7.1

Person	City	Height (cm)	Chest (cm)	Mass (kg)	IQ
Adams	Brisbane	175	100	77	100
Brisbane	Sydney	182	91	80	120
Collins	Sydney	173	80	67	100
Darwin	Darwin	175	95	90	95

example, subjectcode might be defined as {aaddd}, that is, the set of all strings containing two letters followed by three digits.

It can be argued that such label type constraints are an external rather than a conceptual matter. For example, we might want to specify different external interfaces to allow subjects to be referenced by alphanumeric codes, letter codes, numeric codes, English titles, Chinese titles etc. Who is to say which is the "correct" conceptual label type? In spite of this argument, it is important to clearly distinguish between lexical objects (labels) and non-lexical objects (entities), and to ensure that the mutual exclusion between primitive entity types is somehow enforced within the knowledge base.

Moreover, interactive validation of a conceptual schema is best handled in parallel with the design, and this requires populating the fact tables with "acceptable" labels. For these reasons, we pragmatically choose a labelling scheme suggested by the "external level" output reports and stick with this in our conceptual discussion.

If you look at Table 7.1, you will notice that the same label may be used in referring to a person or a city (e.g. "Brisbane" and "Darwin"). The notations "(surname)" and "(name)" used in the schema diagram (Figure 7.1) indicate the reference modes. The reference mode names (e.g. "surname") have meaning only for humans, who also have the task of enforcing the constraints on the reference types. If the humans have done their job properly, the system can enforce the constraints on the fact type.

Conceptually, the label type "surname" is the set of all possible surnames, and the label type "cityname" is the set of all possible names of cities. But it is doubtful whether these label types can be specified in any way that is both natural and simple. For example, we would probably reject strings like "ZZZZZZZZZZZZZZZZ" and "D-M'AR-C'o" as possible citynames in the UoD, but it would be very difficult to come up with some formal lexical constraint to exclude all such "silly" names. In practice, label types are usually defined for the system in a simple, if artificial way. For example, suppose we restrict surnames to strings of up to 20 characters and city names to strings of up to 30 characters. Using the notation {cn} to indicate the set of strings of up to n characters, this choice is set out explicitly in Figure 7.2.

Notice that the label types overlap: {c20} is a proper subtype of {c30}. For example, the label "Brisbane" occurs in both label types. This schema causes the system to reject surnames longer than 20 characters and citynames longer than 30 characters. If we did want to show the label types explicitly like this, the subtype arc could be omitted since it is implied by the lexical constraints {c20} and {c30}. Usually however we would abbreviate this schema to that of Figure 7.3.

Assuming the population shown in Table 7.1, and an appropriate query language, the CIP would respond to the following queries as shown:

Q: Who lives in a city with the same name as his/her surname?
A: Darwin
Q: Which person is a city?
A: None: Entity types Person and City are mutually exclusive

Although it is meaningful to compare the labels for Person and City it is not sensible to compare persons and cities since they are different types of entity. Now consider the second fact from our output report:

Person with surname 'Adams' has height of Length 175 cm.

To begin with, we might display this fact type as in Figure 7.4. We have used "Length" to name the entity type on the right rather than "Height" because presumably we may want to compare heights with chest circumferences, which are both lengths.

In this diagram we have not specified any lexical constraints. This subschema allows the same label to be both a surname and a cm value. In practice, we would usually want to constrain the label types further. For instance we might add lexical constraints to give Figure 7.5. Here {a20} is the set of labels with from 1 to 20 letters, while {'100'..'200'} is the set of labels {'100','101',...,'200'}. Note that we have now made a deliberate decision to ignore any fractions of a centimetre when we record lengths.

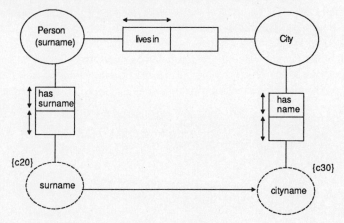

Figure 7.2 Lexical constraints are specified for Figure 7.1

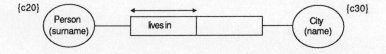

Figure 7.3 Abbreviated version of Figure 7.2

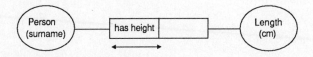

Figure 7.4 Another fact type from Table 7.1

Now while this makes the label types disjoint, it still does not capture the semantics that we would usually wish to employ for the entity type Length. In typical applications, we would want to make use of the *numeric* aspect of Length. For example, we might like to include a derivation rule like:

Person is-tall **if** Person has-height-of Length > 180 cm

or permit queries like:

Whose height length is twice their chest measurement?
Whose height is above the average height of the people?

Here we are using the idea that Length is a physical dimension, which can be operated on in a way analogous to the way numbers can be manipulated. At the abstract level we model the operation of adding two lengths in terms of adding two numbers. If we wish the information system to handle such operations for Length we need to infor.⁀ it that such operations are permitted. One efficient way of doing this kind of thing is to ₁mport into the conceptual schema a predefined *abstract data type*, such as WholeNumber, which has the relevant operations defined.

For example, the reference type for Length in Figure 7.5 is refined into a fact type (Length has cm value WholeNr) and a reference type (WholeNr is denoted by Hindu-Arabic-decimal-numeral). The lexical constraint {'100'..'200'} now applies to the label type Hindu-Arabic-decimal-numeral, while operations such as addition, multiplication etc. are defined on WholeNr, which model analogous operations on Length (e.g. a derived fact type might permit area values to be computed by multiplying length values).

An abstract data type (ADT) is basically a set of values with a well defined set of operations. ADTs are implementation-independent and may be specified conceptually

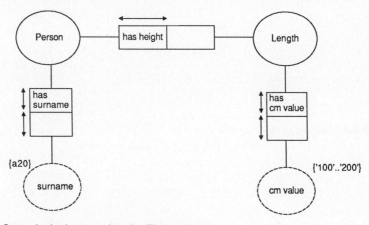

Figure 7.5   Some lexical constraints for Figure 7.4

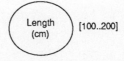

Figure 7.6   Square brackets show numeric operations are allowed

(e.g. binary addition may be set out in terms of a derived homogeneous ternary predicate .. + .. = ..). When the schema is actually implemented a particular implementation data type is chosen (e.g. SQL smallint or Pascal integer). Rather than clutter the schema diagram with nodes and roles for ADTs, we use abbreviated notations. Some of these have already been introduced. For example, in Figure 7.6 square brackets, and the absence of quotes around "100" and "200", emphasize that common numeric operations are permitted.

Even if no such operations are to be used, since interactive validation of a schema can only be done at the external level some decision is usually needed in practice as to whether values are numeric or not, since most languages distinguish syntactically between "numeric constants" and "string constants" by demanding quotes for the latter. For instance, in SQL the queries:

select person **from** Personnel **where** height = '175'
and
select person **from** Personnel **where** height = 175

are different: only the second treats height as numeric. The first form is OK provided the user does not want to apply numeric operations on height. However this would be the exception rather than the rule. If the user wishes to treat an entity type numerically, we have encouraged the early signification of this intention at step 1 by omitting quotes around the value when writing down the fact in natural language.

With respect to the output report shown earlier, suppose the user makes requests like the following:

List the people in alphabetic order of surname.
List all cities with names starting with 'S'.

Such requests are not uncommon. But these entail that the user is thinking of the names as objects which can be ordered and which have structure. To let the system handle such requests we need to let it know that such operations are possible. This could be done by including in the reference chain an ADT such as CharString, which has a set of predefined operations such as "<" for ordering and "substr" for extracting substrings. If we wish to specify that such string operations are permitted we use angle brackets instead of braces in the lexical constraint (see Figure 7.7).

Notice that ordering operations are defined both for Numeric and CharString ADTs, but each has special operations suitable to its nature. Consider reference modes such as StudentNr, Employee#, and RoomNr where the labels comprise only digits, for example, "517". If these are used only to provide identifying labels, then there is no need to mention any ADT. If we desire to apply ordering operations then we would usually make a connection to an appropriate ADT. If as well we want to apply specifically numeric operations (such as addition) then we should indicate a numeric ADT.

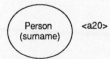

Figure 7.7   Angle brackets show string operations are allowed

Let's consider now the whole of the output report in Table 7.1. Assuming that various ordering and numeric operations are to be applied, we may set the conceptual schema out as shown in Figure 7.8. There are several things worth noting about this schema. First note that IQ is dimensionless and hence its reference mode is just Nr. We do however specify that IQs lie in the numeric range 0..200.

Unlike IQ, Length and mass are physical quantities which require both a number and a unit (e.g. cm, kg) for their identification: these two aspects are specified separately. The subrange constraint [50..200] on Length covers the union of the height and chest measurements. If desired, separate constraints could be placed on the relevant roles (e.g. [100..200] for height and [50..150] for chest).

Notice how the typing and reference schemes determine which comparisons and operations make sense. For example, assuming an appropriate query language, each of the following queries would be rejected:

List persons whose mass is strictly equal to their height.
List persons whose mass is less than their IQ.
List height + mass for each person.
List avg(surname).

Here the term "is strictly equal to" means "is the same object as". A mass can never strictly equal a height since these belong to different, primitive entity types. Although label types often overlap, primitive entity types are mutually exclusive. As an exercise, explain why the other preceding queries are rejected, while each of the following queries is accepted. You may take it that the standard reference schemes for the entity types have been specified, and the system assumes them by default.

List persons whose mass is numerically equal to their height.
List persons whose mass is numerically less than their IQ.
Whose height measure is twice their chest measure?
List height measure + chest measure for each person.
List avg(height).

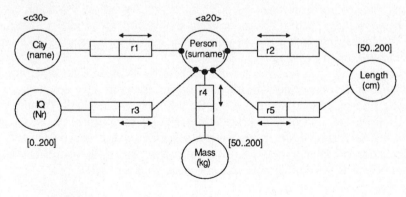

Figure 7.8   The conceptual schema for Table 7.1

Table 7.2

	Student	Subject
	Anderson P	CS100
	Anderson P	PD102
	Jones EA	CS100
	Jones EA	CS112
	Jones ET	CS112

7.2 CSDP step 7: Entity identification schemes

Usually, a single 1:1 naming convention is used to identify entities of a given type. Sometimes however, the identification scheme is more complex. In each case, we need to ensure that the means by which entities are referenced are clearly defined, both for the system and for the user. Checking this is the next step in the conceptual schema design procedure.

CSDP *Step 7: Check that each entity can be identified*

Let's begin by reviewing the simple 1:1 case, using a familiar example. Table 7.2 is an extract from an output report indicating subjects studied by students.

Each student has a single, distinct name and each subject has a single, distinct code. These 1:1 reference schemes are specified by naming the reference modes in parentheses (see Figure 7.9). We might also specify lexical constraints as shown.

The lexical constraint on student names is quite weak, for example, we have not excluded student names like "CS100". You may wish to strengthen the constraint to prevent this. For example, {a17 a2} denotes a string of 1 to 17 letters followed by a space followed by one or two letters: in this context you might widen the notion of a letter to include characters like apostrophes and hyphens to allow names like "O'Gorman J" and "Smythe-Jones A".

Entities in the real world are identified by singular terms in the knowledge base. Fundamentally, such singular terms are always definite descriptions. For example, a particular student in the real world is identified by the term "the student with name 'Anderson P'". However, within the context of a reference type, a label is said to be an *identifier* for an entity if the label denotes only one entity of that type.

While names and codes serve to identify students and subjects, humans tend to read more into these reference schemes than Figure 7.9 suggests. For example, when we look at the name "Anderson P" we tend to assume that "Anderson" is a surname and "P" is the first initial of the student. So long as we don't require the system to possess this deeper

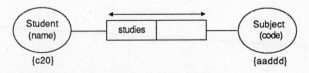

Figure 7.9 A conceptual schema diagram for Table 7.2

Table 7.3

	Student		Subject
	Surname	*Initials*	
	Anderson	P	CS100
	...	...	...

insight into the naming convention, we can leave the schema as it is. Suppose however that we wanted to issue a query like:

List all students with the surname 'Jones'.

With the schema of Figure 7.9, the system can't provide the required answer since it doesn't know anything yet about how surnames fit into the notion of student names. There are several ways in which we might formalize the additional semantics for the system. One way would be to split student names into two components as shown in Figure 7.10.

For this UoD, surnames are not identifiers (e.g. there are two students with the surname "Jones"); nor are initials (e.g. there are two students with the initial "P"). However, the *combination* of surname and initials does provide an identifier since this combination refers to only one student, as indicated by the inter-reference type uniqueness constraint. This kind of reference scheme is fairly common. The need for such a scheme should usually be picked up at step 1, by examining the output reports and sample queries. In many cases, the separation of name parts will be shown explicitly in an output report. For example, instead of the previous table we might have one like that of Table 7.3.

We may abbreviate this kind of reference scheme by enclosing the partial names in parentheses with "+" to indicate the combination. For example, the reference scheme of Figure 7.10 may be abbreviated as in Figure 7.11. If desired, the lexical constraints could also be specified as shown.

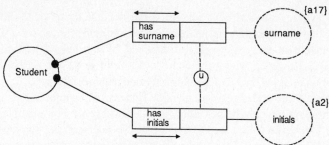

Figure 7.10   A reference scheme requiring two labels

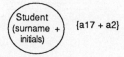

Figure 7.11   Shorthand notation for Figure 7.10

Table 7.4

Physics:	Subject	Semester
	Electronics	1
	Mechanics	1
	Optics	2

Table 7.5

Maths:	Subject	Semester
	Algebra	2
	Calculus	1
	Mechanics	1

As an alternative to having surname and initials stored explicitly as separate components, one could store student names as character strings and provide derivation rules for extracting the surnames and initials. This would be particularly appropriate if in most output reports the student names were left intact, and only on rare occasions was there a need for information about surnames and initials. For example, with this approach the earlier query could be specified in SQL by a command like: **select** name **from** Student **where** name **like** 'Jones %'.

Identification schemes are relative to the particular UoD. Often, a simple scheme which works for a given UoD fails to work in a UoD of wider scope. This is important to bear in mind when merging subschemas into a larger schema. For example, suppose that within a given University department each subject offered by that department can be identified by its title. For instance, consider the output report in Table 7.4, which indicates for the Physics Department which subjects it offers in which semesters.

In designing a schema for the Physics Department we have a 1:1 correspondence between subjects and their titles. So the schema of Figure 7.12 is appropriate.

A similar schema could be used for the Mathematics Department, a sample output report for which is shown in Table 7.5. But now suppose we need to integrate such schemas into an overall schema for the whole university. The schema of Figure 7.12 will no longer work because within this wider UoD, subjects cannot be identified by their title. For example, the subject Mechanics offered by the Physics Department is different from the subject Mechanics offered by the Mathematics Department.

The way we just verbalized the distinction between these two subjects suggests one way of providing an identification scheme. We can combine the title with the Department name. For instance, a combined output report would look like Table 7.6.

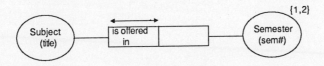

Figure 7.12 A conceptual schema diagram for Table 7.4

Table 7.6

Department	SubjTitle	Semester
Physics	Electronics	1
Physics	Mechanics	1
Physics	Optics	2
Mathematics	Algebra	2
Mathematics	Calculus	1
Mathematics	Mechanics	1

Table 7.7

Subject	Title	Department	Semester
PH101	Electronics	Physics	1
PH102	Mechanics	Physics	1
PH200	Optics	Physics	2
MP104	Algebra	Mathematics	2
MP210	Calculus	Mathematics	1
MA109	Mechanics	Mathematics	1

One way of schematizing this is shown in Figure 7.13. Though conceptually this picture is illuminating, in practice its implementation is somewhat awkward, since we effectively need two labels (one for the department and one for the title) to identify a subject.

In such cases, a new identification scheme is often chosen which provides a simple 1:1 reference. For example, each subject may be assigned a unique subject code, as shown in Table 7.7.

In this output report there are two candidate identifiers for Subject. We could identify a subject by its code (e.g. "PH102") or by combining its title and department (e.g. "Mechanics - Physics"). We choose one of these as the *primary identifier*, that is, the standard identifier. In this case, we would usually pick the subjectcode as the primary identifier: though it is artificial it is simpler to work with. To indicate this choice on the schema diagram we parenthesize the standard reference mode and treat the relationship type between Subject and SubjTitle just like any other fact type (see Figure 7.14).

In some situations we may choose two equally attractive candidate identifiers. For example, suppose that within the UoD no two subjects have the same title, yet subject codes have still been introduced (e.g. to provide a quick means of identification). In this case we have potentially two 1:1 reference schemes, one based on subject title and one on subject code. We deal with such cases in the same way. We pick one as the primary

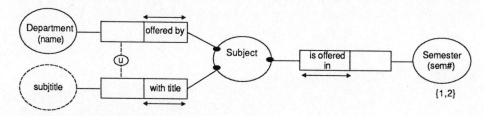

Figure 7.13   One way of schematizing Table 7.6

identifier, even if we have to toss a coin to decide. This example is said to involve "heterogeneous synonyms", since two different label types (subject title and subject code) might be used for identification. Another example is where authors might be identified either by their real name or or by a pseudonym (e.g. Charles Dodgson and Lewis Carroll).

If different identifiers are available using the same naming convention we have a case of "homogeneous synonyms". Such situations are fairly rare. One case of this is that of personal nicknames, where a person with red hair might be identified as "Rusty" or "Bluey". A related case is that of common names (as distinct from scientific names) for plants and animals. For instance the bird kind identified by the scientific name of *Dacelo gigas* may also be identified by any one of the following common names: "laughing kookaburra"; "great brown kingfisher"; "laughing jackass"; "bushman's clock". As a botanical example, "gorse" and "furze" refer to precisely the same plant.

The simplest solution to the problem of synonyms is to choose one as the standard identifier and handle the others in terms of ordinary facts. It might be argued that the selection of a primary identifier out of several candidate identifiers is not a conceptual matter. However it is often clear from output reports that a primary identifier has already been agreed upon by all the users: in such a case it is useful to incorporate this choice in the schema; if this decision needs to be changed at a later stage it can be dealt with by means of a schema transformation.

In the informations systems literature the term "homonym" is used to describe a label which refers to more than one entity. For example, with our earlier example of Table 7.2 the same surname may refer to more than one student, (e.g. "Jones"). Since "homonym" has different grammatical senses, another term such as "non-identifying label" is preferable. At any rate an obvious solution to the "problem of homonyms" is to combine the non-identifying reference type with other reference or fact types until identification is achieved (e.g. the combination of surname and initials discussed earlier).

The reference types discussed so far have been 1:1, 1:many or many:1. For completeness we cite given names as a many:many case. A person may have many given names (e.g. "Johann" and "Sebastian"), and a given name may apply to more than one person. Obviously such a naming convention fails to identify.

Sometimes an entity may be identified by means of one or more fact types. Perhaps the most familiar example is identifying an entity by means of its temporal or spatial location, for example:

The letter dated 1987 Nov 30.
The warehouse located in Brisbane.

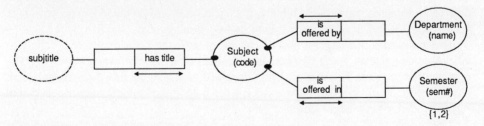

Figure 7.14   A conceptual schema diagram for Table 7.7

Table 7.8

	Subject	Discipline	Level
	CS112	Computer Science	1
	MP104	Pure Mathematics	1
	CS213	Computer Science	2

Table 7.9

	Lumbercode	Length (m)	Breadth (mm)	Depth (mm)
	A5	3	100	100
	B7	2	100	75
	C7	5	200	100

Such reference schemes are sometimes described as "information bearing". The status of this concept is somewhat debatable. At any rate, if we as humans "see" information buried in the names or descriptions of objects and we want to communicate to the system about this information, we need to make this explicit in our schema. For example, the subject codes used at the University of Queensland are at least partly information bearing to humans familiar with the rationale behind the coding scheme. Each code is a sequence of two letters followed by three digits. The letters designate the discipline area of the subject, the first digit the level of the subject, and the last two digits comprise a serial number to distinguish between subjects in the same discipline and level, (e.g. see Table 7.8).

Now suppose we want to be able to extract an output report like Table 7.8 from an information system, or issue a query like:

List all level 1 subjects in the discipline of computer science

Somehow we must convey the appropriate semantics to the system. As an aid to understanding the rationale of the coding system we might draw up a schema in which Subject is identified by three binaries (being in a discipline, at a level, with a serial#) and Discipline also plays the role of having a title (as an exercise draw this). This makes explicit the three components that go into this identification scheme for Subject.

When it comes to actually implementing these semantics however, and catering for the standard external view in which users wish to see subject codes in the form shown earlier, a different schema is more appropriate. In this schema, Subject would be identified by code. If required, information about disciplines and levels of subjects can be derived by means of rules. For example, if subject codes are specified as <aaddd>, then Subject xy--- is in Discipline xy, and Subject --x-- is at Level x.

One nasty case that requires special consideration is the situation where a variety of units are employed by users for the same physical quantity. For example, in Australia pieces of lumber have their longest length specified in meters but their breadth and depth are measured in millimeters. Because this is a standard in the building industry, an output report on lumber sizes might look like Table 7.9.

One might propose a schema like Figure 7.15 to deal with this. This schema is versatile enough to allow comparisons of breadth and depth (e.g. to determine lumber with square cross sections) and perform various arithmetic operations (e.g. computation of average lengths or cross sectional circumferences though derivation functions).

However suppose we want to compare a length with a width. For example:

Which kinds of lumber have length 20 times as long as breadth?

This kind of query suggests that we collapse Length and Width into the same entity type, say "Length" used in the more general sense. But there are two units involved so the naming conventions differ. One way around this problem is to specify a standard conceptual unit (e.g. meters) and provide a conversion rule between the units. This also allows the results of mixed computations to be specified in standard units (e.g. computation of volume in cubic meters). We indicate this conversion capacity with a double arrow as shown in Figure 7.16. The different units may be specified on the arcs for the relevant fact types. If we take it that the first unit mentioned is the standard this default unit may be omitted from the relevant arcs.

In situations like this there are many possible ways of approaching the problem. Often values of the same general dimension might never be equated even though they might

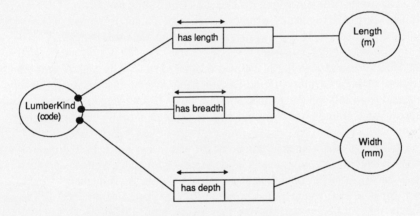

Figure 7.15 A conceptual schema diagram for Table 7.9

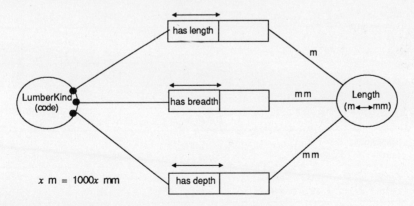

Figure 7.16 This schema allows all lengths to be compared

coexist in the same UoD (e.g. stellar distances measured in parsecs, and telescope diameters measured in centimeters). However conversion rules via a standard unit make it possible to compute ratios etc. which might be vitally needed.

In some cases the capacity to work in completely different unit systems is required. For example, we may need both metric and imperial measures to be displayed as users gradually move from one unit system to a newer one. In such a case the cleanest way out is to store the values in the new system and provide derivation rules to convert these into the older units as required (e.g. centimeters to inches).

Exercise 7.2

1. It is desired to identify a warehouse by its physical location. Design an appropriate identification scheme for the each of the following *contexts*:

   (a) UoD restricted to one suburb. The street in which the warehouse is located is identified by its name.
   (b) UoD restricted to one city. Each suburb is identified by its name.
   (c) UoD restricted to one country. Cities are identified by name.
   (d) UoD restricted to planet Earth. Countries are identified by name.
   (e) UoD restricted to Milky Way galaxy. Planets are identified by name.

2. The UoD is restricted to Earth, and it is desired to store facts of the form: Warehouse contains Item in Quantity. Is the identification scheme discussed in Question 1(d) practical from the implementation point of view? If not, suggest a better scheme and support your scheme by comparing a sample population for the two approaches.

3. The following table indicates the common names by which beer drinks of various volumes may be ordered in hotels in the States of Australia. Volumes are measured in fluid ounces (oz). The population of the table is significant. A hyphen "-" indicates that beer drinks of that volume are not on sale in that State. For instance, in Queensland exactly three different beer drinks may be ordered. Draw the conceptual schema diagram for this UoD.

	4oz	5oz	6oz	7oz	8oz	10oz	15oz	20oz
Qld	-	Small beer	-	-	Glass	Pot	-	-
NSW	-	Pony	-	Seven	-	Middy	Schooner	Pint
Vic	-	Pony	Small	Glass	-	Pot	Schooner	-
SA	-	Pony	-	Butcher	-	Schooner	Pint	-
WA	Shetland Pony	Pony	-	Glass	-	Middy	Schooner	Pot
Tas	Small beer	-	A Beer or a Six	-	An Eight	Pot or a Ten	-	-
NT	-	-	-	A Seven	-	Handle	Schooner	-

⑧ Even more constraints

8.1 CSDP step 8: Further constraints

In our efforts to describe the universe of discourse we began by isolating the kinds of fact that we wanted to discuss. We specified the kinds of entity that were of interest, their identification schemes, and the roles played by them. We picked meaningful names for the entity types and roles so that the schema could be interpreted by humans in terms of the real world.

Since the information system lacks such natural interpretation powers we had to formalize the relevant semantics for it. This was partly achieved by specifying the stored fact types and derivation rules. It was also necessary to formalize several kinds of constraints on the stored fact types.

So far we have seen how a variety of constraints can be specified. These include uniqueness constraints, entity type constraints, mandatory roles, subtype constraints and occurrence frequencies. Such constraints hold for all states of the database, and are enforceable by the system. Although these cover the vast majority of constraints that are of practical significance, other kinds of constraint sometimes need to be applied. The specification of these further constraints is the next step in the conceptual schema design procedure.

CSDP *step 8: Add equality, exclusion, subset and other constraints*

This chapter examines such constraints. In the next section we discuss equality, exclusion and subset constraints. Then we consider some special constraints for homogeneous binaries. In the final section we discuss some other constraints that are sometimes met.

8.2 Equality, exclusion and subset constraints

Suppose a health club maintains an information system concerning its members, and that Table 8.1 is an extract of an output report from this system. As usual, we use "?" for a null value, although in reports a blank is often used instead. The almost empty fourth row refers to the member with surname "Fit" and initials "IM". She plays two sports: aerobics and tennis. Try to schematize this yourself before looking at the schema supplied (Figure 8.1).

171

172   *Chapter 8*

Table 8.1

Member	Sex	BirthYr	Sport	Reaction Time (ms)	Resting Heart Rate (beats/m)
Anderson PE	M	1940	golf	250	80
Bloggs F	M	1940	golf	?	?
Fit IM	F	1960	aerobics tennis	250	80
Hume PE	F	1946	golf	305	93
Jones T	M	1965	tennis	?	?

Notice that the reaction time and heart rate information is optional. You may have been tempted to introduce a subtype for these two fact types but this would be wrong. The null value "?" (meaning "not recorded for this state ") is quite different from our special "–" value for "not to be recorded for any state". If you look at the first and second rows, you will find nothing to let the system know that reaction time and heart rate should be recorded for Anderson but not for Bloggs (let us agree that the structure of a member's name cannot be used to determine whether these values are recorded). Since the system has no well-defined reason for deciding whether these roles should be recorded, we simply leave them as optional roles attached to Member rather than attempt subtyping.

But, assuming the report is significant in this respect, reaction time is recorded for a member if, and only if, the resting heart rate is. We can imagine a scenario in which this constraint makes sense. Both these figures are measures of fitness. If a member feels inclined to take one of these tests the health club arranges for that member to also take the other test so as to ensure a balanced view of fitness rather than an incomplete one. When the test data are entered, a compound transaction is used to enter both figures. We express this constraint diagrammatically by means of a double headed arrow between the relevant roles (see Figure 8.1). If desired, both the arrow heads may be omitted.

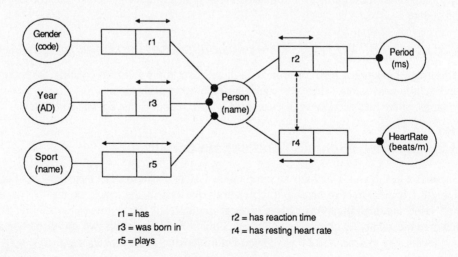

r1 = has
r3 = was born in
r5 = plays

r2 = has reaction time
r4 = has resting heart rate

Figure 8.1   A conceptual schema diagram for Table 8.1

Such a constraint is called an **equality constraint**, since for any state of the database the set of people for which r2 is recorded *equals* the set of people for which r4 is recorded. Another way of expressing this is to say that for any person, r2 is recorded *if and only if* r4 is recorded. One reason for using a double arrow to mark this constraint is because a double arrow "↔" is often used in logic for "if and only if". Note however, that an equality constraint applies to what is *stored*: it does not say that one of these fact types can be derived from the other.

One might argue that the schema could be expressed instead by subtyping in the following way. Leave the schema the same for roles r1, r2, r3, and r5 but create a subtype RTperson with r4 attached as mandatory, where RTperson is defined as Person who has r2 recorded. Although this is semantically equivalent to our earlier schema we recommend against such a portrayal because it is messier and because it arbitrarily gives pictorial prominence to r2 over r4 (one may equally well attach r2 to a subtype HRperson defined in terms of r4). The general notion of semantic equivalence is discussed in a later chapter.

Figure 8.2 formalizes the notion of an equality constraint. Here r1 and r2 are any two roles played by an entity type A. Although r1 and r2 will usually occur in different fact types, we allow that they could be within the same fact type. Here *a* is any member of A.

In terms of the associated fact columns, this constraint means that the set of values in column r1 is always identical to that of column r2 (i.e. for each state, pop(r1) = pop(r2)). It doesn't matter if there are duplicates in the columns: we only require that the sets are equal, not the bags.

If both roles r1 and r2 are mandatory, then clearly an equality constraint between these roles is implied, since for each state of the database the whole population of A plays both roles (see Figure 8.3). To explicitly include this constraint would lead to a cluttered diagram, and to more overhead if we forgot that the constraint is already enforced by the two mandatory role constraints. Hence, such implied constraints should be omitted from the schema.

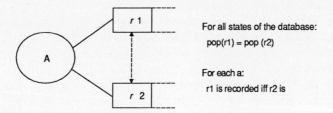

For all states of the database:
pop(r1) = pop (r2)

For each a:
r1 is recorded iff r2 is

Figure 8.2 An equality constraint

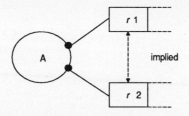

implied

Figure 8.3 The implied equality constraint should not be shown

Table 8.2

Employee	Gender	Parking bay	Parking claim ($)
Adams B	F	C01	-
Bloggs F	M	-	200
Collins T	M	B05	-
Dancer S	F	-	250
Egghead E	M	?	?

Clearly, for an equality constraint to apply between two roles, both roles must be attached to the same entity type (Why?). If one role is mandatory and the other is optional, then an equality constraint does not apply since it is possible to have a state in which only some of the population has the optional role recorded. If neither role is mandatory but their disjunction is, then we do not have an equality constraint because if we did both the roles would then be mandatory (Why?). In general, we need to ask ourselves whether an equality constraint between two roles needs to be specified, only for the situation where both are optional roles attached to the same entity type (see Figure 8.4). Here we have indicated that there must be another role or role disjunction that is mandatory (Why?).

Now consider the output report of Table 8.2. In this UoD employees may request a company parking bay or a refund of their parking expenses but not both. Also, employees might make neither request (e.g. they might not have a car, or they might simply want more time to decide). We invite you to try your hand at the schema before checking the solution provided.

Here we have two kinds of null values. The "-" value indicates "not to be recorded" (because the other option is chosen). The "?" value simply indicates "not recorded": an actual value might still be recorded for the employee "Egghead E" at a later stage (e.g. once he buys a car or makes up his mind to make a request); once such a value is recorded however, the system must assign a "-" value to the other option. This leads to the schema of Figure 8.5. We use a dotted line with an "×" to indicate an **exclusion constraint** between the roles r1 and r3. This indicates that for each state of the database no employee can be recorded as playing both these roles, that is, the populations of r1 and r3 are *mutually exclusive*.

Again, one might argue for an alternative diagram using a subtype. For example, we might leave the schema for r1 and r2 unchanged but introduce a subtype PossibleFeeClaimer to which r3 is attached as optional, where PossibleFeeClaimer is

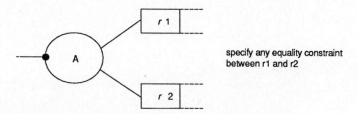

Figure 8.4   In this case, any equality constraint should be shown

defined as Employee who has *not* been (recorded to be) assigned a parking bay. However we recommend against this portrayal since it arbitrarily gives precedence to parking bay allocation (over parking fee claims) and is more complex. Figure 8.6 formalizes the notion of an exclusion constraint (recall that { } is the null set).

If r1 and r2 are played by different (primitive) entity types then an exclusion constraint between them must apply since the entity types are mutually exclusive by definition: we do not include an exclusion constraint in such cases since it is implied. If r1 and r2 are played by the same entity type but at least one of these roles is mandatory then clearly an exclusion constraint cannot apply between them (Why?). So in general, we need to ask ourselves whether an exclusion constraint between two roles needs to be specified, only for situations where both are optional roles attached to the same entity type (including the case of mandatory disjunction). See Figure 8.7.

An exclusion constraint between two roles is more common with homogeneous fact types. Consider Figure 8.8. In this UoD people are identified by their first names. We do not record a person's gender. However, the exclusion constraint indicates that nobody is both a husband and a wife. Each person can be a husband or a wife but not both. This is a case of *exclusive or*.

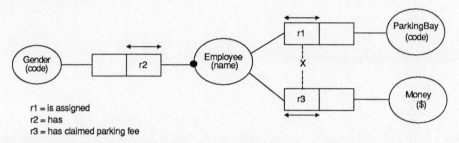

r1 = is assigned
r2 = has
r3 = has claimed parking fee

Figure 8.5 A conceptual schema diagram for Table 8.2

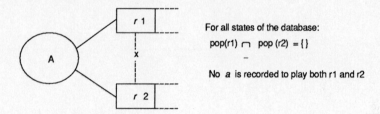

For all states of the database:

pop(r1) ∩ pop (r2) = { }

No *a* is recorded to play both r1 and r2

Figure 8.6 An exclusion constraint

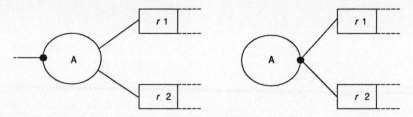

Figure 8.7 Specify any exclusion constraint between r1 and r2

Contrast this marriage fact type with the parenthood fact type of Figure 8.9. The occurrence frequency constraint "1..2" indicates that nobody has more than two parents. Here each person can be recorded as being a parent or child or both. This is a case of *inclusive or*.

Figure 8.10 summarizes how an exclusion constraint is used to distinguish between inclusive and exclusive disjunction. Here the roles may belong to different fact types or the same fact type.

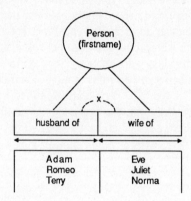

Figure 8.8   No husband is a wife

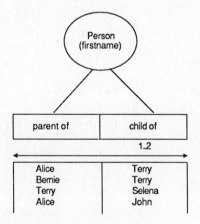

Figure 8.9   A parent may be a child of another parent

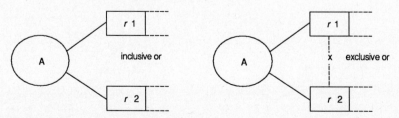

Figure 8.10   Inclusive and exclusive disjunction

Now consider the general case where two roles r1 and r2 are played by entities of type A. Since the populations of r1 and r2 are both subsets of A it is meaningful to compare them. So far, we have considered the cases where these populations must be identical and where they must be disjoint. But these are only the two extreme cases that arise in comparing two sets. The three other classic set comparisons (proper subset, proper superset, and proper overlap) are not relevant in practice for database constraints since the "proper" aspect demands existence of entities (constraints apply to all states of the database, including the initial state which is typically empty).

However there is one other set comparison which does need to be considered, and that is subsethood. We use a dotted arrow to indicate a **subset constraint** as set out in Figure 8.11. Again, *a* denotes any member of *A*. The choice of the arrow for the subset constraint is consistent with the use of an arrow for a subtype constraint. It also reminds us of the link to the "if-then" operator of logic, which is often shown as "→"; however a subset constraint is a database constraint, not a derivation rule. In a later chapter, this arrow also provides a convenient notation for specifying subset constraints between tables in a relational database.

Although we have introduced the subset constraint in the context of specifying a necessary comparison between the populations of two roles, in a conceptual schema the subset constraint is rarely used for this purpose. Consider Figure 8.11. If r1 and r2 are mandatory then we have an equality constraint: this implies a subset constraint in both directions (as suggested by the double arrow). If only one role is optional (see Figure 8.12) then its population must be a subset of the other's (Why?).

For reasons discussed earlier, such an implied constraint should not be shown (however, we will later make use of this implication in our mapping to an ONF relational schema). Now consider the case where both r1 and r2 are optional (see Figure 8.13). The subset constraint in (a) is equivalent to the subtype constraint in (b) if the strongest

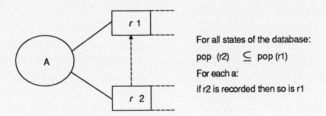

For all states of the database:

pop (r2)   ⊆   pop (r1)

For each a:

if r2 is recorded then so is r1

Figure 8.11   A subset constraint

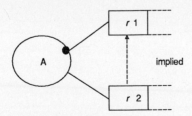

Figure 8.12   The implied subset constraint should not be shown

Table 8.3

Person	Sex	CarsOwned	CarsDriven
Fred	M	272NCP, 123BOM	272NCP, 123BOM
Sue	F	272NCP, 123BOM	272NCP
Tina	F	105ABC	?
Tom	M	?	?

definition we can provide for B is B = A playing r1 (e.g. Person having *some* Gender). If a stronger definition is available for B (e.g. Person having Gender 'M') then we must subtype: in this case the subset constraint is weaker and is not shown since it is implied. In those rare cases where we can't get a stronger definition for B we may choose the subset representation.

Why mention subset constraints at all then? Partly because the notion is useful even for this simple case when we later consider mapping to relational schemata. But more importantly, subset constraints between *tuple* populations often *do* need to be specified. We now turn to a consideration of subset, exclusion and equality constraints for such cases. Consider the output report of Table 8.3, which provides details about people and the cars they own or drive. Try to schematize this yourself before checking with the schema-base diagram provided.

Each car is identified by a registration number stamped on its licence plate (if we allowed a car to change its licence plate we would need to pick some other identifier, e.g. its compliance plate number). The ownership fact type is many to many (a person may own many cars and the same car may be owned by many people, e.g. Fred and Sue might be married and co-owners of two cars). The drive fact type is also many to many. Note that although Fred and Sue both own car 123BOM, only Fred drives it. (For example, it might be Fred's "pride and joy" and he won't let Sue drive it; or perhaps it is a "bomb" of a car and Sue refuses to drive it!). Tina owns a car but doesn't drive it (maybe she has a chauffeur). Tom neither owns nor drives a car.

Assuming the sample database is significant, each car a person is recorded as driving is a car he or she is recorded as owning. Taking a closed world view, for this UoD people own every car that they drive. We indicate this by the subset constraint shown (see Figure 8.14). This asserts that, for each state of the database, the set of *tuples* in the Drives fact-table is a subset of the set of tuples in the Owns table. You may think of a tuple as a sequence of values occurring on the same row of a fact table. Here, each tuple is an ordered pair. We use "order" in a general sense here to include the case where roles are identified by name rather than position.

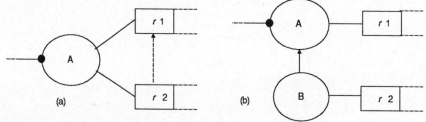

Figure 8.13   Choose representation (b) unless B = A playing r1

For the database state shown, the Drives table has three tuples: (Fred,272NCP); (Fred,123BOM); and (Sue,272NCP). The Owns table has five tuples. We see that each tuple in the Drives table is also in the Owns table: the subset constraint indicates that this is true for each state of the database. To indicate that the subset constraint applies between role tuples rather than single roles, each end of the arrow is positioned at the division between the two roles involved in the tuple. The general idea is formalized in Figure 8.15.

Notice the notation for populations of *role sequences*. In terms of the UoD, "pop(r1,r2)" means the set of entity tuples referenced in the fact columns for r1 and r2, where the first entity is referenced in the column for role r1 and the second is referenced in the column for role r2 (on the same row). In terms of the knowledge base, we have a corresponding population of label (column entry) tuples: so we may think of pop(r1,r2) as the *projection* on columns r1 and r2 of the fact table.

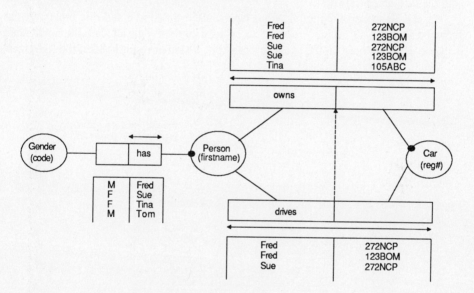

Figure 8.14 A schema-base diagram for Table 8.3

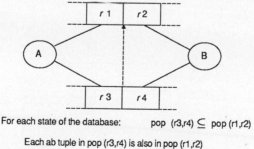

For each state of the database: pop (r3,r4) ⊆ pop (r1,r2)

Each ab tuple in pop (r3,r4) is also in pop (r1,r2)

Figure 8.15 Subset constraint between tuple populations

Note that the direction of the subset constraint is quite important. With our present example, if the arrow pointed instead to the Drives fact type this would signify that each person who owns a car also drives that car, which is quite a different assertion. For the case where people own a car if and only if they drive that car, we have subset constraints in both directions: this amounts to an equality constraint. Whether equality constraints between tuple-sets are useful is debatable; we can however display them as shown in Figure 8.16.

Similarly, exclusion constraints can be specified for tuples. Suppose we want to record information about cars that people own and cars that they want to buy. Clearly, nobody would want to buy a car that they already own: we can indicate this by the exclusion constraint shown in Figure 8.17. Notice that this constraint is weaker than an exclusion constraint between the Owns and Wants-to-buy roles (which would instead say that no car owner wants to buy any car, and hence would disallow Fred's appearance in both the fact tables shown).

We may summarize the implications between the single role and role tuple cases as shown in Figure 8.18., using "⇒" for "necessarily implies". In each case the implication is in one direction only. In the exclusion example, a similar result holds if the right hand

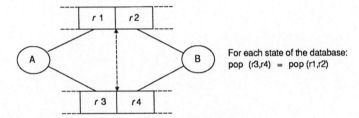

Figure 8.16   Equality constraint between tuple populations

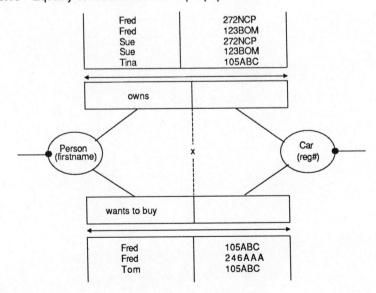

Figure 8.17   Exclusion constraint between tuple populations

constraint is between the other pair of roles. We leave the proof of these results as an exercise: if you have trouble here, try inventing some counterexamples to equivalence claims. For example, if pop(r1,r2) = {(a1,b1), (a2,b2)} and pop(r3,r4) = {(a1,b2), (a2,b1)} then pop(r1) = pop(r3) and pop(r2) = pop(r4) but pop(r1,r2) ≠ pop(r3,r4).

Note that the question of whether an equality, subset or exclusion constraint between role tuples needs to be explicitly specified arises only for those cases where the role tuples are connected to the same entity type tuples. If the roles are not displayed as contiguous or if the arity of the tuples exceeds 2, then dotted lines are used to show the relevant tuples (e.g. see Figure 8.19).

Exercise 8.2

1. Draw the conceptual schema for the UoD described by the following output report about employees and the company cars they use.

Employee	Sex	Car	Driver's licence
Adams	M	111ABC	C5400
		123HAP	
Brown	F	111ABC	A6742
Collins	F	?	?

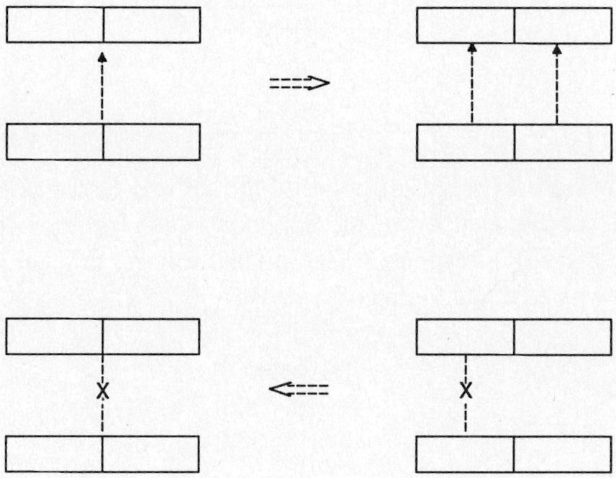

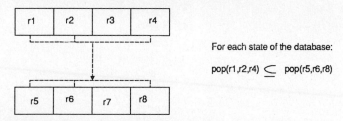

Figure 8.18 Some implications between constraint patterns

For each state of the database:

pop(r1,r2,r4) ⊆ pop(r5,r6,r8)

Figure 8.19 Dotted lines are used with longer tuples

2. The conceptual schema for a particular UoD is shown below. Reference modes have been omitted for simplicity. Fact tables are shown below their corresponding fact types. Predicates are identified as R..U, and constraints as C1..C10.

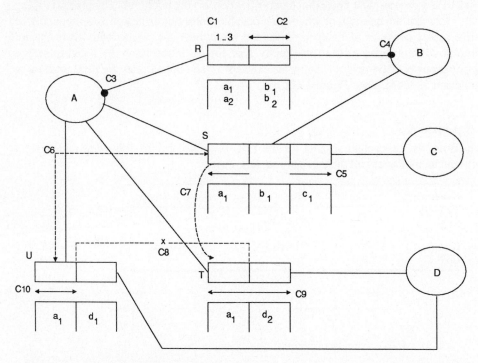

Each of the following user requests applies to the **same** database population as shown, that is, treat each request as if it was the first to be made for this population. For each request, indicate the CIP's response. If an update request is legal, write "accepted"; otherwise indicate a constraint violated.

(a) add: a_1 T d_2

(f) begin
    add: S a_2 b_1 c_2
    add: a_2 U d_2
    end

(b) add: a_2 T d_2

(g) add: S a_1 b_3 c_2

(c) del: a_1 U d_1

(h) add: a_3 R b_1

(d) add: a_1 T d_1

(i) del: a_2 R b_2

(e) add: S a_1 b_2 c_1

(j) begin
    add: a_1 R b_3
    add: a_1 R b_4
    add: a_1 R b_5
    end

3. Draw the conceptual schema diagram for the UoD described in Exercise 2.2 Question 2, adding constraint labels C1..C5 to the relevant constraints marked on the diagram.

8.3 Homogeneous binaries

In this section we focus our attention on constraints of special relevance to homogeneous binaries, that is, binary fact types where both roles are played by the entities of the same type, as indicated in Figure 8.20. Here we have an entity type A, and a binary fact type with two roles r1 and r2. For each state of the database we have a relation defined by the set of tuples in the fact table, that is, pop(r1,r2). The relation type R may be defined as the set of all such possible relations, or as a variable whose value at any given state is a relation. We allow derived as well as stored relations.

We make use of the infix notation "xRy" (read "x Rs y") to denote a relationship between x and y, where x and y are placeholders for roles r1 and r2 respectively. This notation is convenient for defining various properties of relations such as reflexivity, symmetry and transitivity. We discuss such notions by way of example. Consider the schema-base diagram of Figure 8.21.

Here we have used nouns for the role names ("liker" = one who likes; "likee" = one who is liked). Given the context that the entities are people identified by their firstnames, the population of the database comprises three facts: Ann likes Ann; Ann likes Bill; Bill likes Bill. Notice that each person likes himself/herself. If we updated the database by adding the fact that Colin likes Ann, there is now one person (Colin) who is not known to

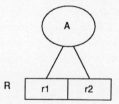

Figure 8.20 A homogeneous binary

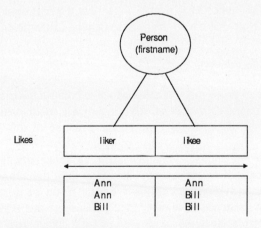

Figure 8.21 A schema-base diagram for the Likes fact type

Table 8.4

Likes:	*liker*	*likee*
	Ann	Bill
	Bill	Colin
	Ann	Colin
	David	Ann
	David	Bill
	David	Colin

like himself. Suppose however that we have a UoD in which all people do like themselves, and we want the system to know this. That is:

    for each state of the knowledge base
      for each person x
        x likes x

In this case the relation type Likes is said to be *reflexive* over Person. In general, reflexivity of a relation type R over an entity type A may be defined thus:

    R is **reflexive** over A iff for all x in A   xRx

Now suppose that for the UoD under consideration, anybody who likes another is liked by that other person. For example, one satisfying population comprises the three facts: Ann likes Bill; Bill likes Bill; Bill likes Ann. Here given any persons x and y, if x Likes y then y Likes x. If this is always the case, we say that Likes is *symmetric*. Using "$\rightarrow$" for "implies", we may define this notion for any relation type R as follows:

    R is **symmetric** iff for all x,y   xRy $\rightarrow$ yRx

Now suppose that for our UoD if one person likes a second, and the second person likes a third, then the first person must like the third. In this case we say that likes is *transitive*. The relation in Table 8.4 illustrates this property.

In general, transitivity of a relation type R may be defined as follows. Here we use "&" for "and", and give "&" precedence over "$\rightarrow$" (so that the & operation is evaluated before the $\rightarrow$ operation). Note that we do not assume that the instantiations of x, y and z are distinct.

    R is **transitive** iff for all x,y,z   xRy & yRz $\rightarrow$ xRz

We leave it as an exercise to prove that a relation which is both symmetric and transitive must also be reflexive. A relation which is reflexive, symmetric and transitive is called an "RST relation" or "equivalence relation". The classic example of this is the identity relation "=".

In the general sense, relational properties such as reflexivity, symmetry and transitivity might be thought of as constraints, since they limit the allowable relations. However, we will describe such properties as **positive** since, given the existence of one or more facts they posit the existence of another fact. Because of this feature it is often better to treat such properties in terms of *derivation rules* rather than as part of the constraint section of the conceptual schema.

Table 8.5

Word	Synonyms
abandon	leave, relinquish, forsake
abate	diminish, lessen, reduce, decline
abbreviate	shorten, reduce, condense
:	:
condense	compress, consolidate, abridge
:	:
reduce	shorten, weaken, abate
:	:

Let's look at an example. Consider the problem of designing an information system for synonyms. Recall that a synonym for a word has roughly the same meaning as that word. A sample taken from a book of synonyms is shown in Table 8.5.

An incomplete schema is set out in Figure 8.22. Notice that here we have an entity type which is also its own label type. For practical reasons we have chosen different role names to distinguish (somewhat artificially) between the roles. Since we have a homogeneous binary we might ask ourselves whether the relation type is reflexive, symmetric or transitive. From the output report it is clearly not reflexive. Although one might argue that each word is a synonym of itself, this is a trivial result that humans are not usually interested in seeing. So let us agree to think of the relation in such a way that no word is its own synonym (this actually indicates that the relation is *irreflexive*; but let us postpone discussion of this kind of constraint till a later example).

From our human understanding of the term, we would agree that if one word is a synonym of another then the other is a synonym for it. In other words, the real world relation of synonymy is symmetric. But if you look at the output report, which was taken from a book of synonyms, you will see that this condition has not been enforced. For example, the pair ("abbreviate","reduce") appears in this order only: so if we look up the word "reduce" we won't find out that "abbreviate" is one of its synonyms. This is a defective feature of the synonym book which one would wish to avoid with a computerized synonym system.

One way to proceed here would be to add the following assertion to the constraint section of the conceptual schema, using "hasSynonym" as the predicate name:

sym(hasSynonym)

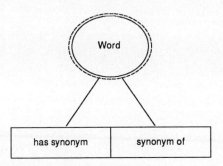

Figure 8.22 An incomplete schema for Table 8.5

The notations "reflex(R)", "sym(R)", and "trans(R)" are used to assert that R is reflexive, symmetric and transitive respectively. The system would now enforce this constraint on the database. For example, suppose the following update is attempted:

add: hasSynonym('abbreviate', 'shorten')

A naively programmed CIP may simply reject this as violating the symmetry constraint. A more sophisticated CIP would give the user the option of either adding this as well as the converse fact: hasSynonym ("shorten","abbreviate"), or of cancelling the update. A consistent scheme would be adopted for the delete operation. While such an approach has the advantage of access efficiency it has the disadvantage of substantially increasing the size of the database, since each pair of synonyms is stored twice, once for each ordering.

An alternative approach would be to allow the database synonym relation to lack symmetry but to add a derived fact type to provide a symmetric synonym relation. For example, we might define this derived relation in Prolog as follows. In a simple setup we might require users to perform updates through the hasSynonym relation but to issue queries through the areSynonyms relation.

areSynonyms(X,Y) if hasSynonym(X,Y).
areSynonyms(X,Y) if hasSynonym(Y,X).

If we decide on this kind of approach our conceptual schema diagram looks like Figure 8.23. Here we have used the notation "qo" and "uo" to indicate the fact types are for "query only" and "update only" respectively. Though "updatable views" are sometimes used, derived fact types should generally be considered to be "query only".

Although the derivation rules may be written in a conceptual notation similar to that of Prolog, any suitable language may be used for implementation. For instance, this approach may be implemented in SQL using a stored query. For example, suppose the stored relation is called "hasSynonym" and has columns named "word" and "alias". This table can be used for updates while the following query (stored under the name

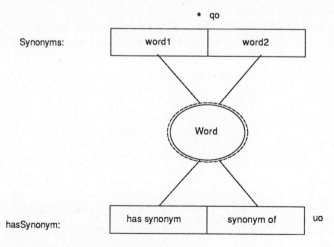

Figure 8.23   One way of schematizing Table 8.5

"synonyms") may be used to access the synonyms of any word passed as a parameter to be substituted for the placeholder "&1". Besides saving on storage space, this implementation can be made access efficient by using an index for each of the columns.

```
select alias from Synonyms where word = '&1'
union
select word from Synonyms where alias = '&1'
```

Thus, one sometimes has a choice as to whether to capture an aspect of the UoD in terms of a database constraint or as a derivation rule. Notice that here we distinguished the stored and derived fact types by name. In the next chapter we consider the possibility of having the same fact type partly stored and partly derived.

Now what about transitivity of synonymy? This issue is not so easily decided. You are probably familiar with the "bald-hairy paradox" based on the premise: in all cases if we add one hair to the head of a bald man he is still bald (where is the paradox?). A similar acervus argument can be proposed to argue against transitivity (sequences of approximations finally lead to non-approximations). Moreover there is the problem that the same word may have different meanings leading to different groups of synonyms. If we do want to pursue with some measure of transitivity we might include a derivation rule for transitivity of the synonym relation but constrained by an upper bound for the length of the transitivity chain and relativized to group meanings. We do not pursue this matter further here.

We now turn to a study of **negative** relational properties such as irreflexivity and asymmetry. We call these negative since given the existence of some facts, such properties posit the *non-existence* of certain other facts. In general such properties tend to be better handled as simple constraints rather than as derivation rules. In previous work we have considered a schema for parenthood, but the schema was incomplete. Have a close look at the schema-base diagram in Figure 8.24, and see if you can spot anything that seems wrong:

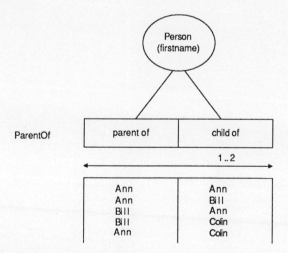

Figure 8.24 What is wrong here?

First note that formally the population shown is consistent with the constraints specified in the conceptual schema. But as you no doubt noticed, some of the facts in the table are inconsistent with the real world concept of parenthood. What we need to do is formalize this concept further by providing more constraints so that the information system is able to reject such erroneous populations.

To begin with, the first fact (Ann is parent of Ann) has to be rejected since nobody can be his/her own parent. We say that the parenthood relation is *irreflexive*. In general, for any relation type R:

R is **irreflexive** iff for all x   ~xRx

Here we use tilde "~" for "not". We want to say that for every state of the database the ParentOf relation is irreflexive. We could specify this constraint by writing "irreflex(ParentOf)" beside the diagram. But to save writing and avoid cluttering the diagram we simply write "ir" (for "irreflexive") beside the fact type (see Figure 8.25).

Irreflexivity is unusual in being an intra-tuple constraint; that is, violation of the constraint can be determined simply by examination of the tuple itself, irrespective of what other tuples exist in the relation. The constraint means that no entity may be referenced in both columns of the same row. Note that "irreflexive" is much stronger than "not reflexive". For example, if Likes is irreflexive then nobody likes themselves; if some but not all people like themselves then Likes is not reflexive and not irreflexive. With homogeneous binaries, exclusion constraints are sometimes confused with irreflexivity constraints. To explain the distinction we recall the example reproduced in Figure 8.26.

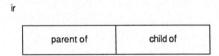

Figure 8.25   Parenthood is irreflexive

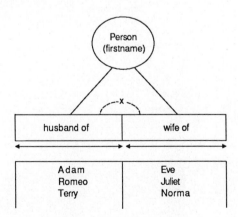

Figure 8.26   The exclusion constraint implies irreflexivity

Here the exclusion constraint says that no entry in the husband column may appear *on any row* of the wife column. This of course implies that no entry may appear in both positions on the same row. So the *exclusion constraint implies irreflexivity*. However the converse does not hold, that is, if the relation is irreflexive this does not imply the exclusion constraint. For example, the parenthood relation is irreflexive but not exclusive (e.g. Bill may appear both as a parent of Colin and as a child of Ann). If we added the fact that Eve is the husband of Fred to this table this would violate the exclusion constraint but not irreflexivity.

Returning to our parenthood example and adding the irreflexive constraint, the system now rejects the first row (Ann parent of Ann). This leaves us with Figure 8.27. Can you spot any problems with this?

If we accept the first row we ought to reject the second row. If Ann is a parent of Bill then it cannot be true that Bill is a parent of Ann. This is because the parenthood relation is *asymmetric*. In general, for any relation type R:

R is **asymmetric** iff for all x,y   xRy → ~yRx

That is, if the first item Rs the second item then the second item cannot R the first. Here, if one person is parent of another then that other cannot be parent of the first. Classifying a relation as asymmetric is stronger than saying the relation is not symmetric (we leave the proof of this as an exercise). We specify the constraint that, for each state of the database, the ParentOf relation is asymmetric (i.e. asym(ParentOf)) by adding the notation "as" (for "asymmetric") beside the fact type on the diagram (as shown in Figure 8.28). With this constraint enforced, the legal population has been reduced as shown.

Notice that the irreflexive "ir" constraint is not displayed in Figure 8.28. Is this a mistake? No. It is easy to prove that any relation which is asymmetric must be irreflexive (we leave the proof as an exercise: note that x and y need not be distinct). The converse does not hold. There are some irreflexive relations which are not asymmetric. To avoid showing implied constraints, we should omit "ir" if "as" applies.

There is still a problem with Figure 8.28. Can you spot it? If Ann is parent of Bill and Bill is parent of Colin then Ann cannot be parent of Colin (she would be a grandparent

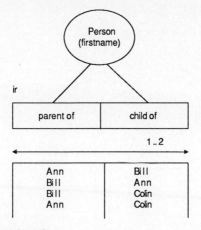

Figure 8.27   What is wrong here?

instead). We say that the parenthood relation is *intransitive*. In general, for any relation R:

R is **intransitive** iff for all x,y,z   xRy & yRz → ~xRz

Here, if one person is a parent of a second and the second person is parent of a third, then the first person cannot be parent of the third. To signify that the parenthood relation is intransitive for all states of the database we write "intrans(ParentOf)" or add "it" (for "intransitive") beside the fact type. This leaves us finally with Figure 8.29.

The term "atransitive" is sometimes used instead of "intransitive". Saying a relation is intransitive is stronger than saying the relation is not transitive. Again we leave the proof of this as an exercise. Note that asymmetry and intransitivity are not intra-tuple constraints, since their enforcement requires comparing the tuple in question with other existing tuples.

Other properties of relations are sometimes used in describing homogeneous binaries (e.g. antisymmetry and connectivity) but we do not discuss them here. It should be noted that what we have said about homogeneous binaries may be extended to cases where such binaries occur within the context of a larger fact type. The classic case of this is the so called "Bill of Materials" or "Parts Explosion" problem, that you may have met in an earlier Exercise (i.e. Part contains Part in Quantity). You are invited to provide a more complete solution to this problem in the exercise that follows.

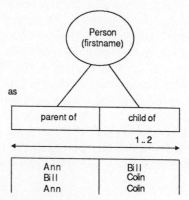

Figure 8.28   There is still something wrong

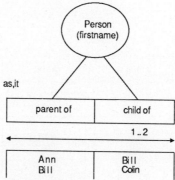

Figure 8.29   A correct schema-base diagram

Exercise 8.3

1. For each of the following relation types, state which, if any, of the following properties hold for it:

reflexive, irreflexive
symmetric, asymmetric
transitive, intransitive

(a) has same age as
(b) is brother of
(c) is sibling of
(d) is shorter than
(e) is an ancestor of
(f) is at least as clever as
(g) lives next to

2. Specify the conceptual schema for the UoD described by the following output report, which indicates the composition of items (e.g. Item A contains 2 B parts and 3 C parts). For this exercise read "contains" as "directly contains" (e.g. A does not contain D). We take a more general reading for "contains" in a later exercise.

Item	Part	Quantity
A	B	2
A	C	1
B	D	1
B	E	3
C	E	3
C	F	2
C	G	3

3. If you are familiar with predicate logic, prove the following theorem.

irreflex(R) & trans(R) $\Rightarrow$ asym(R)

8.4 Other constraints

We have seen how to express a large variety of constraints on a conceptual schema diagram. These cover most of the constraints that are met in practical situations. Although we could invent new notations for marking further constraints on a CS diagram, we will typically choose not to do so, since one of the main reasons for drawing a CS diagram at all is to provide a simple, concise picture to help humans obtain an overview of the structure of the UoD. If we continue to add more marks on the diagram to cover rarely encountered constraints, both our notational system and the diagram itself are likely to become so cluttered that this simplicity is lost.

Sometimes CS diagrams become somewhat cluttered anyway. This is particularly the case with very large schemas where all constraints right down to the lexical level are

Table 8.6 Two ways of specifying transition constraints

From\To	Spring	Summer	Autumn	Winter
Spring	0	1	0	0
Summer	0	0	1	0
Autumn	0	0	0	1
Winter	1	0	0	0

displayed. In such cases we typically allow users to control the amount of detai shown by the diagram. For example, a user may wish to see only a subschema related to part of the application, or perhaps just an overview of the whole schema where "minor" fact-types are omitted (e.g. omit nodes playing only one role), or perhaps the schema with all reference modes omitted. Such controlled *information-hiding* is facilitated by having an automated conceptual schema design workbench.

Recall that the conceptual schema diagram is not to be equated with the conceptual schema. The *CS diagram provides a human-oriented, unambiguous but typically incomplete specification of the UoD structure*. The aspects of the UoD that cannot be captured by the CS diagram should be set out clearly in other notations which are easy for humans to follow (e.g. formalized natural language or other kinds of diagram). Once humans have agreed upon the conceptual schema, a more formalized language may be used to communicate the schema to the system. In practice a variety of such formalisms are used (e.g. various systems of formal logic and set theory, Prolog, Z and even special graphical languages like our own).

Constraints not covered by our diagram notation may be written below the CS diagram if there is room, or on an extra sheet (just as derivation/inference rules are added). Initially we should express these constraints in natural language. If we can think of a more concise way of formulating them without losing clarity or human-readability, this way can be used; otherwise we stick with the natural language formulation.

As indicated in an earlier chapter, dynamic constraints (those that are concerned purely with restricting the possible transitions between database states) are usually not included in our CS diagram. For instance, to specify a constraint such as "No person can be demoted in salary" we might simply write this sentence down. Besides natural language, transition tables and graphs may be used to express dynamic constraints. For instance, the possible transitions between seasons may be expressed by either formulation in Table 8.6 (in the table, "1" and "0" indicate allowed and forbidden transitions respectively; in the graph, arrow heads indicate permitted transitions).

Occasionally, we run into static constraints that are not catered for by the CS diagram. For example, "the number of members of a committee must be odd". As another example, consider a UoD in which everybody watches at least one soap opera but only the women are allowed to watch more than one! In this case the uniqueness constraint on the watches role is shown as many to many, as indicated in Figure 8.30.

Here the constraint on males watching soap operas needs to be stated separately, as shown. This specification is informal: it is clear enough for humans, but some more formal notation would be needed for the system (e.g. "Person having Gender 'M' watches only-one SoapOpera" assuming the notion "only-one" has been formalized elsewhere).

We conclude the chapter by discussing a graphical output report which introduces some other kinds of constraint. Suppose Figure 8.31 provides a topological picture of a local area network of computers (i.e. it shows which computers are connected to which but not their distance apart or directional pattern).

This is commonly referred to as a "bus network". Here we have a network of five nodes, comprised of a file server connected via a bus to four work-stations. The main memory of each node, and the hard disk capacity of the file server are recorded. As simple as it is, this diagram actually packs in a lot of information. Our task is to design an information system to record this information in a textual form so that users can extract as much information from this system as they could extract from the diagram itself. You might like to have a go at solving this problem yourself before reading on.

There are several ways in which one might handle this problem. We discuss two of these briefly. Starting at step 1 we try to read off the information in terms of elementary facts. From the box notation and legend we determine the kind of node. For example:

Node (code) 'A' is of NodeKind (name) 'FileServer'.
Node (code) 'B' is of NodeKind (name) 'WorkStation'.

Since the identification scheme for nodes has been determined, we can safely leave it unstated from now on. The facts about storage capacity of main memory and hard disk are easily stated. For example:

Node A has main memory with Storage of 10 (Mb).
Node A has a hard disk with Storage of 300 (Mb).

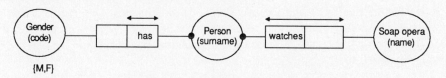

Each male person watches only one soap opera.

Figure 8.30   A conceptual schema including a verbal constraint

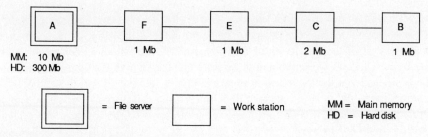

Figure 8.31   A bus network

So far we have catered only for the information about individual nodes which is independent of how they relate to other nodes. Now comes the hard part: how do we describe the actual configuration of nodes? Depending on what we choose to be our primitive predicates, there are a number of choices. We might find it hard initially to express the information in terms of elementary sentences. To get the ball rolling we might just jot down samples of whatever comes to mind. For example:

1. Node A is directly connected to node F.
2. Node F is directly connected to node A.
3. Node A is indirectly connected to node E.
4. Node E is 2 nodes away from node A.
5. Node A is an end node.
6. Node F is an intermediate node.
7. There is at most one link between each pair of nodes.
8. There is at least one link between each pair of adjacent nodes.
9. No link connects a node to itself.
10. Each node is directly connected to at most 2 nodes.

Let's stand back from the problem for a minute. If we look at the diagram from our human background there are two basic aspects about the configuration that need to be captured somehow. Firstly, the nodes all lie along the same *continuous line segment* (in contrast to other shapes such as star networks, ring networks, fancy loop structures, separate segments, etc.). Secondly, the nodes are *positioned in some order* on this line. Sentences 1–4 above seem to be mostly about this positioning while sentences 5–10 seem to be mostly about the structure being linear.

If we consider the linearity of the structure to be a *constraint* then we can focus our attention initially on expressing how the nodes are ordered. Given that the nodes are positioned on a line, and that the file server is at one end of this line, let's first establish a *direction* for the line by saying the line starts at the file server. One major benefit of choosing a direction is to avoid the problems of dealing with symmetric relations. For instance, a relation like is-just-before is easier to handle than a symmetric relation like is-directly-connected-to.

There are two basic approaches we might adopt to specify the ordering. We might consider the notion of *position* to be primitive, or we might define this notion in terms of some other notion such as *directed linkage* (e.g. just-before). This is partly related to the question of whether to give priority to the nodes or to the links. We consider each of these approaches in turn.

First let's assign each of the nodes a position on the line. Whole numbers provide a simple identification scheme for position. Since we have agreed that the file server is always at the start of the line let's call this position "0", and number each of the other positions 1, 2, 3, etc. as we move along the line. For the sample configuration we thus have the positions identified as shown in Figure 8.32.

As we will see, all the information to do with ordering can be now derived by simple rules. It helps to construct a table for the stored information before we draw the schema diagram (see Table 8.7). Here "–" as usual means "not to be recorded". Let us agree to shorten the identifiers for NodeKind by using the codes shown.

Table 8.7

Node	Kind	Position	MainMemory (Mb)	HardDisk (Mb)
A	FS	0	10	300
F	WS	1	1	–
E	WS	2	1	–
C	WS	3	2	–
B	WS	4	1	–

Constructing the basic conceptual schema diagram is now fairly straightforward. Let us agree to set upper limits of 31 nodes and 1000 Mb for individual storage capacities.

Notice the "1" beside the subtype node: this is a "cardinality constraint" indicating the maximum number of file servers is 1. This implies uniqueness constraints on r4 and r4'. The dot above "FS" is a "mandatory entity constraint" indicating that the NodeKind "FS" must be present in any non-null population of NodeKind (if the network contains only one node it must be the file server). The diagram however is still incomplete. This can be seen by trying to capture the information expressed in sentences on the diagram. Another way is to try to invent some counterexamples (i.e. sample data sets that are consistent with the schema but not with the actual UoD). For example, the positional data of Table 8.8 are consistent with our current schema.

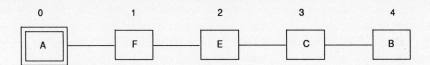

Figure 8.32 Node positions have been numbered

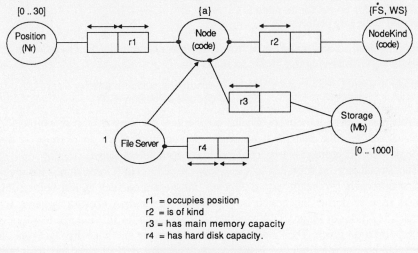

r1 = occupies position
r2 = is of kind
r3 = has main memory capacity
r4 = has hard disk capacity.

FileServer = Node of kind 'FS'

Figure 8.33 A conceptual schema based on Table 8.7

Table 8.8   A counterexample showing Figure 8.33 is incomplete

Node	Kind	Position
A	FS	2
F	WS	1
E	WS	0
C	WS	6
B	WS	7

The first row must be rejected because we have agreed that the file server is at the end numbered 0. Secondly, the data suggest that there are gaps in the network since there are no nodes recorded for the positions between 2 and 6. We can eliminate these defects in our schema by adding the following constraints below the diagram:

The file server occupies position 0.
All positions 0..n-1 are occupied, where n = number of nodes.

Together, these imply the mandatory "FS" constraint. It might be argued that we now have some redundancy in our schema since the kind of node can be also determined from the node's position. We may modify the schema by marking the kind-of-node fact type as derived and providing an appropriate rule for this (which would subsume the first additional constraint above).

For most practical purposes we now have a reasonably complete constraint picture, particularly if we assume humans interpret "occupies position" in terms of their background understanding of the linear bus structure and hence have no interest in posing queries such as "How many links are there between adjacent nodes?". Instead let us focus our attention on the ability of the schema to deal with more likely queries such as:

Which node comes just before node C?
Which nodes are adjacent to node C?
How many nodes come between nodes F and B?
Which nodes come before node C?
Which is the last node?

Clearly we need to add some derivation rules. For example, to handle the first query a rule such as the following might be specified:

Node X is just before Node Y **if** Node X occupies Position n **and**
Node Y occupies Position n+1.

This rule can be used to help specify the other rules. We leave this as an exercise for the interested reader. One point that becomes apparent from such an exercise is that the notion of numeric position is very convenient for such derivations.

The second general approach to specifying the positional information is the reverse of the first approach. We begin with a directed linkage notion such as just-before: this can then be used to derive the notion of position if required. A skeleton schema for this approach is set out in Figure 8.34, together with the table for this linkage fact type based on the population given. The kind-of-node, main-memory and hard-disk fact types are as before. Derivation rules may be listed for the kind-of-node fact type, but are somewhat clumsier than before. For example, a node is respectively a Workstation or FileServer accordingly as it plays or doesn't play the just-after role.

Notice that this fact table stores information about only the direct or immediate links: this reduces the size of our database as well as avoiding the problems of symmetry and transitivity. Note that the fact type has been specified as irreflexive, asymmetric and intransitive: convince yourself that these constraints are needed. Information about which nodes come before which can easily be derived from the just-before fact type. For example, the following recursive formulation is typical:

X before Y **if** X just-before Y.
X before Y **if** X just-before Z **and** Z before Y.

There are still some constraints left to specify. For example, to guarantee there are two ends and no gaps we might specify that one node plays just the just-before role, one node plays just the just-after role, and all other nodes play both these roles. We also need to specify derivation rules to cater for queries as discussed earlier. This is left as an exercise.

This kind of problem is an interesting one to discuss from the aspect of *updates*. For example consider how each approach would deal with the requirement to add nodes, delete nodes or swap nodes. With the position approach, global changes to positional information would be required for insertion or deletion of a single node. For instance if we add a node, say D, between F and E then not only will D be assigned the position 2 but nodes E, C and B will all need to have their position numbers increased by 1. With the other approach, only a local change would be needed. Swapping nodes is simple with both approaches. As an exercise, set out the compound transactions involved for some sample updates.

Conceptually, both approaches can be filled out to completely specify the same UoD, and are then semantically equivalent. At the implementation level, the position approach tends to be less efficient for updates but more efficient for queries requiring derivation. Either approach may be used for the initial conceptual schema. When it comes to implementation, the conceptual schema may if desired be transformed to the other before mapping down to the implementation language. A later chapter discusses the notion of schema transformations in some detail.

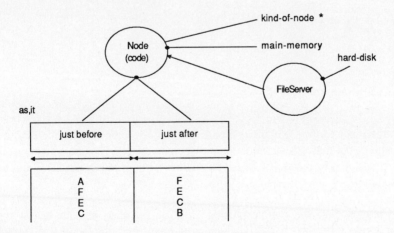

Figure 8.34 Another way of schematizing the bus network

Other constraint notations have been devised to handle additional cases that sometimes occur (e.g. involving joins or restrictions), but these will not be discussed in this introductory work.

Exercise 8.4

1. Undergraduate Science students at a particular university are classified as Year 1, 2 or 3 students. Although it is possible for students to repeat a year, no student may be demoted a year. Draw a transition diagram to specify this constraint.

2. A *star network* has a centrally located file server directly linked to zero or more work-stations. A sample star network is shown. For each node the kind of computer is recorded (XT, AT or PS/2). Only for the file server is the processor type recorded. The maximum number of work-stations is 20. The cable distance (in metres) of each node from the file server is shown beside each link.

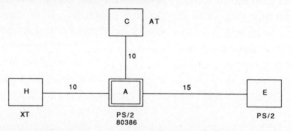

Specify the conceptual schema for this UoD. You may assume that the basic star configuration is understood by humans using the system.

3. A *ring network* has a central file server with work-stations arranged in a ring. A sample configuration is as shown. Details are as for question 2, except no metric information is required, and the information system should enforce the basic topological constraints. Specify the conceptual schema for this UoD.

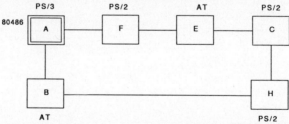

4. With reference to the Community-Roads UoD of Exercise 6.7, assume that roads are continuous, but may connect more than two communities. Discuss whether or not it is appropriate to use a ternary fact type of the form: Road connects Community to Community.

5. With reference to the Parts-explosion UoD of Exercise 8.3, an output report is required which displays parts contained at all levels (e.g. the fact that A contains part D is to be shown). Design a conceptual schema for this UoD.

Final checks

9.1 CSDP step 9: Final checks

Our conceptual schema design procedure facilitates early detection of errors by various checking arrangements including ongoing feedback to the user by way of examples. Nevertheless, it is still wise to include a final check to pick up any errors that might have slipped through. This step comprises three main phases as set out below.

CSDP *step 9: Check that the conceptual schema is consistent with the original examples, has no redundancy, and is complete*

We test for consistency by populating the schema with the original examples and confirming that this population is acceptable to the schema. The redundancy check involves ensuring that no elementary fact can appear twice. Our test for redundancy should encompass derived facts as well as stored facts. We check that the schema is complete by searching for an aspect of the problem being modelled which has yet to be formally captured in the conceptual schema (in particular, is there some constraint which we can express informally but which has as yet no counterpart in the schema?).

Step 9 is the last step in our conceptual schema design procedure. In the rest of this chapter we discuss each of its three stages in some detail. Although this is the last step in the design procedure, it is possible to design different but equivalent conceptual schemas for the same UoD. When it comes to implementing the conceptual schema efficiently on a particular software/hardware configuration, some versions provide a more direct mapping than others, and hence we may wish to perform a conceptual schema transformation before performing this mapping: this topic is addressed in the next chapter.

9.2 Population check

The first step of our CSDP was to express the information contained in a set of familiar examples in terms of elementary facts. These examples were typically output reports with small, but hopefully significant, sample populations. In step 2 we drew a draft schema

Table 9.1

	Person	Subject	Degree
	Ann	CS112	BSc
	Ann	CS100	BSc
	Bob	?	BA
	Sue	CS112	BA
	Tom	CS213	BSc

diagram and populated it with some of the original examples as a check that we had captured the fact types. In later steps various constraints were specified on the possible populations of these fact types. During these stages we often make use of schema-base diagrams to check our constraint specifications.

If not already done, we can perform a final check on the constraints by populating the schema-base diagram with the sample data, and looking to see if some constraints have been violated by the population. If they have, then the constraints are *too strong* in this respect, since they reject examples that are quite legal for the UoD. We should then modify the schema, typically by removing or softening some constraints, until the population is permitted. As a simple illustration, consider the UoD of Table 9.1. Notice the null value on row 3. We know that Bob seeks a BA degree but we do not know any of Bob's subjects.

Now suppose that we come up with the schema of Figure 9.1. Let us also suppose that we have performed step 1 properly, so the fact types are correct. But what about the constraints?

To help us decide, let's populate the fact tables with our sample data. This gives Figure 9.2. Consider first the uniqueness constraint on the Studies fact type. This asserts that each entry in the person column is unique (i.e., each person studies at most one subject). However, the entry "Ann" appears twice here. So this constraint is wrong. The population of the fact table makes it clear that the uniqueness constraint should span both columns.

Figure 9.1   Is this a correct conceptual schema for Table 9.1?

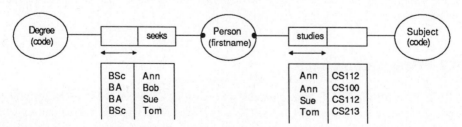

Figure 9.2   The constraints are inconsistent with the population

Now consider the uniqueness constraint on Person seeks Degree: this asserts that each entry in the degree column is unique. But the entry "BSc" appears twice there, and so does the entry "BA". The presence of either of these cases proves that this constraint is wrong. This does not imply that the correct uniqueness constraint should span both columns: although the population is consistent with this weaker constraint, it is also consistent with a uniqueness constraint over the Person column.

To decide between the two possibilities we need to know that the population is significant in this respect, or have the appropriate background knowledge. If the population is significant or we simply know that persons seek at most one degree then we should replace the old uniqueness constraint with one across the Person column for this fact type.

So while populating the schema with the original examples may detect constraints that shouldn't be there, this will not automatically reveal missing constraints. In other words, while this check can pick up aspects of the constraint section that are too strong, we require significant examples or background knowledge to determine whether the constraint section is *too weak* in other respects.

As a final illustration of this point, the null value in the output report has no explicit counterpart in the schema-base diagram, since elementary facts cannot have null values. But this itself reveals that the mandatory role constraint on Studies is wrong: so this role is optional. Of course, if we had correctly followed the design procedure at earlier stages, there would be no such errors in need of elimination. The corrected schema is set out in Figure 9.3.

Exercise 9.2

1. From the sample output report shown, a student draws the conceptual schema diagram shown. Check to see if the data in the original report can be a legal population of this schema. If not, modify the schema accordingly.

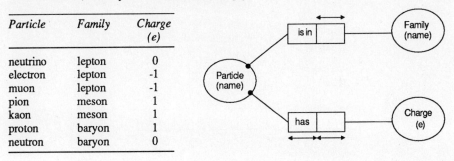

Particle	Family	Charge (e)
neutrino	lepton	0
electron	lepton	-1
muon	lepton	-1
pion	meson	1
kaon	meson	1
proton	baryon	1
neutron	baryon	0

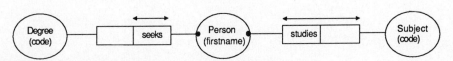

Figure 9.3 A correct conceptual schema for Table 9.1

9.3 Redundancy check

In our conceptual schema design procedure we have stressed the importance of avoiding redundancy. As explained in an earlier chapter, this is primarily motivated by a desire to avoid update anomalies, or inconsistencies that might arise as the facts in the database are changed. Most update anomalies can be tracked down to a redundancy of some kind.

The elimination of redundancy is also important for implementation, since the size of the database is thereby minimized. A tradeoff between this "space efficiency" and the "time efficiency" of execution speed may in practice favour some controlled redundancy in an actual implementation. But these are lower level concerns: at the conceptual level we should strive to eliminate redundancy completely. Firstly, we focus on getting a correct design: this is the hardest and most important aspect of the overall software development; later on we can consider issues such as speed.

There are two main kinds of redundancy that we should be on the look out for. The simplest case is *stored redundancy*. Here the same fact is actually stored more than once. At the fifth generation level, all recorded facts are elementary, and of course, no fact is recorded more than once. So provided our conceptual schema is correct, there will be no stored redundancy. However an incorrect conceptual schema can permit stored redundancy: this can happen if we have incorrectly included some non-elementary fact types in the schema.

In the arity checking step of our CSDP we provided a number of ways of checking whether fact types were elementary or not. One such method was to look for redundancy. Consider Figure 9.4, for example. The population shown is not fully significant, but let us proceed with it anyway.

The uniqueness constraint covers all but one role, so we cannot use this to determine splittability. However, a glance at the population reveals that various embedded tuples are repeated. For example, (105, Production) and (Accounts, BCom) each occur twice. This does not by itself entail redundancy. For any given state of the database, stored

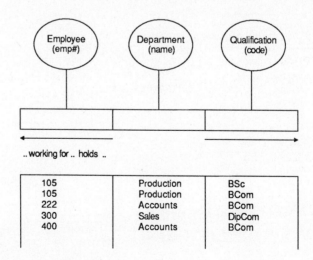

Figure 9.4 Is there redundancy here?

redundancy occurs if and only if an elementary fact is stored more than once. If the same tuple occurs twice we need to determine whether each occurrence of this tuple involves the same elementary fact: if so, we do have redundancy.

Now from the formal viewpoint of the system, until we specify an elementary fact type within the conceptual schema it doesn't make sense to say that facts of this type are repeated (because there are no facts of this type). So unless we have defined a binary fact type for one of the three binary tuple associations embedded within the ternary under discussion, tuple duplication does not mean redundancy.

If we have included a stored binary fact type whose entity types match two of those for the ternary, then we should have also included any equality, subset or exclusion constraint between this fact type and the embedded association. For instance, if we store the fact type Employee works-for Department we have an equality constraint between this and the embedded Employee-Department association. This really is redundancy. Even with a subset constraint we still have redundancy. A procedure for handling such cases is discussed in the next chapter.

If we wish to treat such an embedded association as a fact type to be *derived* from the host fact type then we simply include a rule for this. For example, using an extended Horn clause notation which supports both types and distfix operators, we might include the following rules:

Employee works for Department **if**   Employee working for Department
holds Qualification

Department has a worker with Qualification **if**   Employee working for Department
holds Qualification

With this arrangement it might be argued that whenever the relevant stored tuple is duplicated we have a very weak kind of "unavoidable redundancy". For example, the fact that the Accounts department has a worker with a BCom degree can be derived from either the third or fifth rows of the fact table shown. However, this kind of tuple duplication is harmless: it cannot lead to any update anomalies since such derived fact types are used only for queries, not for updates. From the system's viewpoint it is not actually storing the same fact twice, so it better not to call this redundancy at all.

Embedded tuple duplication is of particular interest when we consider schema transformations and relational database tables whose rows may comprise a conjunction of elementary facts. But for our present purposes such duplication is of little interest. As you no doubt noticed there is something wrong with the fact type under discussion: it is not elementary. If you can't see this yet, you may want to reread some of the chapter on arity checking until you can spot the problem.

Recall that a fact is elementary iff it can't be expressed as a conjunction of simpler facts. Now as a human familiar with the application it should be clear that a fact of the form:

Employee working for Department holds Qualification

can be rephrased as:

Employee works for Department **and**
Employee holds Qualification

So we really have two elementary fact types, not one. This linguistic approach utilizing human ability is the best way to perform the split. Alternatively, we might argue for splittability on a purely formal basis. For example, in the population of Figure 9.4 Department is functionally dependent on Employee. The formal approach relies on the population being significant. While the population is significant with respect to this FD (an employee can work for only one department), it is not significant in other respects. Formally, the projection-rejoin technique leads to other splitting possibilities (e.g. Employee-Department and Department-Qualification). The UoD expert should be consulted to reject such an alternative or add further data until the population is significant. For example, part of the meaning of row 1 of Figure 9.4 is that employee 105 holds a BSc degree.

In most cases it is easier for a human familiar with the application to perform the rephrasing than to provide a significant population. Typically, to be sure that a population is significant requires an understanding at least as thorough as that required for the rephrasing task. At any rate, we can now set out the correct schema (see Figure 9.5).

We note in passing that the embedded tuple duplication present in the original ternary has now been eliminated. As we have stressed however, it is still possible to have such duplication in legitimate elementary fact types. For example, the ternary in Figure 9.6 should be left as it is even though the subtuples (105,Harvard) and (Stanford,BCom) occur twice.

Except for the last row, Figure 9.6 has the same structure as Figure 9.4: only some of the identifiers have been changed. However, the last two rows show that an employee can receive qualifications from different universities. If instead we knew that each employee could attend only one university then of course the fact type would be splittable (how?).

Now let us turn our attention to *derived redundancy*. The most common case of this is when a recorded fact can be derived from other facts by means of specified derivation rules. The task of identifying derived fact types was introduced at step 3, where the markup of an article was derived by subtracting its wholesale price from its retail price.

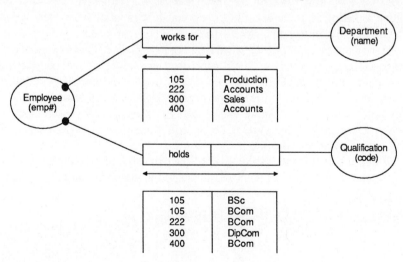

Figure 9.5   The correct schema-base diagram for Figure 9.4

Here, however, it would be redundant to store the markup values. If markup values are not stored then they need to be computed upon request: this has the disadvantage of adding slightly to the response time for markup queries.

If markup values are stored this takes up extra storage space. Moreover, if either the wholesale price or the retail price of an article is changed, then failure to update markup accordingly leads to an inconsistent database. If such an update anomaly can occur then the redundancy is "unsafe".

One can arrange for "*safe redundancy*" or "*controlled redundancy*" by having the derivation rule triggered by relevant updates. For example, the system can be configured to automatically "recalculate" the markup values whenever wholesale or retail prices are updated (we assume markup values may not be updated directly: this avoids the further overhead of a mutual recalculation between the three values). This kind of approach is often used with spreadsheets.

Before considering some more complex cases of derived redundancy, it will help to underline the difference between the open world and closed world assumptions, and to clearly distinguish between derivation rules and constraints.

The *open world assumption* (OWA) allows that the system may have *incomplete knowledge* about the UoD (where we take the UoD to embrace those aspects of the real world that we wish to model in the system). This assumption may be expressed as follows. Given any fact or proposition *p* about the UoD:

p is true **if** *p* is stored or derivable

Here "stored" means "expressed by sentences recorded in the database" and "derivable" means "definitely derivable by the system" (the system has an algorithm for deriving the fact). This assumption provides a sufficient but not a necessary condition for truth: there may be some true propositions about the UoD which are neither stored nor derivable (by the system). In contrast, the *closed world assumption* (CWA) demands that the system

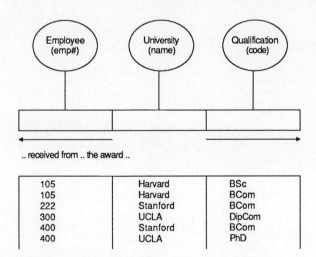

Figure 9.6 An elementary fact table can have duplicate subtuples

must have *complete knowledge* about the UoD. That is, given any proposition *p* about the UoD, the following biconditional holds:

> *p* is true **if and only if** *p* is stored or derivable

Let us agree that, without qualification, the terms "knowledge" and "known" refer to the *system's knowledge* of the UoD. Thus, given any proposition *p* about the UoD:

> *p* is **known** iff *p* is stored or derivable

The open and closed world assumptions may now be briefly defined as follows. Given any proposition *p* about the UoD:

> open world: *p* is true **if** *p* is known
> closed world: *p* is true **iff** *p* is known

Clearly the closed world assumption is stronger than the open world assumption. In NIAM, the open world assumption is understood by default. Unless explicitly stated otherwise, we allow that the system's knowledge of the UoD may be incomplete. Recall the example reproduced in Figure 9.7.

Notice the null values in the output report. With the open world assumption a "?" indicates that an actual value may exist but be unknown by the system. For example, it is possible that Tina drives the car 105ABC. With the closed world assumption a "?" indicates that no actual value exists. Thus if the following query is posed:

> Person Tina drives Car 105ABC?

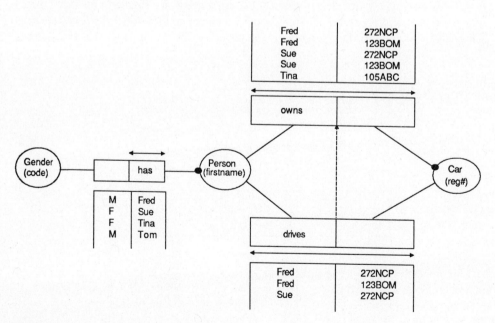

Figure 9.7   A UoD discussed in Section 8.2

the open world assumption yields the answer "Unknown" or "I don't know", whereas the closed world assumption yields the answer "No". With respect to any fact about the UoD, the open world assumption allows three possible answers (Yes, No, Unknown) whereas the closed world assumption allows only two (Yes, No).

The subset constraint in the schema may be expressed thus:

| **if** | Person drives Car | *is stored* |
| **then** | Person owns Car | *is stored* |

If the fact that a person drives a car is stored, then the fact that that person owns that car must also be stored. Like all other constraints, subset constraints are enforced whenever a relevant *update* operation is attempted. For example, if we wish to add the fact:

Person Tom drives Car 345ABC

then in the same transaction we must also add the fact:

Person Tom owns Car 345ABC

since this latter fact was not already stored. Let us suppose that we know from our human background that in this UoD people own the cars they drive, that is, if anybody drives a car then that person also owns that car. We may refer to such human knowledge as a *re[?] world constraint*, as distinct from a database constraint. We might state this real world constraint as follows:

RC1: Person owns Car *is true* if Person drives Car *is true*.

Now in modelling the UoD we want if possible to capture this real world constraint by means of some formal component of the conceptual schema. We can attempt to do this by means of a database constraint or a derivation rule or both. Let's examine these alternatives.

First let us consider using just a database constraint. This means that facts of the form *Person owns Car* and *Person drives Car* are only stored (not derived). Given this storage-only assumption, if we adopt the closed world viewpoint for this aspect of the UoD it is easily shown from our earlier definitions that the real world constraint RC1 is equivalent to the following subset constraint on the database:

C1: Person owns Car *is stored* if Person drives Car *is stored*.

We leave the proof of this equivalence as a simple exercise. If we adopt the open world viewpoint, then obviously RC1 cannot be enforced by the system (since its knowledge may be incomplete); however, given the storage-only assumption we can at least have the system enforce RC1 to the extent of its knowledge about people driving cars, again by enforcing the subset constraint C1.

Note that *C1 is a constraint, not a derivation rule*. C1 is used by the system only for checking updates of the following kinds: addition of a fact of type Person drives Car; deletion of a fact of type Person owns Car. It is sometimes argued that a subset constraint necessarily involves redundancy. But in the absence of a derivation rule, this does not follow. Although the tuple (Fred,272NCP) occurs in both the Drives and Owns fact tables, we have here two different facts, not two instances of the same fact.

However, from an implementation rather than a conceptual concern, you may wish to reduce the size of the database by introducing a derivation rule to avoid such duplicate tuples. To cater for RC1 we might introduce the derivation rule:

D1:   Person owns Car **if** Person drives Car.

At first glance, this approach seems fine. If we have recorded the fact that a person drives a car there is no need to record the fact that that person owns that car (since this can be derived). However, such an approach requires a great deal of care. Before discussing some of the possible pitfalls, let us clarify our derivation rule notation. Derivation rules are to be understood in terms of system knowledge. For instance, D1 should be interpreted as:

Person owns Car *is known* **if** Person drives Car *is known*

where "known" as usual means "known by the system", stored or derivable. From the closed world viewpoint, D1 is equivalent to RC1 since truth is then equivalent to knowledge. From the open world viewpoint, knowledge implies truth but not conversely; so as with the subset constraint approach, RC1 can be captured by D1 only to the extent of the completeness of the Drives knowledge (Person owns car is true if Person drives Car is known). In general, a derivation rule of the form:

q **if** *p*

is understood as   *q* is known **if** *p* is known

which implies   *q* is true **if** *p* is known

and in a closed world is equivalent to   *q* is true **if** *p* is true

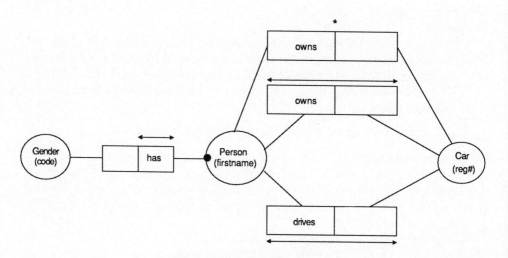

* Person owns Car   **if**   Person drives Car

Figure 9.8   Car ownership details are stored or derived

Note that derivation rules are different from database constraints. A database constraint places a restriction on facts that are stored, and is imposed by the system whenever a relevant update operation is performed. In contrast, a derivation rule indicates how a fact type may be derived and is used by the system to answer queries about that fact type.

Returning to our example, using the derivation rule D1 to cater for the real world constraint RC1 we might set out the schema in Figure 9.8. Notice that for the first time we have a fact type that is both stored and derived viz. Person owns Car. In this universe it is possible that a person owns a car but does not drive it. With our sample the fact that Sue owns car 123BOM has to be stored since it can't be derived (it is either unknown (OWA) or false (CWA) that she drives this car).

So far we have not specified any constraint between the stored fact types Person drives Car and Person owns Car: if we allow these to have intersecting tuple populations then we now have a case of derived redundancy. For instance suppose we store the following facts:

Person Fred drives Car 272NCP
Person Fred owns Car 272NCP

and later pose the query:

Person Fred owns Car 272NCP?

Clearly the system will answer "Yes". But the fact that Fred owns 272NCP is not only stored: it can be derived from the fact that Fred drives this car. In this case it is redundant to store the fact that Fred owns 272NCP since it can be derived. When confronted with such redundancy what should we do?

One possibility is to simply leave things as they are. We do not bother specifying any constraint between the two stored fact types. This permits the tuple populations to intersect, but apart from using up more memory this does no harm. The redundancy is safe because it cannot lead to update anomalies. For instance, when we add a Drives fact it doesn't matter whether or not we add the corresponding Owns fact: if we do, this takes up extra space but if the space is available this is alright; if we don't, then the Owns fact is still catered for by the derivation rule D1.

While it is safe to implement RC1 in this way, it is conceptually not as clean as the subset constraint approach discussed earlier. Nevertheless this kind of implementation is commonly used by Prolog programmers: when a fact type is partly stored and partly derived and a query requires a search of this fact type the stored part is typically searched first.

A second possibility is to add an exclusion constraint to prevent the same tuple appearing in both the stored Drives and Owns fact types. This leads to the schema of Figure 9.9. In this case there is no derived redundancy. Moreover, the fact storage space is minimized. But update anomalies can occur unless special update handling mechanisms are also specified.

To illustrate this point, consider the following sequence of user-CIP interactions, assuming that the population of the fact types is initially empty. The default reference modes (firstname and reg#) have been omitted. Assume the subset constraint is labelled "C1".

User	CIP
1. add: Person Fred has Gender M	accepted
2. add: Person Fred drives Car 272NCP	accepted
3. add: Person Fred owns Car 123BOM	accepted
4. add: Person Fred owns Car 272NCP	rejected: violates C1
5. del: Person Fred drives Car 272NCP	accepted
6. Person Fred owns Car 272NCP?	No

Check for yourself that requests 1–3 should be accepted. Request 4 is rejected in order to prevent the same tuple being stored in both the Drives and Owns fact tables (which would violate the exclusion constraint, and mean the fact that Fred owns 272NCP is both stored and derivable). Suppose now that although Fred still owns 272NCP, he no longer drives it (e.g. he may have failed his licence renewal test): to indicate this change in the UoD request 5 is made, and accepted. This simplistic response by the CIP leads to problems. For example, request 6 now yields the wrong answer.

Clearly, if we wish to pair a derivation rule with an exclusion constraint in this way, we will have to specify a *special dynamic constraint* to prevent such anomalies occurring. This additional constraint can be expressed in words as follows:

> Before deleting any fact of the form Person drives Car, check with the user whether the corresponding fact Person owns Car should now be stored.

Note that, unlike the constraints we usually discuss, this is not a static constraint; nor is it a simple transition constraint, since it requires dialogue with the user. We may think of it as a special dynamic constraint that specifies an action to be taken when a particular kind of update is attempted. In a later chapter we introduce other concepts to describe this situation (e.g. a process being *triggered* by an event). As a reminder that the constraint

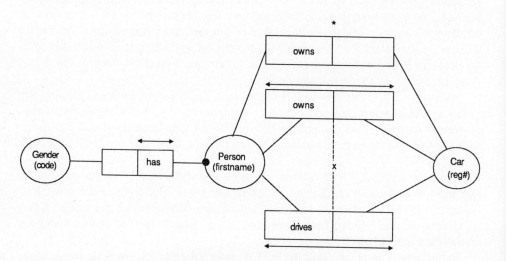

* Person owns Car **if** Person drives Car

Figure 9.9 This approach reduces storage but complicates updates

between the Owns and Drives fact types is more than just a simple exclusion constraint, we add a plus sign "+" to the exclusion constraint symbol:

$\times^+$

The additional details describing this constraint should be included in textual form below the schema diagram (together with the related derivation rule). With this arrangement, the previous user-CIP interaction sequence remains the same for requests 1–4, but the rest is altered as shown, assuming the user responds in the affirmative:

User:	del: Person Fred drives Car 272NCP
CIP:	Should I store: Person Fred owns Car 272NCP?
	(not derivable after delete)
User:	Yes
CIP:	deletion accepted; formerly derivable fact now stored
User:	Person Fred owns Car 272NCP?
CIP:	Yes

Although this approach now works, it is more complex than the subset constraint approach, particularly with respect to the managing of updates. As the following interaction makes clear, no special dynamic constraints are required for the subset constraint approach:

User	*CIP*
1. add: Person Fred has Gender M	accepted
2. add: Person Fred drives Car 272NCP	rejected: violates C1
3. begin	
add: Person Fred owns Car 272NCP	
add: Person Fred drives Car 272NCP	
end	accepted
4. add: Person Fred owns Car 123BOM	accepted
5. del: Person Fred drives Car 272NCP	accepted
6. Person Fred owns Car 272NCP?	Yes

So unless memory space is at a premium, the subset constraint approach has much to recommend it. From the *external* rather than the conceptual viewpoint, a user interface may be constructed to have the system add the required superset fact when required. For example, the following kind of interaction may be more convenient for the user:

User	*CIP*
1. add: Person Fred has Gender M	accepted
2. add: Person Fred drives Car 272NCP	also add: Fred owns 272NCP?
Yes	Both facts added
3. add: Person Fred owns Car 123BOM	accepted
4. del: Person Fred drives Car 272NCP	accepted
5. Person Fred owns Car 272NCP?	Yes

Here if the user had replied "No" at step 2 the system would reject the update.

Apart from stored and derived redundancy, redundancy can occur within the set of derivation rules. For instance, it might be possible to derive a fact in more than one way, using different rules. Moreover, some rules might be derivable from more primitive rules.

This situation is fairly common in formal inference systems, for example computer aided reasoning systems.

In a wider context, redundancy can sometimes be very useful from the point of view of information retrieval, understanding (e.g. human communication), and coping with partial system failure (e.g. backup systems). This book itself exhibits a great deal of redundancy (e.g. by repeating important points). Although this makes the book longer, it should make it easier to follow.

Exercise 9.3

1. Is the following schema guilty of redundancy? If it is, modify the schema to remove this defect.

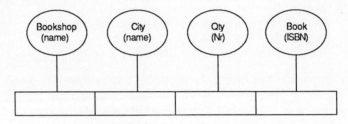

.. located in .. has ordered .. copies of ..

Bookland	New York	100	300705
Websters	New York	100	300705
Bookland	New York	50	123555
OKBooks	London	200	123555

2. With respect to the previous question, suppose it is now possible that bookshops in different cities have the same name. For example, the following population is legal:

Bookland	New York	100	300705
Websters	New York	100	300705
Bookland	New York	50	123555
Bookland	London	200	123555

Draw the correct conceptual schema diagram for this UoD.

3. Consider the following extract from an output report about people's eating habits.

Person	*Diet*	*Food*	*Foodclass*
Ann	NV	beef	meat
		chicken	meat
		beans	vegetable
		apple	fruit
Bob	V	beans	vegetable
		peas	vegetable
		apple	fruit

V   = vegetarian
NV = nonvegetarian

You may assume that for this UoD a diet is nonvegetarian iff it includes the foodclass meat. Set out the conceptual schema for this UoD:

(a) making the closed world assumption
(b) making the open world assumption (the sample is not significant)

4. Consider the following output report about programmers, the languages they use, know (are fluent in), and like.

Programmer	Uses	Knows	Likes
Ann	C COBOL SQL	BASIC C COBOL Pascal SQL	Pascal SQL
Bob	Pascal SQL	C Modula Pascal SQL	Modula Pascal SQL

Assuming the population is significant, specify the conceptual schema for this UoD:

(a) making no use of derivation rules
(b) making use of derivation rules (discuss the issues of redundancy and avoidance of update anomalies)

5. In Prolog, relations are often partly stored and partly derived. For example, at one state the knowledge base might consist of the following facts and rules:

```
parent_of(ann,bob).
parent_of(bob,chris).
grandparent_of (david,chris).
grandparent_of (X,Y) if parent_of(X,Z) and parent_of(Z,Y).
```

Discuss this situation making reference to the notion of derived redundancy.

6. An information system is to deal with various colours which are classified as primary (P), secondary (S) or tertiary (T). There are three primary colours: blue; red; and yellow. A secondary colour is comprised of a mixture of exactly two primary colours. A tertiary colour is comprised of exactly three primary colours.

Each colour has a unique, identifying trade name (e.g. "forest green"). The trade names of the primary colours are "blue", "red" and "yellow". Each colour has a (perhaps zero) percentage of blue, red and yellow. This percentage is expressed as a whole number in the range 0..100. For example, forest green is 70 percent blue and 30 percent yellow but has no red. The following extract from a sample output report indicates the sort of information that needs to be accessed.

Colour	% blue	% red	% yellow	Class
forest green	70	0	30	S
mud brown	30	30	40	T
red	0	100	0	P

It is required that the size of the database be minimized as much as possible by using derivation rules. For example, the percentage of a given colour that is yellow should be derived from the percentages for blue and red. Draw the conceptual schema diagram for this universe of discourse, clearly indicating all constraints. State clearly each derivation rule. In stating the rules you may use obvious abbreviations (e.g. "%B", "%R" and "%Y"). So long as circularity is avoided, the rule for computing the percent yellow may be assumed in formulating other rules (i.e. other rules may use the term "%Y").

9.4   Completeness check

In coming to the end of our conceptual schema design procedure, recall that in the software life cycle, design is traditionally preceded by specifying what tasks are to be performed by the information system. Now that the conceptual schema has been designed we should check that it provides an accurate and complete model of the UoD.

In particular we should look carefully to see if all the relevant UoD aspects have been catered for in the schema. One systematic way of performing this check is to draw up a table of two columns. In the first column, place a numbered list of all the UoD aspects (i.e. the relevant real world constraints and features): these may be expressed informally. Then label each of the constraints and derivation rules in the conceptual schema as "C1", "C2", "D1", "D2", etc. These should include all the constraints marked on the schema diagram as well as those expressed by other means (e.g. verbally or by a transition table), and the derivation rules.

For each row of the table, enter in the second column those aspects of the schema corresponding to the UoD aspect specified in the first column. The following illustration gives the general idea.

UoD aspects	Conceptual schema counterparts
1. Each person has exactly one gender	C3, C4
2. Gender is male or female	C2
...	...

Here C3 and C4 are uniqueness, and mandatory role constraints within a Person has Gender fact type: the labels "C3" and "C4" can be added beside these constraints on the schema diagram. As discussed in earlier work, sometimes we deliberately decide to make a constraint on the knowledge base different from its counterpart in the real world (e.g. we record only one phone number even if the person has more). Such differences should be spelt out here explicitly, and the reason for the difference documented.

If after performing this exhaustive check we find that some UoD aspects have been overlooked, we should find some way of catering for them in the conceptual schema, preferably on the schema diagram.

This completes the first run through of our conceptual schema design procedure. In terms of the software life cycle there are still several things to be done: transforming the design into one that can be implemented directly; external and internal schema design; implementation; testing; and maintenance. However, the most crucial and important stages of the cycle have now been considered.

10 Conceptual schema transformations

10.1 Conceptual schema transformations

In previous chapters we studied how to design a conceptual schema for a given application. In the next chapter we consider how to implement a conceptual schema by mapping it onto a relational schema. We have already noted that the same application may be modelled by more than one conceptual schema. For example, we might express a ternary fact type in either flattened or nested form. Conceptual schemas which describe the same UoD are said to be *semantically equivalent*.

> Given any two conceptual schemas A and B, we say that A is **equivalent** to B if and only if every state of affairs and state transition permitted by A is permitted by B, and vice versa.

This definition is rather informal. The notion of schema equivalence can be formalized in terms of logical equivalence by introducing an appropriate model theory and calculus. Similarly, other modalities such as implication and inconsistency can be given a firm logical foundation. However, it is our intention in this introductory text to place only minimal mathematical demands on the reader. Hence we deliberately avoid any serious attempt at full formalization.

If we design two different but equivalent conceptual schemas for the same application, then *conceptually* it doesn't really matter which one we pick. They both model the same UoD, and from the logical viewpoint both exhibit precisely the same behaviour: any update accepted/rejected by one is accepted/rejected likewise by the other; for the same query, both give the same answer. However, as will become apparent in the next chapter, from the *implementation* viewpoint, equivalent conceptual schemas are not necessarily equally *efficient*. For instance, some map directly onto relational database structures which are easier to work with.

The act of reshaping a conceptual schema into an equivalent one is said to be a **conceptual schema transformation**. A knowledge of schema transformations is important because it gives us flexibility in designing a schema. Such flexibility is often

Table 10.1

	Lecturer	Gender
	Halpin	M
	Nijssen	M
	Orlowska	F
	Raymond	F

Table 10.2

	Lecturer	Male	Female
	Halpin	1	
	Nijssen	1	
	Orlowska		1
	Raymond		1

needed if we are to merge subschemas. In practice, the most important application of schema transformations is in reshaping schemas into ones that provide direct mappings onto more efficient implementations.

In this chapter we investigate some of the main kinds of conceptual schema transformations. Although some of the ideas discussed here have been introduced earlier, we now provide a more detailed and systematic treatment. In particular, we discuss conversions between entity types and fact types, and objectification by composite definite descriptions as well as by nesting.

10.2   Entity type: Fact type conversions

In a certain university department, lecturers may be identified by surname. Table 10.1 is an extract from an output report listing the surname and gender of the lecturers.

This kind of example is familiar. We would typically read off the information on rows 1 and 3 as:

Lecturer (surname) 'Halpin' has Gender (code) 'M'.
Lecturer (surname) 'Orlowska' has Gender (code) 'F'.

which leads to the schema shown in Figure 10.1. Here we have two entity types but only one fact type. Given the format of the output report, this modelling by means of a binary fact type is natural.

Suppose however the output report was set out as in Table 10.2. Here a "1" indicates the lecturer is of that gender.

(S1)

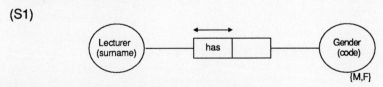

Figure 10.1   A conceptual schema for table 10.1

It is more natural now to read off the information in terms of unary facts. For example:

Lecturer (surname) 'Halpin' is-male.
Lecturer (surname) 'Orlowska' is-female.

This approach leads to the schema of Figure 10.2. Here we have two unary fact types but only one entity type. As humans we would usually regard these two schemas S1 and S2 as being equivalent. Although different, they appear to model the same aspects of the real world. For instance, the real world constraint that each lecturer has at most one gender is captured by a uniqueness constraint in S1 and by an exclusion constraint in S2. The constraint that gender must be recorded is handled by a mandatory role in S1 and a mandatory role disjunction in S2.

However, in agreeing that these two schemas are equivalent we have in fact used some background knowledge (e.g. that male and female are the only instances of gender, and that the codes "M" and "F" abbreviate "male" and "female"). Formally, the important aspect of these schemas which allows one to be transformed into the other is the fact that Gender has exactly two values. The underlying transformation rule T1 is set out in Figure 10.3, where A, B are entity type variables and r, r1 and r2 are role variables.

Although the schemas in our present example fit the pattern of this rule, we have used additional human knowledge to provide more natural identifiers. To the system, an identifier is just an uninterpreted character string. If presented with the schema S1 it can recognize that it is of the form of left hand schema in T1, by performing the substitutions:

A   =   Lecturer
B   =   Gender

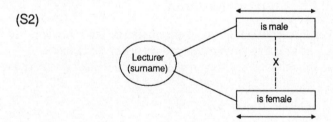

Figure 10.2   A conceptual schema for Table 10.2

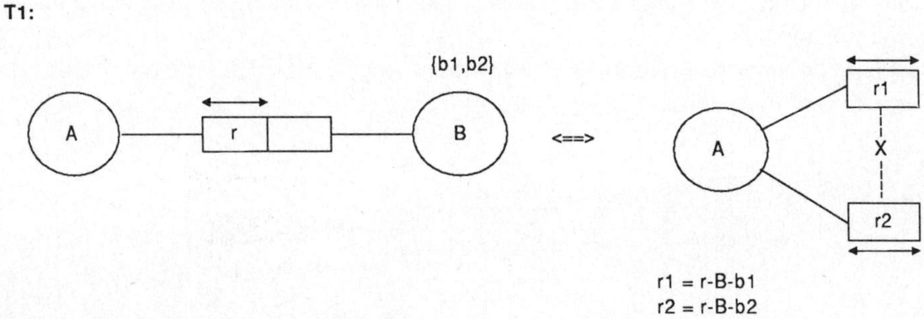

T1:

r1 = r-B-b1
r2 = r-B-b2

Figure 10.3   Two equivalent schema forms

```
r   =  has
b1  =  M
b2  =  F
```

Using T1 it can transform S1 into a schema with the structure of S2. However the role identifiers will be more stilted. Instead of "is-male" and "is-female" it will obtain, by substitution into r1 and r2, the schema S3 (see Figure 10.4).

Unless the system possesses a language translation facility this is as far as it can go unaided: it cannot generate the identifiers used in S2. However, the system can be easily programmed to request more natural identifiers from the human designer: with human input, S2 can then be produced.

Now consider the transformation of S2 into S1. S2 has the shape of the right hand schema in the rule T1, where:

```
A   =  Lecturer
r1  =  is-male
r2  =  is-female
```

Let us assume that the system knows that any is-value expression can be reworded in terms of a has-object-type-value expression. This entails that the system knows that S2 is equivalent to a schema with the shape of S1. Depending on the sophistication of the system's translation facility however, the resulting identifiers might turn out to be awkward (e.g. see Figure 10.5).

To carry the transformation all the way into S2 requires better identifiers (e.g. "Gender" instead of "MaleOrFemaleStatus"). This information can be provided simply through interaction with the human designer, or, with more programming overhead, through a more substantial translation facility. In spite of the fact that S1 and S2 may require further refinement of identifiers on top of the use of the transformation rule T1, we will in most cases speak of them as equivalent, since such translation refinements are

(S3)

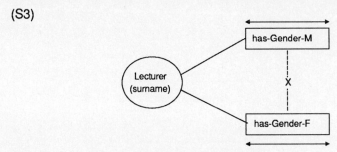

Figure 10.4   The result of applying T1 to schema S1

(S4)

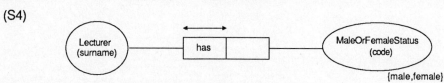

Figure 10.5   The result of applying T1 to schema S2

typically obvious to humans. Formal justification of such transformation rules requires use of definitions to map one theory onto another; for such proofs it is convenient to give primacy to the schema form with more object types.

The transformation rules apply to subschemas not just whole schemas. For example, suppose we record the birth year of each lecturer, and optionally their gender. In this case, schema S1 is a subschema of a larger schema in which the role born-in is mandatory for Lecturer but has-gender is optional. The subschema S1 may still be transformed into the subschema S2. In almost all practical applications the full schema will be much larger than the forms appearing in transformation rules. Care is sometimes required to ensure that transformation of subschemas does not generate problems with the global schema. A detailed treatment of this matter is beyond the scope of this book.

The transformation rule T1 is the simplest example of **entity type - fact type conversion**. Here *an entity type with a small number of values is replaced by an equal number of fact types, or vice versa.* Replacing or introducing the entity type respectively increases or decreases the arity of the fact types involved. By introducing an entity type, several unary fact types may be replaced by a single binary. For the unary case, the conversion to binary is generally preferred for a number of reasons. To begin with, this typically makes it easier to enforce the constraints (e.g. compare S1 with S2). The larger the number of possible values, the stronger this argument becomes. For example, compare the schemas in Figure 10.6 (reference modes have been omitted for simplicity).

Consider enforcing the constraint that each person belongs to at most one work class. With schema S5 this is neatly handled by the uniqueness constraint. With schema S6 three exclusion constraints are needed, two of which have to be checked each time a fact

(S5)

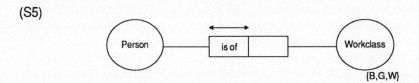

(S6)

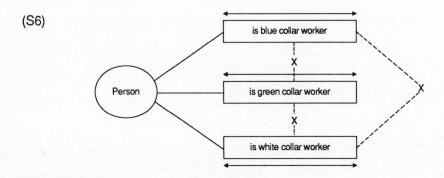

Figure 10.6   The binary version is preferable

is added to the database. In general, if there are *n* mutually exclusive options then the number of exclusion constraints needed is *1 + 2 +...+ n-1*. As an exercise show this.

When the number of unaries to be replaced is large, the binary version has the advantage of yielding a more compact schema. Moreover when the conceptual schema is mapped onto a relational schema (see next chapter) the binary approach leads to a more compact database. Compare Table 10.1 with Table 10.2. Unaries attached to the same entity type are typically mapped onto one table. Apart from a column for the entity type, each unary fact type requires another column in the table.

Another disadvantage of the unary approach is that update operations can become more complex. For instance, suppose we need to update a person's work class from blue to white. With the binary version, the conceptual deletion and addition is handled by a simple modify operation where a "B" value is replaced with "W". If the unary version is mapped onto a single table, two values in different columns need changing. If a different algorithm is used which maps each unary onto a separate table the situation is even worse: the update would require deletion of a fact from the blue collar table followed by addition of a fact to the white collar table. Such "jumping" between columns or tables is inefficient.

This criterion of avoiding jumping transitions should not be taken too strongly. It is of little relevance if the entity values involved are reasonably stable. For example, changes of workclass status might happen only very infrequently and changes of gender are certainly very rare!

While having separate tables for the unary fact types is less efficient for updates, it is more efficient for queries which require just one of these tables to be searched (e.g. list all the white collar workers). This kind of situation is typical: making an implementation more efficient in one way often makes it less efficient in other ways. In practice a good estimate of the likely frequencies of the relevant updates and queries is often used to determine the best trade-off for the given application.

With certain logical applications it is sometimes preferable to adopt the unary approach. For example, if doing so means that there is only one entity type in the UoD (e.g. Person or Number), then a simpler identification scheme is obtained, as well as simpler formulae within unsorted logic.

As indicated earlier, in practice the schemas to which we apply the transformation rules are just fragments within much larger schemas. It is often the case that a transformation on part of an overall schema has an impact on the rest of the schema. So in considering whether to apply a transformation we may need to look at the surrounding schema.

From all this you may have gathered that it is not always immediately clear which of a variety of equivalent schemas should be chosen for a particular application. This is true. However, by acquainting ourselves with the relevant criteria for making such a design decision, and using practical knowledge of the application's likely update/query pattern, we are in a position to make an informed selection. In some cases, the final selection is made only after testing a few prototypes.

So far we have considered two examples of entity type - fact type conversion. One of these involved two unaries and the other three. The transformation rule T2 expresses an obvious generalization to the case of *n* unaries (see Figure 10.7). To make it easier to express the fact that an exclusion constraint exists between each pair of unaries, we introduce a *circled cross notation to denote mutual exclusion among the connected roles.* Roles r_1 through r_n are mutually exclusive if and only if, given any state of the database,

$$pop(r_1) \cap pop(r_2) = \{ \} \ \& \ pop(r_1) \cap pop(r_3) = \{ \} \ \& \ .. \ \&$$
$$pop(r_{n-1}) \cap pop(r_n) = \{ \}.$$

Entity type - fact type conversions are also possible with fact types of higher arity. To illustrate this, we return to the Olympic UoD discussed in an earlier chapter. A sample output report is shown in Table 10.3.

In earlier work we portrayed this UoD in terms of the ternary fact type shown in Figure 10.8.

Notice that MedalKind has only three possible values. This gives us the opportunity to eliminate this entity type by replacing the ternary with three binaries, one for each of the three kinds of medal, as shown in Figure 10.9.

T2:

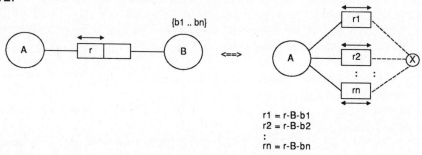

Figure 10.7   The general transformation for the unary case

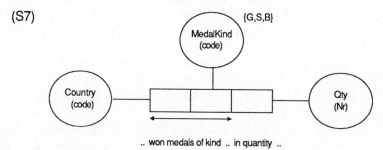

Figure 10.8   A conceptual schema for table 10.3 (ternary version)

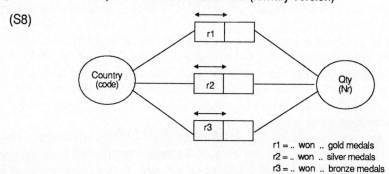

Figure 10.9   A conceptual schema for Table 10.3 (binary version)

Table 10.3

	Country	Medal	NrWon
	Japan	G	1
	USA	G	1
	USA	B	2
	USSR	S	2

We may generalize this kind of transformation by the rule T3 (see Figure 10.10). Note that if the role r is mandatory then so must be the disjunction of roles $r_1..r_n$.

Now look back at the output report (Table 10.3). We need to make a decision as to whether this is to be interpreted in terms of the open or the closed world assumption. Consider for instance the query:

How many bronze medals has Japan won?

If we adopt the open world viewpoint then our knowledge may be incomplete; so our reply to this question is "I don't know". In this case both the schemas S7 and S8 (Figures 10.8 and 10.9) are correct.

Suppose however we interpret the output report in terms of the closed world assumption. In this case our reply to the above question is "0". With this interpretation the previous schemas are incorrect. How should the schemas be set out for the closed world viewpoint? There are basically two ways of handling this. Recall that our standard method of enforcing aspects of complete knowledge is to add occurrence frequency constraints.

Before discussing this standard approach however, we note that another possibility is to simply indicate that the particular fact type is to be interpreted in terms of the closed world assumption. For example the notation "*cw" could be placed next to the fact types on the diagram; no corresponding notation is needed for the open world assumption since this is the default. With this addition to S7 and S8, the schemas may now be considered correct for the closed world view. The advantage of this approach of course is to eliminate the space and time requirements needed for recording results such as "Japan has won no bronze medals".

T3:

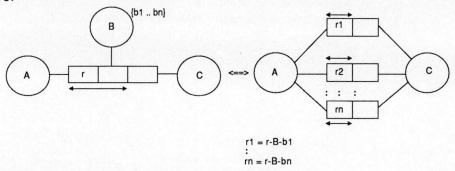

Figure 10.10 The general transformation for the binary case

Table 10.4

Country	Medal	NrWon
Japan	G	1
Japan	S	0
Japan	B	0
USA	G	1
USA	S	0
USA	B	2
USSR	G	0
USSR	S	2
USSR	B	0

Now let's consider our standard approach to enforcing aspects of complete knowledge. Let us agree that, for any country that has won a medal we must have complete knowledge of their medal wins. In other words we interpret Table 10.3 to mean the same as Table 10.4.

Let us also agree that we will not make use of derivation rules enabling zero wins to be deduced from absence of recorded wins. We are now forced to record the information in full. To cater for this, the ternary fact type in schema S7 needs to have an occurrence frequency (of 3) constraint added (consider Table 10.4). Moreover, let us assume that the the population of Country must participate in this fact type. This yields schema S9 (see Figure 10.11).

Notice the "*mandatory role dot*" in schema S9. If S9 is the global schema then this dot is redundant. If S9 is only a subschema of a global schema in which Country may play other roles, this dot asserts that the role is "*mandatory in the global schema*". To transform schema S9 into the binary version we now need to indicate that each of the three binaries must be recorded for each recorded country. This requires that each of the roles r1..r3 are mandatory, as shown in Figure 10.12.

Of course, if the role played by Qty in schema S9 is mandatory then so is the disjunction of roles played by Qty in schema S10. This kind of transformation may be generalized in terms of rule T4 (see Figure 10.13).

Now look back at schema S9, and suppose that the explicit mandatory role constraint does not apply. For example, the global schema might include a fact type in which all countries on our planet must have their capital city recorded. In this case, the transformation into three binaries can be made as in schema S10, but instead of roles r1..r3 being mandatory we assert the weaker condition of equality constraints between

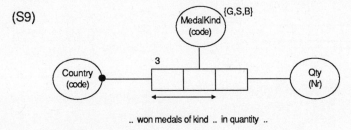

Figure 10.11   A schema for Table 10.4 plus explicit mandatory role

them. As an exercise, generalize this kind of transformation (call it rule T4') and draw a diagram to summarize the rule.

In deciding whether to apply transformation T3 or T4 to a schema fragment, it is important to consider how the fragment connects to the rest of the schema. For instance, if B plays other roles then the ternary version may well be preferred (Why?). On the other hand, if A plays other roles which are governed by a simple uniqueness constraint then the binary version may well be better since it reduces the number of tables required in a relational schema (this is discussed in the next chapter).

Exercise 10.2

1. A company committee has to decide on whether to increase its budget on staff training. With respect to this issue the current views of the committee members are indicated below:

For	Against	Undecided
Alan	Betty	Chris
David	Eve	Fred
Gerty		

(a) Set out a conceptual schema diagram for this UoD using only unary fact types.
(b) Transform this into an equivalent schema with no unaries.

(S10)

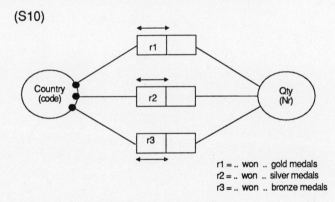

r1 = .. won .. gold medals
r2 = .. won .. silver medals
r3 = .. won .. bronze medals

Figure 10.12 A schema equivalent to that of Figure 10.11

T4:

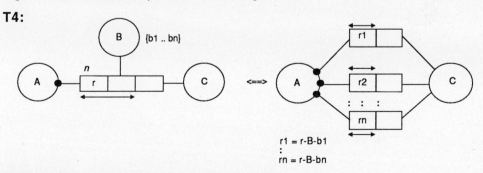

r1 = r-B-b1
:
rn = r-B-bn

Figure 10.13 A special case of the T3 transformation

2. The following table is an extract from an output report indicating quarterly sales figures for software products marketed by a particular company.

Software	Quarter	Sales ($)
database	1	200 000
	2	500 000
	3	500 000
	4	700 000
wordprocessor	1	90 000
	2	150 000
	3	155 000
	4	200 000
...		

(a) Draw the conceptual schema diagram for this UoD using a ternary fact type.

(b) Transform this schema into an equivalent one with smaller fact types.

3. The following conceptual schema is used for storing information about the amount of rain and sunshine in four states of Australia (New South Wales, Queensland, Victoria and Western Australia). Transform this schema into an equivalent one having the minimum number of fact types.

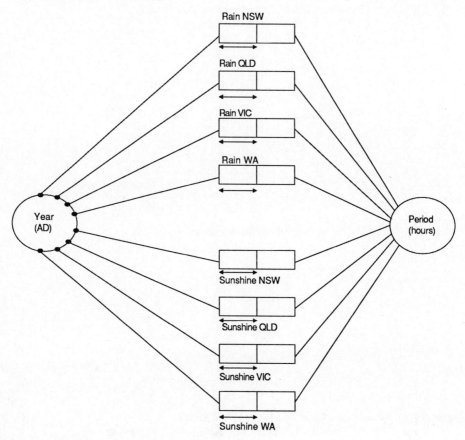

Table 10.5

	Student	Subject	Rating
	Adams	CS112	7
	Adams	CS100	6
	Adams	MP104	7
	Brown	CS112	6
	Brown	MP104	7

10.3 Nesting and flattening

In this section we discuss in some detail the nesting-flattening transformation. Simple examples of this transformation were considered in earlier chapters. For instance, from the output report of Table 10.5 we developed two alternative schemas.

The flattened version is reproduced as schema S11 (see Figure 10.14). The nested version is set out as schema S12 (see Figure 10.15). The underlying principle here is that a relationship between two or more objects may itself be regarded as an object: in this case we have an *objectified relationship*. Looking at the ternary fact type we may choose to treat the embedded association between Student and Subject as an object type which participates in a binary association with Rating: this leads to the nested version.

(S11)

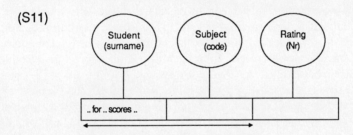

Figure 10.14   A schema for Table 10.5 (flattened version)

(S12)

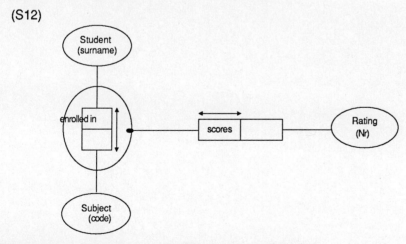

Figure 10.15   Another schema for Table 10.5 (nested version)

There are a number of points about this transformation that need to be well understood. Firstly, the formal equivalence between schemas S11 and S12 is based on permitted tuple populations involved rather than the identifiers used. In fact the provision of meaningful identifiers such as "enrolled in" to name the roles and object types is fundamentally a human rather than a system task (although part of this task can be automated). To clarify this it will help if we return to step 1. Consider the first line of the output report. One way of expressing this information is:

(F1)   Student (surname) 'Adams' for Subject (code) 'CS112' scores Rating (Nr) 7.

This leads to the flattened version. Another way of expressing the information is:

(F2)   Student (surname) 'Adams' enrolled in Subject (code) 'CS112'.
(F3)   *This relationship* scores Rating (Nr) 7.

This leads to the nested version. Here we use the term "relationship" (instead of "relation") to indicate a particular association between particular objects. The reference of the term "this relationship" above is the enrollment relationship between Adams and CS112. This reference is determined by the sequencing of the two sentences (and the conventions of English). Notice that because of the juxtaposition of the sentences there was no need to name the relationship.

Similarly, on a conceptual schema diagram, the ellipse around the relevant role boxes serves to identify the type of relationship being objectified. Moreover, the reference mode for this objectified relationship type is understood to be the concatenation of the reference modes involved. If it is desired to speak about the objectified relationship type, independent of the diagram, then it is convenient to add an object type identifier and make the reference mode explicit (see Figure 10.16).

Similarly, to specify a schema in textual rather than diagrammatic form one would normally name all fact types (alternatively, if all "primary" role names are unique these could be used for predicate names). From the point of view of a human examining a schema diagram however, such additional text is superfluous. Diagram S12 is usually preferable to S12' since it is less cluttered.

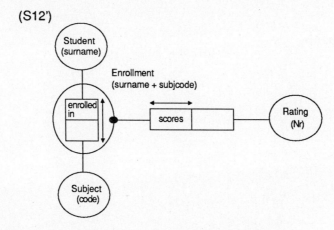

Figure 10.16   Reference included for objectified relationship type

Now consider the constraints in the nested version. The uniqueness constraint across the objectified relationship is consistent with the notion of an object type, and with the concatenated identification scheme: recall from earlier work that the uniqueness constraint for an objectified relationship must span the whole of this relationship. Notice the uniqueness and mandatory role constraints on the Scores role: whenever an enrollment fact (e.g. F2) is entered, a corresponding scores fact (e.g. F3) must be entered as well; also, a scores fact cannot be deleted without deleting its corresponding enrollment fact. By "corresponding" we mean the tuple of the enrollment fact matches the object playing the scores role. For instance, the schema-base diagram for the output report may be set out as shown in Figure 10.17.

Compare this with the schema-base diagram of the flattened version (see Figure 10.18). Using our human understanding of the UoD and the identifiers chosen for the role names, we have been able to populate the fact tables in accordance with the output report.

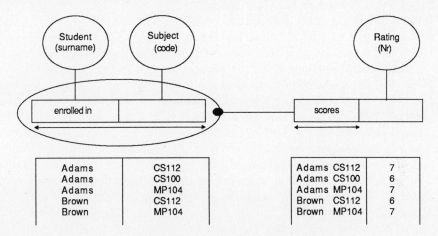

Figure 10.17 Schema-base diagram for Table 10.5 (nested version)

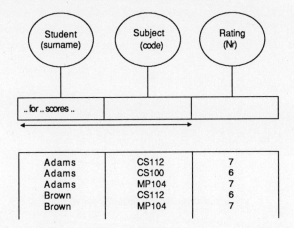

Figure 10.18 Schema-base diagram for Table 10.5 (flattened version)

Table 10.6

	Student	Subject	Rating
	Adams	CS112	7
	Adams	CS100	6
	Adams	MP104	?
	Brown	CS112	?
	Brown	MP104	?

What clearly emerges is a formal connection between the populations of the two schemas. Firstly, the population of the objectified relation matches that of the first two roles of the ternary. Secondly, if the concatenated values of the other binary are separated to become ordered pairs then the population of this binary expands to match the population of the ternary. For example, the tuple (Adams-CS112,7) becomes ((Adams,CS112),7) which expands to (Adams,CS112,7).

It is this formal connection between the populations (the relations in extension) which underlies the claim of equivalence in the nesting-flattening transformation. Using the notation $t(r)$ to denote the tuple vector formed by separating the concatenated values of role r, our current example generalizes to transformation rule T5 (see Figure 10.19).

Notice that this transformation rule does not specify how the role *names* used in one schema might assist in selecting the role names used in the other schema. A formal grammar involving structured identifiers might be devised to have the system make some suggestions here, but for this kind of transformation the task of selecting appropriate identifiers is probably best carried out completely by humans. In choosing identifiers, humans should ensure that the background meaning attached by humans to the identifiers does in fact agree with the formal extension equalities listed in the transformation rule. This still leaves quite a lot of possibilities. For example, instead of the identifier "..for..scores.." one might use "..enrolls in..obtaining.." or "..studies..resulting in a.."; instead of "enrolled in" and "scores" one might use "studies" and "results in".

Let us now consider some guidelines on when to choose between a nested and a flattened approach. If the situation is as simple as that shown in T5 (where a single, mandatory role is attached to the objectified relationship type), then the flattened version is generally preferable because it is simpler. But what if this role is *optional*? For example, suppose null values are allowed in the output report (see Table 10.6).

T5:

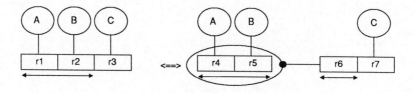

where for all states of the database: pop(r4,r5)   = pop(r1,r2)
                                        pop(t(r6),r7) = pop(r1,r2,r3)

Figure 10.19   Nesting-flattening transformations (2-role key)

There are several interpretations for the null values which might make sense here. For example, perhaps the MP104 exam is still to be held so results for it are not yet in; perhaps Brown was absent for the CS112 exam and has applied to sit for a special exam. At any rate, we now have a different situation. We want to be able to record that a student has enrolled in a given subject without at the same time recording the rating obtained. For instance, the information on the third row may be expressed as:

Student (surname) 'Adams' enrolled in Subject (code) 'MP104'.

This is a binary, not a ternary. So it would be wrong to schematize the output report in terms of a simple ternary (remember that at the conceptual level, null values are not allowed). In general, *the flattening transformation cannot be used if there is only one role played by the objectified relationship type and this is optional.*

For this application it might be argued that we really have two fact types, one concerning enrollment and the other concerning scores. This suggests the schema S13, which is embedded in a schema-base diagram for the output report (see Figure 10.20). Notice the *subset constraint*, indicating that for every state of the database the set of (Student,Subject) tuples recorded in the ternary is a subset of the set of (Student,Subject) tuples recorded in the binary. Check for yourself that the sample populations satisfy this constraint.

In other words, if we record the fact that a student scores a rating for a subject we must have also recorded the fact that the student enrolled in that subject. This is a sensible constraint to prevent us from recording ratings for students in subjects for which they did not enroll.

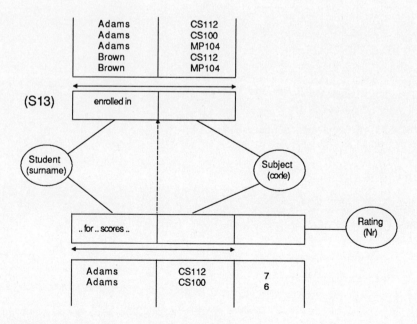

Figure 10.20 A schema-base diagram for Table 10.6

If S13 is a global schema then each of the roles in the binary fact type are mandatory (Why?). If S13 is a subschema these roles may be optional. It should be clear that the schema S13 is equivalent to the schema S14, which is identical to S12 except that the role attached to the objectified relationship type is now optional (see Figure 10.21). Recall that even in a subschema, any role that is mandatory for an objectified relationship type must be explicitly marked with a dot.

This kind of equivalence generalizes to transformation rule T6 (see Figure 10.22). Here, apart from their structural context, the roles r5 and r7 may be regarded as effectively the same. Similarly, in rule T5 the roles r3 and r7 are effectively the same.

With respect to the equivalent schema fragments in T6, the nested version is usually preferable. This is especially the case if the schema is to be implemented in a relational database system by using the ONF algorithm, since here nesting leads to a single table while the flattened version leads to two tables (we discuss this in the next chapter).

From the conceptual point of view, it may be argued that the nested version is preferable since the flattened version comes very close to exhibiting redundancy. Certainly there is duplication of tuples, since any (r3,r4) tuple is also stored as an (r1,r2)

(S14)

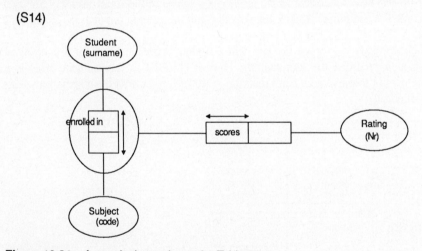

Figure 10.21 An equivalent schema for Table 10.6

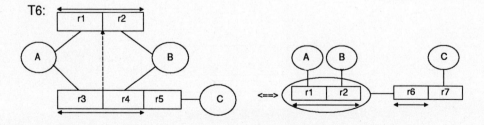

where for all states of the database pop(t(r6),r7) = pop(r3,r4,r5)

Figure 10.22 The transformation when the role r6 is optional

Table 10.7

Subject	CS102		CS113	
Student	Assign	Exam	Assign	Exam
Adams	27	65	25	68
Brown	20	50	20	50
Collins	27	65	25	67
Dancer	10	20	12	20

tuple. However the subset constraint makes this duplication safe; moreover, so long as the roles r3, r4 are treated as different from the roles r1, r2 there is formally speaking no fact redundancy. So while the flattened version in T6 is generally not recommended, we do not rule it out as totally illegal.

With respect to tuple duplication, the nesting transformation of T6 may be considered a special case of the following principle: *whenever overlap between (compatible polyadic) relations is possible, the duplication of the intersection between these relations can be avoided by forming an object type equal to the **union** of the relationship types.*

By "compatible" relations we mean the same entity types are involved with both relations. We allow that the relations may be *partial* (projections of a longer relation); a relation that is not partial is said to be *whole*. For the moment let us restrict ourselves to cases where R and S are binary relations spanned by uniqueness constraints, as indicated in Figure 10.23.

The precise form of the transformation depends on the kind of overlap between R and S (proper, subset or equality) and on whether R or S are partial or whole relations. For the T6 transformation just considered, S is a subset of R (and hence R = R ∪ S), S is partial and R is whole: this is the most common case. Let's have a brief look at some of the other cases now. Consider the output report extract shown in Table 10.7.

Performing step 1 we might express the information as follows (here the reference modes are listed initially and assumed thereafter):

Student (surname); Subject (code); Mark (Nr)
Student 'Adams' in Subject 'CS102' obtains Mark 27 for assignment.
Student 'Adams' in Subject 'CS102' obtains Mark 65 for exam.
Student 'Adams' in Subject 'CS113' obtains Mark 25 for assignment.

...

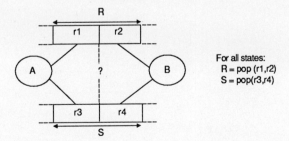

Figure 10.23   How much do R and S overlap?

This suggests the schema S15 involving two ternaries (see Figure 10.24). Notice the *equality constraint* between the partial relations pop(r1,r2) and pop(r4,r5). If Table 10.7 is the only output report for the UoD, then S15 is the global schema. In this case the equality constraint implies that roles r1, r2, r4 and r5 are mandatory. If S15 is a subschema these roles may be optional.

If we use R and S to denote the partial relations connected by the equality constraint, we now have the extreme case of total overlap where R = S. To avoid this tuple duplication we objectify the union (here R ∪ S = R = S) and adopt the nested approach of schema S16 (see Figure 10.25).

Here more than one role is attached to the objectified relationship type: as remarked in earlier work, the nested version is generally preferable to the flattened version in such cases. Of course, if the assignment and exam marks were optional (e.g. we wish to record enrollments before any marks) the flattened version could not be used at all (Why?). In the next chapter we will see that when mapped onto a relational schema the nested schema S16 leads directly to a single table whereas the flattened schema S15 produces two tables.

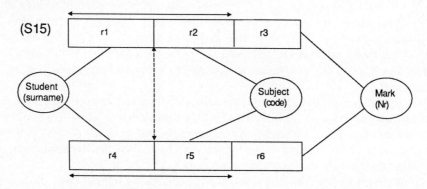

Figure 10.24   A schema for Table 10.7

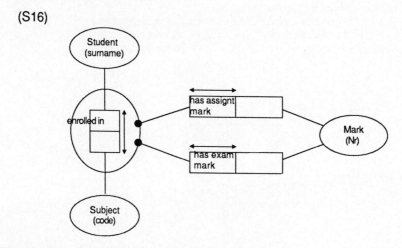

Figure 10.25   A better schema diagram for Table 10.7

Table 10.8

Student	Subjects enrolled	Subjects passed
Adams	CS112,CS100,MP104	CS112,CS100
Brown	CS112,MP104	CS112
Casey	CS112,CS100	?

Sometimes we run into a case where a whole relation must be a subset of another. For instance consider the output report of Table 10.8.

Here we are not interested in the ratings students obtain for subjects: just whether or not they have passed. Schema S17 provides one way of describing this situation (see Figure 10.26). If S17 is the global schema then the subset constraint implies that both roles in the enrollment fact type are mandatory (Why?).

Notice that the Passed relation is whole, as well as being a subset of the enrollment relation. How would you go about eliminating the tuple duplication in this case? See if you can solve this problem yourself before peeking at the equivalent schema S18 (see Figure 10.27).

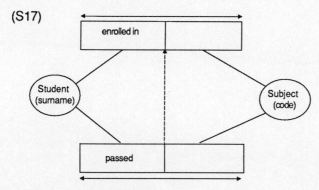

Figure 10.26 A schema diagram for table 10.8

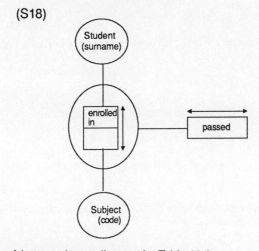

Figure 10.27 A better schema diagram for Table 10.8

Notice how the binary Passed fact type has been replaced by an optional role attached to the objectified enrollment fact type. Again, the nested version is generally preferable to the flattened version. You may be tempted to replace the unary with a binary (e.g. Enrollment obtains Grade, where Grade has two values (pass, fail)). However this assumes that the output report is to be interpreted so that if a student is not recorded as passing then that student has failed. Clearly, the status of absent and null values needs to be determined by the human designer before such a pass/fail fact type can be introduced. The equivalence between schemas S17 and S18 does not depend on such interpretation issues.

The examples discussed should be sufficient to indicate how tuple duplication can be eliminated by objectifying the union of compatible relationship types. For the kinds of situation discussed, a transformation algorithm is briefly sketched in Figure 10.28.

So far we have restricted our attention to objectifying binary relationships spanned by a uniqueness constraint. In the absence of such a uniqueness constraint, the binary can still be objectified but of course the attached fact type can no longer have a simple key (Why?). Compare the transformation rule T7 (see Figure 10.29) with T5 (Figure 10.19).

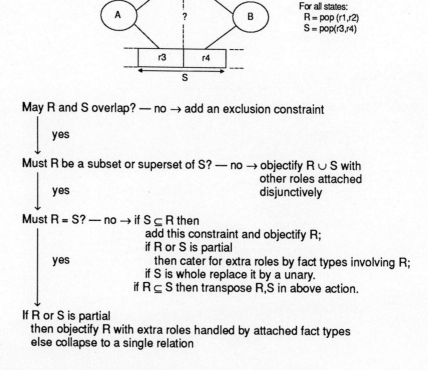

For all states:
R = pop (r1,r2)
S = pop(r3,r4)

May R and S overlap? — no → add an exclusion constraint

↓ yes

Must R be a subset or superset of S? — no → objectify R ∪ S with
other roles attached
disjunctively

↓ yes

Must R = S? — no → if S ⊆ R then
add this constraint and objectify R;
if R or S is partial
then cater for extra roles by fact types involving R;
if S is whole replace it by a unary.
if R ⊆ S then transpose R,S in above action.

↓ yes

If R or S is partial
then objectify R with extra roles handled by attached fact types
else collapse to a single relation

Figure 10.28 A transformation algorithm based on degree of overlap

Recall that the pop operation applied to a table returns a projection (a tuple set with duplicates removed), so the uniqueness constraint across (r4,r5) makes sense; the lack of such a constraint across (r1,r2) is catered for by the lack of one for r6. It should be clear that instead of objectifying the A-B relationship, one may objectify the A-C relationship or the B-C relationship. As an exercise, consider the three ways of applying this transform to the fact type: City in Year has Population.

The transformations discussed in this section can be generalized to n-ary fact types. Consider a flattened fact type of arity n with a uniqueness constraint spanning u roles where $n = u + 1$ (u must be at least n - 1, otherwise the fact type is splittable). The relationship type comprising the u roles may be objectified, with an attached unique role connected to the remaining role. Figure 10.30 gives the basic idea.

In the case where the uniqueness constraint spans the whole of the fact type ($u = n$), the objectification may be made on any role sequence but the uniqueness constraints on both objectified and attached sections must span the whole section, as indicated in Figure 10.31.

T7:

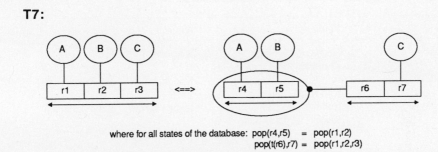

where for all states of the database: pop(r4,r5) = pop(r1,r2)
pop(t(r6),r7) = pop(r1,r2,r3)

Figure 10.29 Nesting-flattening transformations (3-role key)

T8:

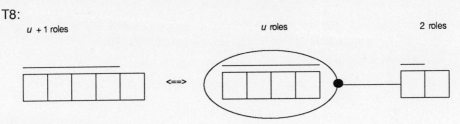

Figure 10.30 Nesting-flattening transforms (shorter key)

T9:

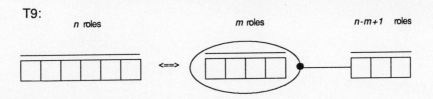

Figure 10.31 Nesting-flattening transforms (full length key)

It should be borne in mind that the transformation rules T8 and T9 may be applied recursively. For example, a flattened quaternary may be nested, and then the result may be nested again, as indicated in Figure 10.32.

Generally speaking, the nested approach has to be used if the attached role is optional, and is preferably used if it avoids tuple duplication. In other cases the flattened approach is usually better. In some cases, the picture is complicated by overlapping uniqueness constraints (e.g. the final equivalence discussed in Section 4.3), mandatory/optional patterns or other features (e.g. the uniqueness constraints on overlapping relations may differ).

Exercise 10.3

1. The following table is an extract from an output report concerning the finals of a recent judo competition. For each weight division, the four clubs which made it to the finals are recorded, together with the results for first and second places. For a given weight division a club can obtain at most one place.

Event	Finalists	Winner	Runner-up
Lightweight	Budokan, Judokai, Kodokan, Zendokan	Kodokan	Judokai
Middleweight	Budokan, Judokai, Kodokan, Zendokan	Kodokan	Zendokan
Heavyweight	Budokan, Kanodojo, Kodokan, Mifunekan	Mifunekan	Kodokan

(a) An information designer schematizes this UoD in terms of three fact types: Club is finalist in Event; Club wins Event; Club is runner-up in Event. Set out this conceptual schema including all constraints.

(b) Using a fact type to entity type transformation, convert this schema into an equivalent one involving one binary and one ternary fact type.

(c) Transform this schema into an equivalent nested version.

(d) Which of the three schemas would generally be preferable?

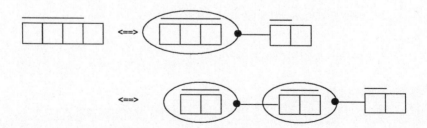

Figure 10.32 Transforms may be applied more than once

2. The following is an extract from a yearly output report giving test results of reaction time (in milliseconds) and resting heart rate (in beats per minute) for members of a health club. As the table indicates, the club may gain or lose members during the year.

Month	Member	Reaction time	Heart rate
Jan	Jones	250	80
	Matthews	320	120
	Robinson	300	100
Feb	Jones	250	75
	Matthews	300	100
Mar	Anderson	250	80
	Matthews	280	85
...	...	...	...

(a) Schematize this UoD in terms of two ternaries.

(b) Transform this by nesting.

(c) Which of the two schemas is generally preferable?

3. The following output report indicates the performance of students in subjects in a given semester. Once a student has failed a subject in the semester, the subject cannot be passed by the student in that semester. As students pass or fail subjects these results are recorded. In certain states it is possible that a student might have neither passed nor failed a subject taken (e.g. the MP104 exam may yet to be held).

Student	Subjects taken	Subjects passed	Subjects failed
Adams	CS100,CS112,MP104	CS100,CS112	?
Brown	CS112,MP104	CS112	?
Casey	CS100,CS112	?	CS100,CS112

(a) Schematize this UoD using three binaries.

(b) Transform this into a schema with an objectified binary with two attached unaries.

(c) Transform the two unaries into a binary.

(d) For this UoD is it possible that the null value for Adams might be updated to an actual value? What about the null value for Casey?

10.4 Composite definite descriptions

In the state of Queensland, electricity bills are issued every three months. Table 10.9 is an extract from an output report concerning the quarterly electricity bills for a particular household.

This may be schematized in flattened form as shown in Figure 10.33.

From our discussion of the nesting transformation, it is clear that this ternary may be transformed into the schema shown in Figure 10.34.

Table 10.9

Electricity bill:	Year	Quarter	Cost($)
	..	..	..
	1987	3	230
	1987	4	200
	1988	1	230
	1988	2	280
	1988	3	300
	..	..	..

Nesting provides one way of objectifying the relationship type between Year and Quarter. Recall that this object type is identified by concatenating the participating reference modes (e.g. "1987 3" is the compound label for one instance). For the case being discussed it is fairly natural to think of Electricity Bill as an entity type. If we think of an electricity bill as being identified here by its year and quarter, then it is easy to see that the schema of Figure 10.35 is equivalent to the nested version of Figure 10.34. Indeed, the difference between these two schemas is basically only cosmetic.

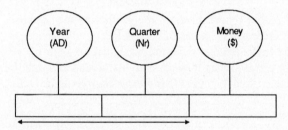

In the year .. for the quarter .. the electricity cost ..

Figure 10.33   A schema diagram for Table 10.9

(S2)

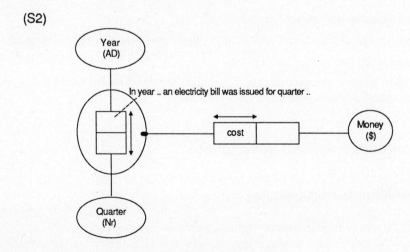

Figure 10.34   A nested schema diagram for Table 10.9

Table 10.10

Bill#	Year	Quarter	Cost($)
..	..	..	..
346	1987	3	230
593	1987	4	200
792	1988	1	230
904	1988	2	280
1090	1988	3	300
..	..	..	..

Notice that the entity type Electricity Bill does not have a simple 1:1 naming convention. Instead it is identified by a *composite definite description*, as indicated by the uniqueness constraints. For example, the first fact listed in the output report may be expressed as:

The Electricity Bill of Year (AD) 1987 for Quarter (Nr) 3
cost
Money ($) 230.

Clearly, for this kind of object type introduction a set of transformation rules holds which are analogous to the objectification transformations discussed for nesting in the previous section. For instance, T5 has the analogous transformation rule shown in Figure 10.36.

So long as the new entity type is standardly identified by a compound definite description, the transformation rules are analogous to the ones for nesting. However, in some cases it is convenient to introduce a standard 1:1 reference scheme for the new entity type. This changes the situation somewhat. For example, suppose that a bill number is used to identify electricity bills. The output report would now be different (see Table 10.10).

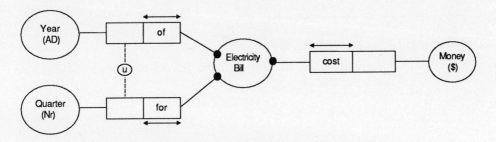

Figure 10.35 Bill is identified by a composite definite desciption

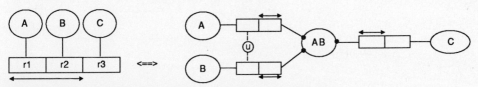

Figure 10.36 Object types may be introduced for convenience

The usual interpretation of such a report is that Bill# is being used as the standard identifier for the electricity bill. Although the combination of year and quarter could in principle also be used to identify the bill, we now have the situation in which the relationships between the entities of type ElectricityBill, Year and Quarter can be expressed in terms of facts rather than references. For example:

ElectricityBill (bill#) '346' was issued in Year (AD) 1987.
ElectricityBill (bill#) '346' was issued for Quarter (Nr) 3.

This change is catered for by including the reference type Bill# in the schema as shown in Figure 10.37.

In this chapter we have considered three basic kinds of transformations which enable a schema to be reshaped into an equivalent schema: entity type/fact type conversions, nesting/flattening, and objectification by composite definite description. In practice these are the most important equivalences. Other kinds of transformation are possible (e.g. those involving other constraints or derivation rules) but will not be detailed in this introductory text.

Exercise 10.4

1. The following table is an extract from a report indicating the rooms and times for lectures in various subjects.

Subject	Time	Room
CS213	Mon 3 pm	B19
CS213	Wed 9 am	A01
CS213	Wed 10 am	A01
EN100	Mon 3 pm	F23
EN100	Mon 3 pm	G24
..		

(a) Schematize this UoD in terms of a ternary fact type.

(b) A lecture may be defined by its room and time. Set out an alternative schema in which Lecture features as an entity type.

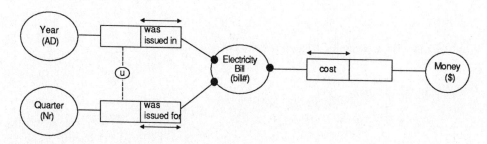

Figure 10.37   Bill identified by bill#

2. The following table indicates where certain objects are placed in three dimensional space (x, y, z are the Cartesian coordinates).

object	x	y	z
A	3	1	0
B	3	1	2
C	0	1	2
...			

(a) Schematize this in terms of three binaries.

(b) Set out an alternative schema using Position as an entity type.

3. The following examples are extracts of output reports from an information system about media channels. Each channel (TV or radio) has a unique, identifying callsign. All TV channels are rated in the range 1..7 in three categories on two surveys. All commercial radio channels have their audience composition assessed (see pie charts). A hyphen "-" means "not to be recorded".

TV channels:

call sign	ownership	ownership details company	% share	head office
ATQ8	commercial	MediaCo	100	Brisbane
CTQ3	commercial	MediaCo	50	Brisbane
		TVbaron	50	Sydney
TVQ3	govt.	-	-	-

Radio channels:

call sign	ownership	ownership details company	% share	head office	modulation	music played
4BZ	commercial	MediaCo	100	Brisbane	FM	rock country
RB3	govt.	-	-	-	AM	-
STR5	commercial	MediaCo	30	Brisbane	AM	country
		OzRadio	70	Cairns		
4AA	govt.	-	-	-	FM	-

TV survey ratings:

channel	survey	news	category drama	sport	totals
ATQ8	A	5	3	3	
	B	4	4	3	22
CTQ3	A	5	3	4	
	B	5	4	5	26
TVQ3	A	3	4	4	
	B	2	4	5	22

Audience composition of commercial radio channels:

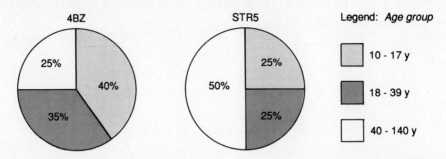

Draw a conceptual schema diagram for this UoD. Include *uniqueness, mandatory role, occurrence frequency* and *subtype constraints*, as well as relevant *label type constraints*. Provide meaningful names and definitions for each subtype. If any fact type is derived, include it on the diagram and provide a derivation rule. Do not nest any fact types. *Minimize the number of fact types* in your solution (if necessary make use of transformation rules to achieve this).

11 Relational implementation

11.1 Implementing a conceptual schema

Now that we have seen how to design a conceptual schema, we turn to the practical question of implementing this schema on a particular software/hardware configuration. The choice of such a configuration is quite important, especially the software. Ideally, an efficient implementation of a truly fifth generation language might be selected.

At the current time, there are a few very high level languages which enable, with different degrees of ease and completeness, a conceptual schema to be added directly to the system. One such language is RIDL (Reference and IDea Language): this allows us to define elementary fact types, constraints and even subtypes directly using schema statements; work statements may then be used to update the database and to issue queries. The terminology of RIDL closely resembles the terminology we have used in our schema design work. For example, consider the simple schema of Figure 11.1.

This schema might be entered in RIDL as follows:

add conceptual schema Staff-payments
add nonlex Employee(emp#), Money($)
add fact Salary
    roles (Employee earning, Money earned-by)
add fact Taxation
    roles (Employee paying-tax-of, Money paid-as-tax-by)
add constraint One-salary-per-employee
    condition Employee earning **only-one** Money **holds**
add constraint One-tax-per-employee
    condition Employee paying-tax-of **only one** Money **holds**
add constraint Each-employee-must-earn-a-salary
    condition Employee **always** earning Money **holds**
add constraint Employee-must-pay-tax
    condition Employee **always** paying-tax-of Money **holds**

Here reserved words in RIDL are shown in bold. Firstly, the entity types and reference schemes were entered, then the fact types, and finally the uniqueness and mandatory role constraints. Every component is named. Role names are often given in the form shown (e.g. "earning" rather than "earns") to make queries appear more like natural English. Facts may be added or deleted, and queries formulated declaratively. For example:

add Employee 'A234' **is** earning Money 40000
list Employee earning Money > 30000

The system responds to the above query by listing the employee numbers of all employees earning a salary over $30,000. Being a hybrid language, RIDL also allows queries to be formulated in a procedural fashion (e.g. by means of **for** loops).

Such very high level languages are not yet widely available. In practice, we usually need to be able to implement our conceptual schema in database languages which are readily available and widely supported today. The most generally suitable of these are the fourth generation languages used with *relational database management systems (RDBMSs)*. Of these, by far the most important is *SQL* (Structured Query Language).

Relational DBMSs are based on a data model which is simpler and easier to use than that of traditional database systems such as inverted list, hierarchic and network models. Recent improvements in efficiency have resulted in a growing acceptance of the relational approach, and SQL has become the dominant relational language used in the commercial environment.

Besides its status as a de facto standard, SQL has recently been adopted by ANSI for standardization. It is available on mainframes, minicomputers and even microcomputers, and runs under the standard commercial operating systems. Most commercial database products that are not built around SQL are at least adding SQL interfaces. For such reasons, our implementation examples will focus on relational database systems and SQL systems in particular.

In practice, SQL is often used in conjunction with other languages such as COBOL, Pascal, C and Prolog, as well as fourth generation application tools. While SQL facilitates many database tasks (e.g. ad hoc queries), other languages may be better at other tasks (e.g. certain kinds of constraint enforcement, screen display and report design). The ongoing development of environments which allow these languages to "talk to one another" is considerably simplifying the overall coding of applications which utilize a combination of languages and tools.

Some basic ideas about relational database systems were introduced in earlier chapters and in the next section we summarize these points and expand briefly on them. We then discuss an algorithm for mapping a conceptual schema onto a relational schema (a set of table definitions, constraints and derivation rules that can be implemented in an RDBMS). The relational schema obtained by this Optimal Normal Form (ONF) algorithm depends on the precise shape of the original conceptual schema. We show how more efficient relational schemas may be obtained by judiciously transforming the conceptual schema before applying the ONF algorithm. The chapter concludes with a comparative discussion of an inferior but popular table design procedure known as "normalization".

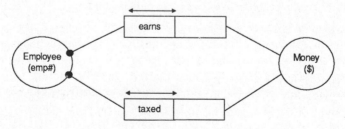

Figure 11.1   A simple conceptual schema

Table 11.1

Member	Gender	Phone	Art	Rank
Adams B	M	2052777	judo	3dan
			karatedo	2kyu
Adams S	F	2052777	judo	2kyu
Brown C	F	3579001	?	?
Collins T	M	?	aikido	2dan
			judo	2dan
Dancer A	F	?	?	?

11.2 Relational schemas

We define a **relational schema** to be a description of the UoD structure in terms of constructs supported by relational database systems. In contrast, a conceptual schema is implementation independent. Once designed, it can be mapped onto a variety of implementations (e.g. network, hierarchic or relational database models). In this section we describe the basic features of a relational schema and introduce a concise notation for setting it out. An algorithm to map from a conceptual schema to a relational schema is discussed in the next section.

Some of the main ideas about relational database systems were introduced in Chapter 2. With such systems, the only essential data structure is the table or relation, which consists of a set of tuples. These tuples are often called "rows" or "records". Visually, a table is divided horizontally into rows and vertically into columns. Tables and columns are named but rows are not. The intersection of a row and column is a field: each field contains a single data value, which may be null. For a given column, all data values are of the same type or "domain". Hence for a given table all rows are of the same type.

To illustrate some basic ideas about relational schemas we consider an information system concerning members of a martial arts club. Table 11.1 is an extract from an output report for this UoD.

Notice the null values. Some members do not have a phone number recorded (e.g. they might not have a phone, or they want their phone number kept private); some members do not have a rank recorded for any martial art (e.g. they may be beginners and hence unranked). Some members are ranked in more than one martial art. In case you aren't aware, black belt ranks are known as dan grades and lower ranks are kyu grades. See if you can set out the conceptual schema before peeking at the solution (Figure 11.2).

There are three fact types. In the conceptual database we thus have three fact tables, each row of which corresponds to a single elementary fact. In a relational database however, as explained in the next section, the two binaries would typically be grouped together into one table (see the Member table of Table 11.2). The names of the tables are shown in bold. Check for yourself that the populations are consistent with that of the original output report. There are several points worth noting here. Firstly, unlike a conceptual fact table but like an output report, one row of a relational database table might be used to represent several facts: this happens here with the Member table but not the Ranks table.

Secondly, relational database tables need not be the same as the tables in the output report. Relational database systems make it easy to produce single output tables which

Table 11.2 Relational database tables for Table 11.1

Member:	Name	Gender	Phone
	Adams B	M	2052777
	Adams S	F	2052777
	Brown C	F	3579001
	Collins T	M	?
	Dancer A	F	?

Ranks:	Person	Art	Rank
	Adams B	judo	3dan
	Adams B	karatedo	2kyu
	Adams S	judo	2kyu
	Collins T	aikido	2dan
	Collins T	judo	2dan

Table 11.3 An illegal table (repeating group in column 2)

Person	Arts and Ranks
Adams B	judo 3dan, karatedo 2kyu
Adams S	judo 2kyu
Collins T	aikido 2dan, judo 2dan

draw information from several tables stored in the database. Moreover, they provide formatting facilities which enable the output reports to be displayed in a variety of ways.

As indicated earlier, only single values may be entered in the fields of relational database tables. For example, it would be illegal to try to store the information of the Ranks table in a table like Table 11.3. Here the Ranks column stores a "repeating group": a single field is used to store one or more groups of Art and Rank values. This is not allowed. Even a table like Table 11.4 is not allowed. Here the Arts column stores a "repeating attribute": more than one art value can be entered in the same field. We may summarize the requirement that no repeating groups or attributes are allowed thus: in a relational database, a field may contain only single values, not sets of values. So the information in Table 11.4 should instead be stored as in Table 11.5.

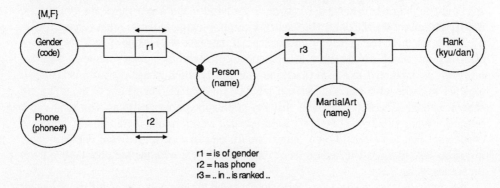

r1 = is of gender
r2 = has phone
r3 = .. in .. is ranked ..

Figure 11.2 A conceptual schema diagram for Table 11.1

Table 11.4 Another illegal table (repeating attribute)

	Person	*Arts*
	Adams B	judo, karatedo
	Adams S	judo
	Collins T	aikido, judo

Table 11.5 A legal table

Plays:	*Person*	*Art*
	Adams B	judo
	Adams B	karatedo
	Adams S	judo
	Collins T	aikido
	Collins T	judo

Of course, this requirement applies to conceptual fact tables as well. Its main advantage is that it provides a simpler picture of the data for humans. It also leads to a simpler and smaller set of data processing operations. Consider for example the two updates:

del: Person 'Adams S' plays Art 'judo'
del: Person 'Collins T' plays Art 'judo'

With the relational model (see Table 11.5), the same delete operation is used for both updates (i.e. delete a whole row). With the repeating attribute model (see Table 11.4), the first delete operation would typically remove the whole row while the second operation would just remove judo from the set of arts played by Collins. A similar comment applies for other operations (e.g. retrieval, insertion and constraint enforcement).

Relational updates are of three kinds: add, delete or modify. The modify operation allows just some of the values in a row to be changed. For example, if Adams B changes his phone number or is promoted to a higher rank in judo then only a value in the final field of the relevant table is changed. The modify operation is provided for convenience rather than necessity, since any modify operation can be expressed using a sequence of delete and add operations.

Let's consider now how to set out the relational schema for the UoD being discussed. To begin with, we set out table equations with the column names enclosed in square brackets:

Member = [name, gender, phone]
Ranks = [person, art, rank]

If desired, the domains for each column may also be specified. In theory the relational model supports semantic domains somewhat like our entity types. In practice however, only syntactic domains are usually supported. For example we might specify maximum length character strings for each of the fields thus:

Member = [name, gender, phone]
           c20   c   c7

Ranks = [person, art, rank]
          c20   c20   c5

Depending on the language being used, various other domain abbreviations can be set out. For example, for SQL's Integer, Smallint, and Varchar(30) we might use "int", "sint" and "vc30". Because the standard data types provided depend on the particular version of the particular language being used, we make no further use of them here. Notice however, that in dropping from a conceptual to a relational schema we have lost some of the natural semantics. For example, unless an exclusion constraint is added we have no way of asserting that Person and MartialArt are different kinds of entity.

Even at the syntactic level, a lexical constraint such as Gendercode = {'M','F'} or Phone# = <d7> is typically not supported in the relational language itself: such constraints are usually enforced by means of additional coding using a procedural language or a special applications tool. Having said this, we now ignore the enforcement of lexical constraints.

We do, however, wish to display the non-lexical constraints in our relational schema. **Uniqueness constraints** are shown by *underlining* the names of the columns spanned by the constraint; arrowheads are used only if the columns spanned are not contiguous. If you look back at the populated Member and Ranks tables, it should be fairly clear that the uniqueness constraints are as set out below:

Member = [name, gender, phone]
Ranks   = [person, art, rank]

In the next section we provide a simple algorithm for determining the uniqueness constraints in the relational schema from those in the conceptual schema. Here, the attribute Name provides a simple key to the Member table, while the pair (Person,Art) provides a composite key for the Ranks table.

Now let's consider **mandatory role** constraints. To help our discussion, we again show the conceptual schema diagram, but this time add two implied subset constraints (see Figure 11.3). Of the three roles played by Person, r1 is mandatory while r2 and r3 are optional. Hence for any state of the database, pop(r2) and pop(r3) are subsets of pop(r1) as shown.

The terms "mandatory" and "optional" are often used in specifying relational schemas. However there is an important difference in the way these terms are used in this context. In a conceptual schema, a role is mandatory or optional according as to whether

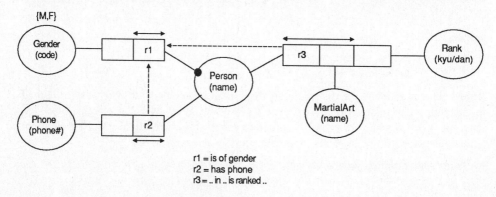

r1 = is of gender
r2 = has phone
r3 = .. in .. is ranked ..

Figure 11.3   Implied subset constraints

or not it must be recorded for each member of the population of its entity type. *In a relational schema, a column is defined to be mandatory or optional with respect to its table:* if the column permits null values it is said to be optional; otherwise it is mandatory or "not null".

Clearly, a role is mandatory if and only if its population must be a superset of that for *each* role played by its entity type. This subsumes the trivial result that if an entity type plays only one role then this role is mandatory. Non-trivially, the constraint that r1 is mandatory for Person can be deduced from the following combination:

(a) the subset constraints running from r2 and r3; and
(b) r2 and r3 are the only other roles played by Person

We now consider implementing the mandatory role constraint for r1 in terms of these conditions. In mapping down to the relational schema, r1 corresponds to the Gender column, and r2 to the Phone column of the Member table. Since both of these roles map to columns of the same table, the subset constraint between them can be declared in terms of this table alone. Relational database systems enable columns of any table to be declared as mandatory or optional (for that table). With the Member table, the Name and Gender columns should be declared mandatory since these must be recorded for each person; since some of the people referenced in this table needn't have a phone number recorded, the Phone column should be declared optional. We may set this out thus:

Member = [name MA, gender MA, phone OP]

In general, *mandatory and optional roles that map onto columns of the same table should be declared mandatory and optional, respectively, for that table.*

As an alternative to "MA", the abbreviation "NN" (not null) may be used. Since each column must be declared mandatory or optional (but not both), we can save writing by adding only the MA declarations: the other columns are then assumed optional. For example:

Member = [name MA, gender MA, phone]

This approach is adopted in SQL (Name and Gender are declared **not null**). However, in practice most columns are usually mandatory; so we can save even more writing by adding only the OP declarations (the other columns are then assumed mandatory). For simplicity, we favour this approach. For example:

Member = [name, gender, phone OP]

Strictly speaking, this definition does not fully express the constraint that r1 is mandatory (for Person), since it is possible that some other instances of Person are referenced in other tables of the database. While r1 maps onto the Gender column of the member table, role r3 maps onto the Person column of the Ranks table. Since r3 is optional (for Person) you might be tempted to express this in terms of an optional column declaration. For example:

Ranks   = [person OP, art, rank]   { incorrect}

However, this says that the Person column is optional for the Ranks table (i.e. null values are allowed in this column). This obviously doesn't make sense, since in our UoD no elementary fact type between MartialArt and Rank has been defined; each row of a table must store at least one fact (not part of a fact). The OP notation can be used only to specify subset constraints between columns in the *same* table. *When different tables are involved, we express a subset constraint between columns by our usual arrow notation*(as used for conceptual schemas). For example:

Member = [name, gender, phone OP]

Ranks   = [person, art, rank]

This indicates that each (non-null) value in the Person column of the Ranks table must also occur in the Name column of the Member table. In general, *a subset constraint between roles that map onto columns of different tables should be expressed as a subset constraint between these columns.* This rule applies not only to the present case where one role is mandatory and the other optional, but also to the case where both roles are optional.

In many cases, subset constraints between tables may be expressed in terms of primary and foreign key declarations. Recall that a key is any column or column-set spanned by a uniqueness constraint. If a table has more than one key these are called *candidate keys*. In the relational model, one key is always selected as the standard identifier or *primary key* for each table. A *foreign key* is a column (or column-set) in one table whose non-null values must also occur in a primary key of some (usually other) table. With our present example, Name is the (primary) key for the Member table, and the Person column of the Ranks table is a foreign key for the Member table.

In the relational model there are two basic integrity rules. The *entity integrity* rule demands that primary key values must not be null; the *referential integrity* rule demands that non-null foreign key values really do occur in the associated primary key. In practice, most relational systems do not support these rules. However, proposed revisions to SQL include primary and foreign key declaration within the table definitions. Currently however, subset constraints between tables are typically expressed as validation rules written in application code.

Rather than get bogged down in language-specific details, we leave our relational schema specification as set out above. To capture the conceptual feature that r1 is mandatory for Person while r2 and r3 are optional, we used a combination of mandatory/optional column declarations and a subset constraint arrow. This is adequate, so long as we know that entities of type Person are referenced only in the Name column of the Member table and the Person column of the Ranks table. In relational systems such knowledge is typically assumed rather than expressed.

It should be clear by now that the relational approach is inferior to the conceptual approach in the handling of entity types, and the primary/foreign key mechanism is unnecessarily restrictive in terms of the reference schemes which users might wish to employ. Despite these deficiencies however, relational systems provide a higher level view of the data than the other main systems in use (e.g. hierarchic and network). To enable the reader to get a feel for the process of implementing a relational schema in a particular language, we show how the martial arts schema might be defined in SQL:

create table Member	(name	**char**(20)	**not null**	**primary key,**
	gender	**char**	**not null,**	
	phone	**char**(7))		

create table Ranks	(person	**char**(20)	**not null**	**references** Member,
	art	**char**(20)	**not null,**	
	rank	**char**(5)	**not null,**	
	primary key (person,art))			

These table definitions are set out in the currently proposed syntax of extended ANSI SQL. The keyword "references" is used for foreign key declaration. In traditional IBM SQL, several changes would be needed. Instead of the primary key notation, *create unique index* statements would be used to enforce the uniqueness constraints on Name and (Person,Art); "char(1)" would be used instead of "char" for gender; and instead of the foreign key declaration, some code would be used to enforce the subset constraint. For example, the constraint is enforced if and only if the following SQL command returns the null set: **select** person **from** Ranks **where** person **not in** (**select** name **from** Member).

Recall that a conceptual schema comprises three sections: fact types; constraints; derivation rules. A relational schema also comprises three sections: table types; constraints; derivation rules. The table types are set out by means of table definitions, which typically also express some but not all of the constraints. With the example discussed in this section, the only constraints we had to cater for were uniqueness and mandatory role constraints. Tables stored in the database are *base tables*. Some derivation rules may be catered for in terms of definitions which show how a *virtual table* or *view* may be derived from other tables.

Just as we used the conceptual arrow notation to express subset constraints between tables, *we may use other conceptual constraint notations in setting out relational schemas*. Sometimes we modify these notations. If two mandatory roles played by the same entity type map onto columns in separate tables we link these two columns with a *broken line* (without arrow heads) to show the *equality constraint* between them.

Some constraints (e.g. subtype constraints) and all derivation rules are set out initially in textual form, below the table definitions. Once the relational schema is set out there are usually several ways in which it may be implemented in the language(s) being used. For example, derivation rules might be set out as views or as stored procedures. In this text our main interest is in arriving at a set of table definitions, and expressing constraints and rules in as simple a way as possible. The basic components of a relational schema are set out below:

Relational schema:

1. *table definitions:*   base table types
                           some constraints
                           virtual table types

2. *special constraints:*   stored procedures to enforce other constraints

3. *special derivation rules:*   stored procedures to derive other facts

11.3   Optimal normal form algorithm

In the previous section we introduced a notation for setting out a relational schema, and discussed an example of mapping from a conceptual to a relational schema. This mapping comprises two main phases: declaring a set of table definitions; writing procedures to implement any additional constraints and derivation rules. The second phase is beyond the scope of this text. To facilitate the first phase we now provide a systematic procedure for grouping the fact types of a conceptual schema into a set of table types of a relational schema: this procedure is known as the *optimal normal form (ONF) algorithm*.

For a given conceptual schema several different table designs might be chosen. The ONF algorithm aims to produce a *simple, safe, efficient design*. The first criterion is simplicity of data structure and operations: hence the relational model is chosen; in particular, each table has a fixed number of fields, and each field can hold only one value (no repeating attributes). Secondly, we wish to avoid update anomalies: hence we aim, at least initially, for no redundancy. Thirdly, in the interests of efficiency, we seek to minimize the number of tables. Reducing the number of tables usually reduces the average time taken for the execution of queries as well as simplifying the formulation of many queries.

Starting with a conceptual schema, the ONF algorithm thus produces a table design satisfying three criteria: (1) no repeating attributes; (2) no redundancy or update problems; (3) minimum number of tables satisfying (1) and (2). In the next section a traditional table design procedure known as *normalization* is discussed. This uses a corrective method to successively refine poorly designed tables into better ones, starting with first normal form and ending with fifth normal form. The ONF algorithm typically generates tables in fifth normal form (5NF); moreover, these are optimized further since the number of 5NF tables in the overall schema has been minimized. For this reason the term "optimal normal form" is used.

It needs to be realized however that the table design produced by the ONF algorithm may often be optimized further for a given application. To begin with, the third criterion of minimum number of tables is *relative to the conceptual schema*. It is possible that even fewer tables may result if a judicious conceptual schema transformation is made before applying the ONF algorithm. Moreover, for a given UoD a number of applications are possible, involving different statistical patterns of queries and updates. A schema optimal for one *query/update pattern* may be less than optimal for another query/update pattern. To cater for this, preliminary conceptual schema transformations can be performed which result in a change to the number and/or shape of the ONF tables. Finally, to achieve the required efficiency it may be necessary to tune the database by permitting *controlled redundancy*.

Thus, the ONF algorithm is not necessarily the last word in table design. Nevertheless, the algorithm is extremely valuable since it does guarantee a simple, safe and reasonably efficient design. Happily, the algorithm itself is simple. Each fact type is mapped *into* only one table, with roles mapping into columns. If a fact type maps *onto* a single table (each row contains only one fact) then all its keys (uniqueness constraints) map onto keys of the table. In the relational model, a primary key (standard identifier for the table) is selected for each table: this is often called "*the* key". Very roughly, tables with simple primary keys list properties of entities referenced by the key; tables with composite primary keys list relationships between entities and perhaps properties about these relationships.

ONF Grouping Algorithm:

1. *For each fact type without a simple key, create a separate table.*
   Select a shortest key of the fact type as primary key of the table.

2. *Group fact types with simple keys attached to a common object type into the same table* with the primary key based on this object type.

3. *For each remaining fact type, create a separate table.*
   Select a key of the fact type as the primary key of the table.

In setting out the table definitions we use the notation introduced in the previous section. Since the natural semantics of entity types and roles has been lost, we should carefully choose meaningful names for the tables and their columns. A table is homogeneous iff all its columns are based on the same domain. With a homogeneous binary table, a fact type name is often used as a table name, with role names used for column names (e.g. Marriage: husband, wife). With a heterogeneous binary table, a role name might be used as the table name. Entity type names are often used as column names if the entity types play only one role in the table (e.g. Speaks: person, language). With wider tables, a table name descriptive of the primary key and perhaps other columns is often used. Sometimes reference mode or label type names are used as column names.

Once the table groupings have been determined, and meaningful names chosen for the tables and columns, keys should be underlined and optional columns marked "OP". Then further constraints may be drawn in as discussed in the previous section. If a table has more than one candidate key, the one selected as the primary key should be distinguished. We use a double underline for this task.

To understand the ONF algorithm it will help to consider several examples. Initially we confine ourselves to cases where all entity types have simple 1:1 reference types, and no subtypes or objectified fact types occur.

ONF step 1 says that each fact type without a simple key should be mapped onto a separate table. If our conceptual schema is correct, a fact type has no simple key iff it is a many:many binary or it has an arity above 2. So each many:many binary goes into a table by itself, and each ternary or longer fact type goes into a table by itself (see Figure 11.4).

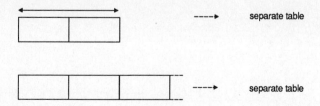

Figure 11.4 Composite keys map to separate tables

Another way to express this is: any fact type whose (shortest) key is composite must go into a separate table. We might picture this as shown in Figure 11.5.

As an example of this, consider the conceptual schema diagram for the martial arts UoD of the previous section. The ternary fact type had to be mapped onto a table of its own (the Ranks table). After ONF step 1 has been performed, any remaining fact type must have a simple key. Each of these fact types must be binary or unary. Unaries are very rare.

ONF step 2 tells us that if an entity type has more than one simple key attached we should group all the fact types involved into a single table, using this common entity type to provide the primary key of the table. For example, if entity type A has two simple keys attached as shown in Figure 11.6 then we should map the two fact types onto a ternary table with the key based on A.

Here the notation "r1/r3" indicates that this field does the job of both roles r1 and r3 in the conceptual schema. Although we speak of mapping roles onto colu. ns, in choosing names for the columns of the resulting table we might focus on the corresponding entity type, reference type or role(s). As discussed earlier, it depends on the particular example as to which is most appropriate. As one example, consider the martial arts UoD of the previous section, where the two binaries mapped onto the ternary Member table. Notice how the common entity type is catered for by the Name field, which is the primary key.

Once ONF step 2 has been performed, the remaining fact types (if any) must have simple keys, and hence be binaries or unaries. Each of these goes into a separate table. A simple example is shown in Figure 11.7. By ONF step 1 we map the right hand fact type onto a separate table (Awarded). No fact types fit the case of ONF step 2. This leaves the left hand fact type, which by ONF step 3 maps onto a separate table (Works_for). Notice the equality constraint, shown as a broken line, between the Lecturer fields of both tables: this is needed since both roles played by Lecturer are mandatory (see previous section).

As another example, consider the schema in Figure 11.8. Here each horse has its gender and weight recorded. Each race has exactly one winner (we do not allow ties). There are no composite keys for ONF step 1 to work on. The gender and weight fact types have simple keys attached to the entity type Horse. By ONF step 2 these two fact

Figure 11.5   The cases in Figure 11.4 summarized

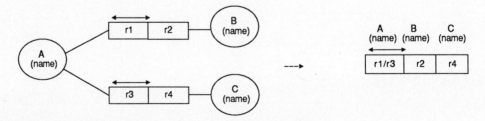

Figure 11.6   The fact types are grouped into the same table

types must be grouped into the same table with the reference to Horse providing the key. The Won fact type also has a simple key, but this key is not attached to Horse (it is attached to Race instead): by ONF step 3 this fact type must go into a table by itself. Notice the subset constraint between the tables. Why is this needed?

We now consider some examples involving *1:1 fact types*. Consider the UoD of Figure 11.9. Each employee has (exactly) one employee number and this is identifying.

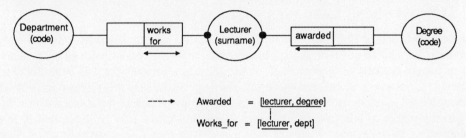

Figure 11.7   Note the equality constraint

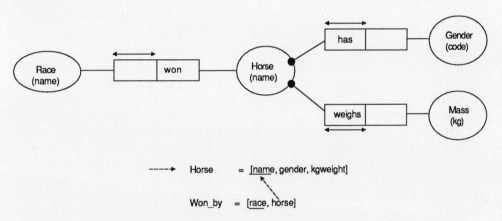

Figure 11.8   Note the subset constraint

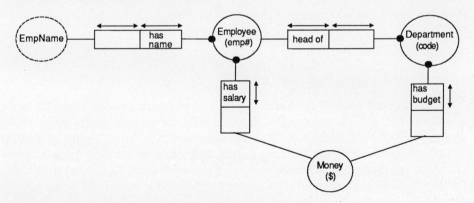

Figure 11.9   How should 1:1 associations be mapped?

Each employee has one name and this is identifying. Each department has one head, and each head is head of one department. Since not all employees are department heads, the head-of-department role is optional.

Let's see how the ONF algorithm works here. There are no composite keys so we proceed to ONF step 2. Looking at the three simple keys attached to the entity type Employee, we might begin by grouping the three fact types involved into one table thus:

Employee = [emp#, name, salary, deptheaded OP]

Notice that each of Emp# and Name are keys and we have used a double underline to indicate our choice of Emp# as the primary key. Emp# is a better choice as the primary key since it is likely to be completely stable whereas a person's name is more likely to change (e.g. when a woman employee gets married). Notice also that we have underlined DeptHeaded, even though it is optional, as this merely expresses the constraint that the *non-null* values of this column are unique. Since null values may be duplicated in this column we do not regard this column to be a key.

Looking at the Department entity type we see two simple keys attached. So we might try grouping these into one table thus:

Department = [deptname, head, budget]

Again we have two candidate keys: DeptName and Head. We use a double underline to show our choice of DeptName as the primary key. However, our design is now faulty since it exhibits redundancy. The information on who is head of what department is now stored in both tables. We should have grouped the head-of-department fact type into only one table. But which one?

If you look at the conceptual schema diagram you will notice that the head-of-department fact type has one mandatory and one optional role. In cases like this it is better to *group on the mandatory role side*. Here this means adding the Head column into the Department table, rather than adding the DeptHeaded column into the Employee table. Since Head is a mandatory column it has no null values whereas the DeptHeaded column is optional and hence does permit null values. Since null values tend to complicate database operations and consume space it is better to avoid them, all other things being equal. So our final relational schema is as shown below. The subset constraint asserts that each head of department is an employee.

Employee   = [emp#, name, salary]

Department = [deptname, head, budget]

Because of the unusual 1:1 nature of the head-of-department fact type, one might consider grouping all the fact types into a single table, for example [emp#, name, salary, deptheaded OP, deptbudget OP]. But this approach has flaws. Firstly, it permits redundancy of the fact dept-has-budget. This fault could be rectified by enforcing a constraint that deptbudget is recorded only on those rows where deptheaded is recorded. Even then, the table is unnatural since although deptbudget is determined by the primary key emp#, one naturally relates this information to department rather than employee. Finally we have the awkwardness of two columns with null values.

The case just considered is one in which there is a 1:1 fact type with only one mandatory role, where both the attached entity types have other simple keys attached. Here we group on the mandatory role side. This refinement to ONF step 2 may be displayed diagrammatically as shown in Figure 11.10.

If, instead, only one of the entity types has an extra simple key attached, we should group around this regardless of how the mandatory role constraints might be distributed. Figure 11.11 illustrates this.

If Bankcard plays only one role then this role is mandatory. In spite of the fact that the has-bankcard role is optional we should group it with the other roles attached to Client rather than making a separate table for it. This leads to the following schema:

Client   = [name, gender, birthyr, bankcard OP]

Here the advantage of getting all the information into one table usually outweighs the disadvantage of null values in the final column. The underlining of Bankcard indicates a uniqueness constraint for its non-null values. One could of course avoid the null values by using two tables:

Client   = [name, gender, birthyr]

Bankcard   = [card#, client]

However, the need to enforce the subset constraint across the tables, and the added overhead involved with queries needing information from the combination of tables weigh against this approach. Of course, one can always imagine an application where this approach might be preferred. For example, suppose there are a billion clients only one of whom has a bankcard. But as a general rule, the single table approach is suggested. This is consistent with ONF step 2.

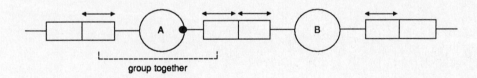

group together

Figure 11.10 Group on the mandatory role side

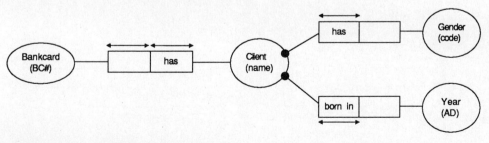

Figure 11.11 Bankcard plays only one role

As another case involving 1:1 fact types, consider Figure 11.12. Here each employee has the use of exactly one company car, and each company car is allocated to exactly one employee. Employees are identified by their employee number and cars by their registration number. The names of employees and the kinds of car (e.g. Nissan Vanette) are recorded, but these need not be unique.

Both roles of the 1:1 fact type are mandatory, and each is attached to an entity type to which another simple key is attached. A first reading of ONF step 2 suggests that the 1:1 fact type be grouped into either an Employee table or a Car table. But which? Unlike the previous example, we now have a symmetrical situation with respect to mandatory roles. An arbitrary decision could be made here. We could group to the left, thus:

Employee   = [emp#, name, car#]

Car   = [car#, model]

or we could group to the right, thus:

Employee   = [emp#, name]

Car   = [car#, model, emp#]

Either of these approaches is safe. One might be tempted to use just one table thus:

EmployeeCar= [emp#, empname, car#, carmodel]

However, this approach is dangerous since, although it is redundancy free, it can lead to update anomalies. For example, to record a change in an employee's car one might update a row by altering just the value of car#. This could result in the wrong value for carmodel.

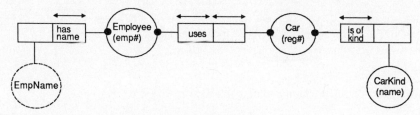

Figure 11.12   How should the fact types be grouped?

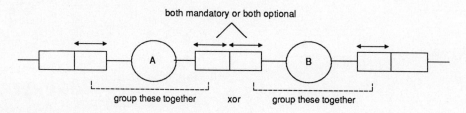

Figure 11.13   Two options are possible in this case

Now what about the case of a 1:1 fact type where both roles are optional? For example, consider a UoD identical to that just discussed except that only some employees are given company cars and only some company cars are used by employees (e.g. some may be reserved for important visitors). ONF step 2 suggests that we create two tables, in either (but not both) of which the 1:1 fact type may be included. This is a safe approach, yielding:

Employee   = [<u>emp#</u>, name, <u>car#</u> OP]

Car   = [<u>car#</u>, model]

or:

Employee   = [<u>emp#</u>, name]

Car   = [<u>car#</u>, model, <u>emp#</u> OP]

In an actual application the percentage of null values is likely to be different in these two designs. In this case the design with fewer null values would usually be preferable. An argument can be made however to use three tables for this case. This argument depends heavily on the percentage of null values resulting. For example, if only 1 percent of employees and 1 percent of cars were involved in the Uses fact type, it might be better to map this fact type into a table all by itself, resulting in three tables for the schema.

However, in the interests of keeping the ONF algorithm simple, we will stay with the two table approach. The essential feature of these cases was the presence of a 1:1 fact type with both roles mandatory or both roles optional, and attached to entity types with other simple keys attached. Our discussion leads to the second refinement of ONF step 2 (see Figure 11.13). Here "xor" denotes "exclusive or", that is, "either but not both".

So far our examples have used only simple 1:1 naming conventions. In cases *where an object is identified by a combination of labels, this combination should always be used to represent the object in a table*. For instance, the conceptual schema in Figure 11.14 is mapped onto the relational schema shown.

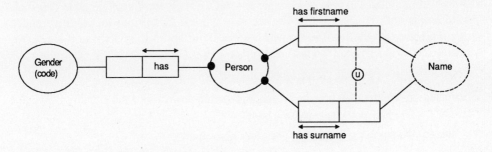

Person = [firstname, surname, gender]

Figure 11.14 A composite key identifies each person

Let us now consider some examples involving nested fact types. If our conceptual schema is correct, each objectified relationship type must be spanned by a uniqueness constraint and must have one or more roles attached. For the purposes of the ONF algorithm, *each objectified relationship type is treated just like any entity type, except that it is represented in its table by the combination of its object types.*

As a simple example, consider the conceptual schema in Figure 11.15. Here each (Student,Subject) enrollment is perceived as an object. Let us refer to the objectified relationship type as Enrollment. First note that ONF step 1 does not entail that we create a separate table for Enrollment. Although Enrollment has a composite key we must think of it as an object type, and focus on the outer fact type in which it is nested. Looked at in this light, we see two binaries each having a simple key attached to Enrollment.

Hence ONF step 2 implies that we group the two binaries into one table, with the primary key based on the Enrollment object type. Of course, this primary key is just the composite key which identifies Enrollment, that is, (Student, Subject). So the relational schema is:

Results = [student, subject, assign OP, exam OP]

Now consider the example shown in Figure 11.16, which you may be familiar with from an earlier exercise. See if you can work out the relational schema for yourself before looking at the discussion.

Firstly, note that the derived fact type may be omitted from the table definitions: a derivation rule like that supplied on the conceptual schema can be appended (this is trivial to implement in a procedure or view, and the details do not concern us here). Now consider the objectified relationship types, which we have called Offering and Award to facilitate our discussion. These should be examined in bottom up order. Since Offering is nested inside Award we look at Offering first.

If you think of Offering as an unstructured object type, it has two simple keys attached. So the two fact types involved must be grouped into the same table using Offering as the primary key. To specify this primary key we unpack Offering in terms of its composite key (Subject, Year). This gives us the table:

SubjectOffering = [subject,year, lecturer, enrollment]

Now think of Award as an unstructured object type. It has only one role attached (ignore the derived role) and this role is a simple key, so we must form a single table based on Award as the key. To specify this key we now unpack Award into its primitive entity types. This yields (Offering,Rating) which unpacks further to (Subject,Year,Rating). We can now set out the second (and last) table thus:

AwardProfile = [subject, year, rating, frequency]

The relational schema may now be set out as shown below. Notice the equality constraint between the (subject,year) pairs in each table:

SubjectOffering = [subject,year, lecturer, enrollment]

AwardProfile   = [subject,year, rating, frequency]

* freq% = 100 × freq/enrlt

As a further refinement to the ONF algorithm we now consider the handling of *subtypes*. Since the notion of subtypes is not directly supported by relational database systems, we need some way of dealing with this kind of constraint. As a simple example, recall the output report of Table 11.6, which was discussed in Section 6.5. In this UoD, the kind of haircover is recorded just for the men (H = hairy, T = thick, B = bald) and

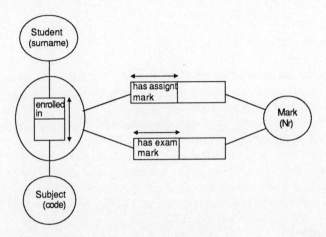

Figure 11.15 Enrollment has two simple keys attached

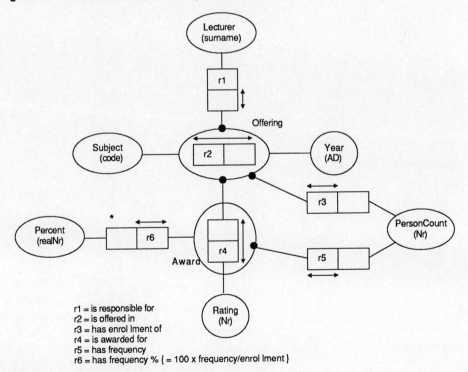

r1 = is responsible for
r2 = is offered in
r3 = has enrol lment of
r4 = is awarded for
r5 = has frequency
r6 = has frequency % { = 100 x frequency/enrol lment }

Figure 11.16 How should the fact types be grouped?

Table 11.6

Person	Sex	Haircover	NrChildren
Jones E	F	–	2
Smith J	M	T	–
Blow J	M	B	–
Lane L	F	–	0
Blossom B	F	–	5

"–" = "not to be recorded"

number of children is recorded just for the women. Since for any person a definite decision can be made whether to record these facts, we have a case of subtypes. In this case we introduced two subtypes as shown in Figure 11.17.

There are two main ways in which subtype constraints can be handled in a relational database. The first approach is to *collapse the subtypes back into their (head) supertype, so that the subtype roles become optional roles attached to this supertype. The grouping of fact types into tables now proceeds in the normal way, and the subtype constraints are expressed verbally.* Although the conceptual schema conversion may be done mentally, we display it here to clarify the process (see Figure 11.18).

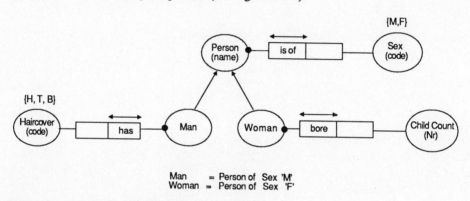

Man   = Person of Sex 'M'
Woman = Person of Sex 'F'

Figure 11.17   How should subtypes be handled?

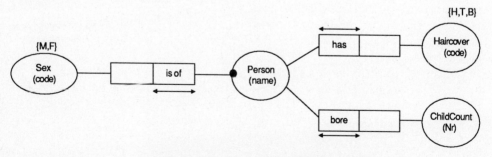

Haircover recorded just for Persons of Sex 'M'
NrChildren recorded just for Persons of Sex 'F'

Figure 11.18   Subtypes collapsed back into their supertype

Applying ONF step 1, the three fact types maps into one table based on Person as the primary key. In setting out the relational schema, the subtype constraints are shown below the table definition. The use of "just for" asserts the subtype constraint ("only for") as well as the mandatory role constraint for the subtype. Thus:

Person = [name, gender, haircover OP, nrChildren OP]

Haircover recorded just for rows where Sex = 'M'.
NrChildren recorded just for rows where Sex = 'F'.

This approach leads to a table matching that of the original output report. It has the disadvantage of generating null values, but the advantage of minimizing the number of tables. Apart from the usual efficiency gains arising from fewer tables, the mapping of subtype roles into the supertype table makes it very easy to implement the subtype constraints since the checking procedure for each row needs to access only that row.

The second main approach is to create separate tables for each subtype, and add the subtype constraints verbally. This leads to the following relational schema:

Man   = [name, haircover]
             | *

Person = [name, gender]
             ↑ **
             |

Woman = [name, nrChildren]

* pop(Man.name)   = pop(Person.name) where gender = 'M'
** pop(Woman.name) = pop(Person.name) where gender = 'F'

Here the notation "Man.name" denotes the name column of the Man table. The subset constraints shown as arrowed lines are implied by the subtype constraints listed below the table definitions; hence these arrowed lines may be omitted. As an exercise, populate these tables with the sample given in the output report. This approach has the advantage of minimizing null values. However, it leads to more tables, and is typically less efficient. In particular, the enforcement of the subset constraints is now more complex since separate tables have to be accessed.

In practice a compromise between the two approaches is sometimes used, but to keep our algorithm simple, we will *standardize on the first approach: collapse the subtypes into their head supertype*.

We end this section with an illustration of the fact that the relational schema obtained by the ONF algorithm is relative to conceptual schema. Consider the output report of Figure 11.19, which indicates for each department the number of male and female staff as well as the faculty to which the department belongs. Graphical reports like these are often used in business. As an exercise, draw your own conceptual schema diagram for this UoD before peeking at the solution provided. Make sure you perform step 1.

There are a number of equivalent conceptual schemas for this UoD. Figure 11.20 provides one solution, based on reading the information in terms of one binary and one ternary.

Applying the ONF algorithm we obtain the following relational schema:

Location   = [<u>dept</u>, faculty]
                      |
                      |
StaffProfile = [<u>dept, gender</u>, number]
                      2

So this approach gives us two tables. However, suppose we transform the conceptual schema into the equivalent version shown in Figure 11.21.

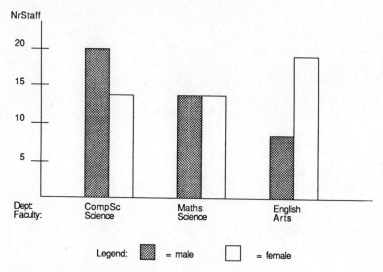

Figure 11.19   A bar graph output report

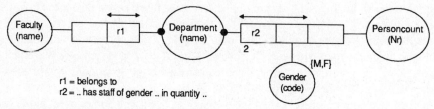

Figure 11.20   A conceptual schema for Figure 11.19

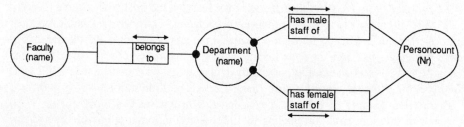

Figure 11.21   Another conceptual schema for Figure 11.19

Now we have three binaries, each with a simple key attached to Department. So applying the ONF algorithm we obtain just one table:

Department = [<u>name</u>, faculty, nrMaleStaff, nrFemaleStaff]

For most applications, this relational schema is much better to work with than the previous one. While the topic of further optimization through preliminary conceptual transformations is an important one, we have no space to pursue it further in this introductory book.

Exercise 11.3

1. Map the following conceptual schema onto a relational schema, using the optimal normal form algorithm. Use descriptive table and column names. Underline the keys, and mark any optional columns as "OP". Indicate any subset or equality constraints between tables.

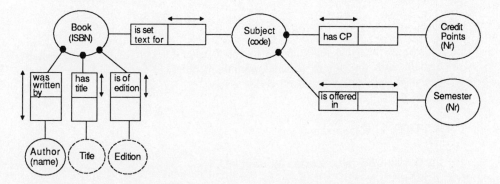

2. Map the following conceptual schema onto an ONF relational schema (as for Question 1).

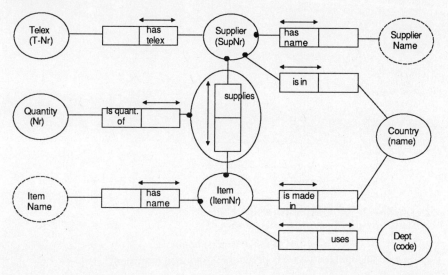

3. (a) The conceptual schema for a given UoD is as shown below.

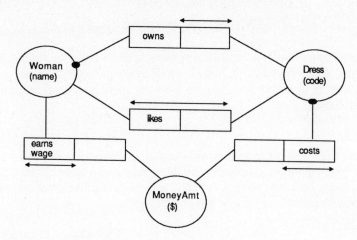

The following table definition is meant to cater for part of this UoD. Briefly explain with the aid of a small, sample population why this table is badly designed. Use the abbreviated codes w1, w2 ... for women and d1, d2 ... for dresses.

Likes = [woman, dress, cost]

(b) Specify an ONF table schema for this UoD.

4. The following conceptual schema was designed to store information about competitors in the most recent Olympic Games.

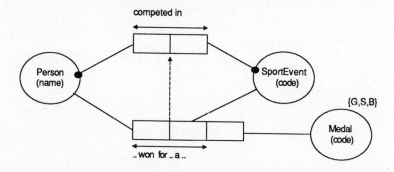

(a) Apply the ONF algorithm directly to this schema.
(b) Transform the conceptual schema by nesting.
(c) Apply the ONF algorithm to this nested schema.
(d) Which conceptual schema is preferable (flattened or nested)?

5. Consider the following UoD about lecturers. Each lecturer has at least one degree and has taught at at least one institution. Each lecturer has exactly one identifying name, and at most one nickname. Each degree is standardly identified by its code, although each degree has exactly one title and degree titles are unique. Each degree is held by at least one lecturer. Institutions are uniquely identified by their names. All these details are to be recorded, as well as the gender and birth year of the lecturers, and the year in which degrees were awarded.

   (a) A beginning student designs a table schema for this UoD which includes the following:

   ```
   Lecturer       = [name, gender, degCode, degTitle]
   Qualification  = [degCode, yrAwarded]
   ```

   Explain, with the aid of a sample population, why these tables are badly designed.

   (b) Draw a conceptual schema for this UoD.

   (c) Map this onto an ONF relational schema.

6. Refer to your conceptual schema diagram for the ProjectManager UoD of Exercise 3.6 Question 1. Set out an ONF relational schema for this UoD.

7. Refer to your conceptual schema diagram for Exercise 3.6 Question 2. Set out an ONF relational schema for this UoD.

8. Refer to the MediaSurvey conceptual schema considered in Section 6.6.

   (a) Collapse the subtypes to produce an ONF relational schema.

   (b) Set out an alternative relational schema with separate tables for each node in the subtype graph. Which schema is preferable?

9. Refer to your conceptual schema for the SolarSystem UoD of Exercise 6.6 Question 4. Collapse the subtypes and set out an ONF relational schema for this UoD.

10. Refer to your conceptual schema for the CommunityRoads UoD of Exercise 6.7 Question 3. Collapse the subtypes and set out an ONF relational schema for this UoD.

11. Map the following conceptual schema onto an ONF relational schema.

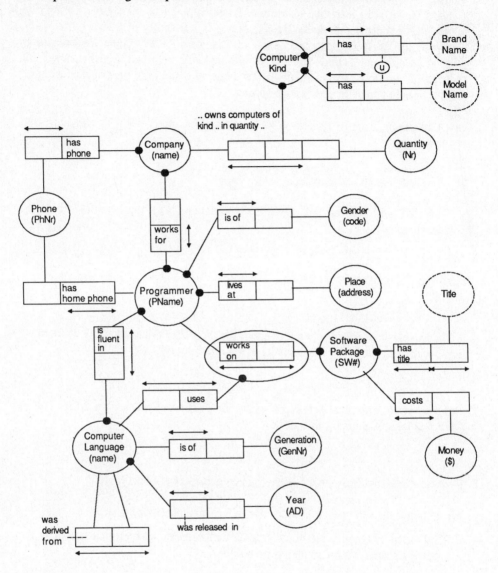

12. Map the following conceptual schema onto an ONF relational schema.

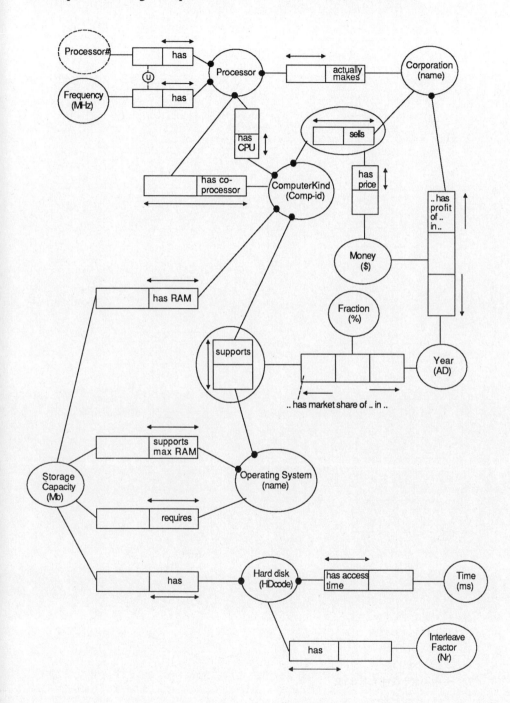

13. A sales company maintains an information system described by the following conceptual schema. Specify the ONF relational schema.

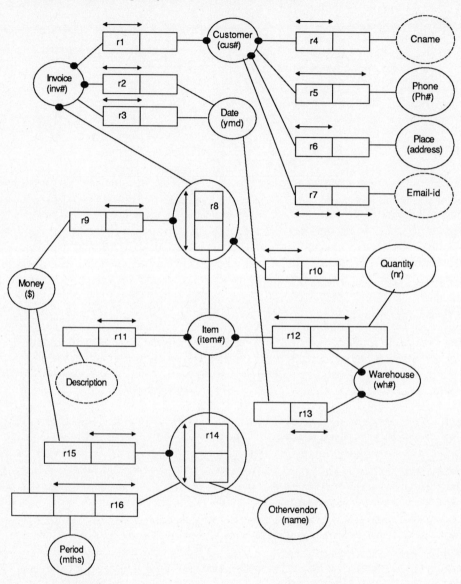

r1 = was issued to
r2 = was issued on
r3 = was paid on
r4 = has name
r5 = may be contacted on
r6 = is located at
r7 = has electronic mail id

r8 = contains order for
r9 = was unit price charged for
r10 = is number of units of item ordered in
r11 = is described as
r12 = .. is stocked in warehouse .. in quantity ..
r13 = had last stocktake on
r14 = is also marketed by
r15 = is price advertised for purchase of
r16 = .. if leased over a period of .. has monthly fee of ..

11.4 Normalization

So far we have discussed two aspects of NIAM: the conceptual schema design procedure (CSDP), and the optimal normal form algorithm (ONFA). The process of mapping from a conceptual schema expressed in elementary fact types to a relational schema expressed in table types is one of **deconceptualization**. This approach facilitates sound design primarily because it emphasizes working from examples, in natural language, and thinking in terms of the natural semantics of the UoD being modelled. Moreover, the conceptual schema may be mapped onto non-relational implementations if desired.

Although NIAM offers many advantages over traditional approaches to relational database design, its practice is not yet widespread in the workforce. Instead, many designers still use a technique known as **normalization**. Since the table design resulting from our deconceptualization is already fully normalized, we do not need to learn about normalization to get our designs correct. However, in this section we have a very brief look at normalization, partly to consolidate aspects of good design and partly to help you communicate with those who use the normalization approach.

Once you have designed the conceptual schema for a UoD, the ONF algorithm enables you to map this straight onto a table schema with no repeating attributes, no redundancy, and a minimum number of tables satisfying these two criteria. Typically some of the constraints in the conceptual schema will not be expressible in terms of relational table definitions, and will need to be coded as separate validation rules. This optimal normal form is typically a version of the fifth (and last) normal form that is obtained by the normalization approach.

There are actually two approaches to normalization. One approach, known as "synthesis", begins with the complete set of attributes and dependencies, and uses formal techniques mainly based on FDs to group the attributes together into tables. The other, more popular approach is called "decomposition", whereby tables that are too large are decomposed into smaller ones that are free of update anomalies. Our discussion deals only with normalization by decomposition. To assist the reader who might be reading this section out of sequence, some relevant concepts developed earlier in the text are briefly redefined.

Instead of working down from a higher level to obtain a table design, the normalization approach proceeds to this goal by starting with what might be a bad design, and then using rules to successively refine this into the desired form. Although various types of *normal forms* are discussed in the literature, we confine our attention to those that focus on eliminating problems with a table by splitting it into smaller ones. There are six such normal forms. In increasing order of acceptability these are: first normal form, second normal form, third normal form, Boyce/Codd normal form, fourth normal form, and fifth normal form. These may be abbreviated as *1NF, 2NF, 3NF, BCNF, 4NF* and *5NF*.

The first three forms were originally proposed by E. F. Codd, who founded the relational model of data. The other forms were introduced later to cater for additional cases. These improvements were due to the work of several researchers including Codd, Boyce, Fagin, Aho, Beeri and Ullman. The basic idea of normalization is to redesign the tables to reduce the chance of update anomalies. An *update anomaly* is a problem that may arise when an update operation (insert, delete or modify) is performed.

One drastic type of update anomaly that can occur is changing just some instances of a standard identifier (e.g. Student# or SubjCode). However, altering the value of a primary key is quite rare. In practice most update anomalies arise because of *redundancy* in the database. There are two main kinds of problem that arise when trying to update a fact that is duplicated in the database. Firstly, it is typically up to the user (rather than being automated by the system) to search out and change *all* instances of the fact. Changing just some instances of the fact leads to the second problem: the database is now *inconsistent*.

A table is *normalized*, or in 1NF, iff its fields are single-valued and fixed. This notion was introduced earlier in the chapter. As an example of an unnormalized table consider the following table definition and sample population:

Studies =   [Student, Subjects REP]

      Fred   CS113, CS102, PD102
      Sue   MP104, CS113

Here the Subjects field may be considered to hold a *set* of values rather than a single value: this structured field is often described, somewhat unfortunately, as a "repeating attribute" (hence the notation "REP"). Sometimes a field may hold a set of grouped values. For example:

Scores =   [Student, [Subject, Rating] REP]

      Fred   CS113 6, CS102 5, PD102 6
      Sue   MP104 7, CS113 6

Such a field is a "repeating group"; this term may be used to include the notion of repeating attribute by allowing degenerate groups with one value. Both the above tables are unnormalized; that is, they are not in any normal form.

Another example of an unnormalized table is the "variant record type" used in languages such as Pascal and Modula. Here different occurrences of the same record type may contain different fields. For instance, a record type about coloured geometric figures may include common fields for figure-id, colour and shape (circle, rhombus, triangle etc.) but have different remaining fields depending on the shape (e.g. radius for circle; side and angle for rhombus; three sides for triangle). Although this provides one way of implementing a restricted notion of subtypes, the record structure used is completely unnormalized.

Table 11.7

Player =   [Person, Sport, Height]

Person	Sport	Height
Fred	tennis	180
Fred	footy	180
Sue	tennis	170

If a table is normalized it will be in at least *1NF* and at most *5NF*. Since any table in a higher normal form is also in all lower normal forms, let us use the term "hNF" to describe the highest normal form of a table.

For a given relation, an attribute is said to be a *nonkey attribute* iff it is neither a key nor a part of a composite key. Given attributes A and B of a relation, *A functionally determines B* iff B is a function of A (i.e. within the relation, for each value of A there is only one value for B). This may be written $A \rightarrow B$, and may also be read B is *functionally dependent* on A. Attributes A and B may be composite.

A table is in **2NF** iff it is in *1NF* and every nonkey attribute is (functionally) dependent on the *whole* of the key (not just a part of it).

Consider Table 11.7. Its hNF = 1 since the nonkey attribute Height is dependent on just part of the key, namely the Person attribute. Notice the redundancy: the fact that Fred has a height of 180 cm has been recorded twice.

By definition, every nonkey attribute is dependent on any key of the relation (Why?). Note that to determine the hNF of a relation we need to have a significant population or be told what the keys are. To avoid redundancy we must split the Player table into the two smaller ones [Person, Sport] and [Person, Height] which are both in second normal form. Check the schema and ONF mapping shown in Figure 11.22 to convince yourself that NIAM automatically caters for such normalization.

Note that although the normalization to 2NF overcomes the redundancy problem in the Player table, this is at the expense of a drop in efficiency for queries which involve all the fields of the original table. For example, if we want to know the name and height of all the footy players the 2NF design means that two tables will need to be searched and have their Person fields matched. This kind of efficiency loss, which is common to each

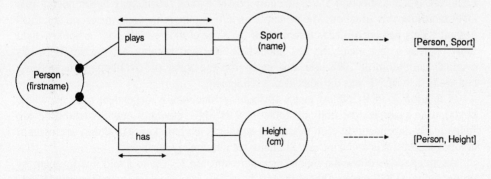

Figure 11.22

Table 11.8

Lecturer	Dept	Building
Halpin	CS	69
Okimura	JA	1
Nijssen	CS	69
Wang	CH	1

Table 11.9

Student#	StudentName	Subject	Rating
831	Smith J A	CS113	7
831	Smith J A	CS102	6

normalization refinement (each involves splitting), is more than offset by the higher degree of data integrity resulting from the elimination of redundancy. For example, if we need to change Fred's height to 182 cm, and record this change on only the first row of the Player table we now have two different values for Fred's height. With more serious examples (e.g. defense, medical, business) such inconsistencies could prove disastrous.

If $A \rightarrow B$, then an update of A entails a possible update of B. Within a relation, a set of attributes is *mutually independent* iff none of the attributes is (functionally) dependent on any of the others. In this case the attributes may be updated independently of one another.

A table is in **3NF** iff it is in 2NF and its nonkey attributes are mutually independent. Consider Table 11.8. Its hNF = 2 since the nonkey attribute Building depends on the nonkey attribute Dept. Another way of expressing this is to say that Building is transitively dependent on the key (Building depends on Dept which depends on Lecturer). Refer to Section 5.2 to see how NIAM avoids redundancy by producing two ONF tables for this situation. The principle underlying the refinement to second and third normal forms has been nicely summarized by Kent (1983) as follows: "a nonkey field must provide a fact about the key, the whole key, and nothing but the key". Codd's original definition of 3NF did not cater for the case of overlapping uniqueness constraints, so BCNF was introduced as a refinement.

A relation is in **BCNF** iff *every* attribute is functionally dependent only on whole key(s). For example, the hNF of Table 11.9 is 3NF. Student# and StudentName are functionally dependent on each other, and neither is a whole key. Since they are parts of composite keys, StudentName and Student# are not nonkey attributes.

As an exercise, show the redundancy here and use NIAM to avoid this problem by producing two ONF tables. Other kinds of cases can arise of tables in 3NF but not BCNF, but all can be resolved by NIAM.

Table 11.10

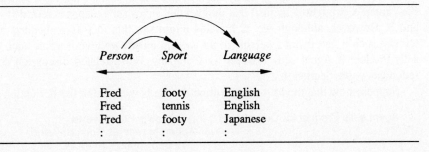

Person	Sport	Language
Fred	footy	English
Fred	tennis	English
Fred	footy	Japanese
:	:	:

Table 11.11

Agent	Product	Company
Jones	sedan	GMH
Jones	4WD	GMH
Jones	sedan	Ford
Smith	sedan	GMH

For a given relation with attributes A, B, and C, attribute A *multidetermines* attribute B iff the *set* of B values paired with any given values of A, C is a function of A only. This is written A —» B, and B is said to be *multivalued dependent*, or *multidependent* on A. In such a case C will also be multidependent on A. A functional dependency is a special case of a multivalued dependency, namely, when the set of dependent values is a unit set.

A relation is in **4NF** iff it is in BCNF and all its dependencies are functional (single-valued) dependencies. For example, Table 11.10 has its hNF = BCNF. It is in BCNF since the only key is the whole row. It is not in 4NF since, for example, sport is multidependent (but not functionally dependent) on Person. A similar comment applies to language. As an exercise, indicate the gross redundancy of which this table is guilty. We take it as obvious for this UoD that sport and language should be treated as independent. As an exercise, use NIAM to produce two ONF tables to eliminate this problem.

Tables in 4NF are almost always in 5NF as well. A table is in **5NF** if and only if it is in 4NF and has no "mutual dependencies" or "join dependencies". Since such dependencies are extremely rare, and the kind of splitting involved has been discussed in earlier work, we do little more than mention them here. The classic example used to illustrate the notion is the situation portrayed in Table 11.11, for which a small sample population has been provided to show that the uniqueness constraint is the weakest possible (verify this constraint for yourself).

The information on the top row in Table 11.11 may be expressed briefly as: Agent "Jones" sells the Product "sedan" for the Company "GMH". Here, if there is no related derivation rule, then any attempt to split this ternary into binaries will result in information loss. For example, from the facts that Smith is a representative for GMH, and that GMH makes the product 4WD, it does not follow that Smith sells the product 4WD. You have studied earlier how to detect such non-facts by projection and regrouping. In this case we simply must leave the table as a ternary, because it does correspond to an elementary fact type.

It has been argued (e.g. by Kent) that we have a kind of unavoidable redundancy here. For example, it might be argued that the fact that Jones sells sedans is repeated on rows 1 and 3. However, although we as humans might see this fact as embedded within the ternary, such a fact is not available to the system unless we give it a rule such as: Agent sells Product **if** Agent sells Product for Company. For a related discussion concerning redundancy, see Section 9.3.

Suppose now that the following symmetric rule is included in our derivation section:

Agent sells Product for Company **if**   Agent sells Product **and**
Agent represents Company **and**
Company makes Product

Clearly, it is now possible to do a 3-way split of the ternary into the three binaries [Agent, Product], [Agent, Company] and [Company, Product], since the derivation rule enables the ternary information to be gathered from the binaries. In this case the ternary table is in 4NF but not 5NF, and we should split it into the three binary tables, which are in 5NF.

Other normal forms have been proposed (e.g. Fagin's "domain-key normal form"). However 5NF is the "last" NF in the sense that 5NF tables are free of update anomalies that can be eliminated merely by taking projections. Considerable research has been conducted in the area of normalization and dependencies. The interested reader is invited to pursue such topics by consulting the references. Kent (1983) provides a very readable introduction. Date (1986a) provides a more formal treatment and includes an extensive bibliography of recent publications in this area (pp 395-402).

Exercise 11.4

1. The conceptual schema for a given UoD is as shown. Some tables designed by various beginners for parts of this UoD are listed below. Indicate briefly, in terms of normalization theory, why each of these tables fails to be fully normalized.

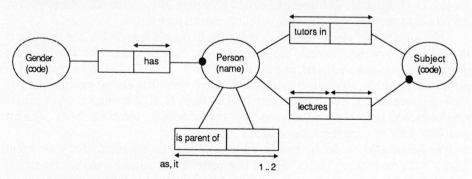

   (a) [Parent, Gender, [Child, Gender] REP]
   (b) [Person, SubjTutored, SubjLectured OP]
   (c) [Parent, Child, ParentGender, ChildGender]
   (d) [Tutor, Subject, Child OP]
   (e) Use NIAM to generate the correct ONF table schema for this UoD.

2. (a) The conceptual schema of Question 1 is actually incomplete with respect to real world constraints. For example, parents of the same child must differ in gender, but nowhere has this constraint been captured. By replacing the parent-of fact type with mother-of and father-of fact types, develop a more complete schema which includes this constraint (Hint: include subtyping).

    (b) Specify the ONF relational schema for your answer to part (a).

References

Date, C. J. (1986a), *An Introduction to Database Systems,* Vol 1, 4th ed. (Reading, MA: Addison-Wesley) Chap. 17.

Date, C. J. (1986b), *Relational Database: Selected Writings* (Reading, MA: Addison-Wesley) pp. 448–53, 461–3, 487–90.

Date, C. J. (1987), *A Guide to the SQL Standard* (Reading, MA: Addison-Wesley).

Fagin, R. (1981), "A Normal Form for Databases that is Based on Domains and Keys", *ACM Transactions on Database Systems 6*, September, pp. 387–415.

Kent, W. (1983), "A Simple Guide to Five Normal Forms in Relational Database Theory", *Communications of the ACM,* **26**, 2 (February).

12 Information flow diagrams (IFD)

12.1 Introduction

So far in this text, we have concentrated on the data perspective of an information system. We have discussed how to specify a conceptual schema starting with a significant set of familiar examples, the primary task being the verbalization of such examples by the user. Once the conceptual schema has been validated by the user, possibly assisted by the professional analyst, one can transform the conceptual schema into a *relational schema*. We recommend that this relational schema is put into an SQL database, together with the facts of the original examples. This permits the user, possibly assisted by the professional analyst, to build a prototype. It is in this stage that the professional analyst can show, in the form of good queries and answers, what the user can expect from the new database.

If the user wants to have elaborate screens or reports, or extensive constraints checked, it is often necessary to get a professional programmer involved. If that person knows that the relational schema has been properly designed, validated and prototyped, he/she can start from a solid foundation when building the application program.

In many cases, the requirements analysis is properly finished with the validated conceptual schema and prototyped relational database. This is in sharp contrast with most other methodologies which primarily expend their energy in specifying processes and their decomposition.

Although we are convinced (as will be discussed in Section 14.2) that proper data analysis is the major and first component of requirement analysis, it is sometimes useful to present an integrated data-process view of the information system. In the next section, we introduce the graphical language to describe an integrated data-process view.

12.2 NIAM information flow diagrams

NIAM conceptual schema diagrams (CSDs) enable us to describe formally, yet in a way easily understood by the user, the major information requirements, (i.e. the kind of information needed, or the data perspective). However, in some cases we need to consider **how** we get from one set of facts to another or how we move facts between the environment and the information system. In this case, we also take the process, or function-oriented, perspective into account. With NIAM, we use a graphical symbolism to express the process-oriented aspect. This symbolism is called an **information flow diagram** or IFD.

In contrast to most other methodologies, NIAM establishes the strongest coupling between IFDs and CSDs (conceptual schema diagrams), thus providing a total integration of the data and process-oriented perspectives. We come back to this point later. Which concepts do we want to express in an IFD? Firstly, of course, the concept of *process* or function. This is represented by the *rectangle* (see Figure 12.1).

We write a short description of the function either inside or next to the function symbol. The next concept we need to represent is the *flow of information*. For this we use an *arrow* whose head points in the direction of the information flow (see Figure 12.2).

Since we are concerned only with information systems, we restrict our attention to processes whose sole purpose is to produce, or move, information. The information flowing into a process is said to be the *input* of that process. The information flowing out of a process is said to be the *output* of that process. The input and output of a process may reside in a *database*. We represent this as shown in Figure 12.3. The name of the database is written inside or next to the symbol.

Suppose we want to represent a situation where one database contains a table of data of which the contents of Figure 12.4 is a significant (but trivial) example:

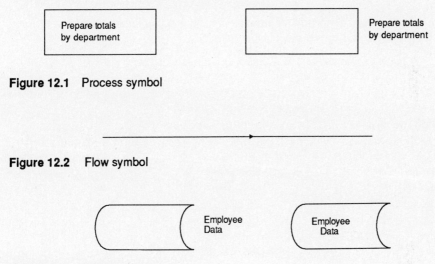

| Prepare totals by department | | | Prepare totals by department |

Figure 12.1   Process symbol

Figure 12.2   Flow symbol

| Employee Data | | Employee Data |

Figure 12.3   Database symbol

Employee	Department
E1	D1
E2	D1
E3	D2
E4	D2
E5	D2
E6	D3

Figure 12.4   Contents of the employee database

A natural language interpretation of line 1, 2, 3 as presented in Figure 12.4, is:

The Employee
    with Employee Number
        E1, E2, E3
works for
the Department
    with Department Number
        D1, D1, D2

The other database, called Department Data, contains a table of data of which Figure 12.5 is a significant example.

A natural language interpretation of line 1, 2, 3, Figure 12.5, is:

The Department
    with Department Code
        D1, D2, D3
has staff size of
    2 ,3 ,1
        persons.

To indicate that a process can compute from the Employee-data the number of employees by department, we could use an IFD as in Figure 12.6. The contents of Figure 12.6 illustrate the basis for nearly all process-oriented methodologies, albeit that different symbols are used to denote processes and input/output.

Department	Number of Employees
D1	2
D2	3
D3	1

Figure 12.5   Contents of the department database

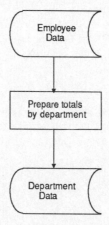

Figure 12.6   Information flow diagram (incompletely described)

The major feature of NIAM's IFDs is the total integration of process and data-oriented views, where all information manipulated by a function is explicitly and completely (in the relational sense) defined on the diagram. In NIAM we represent this integrated view as in Figure 12.7. There we see that not only are the databases completely defined by a relational schema but also (in this case) the function is formally defined. For this definition, we used the language SQL.

NIAM IFDs use exact definitions of the databases involved. This approach differs from most other design methodologies which use functional decomposition with vaguely defined databases (e.g. ISAC, IE, D2S2, Yourdon, Gane/Sarson, DFD).

If information is input (by a human being or robot) to the system, or output from the system via a *screen* we use the symbol as represented in Figure 12.8.

To describe the process which brings facts from the outside world, concerning which employee works for which department, into the information system, we could use the IFD of Figure 12.9. In general such a process should be designed to bring new facts into the database as well as delete facts from the database.

The user requests via flow F1 that the information system stores a new fact instance into the EMPLOYEE table, or EMPLOYEE database. The system will consult (F5) the "law", for the EMPLOYEE database, which is the EMPLOYEE relational schema. If according to this schema and the current population of the EMPLOYEE database (using F3) the fact instance can be added to the EMPLOYEE database (F4), the system notifies the user via F2 that the request has been successfully executed.

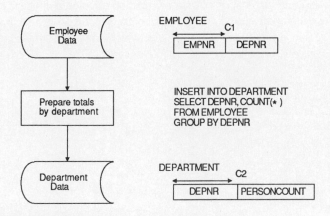

Figure 12.7 Information flow diagram (completely described)

Figure 12.8 Screen symbol

Please note that the relational schema describing the table EMPLOYEE and constraints presented in Figure 12.9 is actually the contents of the database called EMPLOYEE relational schema. To make an IFD less crowded, we omit the schema symbols associated with databases. With a large number of tables, we represent the relational schema on a separate page.

Another concept useful in an IFD is a *report*. The symbol used in an IFD to represent a report is presented in Figure 12.10.

If we have the employee data as in Figure 12.9 and want the department data in an output report, but not stored as permanent facts, we could represent such a situation by the IFD of Figure 12.11.

The conceptual schema associated with the EMPLOYEE DATA database is the same as the one in the upper half of Figure 12.9. But how would we formally describe the contents of the output report called DEPARTMENT DATA? The **select** statement formally describes the information content but it does not describe the positioning of the fact instances on the report, nor the display attributes of the fact instances on the report. These latter aspects are specific characteristics of a report language.

So far we have seen how to represent a:

• function or process,
• database,
• user providing input or accepting output,
• report.

One of the essential aspects of process or function-oriented approaches is the ability to describe the decomposition of a function into other components. In NIAM IFDs, a function may be decomposed into more functions and databases, provided the inputs and

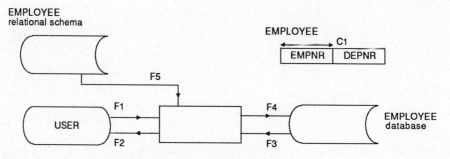

Figure 12.9   Information flow diagram including a screen

Figure 12.10   Report symbol

outputs of the function to be decomposed remain the same at the lower level. Please note that this is a language to describe decomposition—it is not implied that this language automatically helps you to perform good decomposition (e.g. the Pascal language does not force you to write structured programs). Figure 12.12 represents a top level IFD with only one function, F1, which has as input database A and output database B. Figure 12.13 represents a possible decomposition. Here the function F1 is decomposed into three functions (F11, F12 and F13) and two databases (C and D); please note that A and B are the same in Figures 12.12 and 12.13.

Another permitted decomposition of Figure 12.12 is given in Figure 12.14.

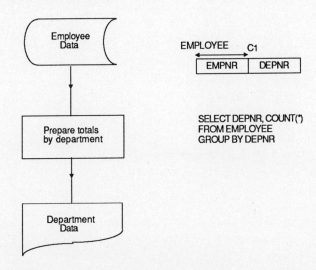

Figure 12.11   Information flow diagram including a report

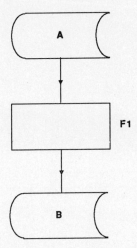

Figure 12.12   Top level IFD

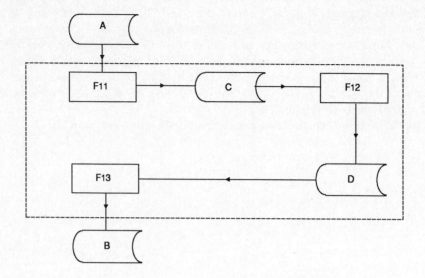

Figure 12.13   Lower level IFD (decomposition of Figure 12.12)

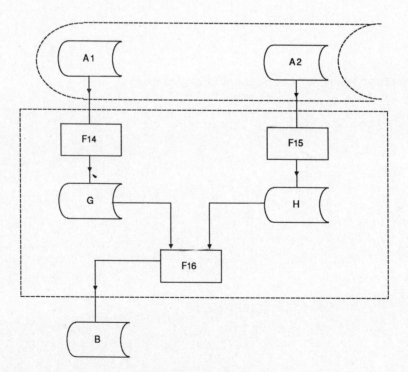

Figure 12.14   An alternative decomposition of Figure 12.12

Please note that F1 has been decomposed into the three functions F14, F15 and F16 and the databases G and H, and that the database A has been decomposed into A1 and A2.

12.3 An application

We illustrate the use of IFDs with a well-known application. Our universe of discourse is a municipal library system where persons holding a library card can borrow books. The library has multiple copies of the more popular books. Books are identified by a six digit number where the last digit is used to identify the specific copy. Hence, the library has decided "never" to have more than ten copies of a book. A library card holder can borrow a book for two weeks. If not returned, a reminder is sent out. A book that is not in stock can be reserved by a library card holder. Borrowers may not have more than four books at any one time. As a service to borrowers, the librarians maintain an author, subject and title index. The acquisition of new books and deletion of old books is outside the scope of this universe of discourse.

In a traditional analysis methodology where hierarchical decomposition (process analysis) was performed before the data analysis was complete, the resulting specifications would include diagrams such as Figures 12.15, 12.16 and 12.17.

By now, it should be clear that there is a more productive way to analyze this universe of discourse. The first step of this analysis should be to ask the user for examples of the (existing or intended) records or forms that show the facts to be recorded in the intended information system. In other words, we first need a significant set of familiar examples of facts about:

- card holders
- loans
- available books
- indexes

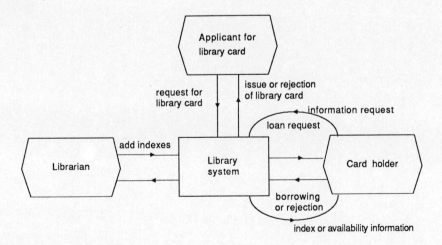

Figure 12.15 Top level IFD for the library system

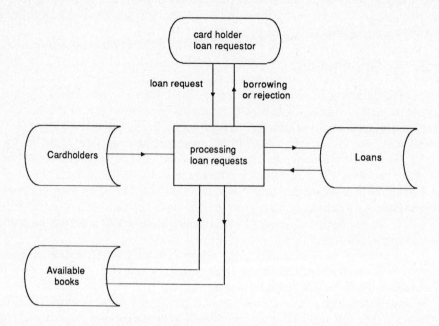

Figure 12.16   IFD for processing loan requests

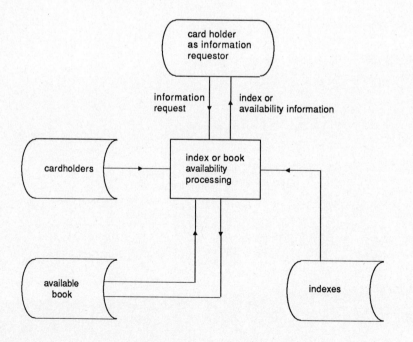

Figure 12.17   IFD for processing index book availability requests

Let us assume the user gives us the following:

Library card information

Card nr:	65257
Surname:	Johnson
Initials:	P.K.
Date of birth:	18.12.1950
Date of issue:	12.05.1988
Addressline-1	
Addressline-2	

Books

Book nr:	37723
Authors:	Spencer J.
	Jones K.
Title:	Parks in Japan
Subjects:	Japan
	Parks
	Tourism

Book edition

Book nr:	37723
Edition nr:	1
Currently available:	yes

Loan record

Book nr:	37723	Library card nr:	65257
Edition nr:	2	On loan from:	15.05.1988

Reminder

Please return this book as soon as possible.

Library card nr:	65257
Book nr:	37723
Edition nr:	2
On loan since:	15.05.1988

Returns

Book nr:	37723
Edition nr:	2
On loan since:	15.05.1988
Return date:	06.06.1988

The design of the conceptual schema and the resulting relational tables is left as an exercise for the reader. In our analysis, the relational tables are specified as in Figure 12.18.

We can now cross-reference the databases in the IFDs with these table specifications to make the IFDs more useful for design.

Database name	Table name
CARDHOLDERS	*Cardholders*
AVAILABLE BOOKS	*Availability*
INDEXES	*Booktitle*
	Bookauthors
	Booksubjects
LOANS	*Loan*

Now the structure of the input and output is precisely defined for each function. This will allow us to reason about these information flow diagrams with precision and to use them as an effective tool for information systems specification.

To summarize:

> Information flow diagrams are used to describe the flow of information. By combining IFDs with relational schemas, one gets a very precise picture of the flow of information in a system.

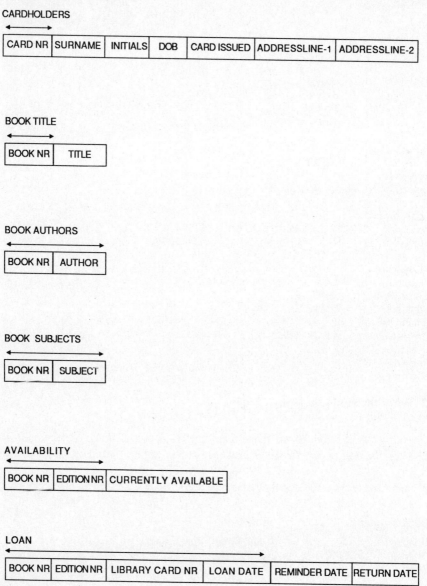

Figure 12.18   Relational database schema for library UoD

13 The conceptual metaschema

13.1 Introduction

In this chapter, we use the conceptual schema design procedure (CSDP) to specify a conceptual schema for a database which has, as its contents, any well-formed conceptual schema.

A conceptual schema itself (see Figure 13.1) is a piece of knowledge which can be expressed in natural language sentences and can therefore be considered to consist of a number of facts. Hence, we may consider the contents of a conceptual schema to be stored in a database. All the permitted states and transitions of such a database are, of course, determined by a conceptual schema which we call the conceptual metaschema.

The NIAM CSDP considers only one kind of input construct, the fact instances, and determines the fact types, roles, entity types, entity subtypes, label types and constraints. A conceptual schema for a user's application is effectively a database about a database, that is, a metadatabase. This means that the NIAM CSDP can be used to analyse the fact instances (that define the conceptual schema or metadatabase) and specify the fact types, roles, entity types, entity subtypes, label types and constraints of the conceptual metaschema (which is the conceptual schema that defines the permitted states and transitions of the metadatabase). Figure 13.1 further illustrates that exactly the same NIAM CSDP can be used to produce an application specific conceptual schema and an application independent conceptual metaschema. Though a CIP is shown twice on the diagram, it is possible to use the same CIP for both tasks. In the metalevel case, the conceptual information processor deals exclusively with the semantics of conceptual schemas (as defined by the conceptual metaschema) in deciding which metadatabase states and transitions are permitted.

13.2 Towards a significant set of familiar examples

The main aim of this chapter is to illustrate the basic notion of *meta* levels (or levels of type abstraction). This can be accomplished by selecting a subset of the concepts in a NIAM conceptual schema. We will therefore limit the conceptual schema language to include only the following:

291

- elementary fact types (irreducible),
- entity types (excluding nominalization or nesting),
- label types (but only in unique and identifying naming conventions),
- intrafact uniqueness (identifier) constraints,
- mandatory role constraints.

However, there is a complete conceptual metaschema for well-formed NIAM conceptual schemas that includes the aspects that have been ignored in this chapter. Although it is not necessary for the development of the conceptual metaschema, we will start at the bottom level which is the database level (or level 1) and build up from there. The current contents of the example database are represented in Figures 13.2 and Figure 13.3.

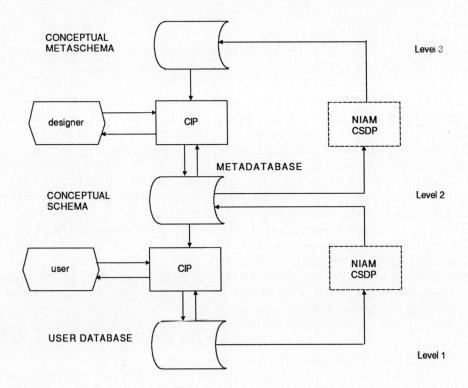

Figure 13.1   Three levels of type abstraction

Person	Birthyear
P1	1946
P2	1952
P3	1938

Figure 13.2   People have birthyears

The user performs the verbalization step for this example, to provide the following well-interpreted sentence instances:

```
The PERSON
     with PERSON-CODE
          "P1", "P2", "P3"
was-born-in
the YEAR
          "1946", "1952", "1938"
     AD
```

Figure 13.3 shows the remaining contents of the example database. The user provides the following interpretation for these facts:

```
The PERSON
     with PERSON-CODE
          "P1", "P1", "P1", "P2", ...
has-spent-so-far-on
the PROJECT
     with PROJECT-CODE
          "R1", "R2", "R3", "R1", ...
the PERIOD of
          "50", "26", "24", "26", ...
     HOURS
```

From this significant set of familiar examples (at the database level), we can conclude that the following constraints exist:

- every value in the person column must be unique (C1) in every table population like Figure 13.2. (Informally, a person has at most one recorded birthyear.)
- the combination of person and project is unique (C2) in every table population like Figure 13.3. (Informally, every person, project pair has at most one value of "hours so far" recorded.)
- if any fact is known about a person in the database, at least his/her birthyear fact must then be known (C3) in the database. (Informally, every person has at least one recorded birthyear.)

The combination of C1 and C3 requires that every person (recorded in the database) has exactly one birthyear (recorded in the database).

Person	Project	Hours spent so far
P1	R1	50
P1	R2	26
P1	R3	24
P2	R1	26
P2	R3	60
P3	R3	40
P3	R2	26

Figure 13.3   People work on projects

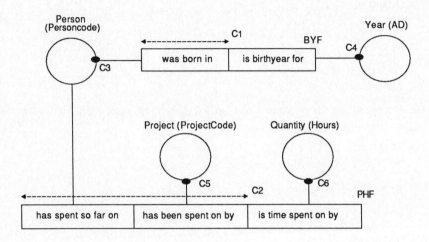

Figure 13.4 Conceptual schema (graphical form)

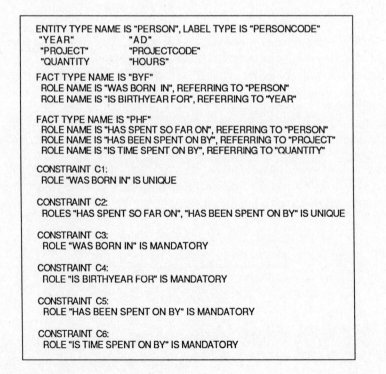

Figure 13.5 Conceptual schema (textual form)

The table populations of Figures 13.2 and 13.3 specify the contents of the user database (at level 1).

The next requirement is to specify the conceptual schema (at level 2) for this database. Of course, we can simply use the NIAM CSDP, together with the previous interpretations and detected constraints to specify this conceptual schema. Figure 13.4 contains a graphical specification of this (level 2) conceptual schema.

This conceptual schema contains two fact types, four entity types, four label types, two uniqueness constraints and four mandatory role constraints.

We could also provide, instead of the graphical conceptual schema of Figure 13.4, an equivalent textual specification (after the style of the CODASYL DDL), as in Figure 13.5.

13.3   The metaschema

Now, to define the conceptual metaschema (level 3) whose permitted population exclusively consists of well-formed (level 2) conceptual schemas, we can apply the CSDP again. In this case, the conceptual schema (of Figure 13.4 or Figure 13.5) is the example population. As usual, we require the user to perform the verbalization step and thus produce the semantic interpretation for the initial examples. Of course, the "user" is the person who is most familiar with the semantics of the application area (the universe of discourse). In this case, the application user is much less familiar with the semantics of conceptual schema diagrams than is the information analyst. For this step, the *information analyst is the user*, and should provide the interpretation. You should understand the semantics of conceptual schema diagrams well enough to provide this interpretation:

```
The Role
      with Role Name
            "was born in", "is birthyear for"
is played by
the Entity Type
      with Entity Type Name
            "Person", "Year"

The Role
      with Role Name
            "was born in", "is birthyear for"
belongs to
the Fact Type
      with Fact Type Name
            "BYF", "BYF"

The Entity Type
      with Entity Type Name
            "Person", "Project"
is identified by
the Label Type
      with Label Type Name
            "Personcode", "Projectcode"
```

The Role
    with Role Name
        "was born in", "*has spent so far on*", "has been spent on by"
is in scope of
the Uniqueness Constraint
    with Constraint code
        "C1", "*C2*", "C2"

The Role
    with Role Name
        "was born in", "*is birthyear for*"
is in scope of
the Mandatory Role Constraint
    with Constraint code
        "C3", "*C4*"

Notice that the same conceptual schema role ("was born in") can play the same metaschema role "is in scope of" in two different fact types. This is a clue that the two roles should be combined into one role, and the distinguishing information preserved by specifying a new fact type.

    The new interpretation for this aspect is:

The Role
    with Role Name
        "was born in", "*has spent so far on*", "has been spent on by", "*was born in*"
is in scope of
the Constraint
    with Constraint code
        "C1", "*C2*", "C2", "*C3*"

The Constraint
    with Constraint code
        "C1", "*C2*", "C3"
is of
the Kind-of-Constraint
    with Kind-of-Constraint-Name
        "uniqueness", "*uniqueness*", mandatory role"

The conceptual metaschema (for this subset of the NIAM concepts) is given in Figure 13.6.

    In Figure 13.7, we have specified the conceptual schema for the level 1 database *as a level 2 database* which conforms to the specification of the level 3 conceptual schema (conceptual *meta*schema).

    A hierarchy of these data levels is presented in Figure 13.8.

    How many levels must there be in this hierarchy? Well, the conceptual schema describes a specific UoD, but the conceptual metaschema describes a UoD which consists only of well-formed conceptual schemas. As the conceptual metaschema is also a conceptual schema, then it should be possible to store the contents of the conceptual metaschema in its own database. If this can be done, then three levels of type abstraction will always be sufficient (because any levels above level 3 must be identical to level 3). In other words, if the conceptual metaschema is considered as a database (the metametadatabase) then this database must be a permitted population of some conceptual schema (named the conceptual metametaschema).

The question is, must the conceptual metametaschema (or, in general, the conceptual meta^n schema for $n > 1$) be *identical* to the conceptual metaschema?

If the answer is "yes", then the hierarchy of metalevels *collapses* after level 3 because all subsequent levels are identical to level 3.

If the answer is "no", then the hierarchy of metalevels continues to *diverge* after level 3 and we will have to construct higher levels in order to obtain the complete picture.

Clearly, the answer to this question depends on the conceptual schema concepts under consideration. We can answer the question empirically, with respect to this limited set of concepts, by trying to store the contents of Figure 13.6 (the conceptual metaschema) *within* the conceptual schema specified by that same figure. The result is presented in Figures 13.9 and 13.10.

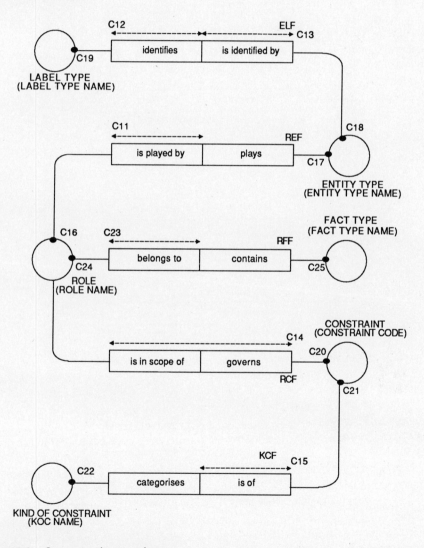

Figure 13.6 Conceptual metaschema.

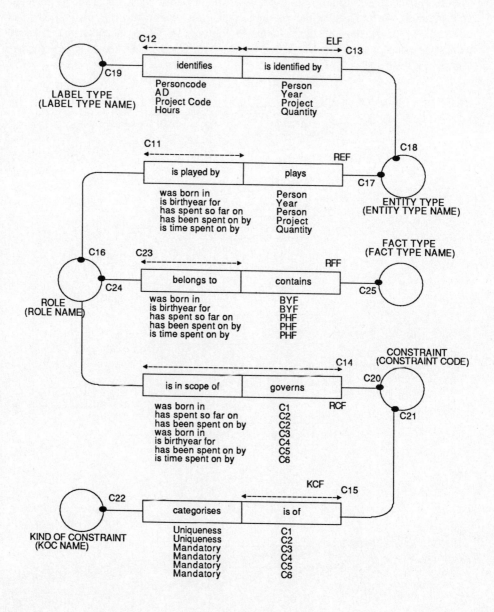

Figure 13.7   Each conceptual metaschema with population

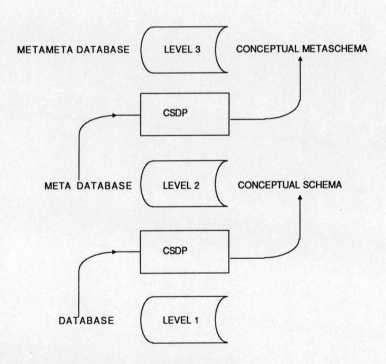

Figure 13.8   Conceptual schema is also a database

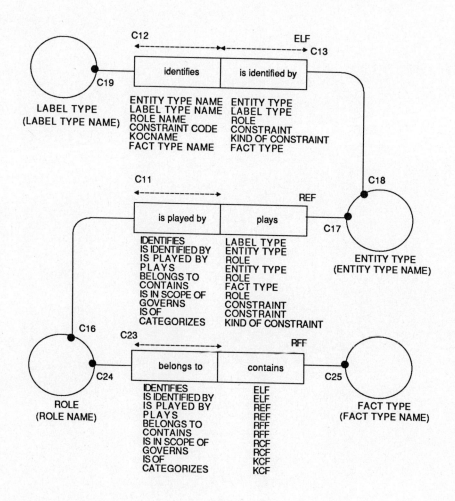

Figure 13.9 Conceptual metaschema populated with itself

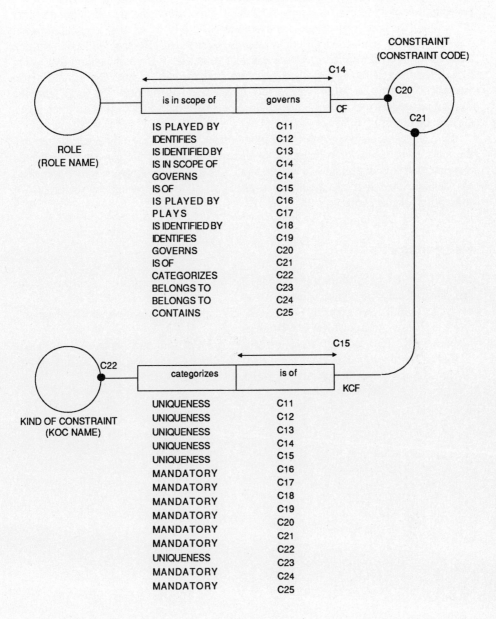

Figure 13.10 Conceptual metaschema populated with itself

We want to call attention to the fact that the role "is in scope of" in Figure 13.10 is optional. Note that the population of the conceptual schema in Figures 13.9 and 13.10 is the definition of that *same* conceptual schema. In other words, the answer to our question is "yes" and the hierarchy collapses at this point: level 4 is the same as level 3 (and level 5 is the same as level 4, which is the same as level 3, etc.). Hence, we have seen that three levels of type abstraction are theoretically sufficient. If the architectural distinction between conceptual schema and database is required, then the three level hierarchy is also theoretically necessary. However, if this architectural distinction is erased (and the conceptual schema and database are collapsed into one big soup) then these three levels may not be necessary in theory.

Of course, this analysis comes with an important *caveat*. It has only demonstrated that the meta level hierarchy collapses after three metalevels in the case of this specific (restricted) set of conceptual schema concepts. Research at the University of Queensland has demonstrated that the argument is also correct for the complete set of NIAM conceptual schema concepts.

References

Olle, T. W. et al. (1988), *Information Systems Methodologies: A Framework for Understanding*, (Reading: Addison-Wesley).

Mark, L. (1985) "Self-Describing Database Systems—Formalization and Realization", Ph.D. Thesis, Aarhus University, Denmark.

Meersman, R. (forthcoming) "Towards Models for Practical Reasoning about Database Design", *Proceedings of DS-2 Database Semantics Conference*, R. Meersman and A. Sernadas (eds), (Amsterdam: North-Holland Publishing Co.).

14 NIAM and other methodologies

In this chapter, we will discuss the traditional information system methodologies and the information system development life cycle. This is then contrasted with a tightly coupled fourth/fifth generation information systems methodology. This combination means that we can use fifth generation analysis combined with fourth generation relational implementation technology.

14.1 Short history of information systems methodologies

The pre-methodology age

In the 1960s and early 1970s, one could hardly detect any principled methodology at use in the design of larger information systems. This statement would be challenged by many accountants, certainly those employed by the large accounting firms or management consultants at that time. What really happened? Let us recall that there were large organizations before the advent of the computer. These large organizations were using (paper) information systems although these were often supported by mechanical accounting and sorting machines before the introduction of batch-oriented computers. Some of the professional accounting and management consulting firms had indeed developed a series of guidelines on how to analyze and implement such paper-based, or partly mechanically supported, information systems. However, these information systems, as well as their associated methodologies, were very rigid and somewhat oriented towards bigger bureaucracies.

It is regrettable that the (extensive) experience with these rigid "paper" systems was not used to develop these new, much more flexible computer-based information systems. Let us add to this a word of caution. Most of the information systems at that time were batch-oriented, and when compared with current technology, are found to be rigid. However, compared with the paper and mechanical systems, these batch systems were much more flexible.

What was happening in the field of the professionals who were experts in the new computer technology? Most computer scientists were interested in systems programming, and the area of information systems was virtually ignored. Indeed, if one looks at university teaching programs in the 1960s and 1970s, most universities were teaching principles of hardware, operation systems, assembler and procedural language programming and compiler construction techniques while some gave a prominent place to numerical analysis. Teaching and research in computer science was part of mathematics or electrical engineering departments, neither of which had expertise in the area of large information systems. This was unfortunate because the lion's share of computer applications was, is, and probably always will be, information systems.

Large information systems, which were successfully providing useful services (like payroll systems, banking systems and airline reservation systems) were considered an unavoidable "COBOL" nuisance by far too many professional scientists during that time period.

The age of structured programming

In the 1970s, a drive was launched to improve "the art of programming". We would welcome a tribute for the people who successfully introduced the structured programming discipline into the professional EDP workforce. Researchers such as de Marco, Gane and Sarson, Jackson, Nassi and Schneiderman, Warnier and Orr, and Yourdon and Constantine made significant contributions in this regard. These "missionaries" had to overcome enormous resistance from the "native" EDP professionals, who had deeply entrenched "pagan" habits. It is worth remarking that nearly all the names just mentioned were primarily interested in application programming.

Now in the late 1980s, one may conclude that structured programming has the same degree of acceptance in the professional programmers' world as the Bible in the Vatican. In the 1970s, most computer scientists believed that large information systems were essentially just large programs. This could probably be attributed to the famous law of Niklaus Wirth:

Algorithms + Data Structures = Programs

Let us analyze why this law covers systems programs but is inadequate for information systems.

In systems programming, the expert in the application (e.g. a Pascal compiler) and the systems programmer are often the same person. Hence, there is a very small semantic gap (if any) between the expert and the systems programmer.

Let us now analyze the area of information systems. Firstly, the expert in a certain area, say accounting (or personnel management, or insurance underwriting, or stock control, etc.), is almost *never* the information technology and programming expert. Hence, in the area of information systems, there is a considerable "grand canyon" between the world of the expert and user and the world of the information technologist.

Secondly, the data structures in systems programming, and particularly in mathematics, are relatively simple. The task of discovering "interesting" fact types about one entity type (such as real numbers) can sometimes keep people busy for years. In the area of information systems, the opposite is the case. The typical information system has very elaborate data structures which are strongly typed. The simplistic distinction between the data types of character, integer and floating point is completely inadequate in that application domain.

Thirdly, the algorithms in most traditional computer science applications were elaborate and therefore received most of the attention. The algorithms in most information systems are straightforward and well- known.

When we summarize these three aspects (Figure 14.1) it becomes clear that methods applicable in one area cannot necessarily be transplanted to the other area. In the 1970s, the computer scientists applied their structured program techniques to the task of information systems analysis design. Unfortunately, they did not realize that these techniques are often inappropriate for the design of information systems.

For information systems, we could rewrite Wirth's famous law to:

	traditional computer science	information systems
semantic gap between application expert and information technologist	small	large
data structure	simple	elaborate
algorithm	elaborate	simple

Figure 14.1 A summary of differences

SEMANTIC ANALYSIS

+

DATA STRUCTURE

+

ALGORITHM

=

INFORMATION SYSTEM

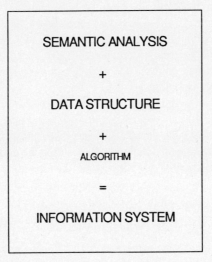

Figure 14.2 A law for information systems development

The real problem for information systems design

In the mid-1970s, a movement started within the International Federation of Information Processing (IFIP) which has tried to suggest that the EDP world is not primarily geocentric (algorithm or process-oriented) but heliocentric (data or knowledge-oriented). With the recent success of structured programming on the mind of every EDP professional in the mid-1970s, this view was often disputed or ignored. Now, in the late 1980s, it is becoming clear that this basic assumption about information systems design methodologies is due for a major review.

14.2   Towards the supremacy of declarative knowledge

Data or knowledge: The most familiar foundation

Present work within IFIP (*Information Systems Methodologies: A Framework for Understanding*, 1988) has indicated that information systems can be viewed from three major perspectives: the data perspective, the process perspective and the behavioral (or event) perspective. There are several reasons to suggest that the data perspective is the most fundamental. For example, all three perspectives can be described using the data perspective concepts but it is not possible to describe the data perspective using the process perspective or behavioral perspective concepts. To express this in more precise terms, it is possible to define a conceptual schema for all possible conceptual schemas, a conceptual schema for all possible information flow diagrams and a conceptual schema for any set of behavioral perspective concepts. However, it is not possible to have an information flow diagram of the conceptual schema. Of course, it is possible to specify an information flow diagram of the conceptual schema *design procedure*. These three perspectives of an information system must be strongly integrated. Once we accept the data perspective as our foundation, a host of new opportunities arises.

Firstly, and most importantly, users deal with examples of data in their everyday work. They are very familiar with examples of data and much less familiar with the definitions of the processes that manipulate that data. This familiarity indicates that examples are the best starting point. Secondly, one can use examples of data to permit the user to validate the data perspective.

The next question is: which data perspective concepts do we choose? As every user is familiar with the natural language used in their application, it is essential that the data perspective concepts are strongly based on the structure of this language. This leads us to choose the fact or sentence based data model to describe the data perspective. This model is one of many (claimed) semantic (or conceptual) data models.

Information systems design methodologies:
A new starting point in analysis

Process-oriented information system methodologies start from a very imprecisely defined basis (to say the least). Some data-oriented design methodologies, like ER database design, have a similarly vague starting point. This means that little effective guidance can be given to the analyst on how to perform the analysis and design process. Hence, the designer often resorts to divine inspiration to perform his design task. Furthermore, since the analysis process uses concepts which are unfamiliar to most users (e.g. normalization), it is almost impossible for the user to effectively validate the design at the early stages of the requirements analysis and design process. Of course, we all realize that errors should be picked up as early as possible. This means that these methodologies often force the analyst to perform his or her task inefficiently.

Perhaps if we built an expert system to select a better starting point, it would conclude that users are very familiar with *examples of the data* that they use in their daily work, expressed in their natural language. As it is possible to have a very precise description of the data perspectives at all levels, then information system design methodologies should accept a different starting point based on examples of data expressed in natural language. Indeed, such an "expert system" has been running in Europe since the late 1970s and its results are now spreading around the world.

The new starting point is to take a significant set of familiar data examples, given by the user, and let the user read these examples aloud, providing the analyst with the major parts of the data perspective. The fact types, entity types and label types can be immediately derived from the well-interpreted facts by a formal procedure and the validation rules (or constraints) can be added. This procedure bridges very efficiently the inevitable semantic gap between the world of the end user and the professional EL analyst. This semantic bridge is essential during the design and validation processes, and is a crucial requirement for user validation not addressed in the ER and normalization approaches to data modelling.

Information systems design methodology: A cookbook

Given this very productive starting point for the design process, it is equally important to have a well-guided procedure ("cookbook") showing how to go from this significant set of familiar data examples to the data perspective design, and when to ask for additional semantic information from the user (by showing the user an example and asking whether this example is permitted). Extensive practical experiments during the last ten years, with an approach that is based on a solid starting point and a precise cookbook, have indicated various refinements to this methodology which have been successfully tested on very large information systems design projects in many different areas.

Expert systems: How to build them effectively

Expert systems are often claimed as a new and very different class of software and it is widely acknowledged that they are very difficult to build. Why? Because most knowledge engineers (or AI analysts) do not realize that expert systems have more in common with information systems than with conventional system programs. As a result, they have been applying inappropriate structured programming techniques and reporting how unproductive these techniques are. If applications requiring expert systems software are fully analyzed, relational databases (with all their proven advantages of query optimization, flexible authorization, concurrency, back-up and recovery) should be an integral component of any expert system. Most of these essential notions in information systems are unknown in too many AI languages. We will illustrate these statements with a series of concrete and practical examples in another textbook, starting with unproductively designed, traditional AI expert systems and showing how our information systems design methodology can be extended and applied to knowledge engineering for knowledge-based systems.

A different cost structure

The cost pattern for requirements analysis (RS) systems design (SD), programming (PR) and testing (TE) is given in Figure 14.3 for third generation methodologies as a straight line and for the combined fourth/fifth generation methodologies as a dotted line. There are two important differences between the costs associated with third and fourth/fifth generation methodologies.

1. The total expenditure is much smaller with fourth/fifth generation methodologies. In fact, the total expenditure for an approach is directly related to the area under the curve for that approach.
2. With fourth/fifth generation, the requirements analysis process is more expensive, while the programming and testing are substantially cheaper.

Why is this the case?

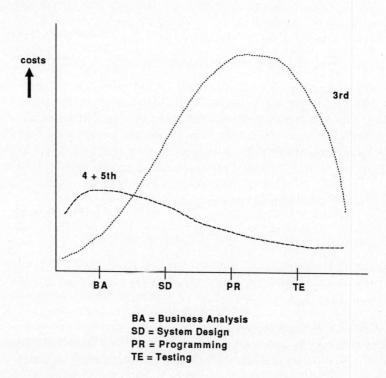

BA = Business Analysis
SD = System Design
PR = Programming
TE = Testing

Figure 14.3   Development costs

In third generation methodologies, the requirements analysis did not include a formal and user validated specification of the information or data to be processed. The reason for this was a (mistaken) belief that top down hierarchical decomposition techniques, which seemed successful for process analysis, were applicable to information analysis. As a result, it is next to impossible to perform an adequate user validation of the desired information during requirements analysis when using these third generation methodologies. This means that serious misunderstandings were detected much later in the cycle with third generation methodologies. Of course, correcting such problems at that late point is an expensive (and often disappointing) experience with third generation methodologies. With third generation methodologies, it was quite common to detect serious misunderstandings between the end user requirements and the understanding of the professional analyst, as late as the programming phase and, quite often, during the testing phase. In fourth/fifth generation fact-based methodologies, not only are the data requirements formally and precisely described during requirements analysis, but the ONF algorithm makes it possible to use relational prototyping to validate the data perspective design. This substantially increases the quality of the user requirements specification.

14.3   A complete fourth/fifth generation methodology

The major difference between third and fourth/fifth generation methodologies is the precise and user validated information requirements in the form of a conceptual schema and a prototype system applying the corresponding relational schema. In third generation methodologies, extensive activity analysis (= process analysis = procedure analysis = (sometimes even) business analysis) was carried out describing functions and their subfunctions, without describing the information required to any acceptable degree of precision. It is now accepted that very little precise guidance can be given on how to decompose a function into subfunctions. As a consequence of this lack of guidance, quite a bit of time can be wasted in third generation methodologies during hierarchical decomposition.

With fact-based fourth/fifth generation methodologies, the various steps are briefly sketched as follows:

1. Management decides to provide a budget for a proper requirements analysis for a certain business area, based on the assumption that introducing a computerised information system would be a good investment. This is the result of the information systems planning phase of the entire life cycle.

2. Divide a large problem area into manageable subareas according to some practical rule. The precise borders have no effect on the final product, so we do not have to worry too much about the division rule.

3. For each subarea, collect a significant number of familiar examples of input or output. In most cases, many of these examples already exist—the business area was not created yesterday, but has evolved gradually. Indeed, most organizations have some form of paper or computer-based information system and have many examples. In the case where an entirely new system is set up, ask the user to provide the "ideal"

examples of information that they need for the jobs/tasks that the information system is supposed to support.

4. For each familiar example:
   (a) specify the conceptual (and relational schema and prototype) if desired;
   (b) specify the IFD;
   (c) specify the event specifications.

5. For each subarea:
   (a) integrate the conceptual schemas for each example, specify associated relational schema + constraints enforced by RDBMS and prototype;
   (b) integrate IFDs for each example;
   (c) integrate the event specification for each example.

6. Integrate (as in 5 above) each subarea into the overall.

7. Specify detailed screens.

8. Specify detailed relational physical layout + constraints enforced by RDBMS.

9. Program the screens including constraints not enforced by RDBMS.

10. Test that the implementation satisfies the specification.

Automatically maintained data dictionary

In most third generation information systems, a user validated conceptual schema or relational schema has never been made, and nor has any relational prototype been made. As a consequence, many of the data descriptions that should have been included in the conceptual schema and validated by the user have been "encoded" in the application or system program maze. As these languages did not require semantic specifications, one usually finds a very short variable name and a low level data type. Some programmers, for whatever reason, did not include comments in their code to enable others to understand the data description. The result is that only the programmer who actually chiseled the data structure in granite holds the Rosetta stone in their mind. What happens when this programmer threatens to leave taking the Rosetta stone?

The obvious solution is to adopt a good data dictionary and enforce the law that all programmers must put their (explained) data descriptions in such a dictionary. This can be an expensive practice. However, with a fourth/fifth generation fact-based methodology, this data dictionary is provided at no extra cost. The result of the analysis is the contents of such a data dictionary, expressed at the conceptual level. Together with the mapping information that relates the conceptual schema to the tables, you have an automatically maintained and complete description of the intended semantics for the relational data structures. As relational technology matures, these intended semantics will be explicitly declared (as part of the relational schema) and automatically enforced by the database manager. So the use of a fourth/fifth generation methodology also paves the way for you to efficiently exploit these "long anticipated breakthroughs" in relational technology.

Effective prototyping

Relational database technology using the SQL language has become a multi-purpose technology. One purpose which has been successfully demonstrated is the use of relational database technology for effective prototyping. With relational database, it is indeed possible to show the users a real prototype quickly and have them working with the prototype. This means that it is now possible to have a prototype of a part of the system at a very early stage in the development cycle, with two important advantages. One is that prototyping very efficiently eliminates misunderstanding between users and analysts, thus contributing to an improved validation process (discussed before). The other is that users can see a working system very early without the frustration of lengthy delays while the analyst comes up with more questions.

Flexibility

One of the nightmares of most of today's computer applications is the relative inflexibility when it comes to changing an existing system. Pre-relational database technology tends to suffer a "cascade effect" from certain changes. With relational database technology, nearly all these detrimental effects are eliminated. This means that the "rusty iron chains" of older software technology need no longer prevent an organization from adjusting its information systems to the changing circumstances.

Decision support

Most organizations have computerised information systems which collect formidable amounts of basic data. In a sense, an organization sits on a valuable mine of data but has problems drilling an additional shaft or hole quickly to be able to use this valuable mineral. With relational database technology, a respectable amount of basic data can be used for management purposes or decision support applications. It is in this new area that most, if not all, managers can introduce substantial productivity increases. Once management comprehends this new opportunity, it is quickly adopted as a major improvement in productivity.

In *Information Systems Methodology: A Framework for Understanding*, the development life cycle is divided into four phases:

1. Information systems planning
2. Business analysis
3. Systems design
4. Construction.

In the new data-oriented methodology, a complete conceptual schema is developed during the business analysis phase. In older methodologies, the complete CODASYL, relational or ER model was only made during systems design. In the much more work is performed during business analysis. In fact, Figure 14.4 gives a point-by-point mapping between the ten points of the new methodology and the four phases of the IFIP report.

14.4   Other methodologies

Decomposition of DFDs

Data flow diagrams (DFDs) are very popular for specifying processes in information systems. This graphical language has been described in many textbooks and is in widespread use. The basic concepts are outlined (in two alternative notations) in Figure 14.5. DFDs are the "target language" for a hierarchical decomposition methodology. A process can be decomposed into two or more subprocesses which can, in turn, be decomposed into subprocesses themselves.

Although this method is often used, it has two major drawbacks.

1. As the data store is only "defined" by a name, there is no unambiguous specification of its contents—this often leads to misunderstandings. Remember that with IFDs, it was mandatory to provide the conceptual schema or relational schema for each database or output/input. It is essential that any data store have a formal definition of the structure of the information contained within it.

Information systems planning	1. Management provides budget
Business analysis	2. Divide problem area
	3. For each subarea, collect examples
	4. For each example, specify conceptual schema, IFD and event specifications
	5. For each subarea, integrate
	6. Integrate each subarea into the overall
Systems design	7. Specify detailed screens
	8. Specify physical tables
Construction	9. Program screens
	10. Test

Figure 14.4   The four phases of information systems design

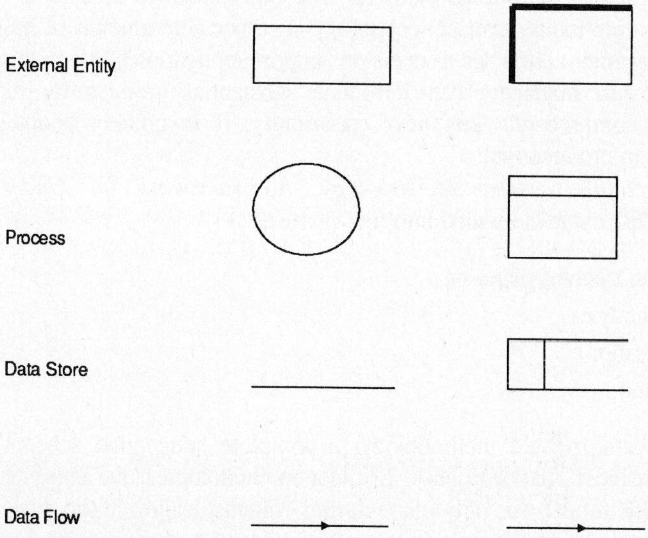

Figure 14.5   Data flow diagram symbols

2. Methodologies which use DFDs are based on hierarchical decomposition of processes. As there are no guidelines on how to decompose a process, it is often a source of unnecessary discussion.

ISAC

ISAC is a process-oriented methodology which was developed in Sweden. It has become reasonably popular in Western Europe. Although ISAC primarily relies on hierarchical decomposition of processes, called activity analysis, it has a few nice methods to systematically record the shortcomings of the present situation. The data-oriented aspects in ISAC are weak and not worth a discussion in this text.

Normalization

One of the most popular techniques for relational database design is normalization. With normalization, one starts with the so-called universal relation. This is a relation which contains the natural join of all the facts involved in a given application. The user is then asked to provide three kinds of constraints in this universal relation, namely, functional dependencies, multi-valued dependencies and join dependencies. These constraints are then used to decompose the universal relation into a set of smaller relations in 5NF (fifth normal form). The ONF form as introduced in Chapter 11 is equal to fifth normal form with the additional two characteristics that the number of tables is minimal and the number of null columns is minimal.

Experience suggests that the universal relation is not a good starting point for *practical* relational database design because of its size. Furthermore, this "bad record" is sometimes difficult to obtain from the users (often the case when starting from graphical data). Proponents of normalization are often impressed by the complexity of normalization theory. In most practical situations of realistic size, it is hardly possible to apply pure normalization as users are often unable to provide multi-valued or join dependencies. Although in such cases one resorts to rules of thumb with their associated dangers, this has not as yet been a reason for most academics to give up their support for normalization. It works well for small and simple applications and these are considered sufficient for teaching purposes. We strongly disagree with this view. The universal relation approach is simply not a practical starting point for relational database design *in the large*. Normalization is primarily a measure of quality for the resulting table design, not a procedure for designing good tables.

ER

Another popular method for database analysis and design is called ER (Entity Relationship) or EAR (Entity Attribute Relationship). It was introduced by Chen in 1976. One problem with ER is that it contains more than one information bearing construct. Hence, designers must know when to encode a fact as a relationship and when to encode a fact as an attribute of an entity. It is widely recognized as a difficult task to determine, once and for all, which facts should be encoded in which way. Furthermore, the ER diagrams were not designed to be used for validation techniques that rely on example populations. Finally, the ER model and diagrams can represent fewer constraints than the NIAM model and diagrams.

References

Olle, T. W., et al. (1988), *Information Systems Methodologies: A Framework for Understanding*, (Reading: Addison-Wesley).

15 Summary, a few questions and conclusion

The preceding chapters describe the first cookbook for a fact-based conceptual schema and relational database design. To the best of our knowledge, the NIAM CSDP and RDDP is a conceptual schema and relational database design methodology which is unique in combining all of the following principles:

1. Input to the design procedure is expressed in the language most familiar to the user: examples of facts the user works with in his job or would like to work with (in case of new information systems).
2. Throughout the design procedure, there are clear signposts indicating what to do next.
3. Validation (or quality control) is not restricted to the end of the production line but is present throughout the whole analysis process.
4. A diagramming technique is used which permits direct reading of combined schema and instance information in natural language, thereby greatly contributing to effective validation by the user.

Let us look at a few questions which have been raised during some of the many seminars for which parts of this text have been used:

Q1. If we are using ER (or EAR) modeling, how could we benefit from introducing the NIAM relational database design procedure?

A1. If, for whatever reason, one cannot give up on ER or EAR, one could use the first seven steps of the NIAM CSDP and then during step 8, transform the NIAM conceptual schema into an ER or EAR schema. With this combination, one still has the NIAM advantages of:

- starting from familiar and significant examples;
- a simple and effective visual-auditory transformation to transform informal examples to formal sentence instances;
- a diagramming technique that shows the instances of a type next to the definition of that type;
- continuous validation in the user's language.

315

Q2. We use IE (or D2S2), and we cannot afford to throw it out now. How could we benefit from introducing the NIAM RDDP?

A2. The NIAM CSDP and RDDP result in much better relational databases than the data modeling component of IE (or D2S2). You could therefore simply replace the IE (or D2S2) data modeling component of these methods with the NIAM CSDP and RDDP.

Q3. We are using ISAC. How could we benefit from introducing the NIAM CSDP and RDDP?

A3. The ISAC methodology has some good components in change analysis and activity analysis. If one replaces the ISAC data design steps with the NIAM CSDP and RDDP so that every message set in an activity graph is described by a conceptual subschema or relational subschema, then the new combination is a better methodology.

Q4. If we are using BSP (ISS), how could we benefit from introducing the NIAM CSDP and RDDP?

A4. IBM's BSP and ISS have their best components in the very early phase of the development cycle. You could easily use the NIAM CSDP and RDDP to replace the BSP component "business data" with better overall results.

Q5. We are using SADT and although SADT can be used for function and data decomposition, in our organisation we only use it for functional decomposition. How could we benefit from introducing the NIAM CSDP and RDDP?

A5. One of SADT's main advantages is the structured way of communication between all of the parties involved and indeed, as you indicated, the functional decomposition notation provided by SADT is among the better candidates. The NIAM CSDP and RDDP naturally fill a gap in the SADT methodology—they provide a design procedure for arriving at the data perspective concepts.

From a very recent IFIP report, (*Information System Methodologies: A Framework for Understanding*, 1988), one can deduce that the data perspective is about to replace the process perspective as the major pillar in information systems analysis and design. This textbook is the result of over seventeen years of experience with a methodology that is primarily data driven. In the 1970s, it was considered heresy not to give primary consideration to the process perspective. Perseverance with the design and use of data perspective methodologies has given us rich insights on how to implement such a methodology in practice and how to teach it. This book reflects those insights, and should equip you to use these techniques in your day to day work.

Good Luck!

Answers
to selected exercise questions

Exercise 1.2

1. B C F G I
2. No: nth generation hardware typically runs generations 1 through n of computing languages.
3. "709T" sounds like "seven oh ninety" and consequently most clients wrote it as "7090". So IBM renamed it to agree with common practice.

Exercise 2.1

1. (a) C (b) A (c) B

Exercise 2.2

1. (a) Ensure database updates are consistent with the conceptual schema. Answer queries about the UoD.
   (b) Declarations of: stored fact types; constraints; derivation rules
   (c) False. With compound transactions only the collective effect of all the component updates is considered.

2. (a) Accepted.
   (b) Rejected. Constraint C1 violated.
   (c) Accepted
   (d) Rejected. Constraint C2 violated.
   (e) Accepted.
   (f) Rejected. Constraint C3 violated.
   (g) Accepted.
   (h) Rejected. Constraint C5 violated.
   (i) Accepted.
   (j) Rejected. Fact type not recognized.
   (k) Accepted.
   (l) Accepted.
   (m) Rejected. Constraint C1 violated.
   (n) Accepted.
   (o) Rejected. Constraint C4 violated.
   (p) Accepted.
   (q) Yes.

317

(r) Chris.
(s) 2.
(t) Ann, Chris.
(u) Integers 1..10.
(v) Question is outside the scope of the UoD.

4. (a) Accepted.
   (b) Rejected. Constraint C1 violated.
   (c) Accepted.
   (d) Rejected. Constraint C4 violated.
   (e) Accepted.
   (f) Rejected. Constraint C2 violated.
   (g) Rejected. Constraint C3 violated.
   (h) Alice.
   (i) X is father of Y **if** X is male **and** X is parent of Y
   (j) X is daughter of Y **if** X is female **and** Y is parent of X
   (k) X is grand-daughter of Y **if**   X is daughter of Z
                                    and Y is parent of Z
   { assuming rule (j) is available }

Exercise 3.3

1. (a), (f), (j)
2. Tutegroup with code 'A' meets at Time with dayhourcode 'Mon. 3pm'.
   Tutegroup with code 'A' is held in Room with room# 'CS-718'.
   Student with student# '302156' belongs to Tutegroup with code'A'.
   Student with student# '302156' has Name 'Bloggs FB'.
   Student with student# '180064' belongs to Tutegroup with code'A'.
   Student with student# '180064' has Name 'Fletcher JB'.

   We begin object type names with a capital letter. A wide choice of type and role names
   is allowed, so long as *humans* interpret them correctly (e.g. if needed we might replace
   "Name" with a more detailed descriptor such as "Surname & initials").

Exercise 3.4

1. This question illustrates the fact that columns with the same name need not have the
   same meaning. In the absence of helpful table names we make an educated guess.
   Here is one interpretation:
   (a) Athlete (name) 'Jones EM' has height of Length (cm) 166.
   (b) Athlete (name) 'Jones EM' pole vaults a height of Length (cm) 400.
2. Person (name) 'Jones EM' has height of Length (cm) 166.
   Person (name) 'Jones EM' was born in Year (AD) 1955.
3. Person (surname) 'Kowalski' is an internal member of AdvisoryPanel (name)
   'Databases'.
   Person (surname) 'Ienshtein' is an external member of AdvisoryPanel (name)
   'Databases'.

4. Person (firstname) 'Colin' was born in City (name) 'Amsterdam'.
   Person (firstname) 'Colin' lives in City (name) 'Amsterdam'.
   Person (firstname) 'David' works in City (name) 'Amsterdam'.
5. Person (firstname) 'Ann' is parent of Person (firstname) 'Colin'.
6. Country (name) 'Disland' has as friend Country (name) 'Oz'.
   Country (name) 'Hades' has as enemy Country (name) 'Oz'.

Exercise 3.5

1. (a) Person (firstname) 'Fred' is male.
        Person (firstname) 'Ann' is female.

   (b)

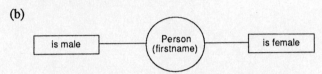

   (c) Person (firstname) 'Fred' has Gender (name) 'male'.
        Person (firstname) 'Ann' has Gender (name) 'female'.

   (d)

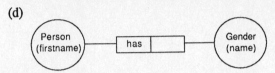

2. (b)

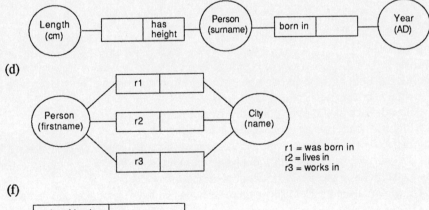

   (d)

   (f)

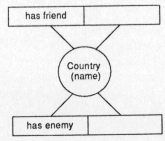

3.

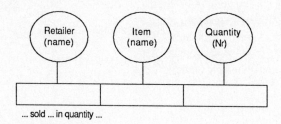

... sold ... in quantity ...

4. Same as for 3.

6.

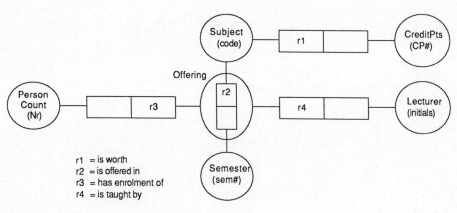

r1 = is worth
r2 = is offered in
r3 = has enrolment of
r4 = is taught by

7. (a) No: here we have 2 binary fact types
   (b) Yes

8. (a) Illegal. Entities must play at least one role. Moreover, joining entity types with an undirected line segment is illegal.
   (b) Illegal. Each role must be played by at most one entity type.
   (c) Illegal. Each role must be played by at least one entity type.
   (d) Legal, for example Person has Gender and was born in Country.
   (e) Illegal. Two entity types must not be linked to the same role.
   (f) Legal, for example Person introduces Person to Person.
   (g) Legal, for example Company employs Person and buys Computer, and Person uses Computer.
   (h) Legal, for example Person gives Present to Person on Day.
   (i) Illegal. Entity types should not be included in nesting ellipse.
   (j) Legal, for example Person has IQ and is parent of Person.
   (k) Legal, for example Student studies Subject, obtaining Score for mid-semester test and final exam.
   (l) Illegal. An extended form of the error in (e).

Exercise 3.6 (Only the diagrams are shown.)

1.

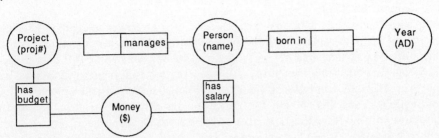

2.

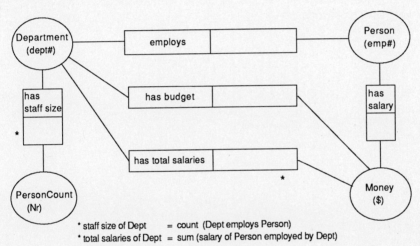

* staff size of Dept   = count (Dept employs Person)
* total salaries of Dept = sum (salary of Person employed by Dept)

3.

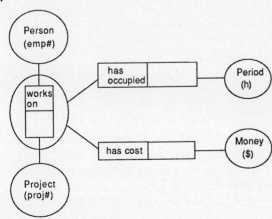

Exercise 4.1

1. Uniqueness constraints apply to: (a) B column; (b) AB combination; (c) A column and B column; (d) A column.
3. Uniqueness constraints apply to: (a) each role; (b) has-gender role; (c) 3.4.1a has-height, 3.4.1b pole-vaults, 3.4.2 has-height, born-in; 3.4.3 is-external-member-of, other fact type is many:many; 3.4.4 born-in, lives-in, works-in; 3.4.5 many:many; 3.4.6 both fact types are many:many; (d) meets-on, meets-at, meets-in {later we see how to specify inter-fact type constraints: the population is consistent with constraints on Day-Room and Hour-Room but these are probably not intended; however a constraint on Day-Hour-Room is likely}; (e) has-manager, manages, born-in, has-budget, has-salary; (f) has-budget, employed-by, has-salary {constraints on has-staff-size and has-total-salaries are implied by the derivation rules}; (g) has-height, has-eyecolour, has-complexion.

Exercise 4.2

1. (a) AB, AC (b) AB, AC, BC (c) ABC (d) AC
3.

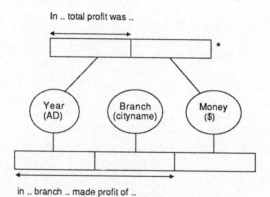

In .. total profit was ..

Year (AD)   Branch (cityname)   Money ($)

in .. branch .. made profit of ..

* total profit in Year = sum (profit of Branch in Year)

* Total profit in Year = sum(profit of Branch in Year)

Exercise 4.3

1. (a) See solution to 3.5.6 and interpret r' as corole of r. Constraints apply to r1, r4, r3 with r2r2' many:many. Some inter-fact type constraints consistent with the population might be intended, for example, between r2' and r4' (in each semester a lecturer can teach at most one subject), but some others are not, for example, between r3' and r4': the Enrollment-Lecturer pair (300,TH) might occur for both CS112 and CS113.
   (b) has-occupied, has-cost; objectified fact type is many:many

2. (a)   (b)

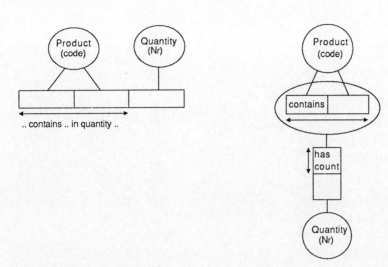

.. contains .. in quantity ..

3.

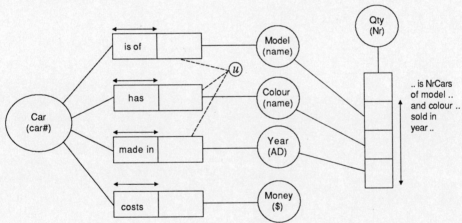

.. is NrCars
of model ..
and colour ..
sold in
year ..

Exercise 5.2

1. Definitely splittable: (a) (b) (d). Possibly splittable: others.
2. The ternary fact type is not elementary, for example, the fact cited is equivalent to the conjunction of the following:

   Flight (flight#) 'T74' has origin City (name) 'Paris'.
   Flight (flight#) 'T74' has destination City (name) 'London'.

The splittability is obvious from the fact that flight# is a key of the table provided (length of key = 1, which is 2 below table length). The correct schema is:

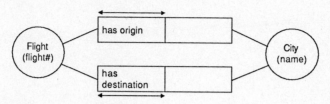

Exercise 5.3

1. (a) Contraints on AC, BC
    (b) Projections: Join:

a_1	c_1		b_1	c_1		a_1	b_1	c_1
a_1	c_2		b_1	c_2		a_1	b_2	c_1
a_2	c_1		b_2	c_1		etc.		
a_2	c_2		b_2	c_2				

X ... unsplittable

(c) AB projection: $a_1\ b_1$ Join gives original table.
                    $a_2\ b_2$ So splittable this way.
     BC projection as above.

(d)

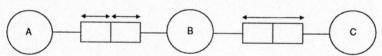

Exercise 6.2

1.

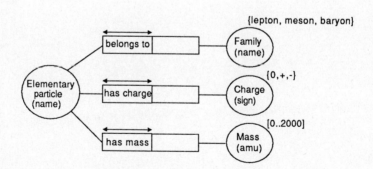

Exercise 6.3

1.

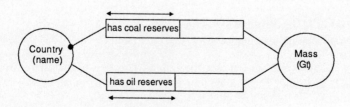

2. See Figure 11.16

Exercise 6.4

1. (a) (i) NIAM demands proper, nonnull subtyping, so any model must satisfy
    $n(B) = 2$ and $n(C) = 1$, e.g. $B = \{1,2\}$ $C = \{1\}$.
   (ii) Must have $n(B) = n(C) = 2$ and $n(D) = 1$. One model is $B = \{1,2\}$ $C = \{2,3\}$
    $D = \{2\}$.
   (b) (i) arcs must be directed (is A subtype of B or vice versa?)
   (ii) graph must be acyclic (*proper* subtype)
   (iii) delete arc for C subtype of A (transitively redundant)
   (iv) graph must be acyclic (*proper* subtype)
   (v) primitive types A and B must be disjoint, which is inconsistent with C being
    a common proper nonnull subtype.

Exercise 6.5

2.

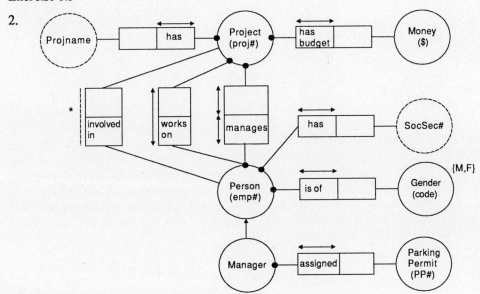

Manager = Person managing **some** Project
* Person involved in Project **if** Person works on **or** manages Project

Parking permit information is recorded just for the managers (E6,E7). Thus we introduce Manager as a subtype. Although two 1:1 naming schemes exist for Project and Person, the cross-referencing between figures suggests that emp# and proj# are chosen as standard identifiers (see Ch 7): hence we parenthesize these but not SocSec# or Projname.

Exercise 6.6

1.

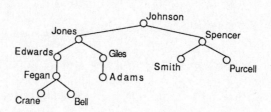

The supervisor hierarchy above shows that Johnson is the chief supervisor (hence the '*'). All of the fact types are about Employee. Taking Employee as the supertype, we obtain the following matrix:

	Dept	Supervisor	MaritalSt	HomePhone	MarriageYr	NrChildren
(1)	1	1	1	1	1	1
(2)	1	1	1	1	0	0
(3)	1	1	1	0	1	0
(4)	1	1	1	0	0	0
		A	A			

A ← A ← B → C ← D

Row (1) caters for rows 1,3,4 and 11 of the output report: row 11 is included here since we must record the fact that Johnson has no supervisor. Row (2) caters for rows 2,8 of the report; row (3) caters for rows 5,7,9 of the report; and row (4) caters for rows 6,10 of the report. A is the supertype, with subtypes B, C, and D. The redundant D ⊆ A relation is eliminated by transitivity. Membership criteria for each subtype must be defined. For C this is obvious (married). For B we need to find a fact type of A which determines whether or not we record HomePhone: just the supervisors have this fact recorded (see above tree). We may now describe B as Supervisor, C as Married Employee and D as Married Supervisor.

2.

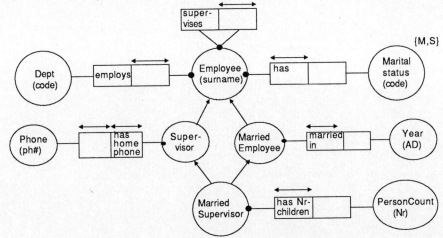

Supervisor   = Employee supervising **some** employee
Married employee   = Employee having Marital status M
Married Supervisor = Supervisor ∩ Married employee

3.

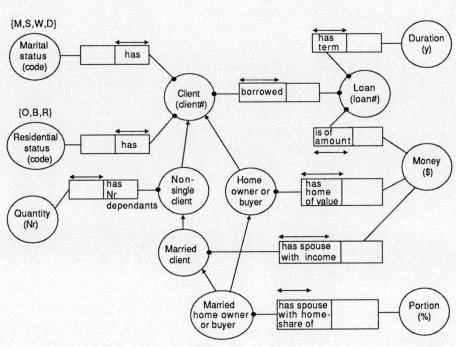

Exercise 6.7

1.

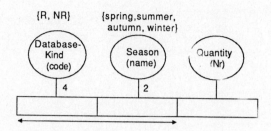

database systems of kind .. in season .. had sales of .. copies

3.

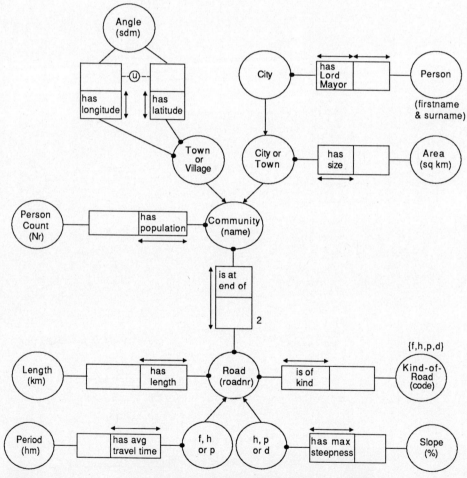

City	=	Community having population count > 100000
Town or village	=	Community having population count ≤ 100000
City or town	=	Community having population count > 10000

Exercise 7.2

1. (a)

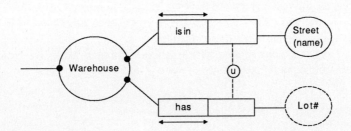

(b) Explode Street node:

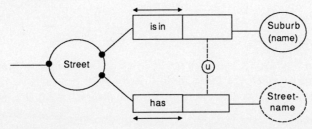

(c) Explode Suburb node:

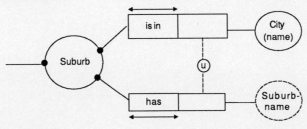

(d) Explode City node:

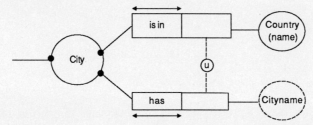

(e) Explode Country node:

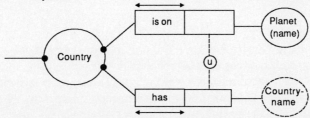

Exercise 8.2

1. Let us interpret the null values in the report thus: a CompanyCar is recorded for an Employee iff the Driver's licence is recorded for that Employee. We may now schematize with an equality constraint as follows.

   Note: In setting out these solutions (and in more complex work) we prefer to omit arrow heads from equality constraints.

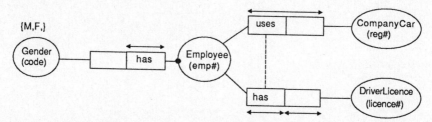

   Alternatively, a subtyping approach might be used, for example, we might define the subtype Driver = Employee using **some** CompanyCar, and attach a mandatory has-DriverLicence role to this. Both methods are equivalent but the first is preferred.

2. (a) C9 violated.   (b) accepted.   (c) C6 violated.   (d) C8 violated.
   (e) C5 violated.   (f) C7 violated.   (g) C4 violated.   (h) C2 violated.
   (i) accepted.   (j) C1 violated.

Exercise 8.3

1. (a) R,S,T   (b) ir   (c) ir,S   (d) ir,as,T   (e) ir,as,T   (f) R,T   (g) ir,S
   (not necessarily intransitive, e.g. a,b,c at vertices of a triangle)

2.

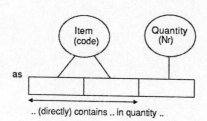

.. (directly) contains .. in quantity ..

(Note: The 'as' (asymmetric) constraint is understood to apply to the homogeneous portion of the ternary.)

Exercise 8.4

4. Let us asssume that Length, Average travel time and Maximum steepness describe the segment of the road between the two communities mentioned (the road connection), whereas the road number reference scheme applies only to whole roads. It is now necessary to objectify the notion of a road connection. Two ways of doing this are sketched:

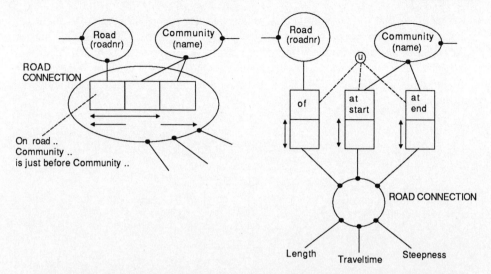

With both approaches, we introduce the idea that the road connections have a direction to avoid problems with symmetric relationships. Only direct connections are stored, with indirect connections, if requested, being derived. For example: R connects X to Y **if** on R X is just before Y; R connects X to Y **if** on R X is just before Z **and** R connects Z to Y. The right-hand schema provides an alternative way of specifying the strict ordering by distinguishing between the start and end of a road connection.

5. The schema is as given previously but with the following derivation rules added:

    X contains Y **if** X directly contains Y.
    X contains Y **if** X directly contains Z **and** Z contains Y.

Exercise 9.2

1. Move uniqueness constraint from r1' to r1.
   Delete uniqueness constraint on r2'.

Exercise 9.3

1. Replace with: Bookshop is located in City.
                   Bookshop has ordered Qty copies of Book.

2.

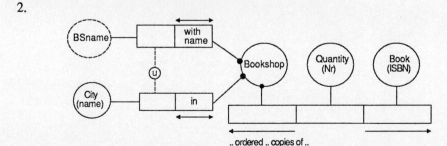

4. Let us agree that the population is significant in suggesting that the only languages that programmers use or like are languages that they know. It is possible that a programmer knows a language but does not use or like it (e.g. Bob, C). In fact, a language may be known by a programmer without being liked or used by *any* programmer (e.g. BASIC). We take it that each programmer uses a language and likes a language.

(a)

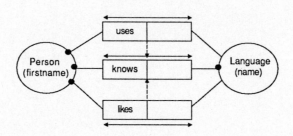

Exercise 10.2

1. (a)

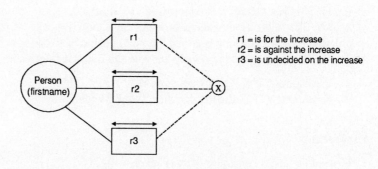

r1 = is for the increase
r2 = is against the increase
r3 = is undecided on the increase

(b)

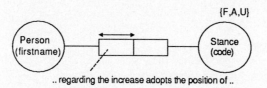

.. regarding the increase adopts the position of ..

3.

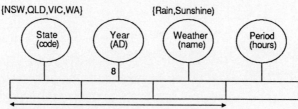

The state .. in the year .. had weather of kind .. for a period ..

Exercise 10.3

2. (a)

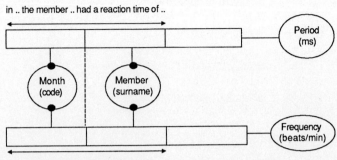

in .. the member .. had a reaction time of ..

in .. the member .. had a heart rate of ..

(b)

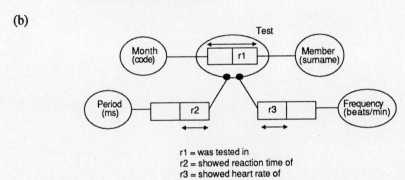

r1 = was tested in
r2 = showed reaction time of
r3 = showed heart rate of

(c) Schema (b) is generally preferable. It leads to one ONF table instead of two.

Exercise 10.4

1. (a)

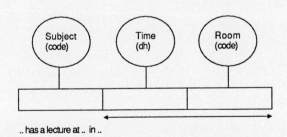

.. has a lecture at .. in ..

(b)

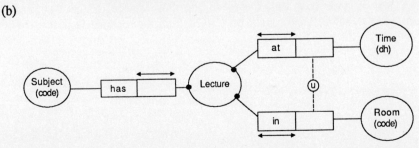

Exercise 11.3

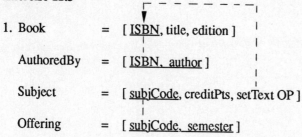

1. Book = [ISBN, title, edition]

   AuthoredBy = [ISBN, author]

   Subject = [subjCode, creditPts, setText OP]

   Offering = [subjCode, semester]

3. (a) The table allows redundancy for example, with the following population the fact that dress d1 costs $30 is duplicated:

   Likes:

Woman	Dress	Cost
Eve	d1	30
Sue	d1	30

   (b) Likes = [woman, dress]

   Dress = [dresscode, cost, owner OP]

   Earns = [woman, wage]

5. (a) The Lecturer table is guilty of redundancy since gender is replicated for each degree studied by the lecturer, and degree title is replicated for each instance of the same degree code, for example:

Name	Gender	degCode	degTitle
Wirth N	M	BSc	Bachelor of Science
Wirth N	M	PhD	Doctor of Philosophy
Smith A	F	PhD	Doctor of Philosophy
...			

   The Qualification table suffers from info-loss caused by splitting the elementary fact type Lecturer is awarded Degree in Year. For instance, the fact that Smith A is awarded a PhD in 1980 cannot be derived from the separate facts that a PhD is awarded in the year 1980 and Smith A has a PhD.

(b)

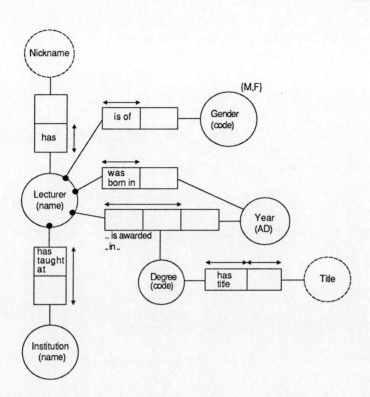

(c) Lecturer   =   [<u>name</u>, gender, birthYr, nickname OP]

Qualification   =   [<u>lecturer, degree</u>, yrAwarded]

Degree   =   [<u>degreeCode</u>, <u>title</u>]

Taught_at   =   [<u>lecturer, institution</u>]

8. (a) Person = [<u>form#</u>, age, TVhrs, newspaperHrs, favChannel OP, favNewspaper OP, prefNews OP]

favChannel recorded just for rows where TVhrs > 0
favNewspaper recorded just for rows where newspaperHrs > 0
prefNews recorded just for rows
    where TVhrs > 0 and newspaperHrs > 0 and age ≥ 18

(b) Person   =   [<u>form#</u>, age, TVhrs, newspaperHrs]
   TVviewer   =   [<u>form#</u>, favChannel]
   NPreader   =   [<u>form#</u>, favNewspaper]
   TV&NPadult   =   [<u>form#</u>, prefNews]

pop(TVviewer.form#)   =   pop(Person.form#) where TVhrs > 0
pop(NPreader.form#)   =   pop(Person.form#) where newspaperHrs > 0
pop(TV&NPadult.form#)   =   pop(Person.form#) where TVhrs > 0
                                       and newspaperHrs > 0 and age ≥ 18

For most applications, schema (a) is preferable.

11. OwnsComputer   =   [company, computerBrand, computerModel, quantity]

     CompanyPhone   =   [phone#, company]

     Programmer   =   [name, employer, gender, address, homePhone OP]

     Fluent_in   =   [programmer, language]

     Ancestry   =   [language, ancestor]

     LanguageUsage   =   [software#, programmer, language]

     Software   =   [software#, title, price OP]

     Language   =   [name, releaseYear, generation OP]

13. Customer   =   [customer#, name, address, email-id OP]

     HasPhone   =   [customer, phone]

     Invoice   =   [invoice#, customer, issueDate, datePaid OP]

     Sale   =   [invoice#, item#, quantity, unitprice]

     Item   =   [item#, description]

     Stock   =   [item#, warehouse#, quantity]

     Warehouse   =   [warehouse#, lastStocktake]

     OtherPrices   =   [item#, otherVendor, advertisedPrice]

     OtherLeases   =   [item#, otherVendor, nrMonthsLeased, monthlyFee]

Exercise 11.4

1. (a) [child, gender] is a repeating group (so not even in 1NF).

(b) The nonkey attribute subjLectured is functionally dependent on just part of the key, viz. Person. hNF = 1.

(c) Each of the nonkey attributes is dependent on only part of the key, e.g. parent → parentGender. hNF = 1.

(d) The attribute child is dependent on only part of the key, viz. tutor. hNF = 3 (not 1, since child is not a nonkey attribute).

(e) Tutors_in   =   [<u>tutor, subject</u>]

Person   =   [<u>name</u>, gender, <u>subjLectured</u> OP]

Parent_of   =   [<u>parent, child</u>] as,it
                        1..2

Index